THE SELLING OF THE SOUTH

JAMES C. COBB

THE SELLING OF THE SOUTH

THE SOUTHERN CRUSADE FOR INDUSTRIAL DEVELOPMENT, 1936–1990

Second Edition

University of Illinois Press
Urbana and Chicago

This book is printed on acid-free paper.

Library of Congress Cataloging-in-Publication Data

Cobb, James C. (James Charles), 1947–
    The selling of the South : the Southern crusade for industrial
development 1936–1990 / James C. Cobb.—2nd ed.
      p. cm.
    Originally published: Baton Rouge : Louisiana State University
Press, 1982.
    ISBN 0-252-01770-6 (cloth : alk. paper).—ISBN 0-252-06162-4 (pbk.)
    Includes bibliographical references and index.
    1. Industrial promotion—Southern States. 2. Southern States—
Economic conditions—1918– I. Title.
HC107.A13C65 1993
338.975′00904—dc20   92-30045
                                                                CIP

For Ben, Lyra, and "Miss Dena"

CONTENTS

TABLES

ACKNOWLEDGMENTS

Any research project is the culmination of the experiences and opportunities that shape the researcher's attitudes and thought processes. Therefore, I am indebted to all my instructors both for their stimulating insights and for their insistence that I attempt to answer many of my own questions. I am particularly grateful to William F. Holmes for his challenging course in recent southern history and the close friendship that developed as we shared our interests in scholarship, country music, and running. Lester D. Stephens deserves my deepest appreciation for the example of character and professionalism he provided for dozens of graduate teaching fellows at the University of Georgia.

I have benefitted greatly from thoughtful, exciting exchanges with my graduate school colleagues. Heated debates in the Leconte Hall lounge were as vital to my intellectual growth as softball games and pizza feasts were to my sanity. I am happy to have maintained especially close ties with former fellow students like Thomas G. Dyer, Harvey H. Jackson, Tennant S. McWilliams, Clarence L. Mohr, and Von V. Pittman, Jr.

I am deeply indebted to Walter Rundell, Jr., whose faith in my abilities gave me the opportunity to pursue the career in teaching and research that was denied many of my deserving contemporaries. My former colleagues at the University of Maryland provided much-needed reassurance and support and my former associates at the University of Northern Iowa have been unfailingly friendly and helpful. Some of the most critical research for this book was supported by a Summer Research Fellowship from the University of Northern Iowa, and I am certain that this project would never have been completed without the cheerful, expert assistance provided by the university's Word Processing Center and the Reader's Services staff at the UNI Library.

As I assume my new duties at the University of Mississippi, I wish to thank my colleagues in the Department of History and the Center for the Study of Southern Culture for making it possible for me to pursue my research and teaching interests in such an appropriate and hospitable setting.

I am grateful for the comments and suggestions provided by Blaine A. Brownell, Richard M. Bernard, and David A. Walker, who read and criticized all or parts of the manuscript. My debt to Numan V. Bartley includes not only the reading of this manuscript but years of patient guidance and firm friendship. No student could ever expect more from his adviser, and no adviser could be held in higher regard by his student.

My greatest debt is to my family, and it is to them that this book is lovingly dedicated. My son, Ben, showed patience and understanding far beyond his years with a father who sometimes allowed an important project to become an obsession. My wife, Lyra, was a tireless typist and skillful editor whose cheerful irreverence and boundless capacity for love and encouragement have made our relationship the most cherished aspect of my life. Finally, I could never adequately express my affection and admiration for my mother, Modena Cobb, who not only made untold sacrifices in my behalf but provided an example of energy, resourcefulness, and strength that I may emulate but will never equal.

Preface to the Second Edition

There are few scholars at any level who have not longed for the opportunity to revise a piece of their written work. In my case, at least, this longing often becomes an all-but-uncontrollable urge. Within a few months after the original version of this book appeared in 1982, I was already fighting a losing battle with the demons of hindsight, especially as emergent economic trends made it increasingly apparent that, in focusing so intently on the regional implications of industrial development policy in the post–New Deal South, I had neglected the pervasive national and international influences that had also played a major role in shaping this policy. A few articles and essays afforded me the chance to revise and redefine my broadened perspective on the history of southern industrial development efforts, but when Dick Wentworth suggested that the University of Illinois Press might be interested in publishing an updated edition of *The Selling of the South,* I jumped at the chance.

I hope that my analysis of the South's economic predicament in the 1980s will remind readers that southern industrial development efforts have always reflected not only the realities of wealth and power at the state and local level but the overriding influences of the larger global and national context that often either exacerbated the region's problems or made them infinitely more difficult to resolve.

THE SELLING OF THE SOUTH

INTRODUCTION

In 1938 President Franklin D. Roosevelt described an already woebegone South as "the nation's number one economic problem." Embarrassed southern spokesmen angrily refused to admit the failure of more than a half century of crusading to build a "New South" through industrialization, but they could find little evidence to refute the president's statement. The Great Depression had been especially damaging to industry-seeking efforts, but World War II resurrected the South's economy and encouraged its leaders to take whatever action was necessary to keep their states from slipping back into the desperate poverty of the thirties. In the postwar period, economic progress became a regional obsession as every southern state expanded and intensified industrial development activities that increasingly absorbed the resources of state and local governments and the energies of public officials and private citizens as well.

Four decades after Roosevelt's pronouncement the South remained the nation's poorest region, but its recent economic gains, excellent prospects for future growth and enhanced regional image were sources of pride to southerners and consternation to representatives of the declining Industrial North. The well-publicized ascendance of the fast-growing, attractive "Sunbelt South" of the 1970s suggested the need to examine the impact of the intensive post-Depression industrial development effort on the region's economy and on the social, political, and institutional deficiencies that, like its poverty, had long kept the South out of the American mainstream.

In the late 1920s and 1930s the Nashville Agrarians warned that the best elements of the region's rural, agricultural way of life would be quickly destroyed as cities and manufacturing plants cluttered the landscape and southerners forsook their farms for the dehumanizing regimen of the factory. While the conservative Agrarians feared that industrialization threatened the elements of the southern way of life most worthy of preservation, in the post-Depression years liberal observers expressed their hopes that the pursuit of a modernized economy would prove incompatible with racial discrimination, reactionary politics, and other less attractive elements of the region's heritage.[1]

Such optimism seemed theoretically sound, but it ignored certain realities of the South's past, particularly the success with which Henry Grady and other "New South" leaders of the late nineteenth century had campaigned for industrial growth without disrupting traditional socioeconomic and political relationships. Manufacturing and commerce were far more advanced in the North by the 1880s and investment capital was relatively scarce in Dixie, but the South was rich in natural resources and blessed with an abundant supply of workers. Consequently, New South promoters aimed their sales pitches at labor-intensive industries that would prepare agricultural products and raw materials for final processing elsewhere. The manufacturing operations they courted employed few skilled workers. Wages were minimal, and many owners preferred rural plant locations where they could draw on a surplus of agricultural labor. Because there was little in the South's pattern of industrial growth to encourage rapid urbanization, accumulation of capital, or the rise of large-scale consumer demand, New South policies failed to produce the industrial and commercial independence that the region had sought since the antebellum period.

Most incoming employers were concerned primarily with getting maximum productivity out of work forces consisting largely of ex-sharecroppers, females, and children, none of whom were likely to complain about wages and working conditions or otherwise develop a well-defined

---

1. For the best-known and most comprehensive statement of the Agrarians' point of view see Twelve Southerners, *I'll Take My Stand: The South and the Agrarian Tradition* (New York: Harper Brothers, 1930). See also I. A. Newby, *The South: A History* (New York: Holt, Rinehart, and Winston, 1978), 450. For the "liberal" perspective, see William H. Nicholls, *Southern Tradition and Regional Progress* (Chapel Hill: University of North Carolina Press, 1960); J. Milton Yinger and George E. Simpson, "Can Segregation Survive in an Industrial Society?" *Antioch Review*, XVIII (Spring, 1958), 15–24.

sense of class consciousness. Industrialists were less interested in schools or hospitals than in low taxes, and responsible political leadership was less important to them than freedom from regulation. The South's closed political system produced public officials disinclined to regulate but eager to protect the interests of industry, particularly in labor-management conflicts. In the name of progress, business leaders encouraged policy-makers to hold down taxes and starve education and services in order to create what they believed was the best possible climate for attracting industry. Thus, despite some indications that the South was enjoying success in encouraging new industrial investments, its facilities and institutions and its human capital remained sorely underdeveloped.[2]

After the Populist challenge to stability had been turned aside in the 1890s, development-oriented southern leaders supported Progressive era programs for improved roads and better schools and even showed a willingness to accept a small amount of regulatory legislation, apparently because they felt that monopoly and railroad abuses actually inhibited economic expansion.[3] The Progressive reform impulse interacted with the desire for industrial development to produce the business progressivism that became a major influence on southern politics in the 1920s.

Business progressivism stressed government's service responsibility and transformed it into "an agent of industrial prosperity." Still, a contemporary observer concluded that "the business class political philosophy of the New South is broad enough to include programs of highway improvement, educational expansion and health regulation. But it does not embrace any comprehensive challenge to laissez faire ideas in the sphere of relationship between capital and labor, and the section is lagging in social support of such matters as effective child labor regulation and compensation legislation." Urban boosters of the 1920s preached progress and businesslike government but insisted that expansion need not pose any challenge to the existing social order. As George B. Tindall noted, the business progressive philosophy assumed not only that race relations were a "settled problem" but that "the larger economic problems of the

2. Joe Persky, "The South: A Colony At Home," *Southern Exposure*, I (Summer/Fall, 1973), 15–22; C. Vann Woodward, "New South Fraud Is Papered by Old South Myth," Washington *Post*, July 9, 1961, p. 3E.

3. For a brief discussion of southern progressivism, see J. Morgan Kousser, *The Shaping of Southern Politics: Suffrage Restriction and the Establishment of the One-Party South, 1880–1910* (New Haven: Yale University Press, 1974), 229–37.

underprivileged farm tenants and factory workers were not its problems; their remedy would come, if at all, through economic expansion."[4]

Although the marriage of boosterism and reform clearly had its limitations, it produced a modified philosophy of industrial development, one that remained socially conservative but nonetheless recognized the importance of an expanded government role in promoting economic growth. Tindall observed that, while it was "severely shaken" by the Great Depression, "the progressivism of expansion and efficiency became by and large the norm of southern statecraft in the decades that followed."[5] Tindall was clearly correct insofar as the pursuit of industrial progress was concerned. The boosterism of the 1920s paled into insignificance after World War II, as competition for new payrolls spawned a host of policies and programs designed to sell the South to industrial investors.

The following survey traces the evolution of efforts to encourage industrial expansion in thirteen southern states (the Confederate South plus Kentucky and Oklahoma), beginning with Mississippi's pioneering bond subsidy program in 1936 and concluding with an analysis of the problems confronting a fast-growing South as it enters the 1980s. In addition to the economic impact of industry-seeking activities, this study focuses on the question of whether the post-Depression South's desire for industrial development became a force for change or reflected the influence of earlier attempts to lead the region toward a prosperous future without jeopardizing the social and political continuity that had characterized its deprived past.

4. George B. Tindall, "Business Progressivism: Southern Politics in the Twenties," *South Atlantic Quarterly*, LXII (Winter, 1963), 96, 106. See also Blaine A. Brownell, *The Urban Ethos in the South, 1920–1930* (Baton Rouge: Louisiana State University Press, 1975).
5. Tindall, "Business Progressivism," 96.

Chapter 1

BALANCE AGRICULTURE WITH INDUSTRY

As a fusion of certain strains of progressivism and New South boosterism, the business progressive phenomenon involved an attempt by southern political leaders to modernize state government and expand and improve public facilities in order to encourage industrial growth. The idea that promotion of economic expansion could be a legitimate function of government gained increasingly wider acceptance in the post–World War II South as competition for new industry became especially heated. Mississippi set the tone for these later development efforts with its 1936 BAWI (Balance Agriculture with Industry) program of industrial subsidization.

The granting of subsidies was already a common practice by the Depression years. In fact, such contributions to economic expansion dated well back into the nineteenth century when, for example, subsidies to railroads indicated a willingness to commit public resources to the support of private commercial and industrial ventures. Prior to BAWI, however, most such grants and concessions had been issued by individual communities acting without, or sometimes in defiance of, legal constraint. By introducing a system wherein the state sanctioned and supervised the use of municipal bonds to finance plant construction, the BAWI program lifted the curtain on an era of more competitive subsidization and broader state and local government involvement in industrial development efforts.

The business progressives felt that governmental participation in the promotion of industrial expansion would make future growth predictable and orderly. The severity of the Depression shattered much of this confidence, however, and left in its place a desperate hunger for new industry at practically any cost. Deciding that propaganda and hard sell were not enough, many local leaders who were already begging for new plants accelerated their efforts to buy and steal them as well.

In Tennessee smaller industry-hungry communities engaged in extreme forms of industrial subsidization with little apparent regard for the state constitution's specific prohibition of such activities. A 1937 survey of forty-one communities revealed that fifty-six plants built in the previous seven years had received some form of subsidy. Many were financed by bond issues authorized by a state legislature that had apparently misplaced its constitutional scruples. Some of these subsidy bills approved by the legislature concealed their true intent in euphemistic language such as "the erection of municipal buildings for public purposes," while others made it clear that the proposed bond issue would provide sites or buildings for new industry. Four of the acts permitted the use of public funds for industrial advertising and training programs as well as for hiring location brokers and collecting assessments from workers.[1]

The latter provision referred to one of the most controversial tactics used to finance new industry, that of forcing the workers to pay for the plant at which they worked through 5 to 7 percent deductions from their salaries. Ralph McGill's files contained one of the salary deduction contracts: "I the undersigned hereby make application for employment at the garment factory erected by the town of Manchester, Tennessee, and agree with the said town of Manchester, Tennessee, that in the event of employment at the said town of Manchester, Tennessee . . . I will pay to the said town of Manchester, Tennessee, 6 percent of my weekly salary."[2] Dickson, Tennessee, captured a Pennsylvania garment plant by offering a free building financed by 6 percent employee salary deductions as well as a five-year tax exemption, and free electric power and water. This mandatory contribution to the building fund must have been particularly painful to the 62 percent of the plant's work force making less than $5.55 per week. Lewisburg followed a similar plan by building a town hall, holding

1. Robert E. Lowry, "Municipal Subsidies to Industries in Tennessee," *Southern Economic Journal*, VII (January, 1941), 317–29; Tennessee State Planning Commission, "Subsidies for Industries in Tennessee," 1947 (mimeo in University of Tennessee Library, Knoxville), 9.
2. Ralph McGill, *The South and the Southerner* (Boston: Little, Brown, 1963), 195.

one meeting in it, and turning it over to the General Shoe Corporation, whose employees were expected to pay half the cost of the building. The willingness of Tennessee communities to meet almost any demand made them particularly susceptible to "fly-by-night" operators like the necktie manufacturer who after occupying a rent-free building and using the services of city-paid trainees for thirty days pulled out with enough ties for the Christmas buying season.[3]

A 1937 survey revealed that subsidization was widespread among Georgia cities. Douglasville provided a building for a garment plant, paid the employees training wages, and granted the company a five-year tax exemption. Washington attracted a shirt factory by raising $20,000 by public subscription, which would be matched with a like sum from salary deductions guaranteed by the promissory notes of workers whose average wages amounted to about $5 per week. Local subsidization was not uncommon in other southern states. Some Arkansas cities interpreted a 1939 statute allowing them to "purchase sites and make other grants" as authorization for municipal construction of industrial buildings. Several counties in South Carolina provided free sites for textile mills, and a few Alabama communities provided land and buildings.[4]

Mississippi, generally regarded as the nation's poorest state, also became heavily involved in various subsidy schemes. In 1935 local leaders in Vicksburg collected $75,000 to construct a factory building for M. Fine and Sons, makers of work shirts. Fine and Sons had formerly been located in Jeffersonville and New Albany, Indiana, and had moved to Mississippi after a history of wage and labor disputes at their previous locations. Some other Mississippi towns managed to supplement local subscription drives by misusing Works Progress Administration funds in order to attract new industry. In Ellisville $26,092 in WPA money went into the construction in 1935 of a "vocational school" on the campus of the Jones County Agricultural High School and Junior College. This new training addition was actually operated by the Vertex Hosiery Company, which had fled Weissport, Pennsylvania, after a siege of labor troubles. Vertex generously agreed to install thirty-six knitting machines in the Ellisville School and to furnish all the raw materials and "instructors."

3. Thomas L. Stokes, *Carpetbaggers of Industry* (n.p.: Amalgamated Clothing Workers of America, 1937), 11–13; Tennessee State Planning Commission, "Subsidies for Industries," 10.

4. Stokes, *Carpetbaggers*, 36–37; William D. Ross, "Industrial Promotion by Southern States" (Ph.D. dissertation, Duke University, 1951), 167, 190, 195.

The company also committed itself to training Jones County student workers for twenty-five years, during which time it would pay no rent and would enjoy the tax exemption given to all the state's educational institutions.[5]

Students of the Ellisville "school" received "on the job training" by actually making hose on one of two 40-hour shifts at a minimum salary of four dollars per week. Theoretically, when a student mastered the art of hosiery making, he or she would become eligible for wages nearly double the training salary, but this day rarely came before graduation, at which time the laborer surrendered his or her job to an underclassman. Their education complete, trained but jobless workers had no other hosiery mill to approach for employment and, thus, had to go elsewhere or pursue another career. WPA money funded another such school at Brookhaven, Mississippi, but before the students received much "training," alarmed officials decided it was best to admit that the establishment was nothing more than a garment plant. They subsequently encouraged the operators to hire adults in order to protect the WPA from charges of subsidizing a sweatshop that employed teenagers.[6]

The Ellisville experiment received considerable publicity and was but one example of the lengths to which an impoverished community would go in order to secure an industrial payroll in the 1930s. Yet, out of this decade of frenzied plant-buying came a more stable, businesslike program that introduced an era of state sanctioned and supervised subsidies to new industry in the South. Mississippi's enduring contribution to publicly subsidized industrial development was the brainchild of Hugh Lawson White, a wealthy lumberman from Columbia, a town of four thousand, which had traditionally depended on local sawmills for its economic well-being. At the peak of its operations the White Lumber Company employed eight hundred men and supplied a payroll that supported local commerce and provided a market for the agricultural products of the surrounding area. The timber companies failed to leave enough trees for reseeding, however, and by the 1920s timber reserves were all but exhausted. Marion County faced a bleak future even before the Depression struck and White retired from lumbering.[7]

5. Walter Davenport, "With Labor Thrown In," *Colliers*, C (November 27, 1937), 17, 79.
6. *Ibid.*
7. Ernest J. Hopkins, *Mississippi's BAWI Plan: An Experiment in Industrial Subsidization* (Atlanta: Federal Reserve Bank of Atlanta, 1944), 11.

Elected mayor in 1929, White accepted some of the responsibility for the joblessness and poverty that afflicted the area and called for a crusade to bring new economic life to Columbia. In addition to encouraging agricultural reform and diversification, he led in the formation of the Marion County Chamber of Commerce and worked feverishly to encourage new industry. A local knitting mill employing seventy-five people was only a start. Soon there was also a canning plant that contracted with farmers for their potatoes, beans, peas, turnips, and tomatoes. These advances relieved some of the local distress, but White was not yet content. He traveled to Chicago and retained Felix Fantus, a relocation engineer, to find a large industrial plant for Columbia. Fantus came up with Reliance Manufacturing Company, a shirt and pajama concern whose executives agreed to establish an operation in Marion County if the community could supply $85,000 for the construction of a plant building. The company pledged to employ at least three hundred workers, mostly females, and pay out $1 million over a ten-year period. When this requirement had been satisfied, the building would become company property.[8]

Realizing that the biggest problem for Columbia was raising the $85,000 in the midst of the Depression, Mayor White summoned the local populace to the city's theater. The mayor urged Columbians to seize the opportunity to save their town and elicited a remarkable response in the form of promissory notes, which were to be payable to a central committee over a thirty-six-month period. White contributed heavily, and his signature on a master note convinced a New Orleans bank to advance the full amount of unpaid contributions.[9]

The only remaining problem was the Reliance Company's doubt that a town of four thousand could supply as large a work force as its operations required. White responded with an offer of a personal bond of $1 million guaranteeing adequate labor. To further allay such fears the community held a labor registration day when, with company officials looking on in amazement, 1,492 women signed applications for jobs.[10]

To prepare this surplus of agricultural labor for industrial employment, White and his associates established a training school, using the manufacturer's equipment in a facility provided and staffed by the community. Trainees received no pay until they reached an agreed-upon level

8. Oliver J. Emmerich, "Balancing Agriculture with Industry," *Nation's Business*, XXV (February, 1937), 23–24; Hopkins, *Mississippi's BAWI*, 12.

9. Emmerich, "Balancing Agriculture," 92; Hopkins, *Mississippi's BAWI*, 12.

10. Emmerich, "Balancing Agriculture," 92.

of proficiency. The plant opened after the National Recovery Act's twelve-dollars-per-week standard had been abandoned and before national minimum wage legislation took its place. One Jackson newspaper reported that the girls toiled long hours for salaries averaging only $9.11 per week, and a New York reporter claimed some of them made nearly $2.00 less. These criticisms notwithstanding, the plant revitalized the area's economy, stemmed the tide of emigration, and by employing rural women, helped to make farm life a bit more bearable in that part of Depression era Mississippi.[11]

The Columbia plan was successful enough to attract statewide attention, and White toured Mississippi explaining to community leaders and chambers of commerce how they might revitalize their towns by the use of an industrial subsidy. Many who were initially skeptical reappraised their positions when Columbia quickly attracted two more plants and Hugh White, flush with success, announced his candidacy for governor in 1931, promising voters that, if elected, he would "Balance Agriculture With Industry" in Mississippi.[12]

White's 1931 bid failed, but he won the governorship four years later with the backing of Senator Theodore G. Bilbo, whose own support rested on a sizable, but ever-shifting group of factions within the state. The 1935 campaign, like most in this era of rough-and-tumble politics, was far from issue-oriented. Instead of extolling the merits of industrialization, White spent most of his time harping on his opponent's alleged ties to Huey Long, the controversial senator from neighboring Louisiana who had become involved in the Mississippi contest in order to save the poor people of the state from "a rapacious millionaire type like Hugh White."[13]

Just before the electorate was to be heard from, the flamboyant Bilbo rushed home from Washington to declare that the sole issue in the race was "President Roosevelt versus Huey Long, the arch enemy of the Democratic Party and the Administration." In such a political climate it was difficult to identify, much less evaluate, major campaign issues, but in the last analysis it is doubtful that either White's loss in 1931 or his vic-

11. *Ibid.*; Hopkins, *Mississippi's BAWI*, 13.
12. Hopkins, *Mississippi's BAWI*, 13; Oliver Emmerich, "Collapse and Recovery," in Richard Aubrey McClemore (ed.), *A History of Mississippi* (2 vols.; Hattiesburg, Miss.: University and College Press of Mississippi, 1973), II, 114.
13. R. G. Jones, "Political and Economic Transition in Mississippi: A Preliminary Survey" (M.A. thesis, Louisiana State University, 1938), 62–65; Martha H. Swain, *Pat Harrison: The New Deal Years* (Jackson: University Press of Mississippi, 1978), 127.

tory in 1935 was closely related to his pledge to promote the "greatest industrialization in this state that has ever been known."[14]

The doubtful significance of industrial development as a campaign issue should not obscure the fact that by the time White began his crusade for new industry many local leaders were ready to go out and do battle to bring new payrolls to their cities. Said the Columbus *Dispatch*: "If the South sits around and waits for Brain Trusters and selfish Northern industrial interests' approval of industrial expansion here, we will never achieve our rightful place in the industry of the nation." The Winona *Times* agreed: "The *Commercial Dispatch* is right. Brain Trusters or Brain Busters, to the contrary notwithstanding, it is high time that the South awakens to the fact we are not going to get anything until we get up 'on our hind legs' and fight for it."[15]

After taking office in 1936, Governor White took pains to acquaint Mississippians with the benefits of industrialization. He had only to cite the case of Columbia where in the last six years per capita business transactions had increased by 26 percent while similar cities showed an average 4 percent decline. White claimed that wherever it had been tried, the Columbia plan had succeeded. Cities using a similar approach had in recent months attracted twenty major industries with $500,000 in investments, five thousand jobs, and total annual payrolls in excess of $2.5 million.[16]

The communities involved benefitted both economically and psychologically from this growth. No longer did sons and daughters or their mothers and fathers have to accept the fact that there were few promising careers for young people in Mississippi. Young adults might now be able to stay near home, earn a better salary, and enjoy an improved standard of living. With a job in even a low-paying industry (which practically all of Mississippi's were), one member might earn more than the whole family's customary farm income. The Magnolia State had a great deal to offer new industry, but its primary attraction was the lower production

14. New York *Times*, September 2, 1935, p. 16; Ralph J. Rogers, "The Effort to Industrialize," in Richard Aubrey McClemore (ed.), *A History of Mississippi* (2 vols.; Hattiesburg, Miss.: University and College Press of Mississippi, 1973), II, 241.

15. Ned Williams, "Financing Industry in the South: Mississippi's Second BAWI Program" (Ph.D. dissertation, Columbia University, 1965), 32.

16. Hugh L. White, *Address of Governor Hugh L. White before the Annual Convention of the Mississippi Press Association at Gulfport, Mississippi, June 12, 1936* (n.p.: n.p., n.d.), 5–6.

costs made possible by an abundance of labor. With a high percentage of "native Anglo Saxons" in its population, Mississippi could offer manufacturers a pool of workers free from the "disturbing elements so common in larger industrial centers."[17]

Given the state's attractiveness as a source of cheap labor, why was it not already overrun with industry? First, Mississippi's allure was not unique. All of the other southern states could brag of abundant labor and raw materials and generally low manufacturing costs. To make matters worse, the rest of the South had a head start. Manufacturing per capita in the region was four times higher than in Mississippi alone. Balancing agriculture with industry in Mississippi would be difficult unless the state had something to offer that would make it more attractive than its southern competitors.[18]

White felt that the Columbia approach provided just what the state needed. The major deterrent to industrial migration from an area of greater to lesser operating expenses was the cost of moving and acquiring the needed buildings and facilities. By providing a tailor-made structure to house an industry, a Mississippi community could make an industrial move relatively painless as far as management was concerned. To that end White called for an act to authorize the governing bodies of counties and municipalities in Mississippi "to erect, build, purchase, rent or otherwise acquire industries, factories, manufacturing enterprises and buildings and business projects, and to conduct and manage these on behalf of the citizens of such counties and municipalities." A second measure proposed to allow cities and counties to issue bonds to finance construction or purchase of these buildings and plants. These bonds would be backed by general revenue funds raised by taxation, and the interest they paid would be tax-exempt.[19]

White knew that a major objection to his proposal would come from low-tax advocates, and he got in the first blow, arguing that, rather than raising local taxes, his plan would actually lower them in the long run. He cited Jackson's existing assessed taxable property valuation of approximately $30 million and noted that twenty new industrial plants with an average investment of $500,000 would add at least $10 million to that figure. With a five-mill levy, in ten years the city could easily retire the $2

17. *Ibid.*, 6.
18. *Ibid.*, 7.
19. *Ibid.*, 8–9.

million in bonds required to construct twenty new industrial buildings. In light of the economic benefits derived from increased employment and the resultant acceleration of the spending cycle, the creation of new industrial jobs seemed a highly justifiable expenditure. "If," White asked, "your community could invest fifty to sixty thousand dollars and secure an average payroll of $200,000 a year, do you not think that would be a real investment for the general public welfare?"[20]

The governor realized that he was launching a bold new plan in what many might have called the most politically conservative state in the Union. He made careful use of terms like *general welfare* and *public interest* that were employed in the language of major New Deal measures that affected Mississippi. White also argued that conditions warranted the bold action he proposed: "If therefore it be a step further than has heretofore been taken, then I, for one, urge the taking of that step to the end that our commonwealth may be saved, may prosper and may continue to shine as one of the brightest stars in Old Glory's field of blue."[21]

White assured his constituents that his proposal was designed to meet an emergency and that if the plan worked it would soon be unnecessary to subsidize industry in Mississippi. To launch Mississippi on its voyage toward industrial prosperity, the governor turned first to the legislature. At his urging, in their regular session in 1936 the lawmakers approved the expenditure of $100,000 to publicize "the agricultural and industrial possibilities of Mississippi." Giving White his "Balance Agriculture With Industry" bonding program was not so simple, however, because the state constitution specifically prohibited the use of public revenue in aid of private individuals, firms, or corporations. The Mississippi Supreme Court had upheld this provision on several occasions, most notably in 1932 when Booneville had attempted to use the proceeds from a $15,000 bond issue to build a garment plant for lease to a privately operated concern. Because this was precisely what White's plan proposed, it seemed that the industrial subsidy program had little chance of surviving a constitutional test. Hoping to find a loophole, however, White secured the services of several prominent Jackson lawyers whom he charged with the responsibility of drafting the desired legislation within the limits imposed by the state constitution.[22]

20. *Ibid.*, 9–10.
21. *Ibid.*, 12.
22. Hopkins, *Mississippi's BAWI*, 16–17.

Taking their cue from the New Dealers, White's own legal brain trust seized upon the principle of general welfare, searching feverishly for precedent for what they wanted to do. They found what they sought in the unlikely state of North Dakota where the government had developed a system of state banks, grain elevators, warehouses, and even flour mills to serve the needs of its wheat-growing citizenry. The framers of the North Dakota measure argued that providing employment was a legitimate means of serving the general welfare. The United States Supreme Court had upheld this bit of reasoning in 1920 by concluding that the local legislative and judicial authorities were best qualified to determine if a program served the general welfare of the state. Thus encouraged, White's advisers drew up the Mississippi Industrial Act, which the governor presented at a special legislative session in mid-September, 1936.[23]

When White outlined his plan to the lawmakers, he spoke of an emergency brought on by population out-migration and shrunken markets for agricultural products. At a time when Mississippi appeared headed for economic collapse, the state faced increasing demands on its fiscal resources as citizens called for an expanded governmental role in social welfare. Without industrial growth, more programs for the poor, aged, and blind would simply be beyond Mississippi's reach. The act began by citing "an acute economic emergency" caused by unemployment and the lack of agricultural markets and declaring that "the present and prospective health, safety, morals, pursuit of happiness, right to gainful employment and general welfare of its citizens demands, as a public purpose, the development within Mississippi of industrial and manufacturing enterprises."[24]

The proposed program to stimulate industrial growth was to be administered by a state industrial commission of three members (one full-time and two part-time). After at least 20 percent of the registered voters of a municipality or governmental subdivision had petitioned directly for a "Certificate of Convenience and Necessity" that would authorize the local government to acquire land and buildings for a new industry, the commission would determine whether a certificate should be issued. In making its decision the industrial commission would have certain guidelines. The community's labor surplus had to be sufficient to supply one

23. *Ibid.*, 18; *Green* v. *Frazier*, 233 U.S. 253 (1920).
24. *Mississippi Senate Journal*, Extraordinary Session, 1936, p. 784.

and one-half applicants for each job. The sale of municipal bonds might be used to raise revenue to provide sites and buildings for new industry although bonds issued could not exceed 10 percent of the town or county's total assessed valuation of taxable property. Finally and perhaps most importantly, the decision had to be based on whether the enterprise showed reasonable prospect of success and would serve the interests of the locality without burdening the taxpayers. To sound out local opinion on the various subsidy proposals White suggested referenda requiring two-thirds approval of the issuance of bonds.[25]

The governor assured the legislature that communities that practiced rigid fiscal conservatism by trimming the fat out of their existing budgets might retire their bonds without increased tax levies. White apparently overlooked the fact that trimmed budgets would likely result in fewer of the social welfare programs he claimed the public was demanding. At any rate, the state industrial commission would be available to assist municipalities in eliminating "unnecessary activities," thereby making it possible to achieve industrial development without "any financial burden upon the citizens of the community." Meanwhile, sale of the bonds would be facilitated by the fact that interest from municipal securities was exempt from federal income taxes.[26]

White justified the $65,000 appropriation needed to administer the BAWI program by alluding to Franklin Roosevelt's philosophy of government spending: "Recently it was stated by President Roosevelt that it would be good economy to expend one million dollars in the drought area to save ten million dollars to the people. Certainly, we can afford to expend this small sum necessary to try out this program, when the returns from the investment are so manifold in their possibilities."[27]

The act passed easily in the house by a vote of eighty-seven to forty-four, but it cleared the senate only by a vote of twenty-two to twenty with seven members absent. Twenty-one of thirty-six farmers in the house and four of eight farmers in the senate opposed the bill, perhaps because they did not wish to pay higher taxes to support an industry likely to lure workers away from agriculture. No other pattern of opposition or support emerged. In the runoff election in 1935 White had carried twenty of the

25. Hopkins, *Mississippi's BAWI*, 19.
26. *Ibid.*, 19–20; *Mississippi House Journal*, Extraordinary Session, 1936, p. 788.
27. *Mississippi House Journal*, Extraordinary Session, 1936, p. 789.

thirty-two counties whose house delegates opposed the act. Geographically, representatives of the poorer hill counties of the northeast and the Piney Woods areas of the south central region voted against BAWI while the Delta and coastal counties, along with the more urbanized areas, gave it their support. This ironic pattern wherein the regions most in need of industry seemed to be rejecting efforts to attract it was probably more the product of political factionalism than any deep-seated opposition to industrialization.[28]

Of the legislators who were willing to explain their votes for the record, only one objected to the BAWI plan because of its socialistic implications. Most withheld their support apparently because they feared that subsidizing industry would break the backs of "already overburdened taxpayers." Others were concerned that a minority of a community's citizens might commit it to an expensive bond issue. On the other hand, one of the supporters of the measure explained that he believed that the "health, morals, prosperity and happiness" of Mississippians should no longer be "wholly dependent on agriculture."[29]

Governor White lost no time in getting the Mississippi Industrial Commission into action. The governor appointed Harry O. Hoffman of Hattiesburg, a railroad executive, as chairman. To serve with Hoffman, the governor picked Frank A. England, an automobile dealer, bank director, and community leader in Greenville, and S. A. Klein of Meridian, a retired merchant. With only two secretarial assistants, the commission received and screened approximately 3,800 inquiries and propositions concerning industrial ventures in Mississippi over a three-year period.[30]

Each prospect expressing significant interest in locating in the state received a thorough investigation. Often the commissioners secured a Dun and Bradstreet rating. On other occasions, they utilized their own connections in the business world to get background information on a particular firm. Power companies and railroads often put their industrial development departments at the state's disposal. By its various screening and sifting methods, the commission reduced its group of apparently

28. Jack Edward Prince, "History and Development of the Mississippi Balance Agriculture with Industry Program, 1936–1958" (Ph.D. dissertation, Ohio State University, 1961), 73–74; Alexander Heard and Donald S. Strong, *Southern Primaries and Elections, 1920–1949* (Freeport, N.Y.: Books for Libraries Press, 1970), 80–81.

29. *Mississippi Senate Journal*, Extraordinary Session, 1936, p. 817; *Mississippi House Journal*, Extraordinary Session, 1936, p. 812.

30. Hopkins, *Mississippi's BAWI*, 21–23.

worthwhile prospects to three hundred. Further screening and company decisions to postpone expansions brought a still shorter list of a hundred firms that the commission hoped to recruit for Mississippi. Of this number sixty companies showed enough interest to send representatives to the state. The Industrial Commission interviewed these emissaries and took them to meet local officials and inspect potential plant sites.[31]

When the company being courted expressed interest in a particular city or community, the commission notified local officials and gave them as many details about their prospective new industry as possible. For example, in 1938 when Miller Industries, a manufacturer of dairy equipment, expressed a desire to locate in Crystal Springs, the commission gave community leaders information regarding the history and soundness of the company and the sort of operation contemplated for Crystal Springs. In this case, Miller wanted to locate in Mississippi to serve the southern market for dairy equipment. The company hoped that Crystal Springs would provide a five-acre site and $65,000 for construction of a forty-thousand-square-foot building and additional expenses related to moving. In return it would guarantee a minimum payroll of $1 million over a ten-year period. Spokesmen promised to have fifty men working within six months after operations began and to hire fifty more in the six months that followed. Because many of these would be skilled jobs, wages might run as high as thirty dollars per week, and the work force would gradually build up to 250 or 300 men "at an equally high wage."[32]

Miller Industries pledged its equipment and assets as security for the payroll guarantee, and in the event it was unable to meet its obligations, it agreed either to make a compensatory payment or surrender the building and equipment to the city. On the other hand, when the company achieved its million-dollar payroll its executives expected to receive an outright deed to the building. Commission Chairman Hoffman later met with the Crystal Springs Board of Aldermen and expressed the opinion that the proposition offered a good investment for the city although he did caution officials that public funds could not be used for moving expenses. In the long run, however, this was one of the many BAWI negotiations

31. *Ibid.*, 24. The papers of the Industrial Commission, housed at the Mississippi State Archives in Jackson, reveal the pains taken to determine that interested industries were sound.

32. E. C. Pfahl to Board of Aldermen, Crystal Springs, Mississippi, June 11, 1938, in Mississippi Industrial Commission Records, Mississippi State Archives, Jackson.

that came to naught because local leaders and Miller Industries could not work out mutually agreeable terms that would also satisfy the program's legal requirements.[33]

Had the community and company been able to agree, Crystal Springs would have petitioned the Industrial Commission for a Certificate of Public Convenience and Necessity. This petition, requiring the signatures of 20 percent of a municipality's registered voters, was normally accompanied by information indicating that the community had ample natural, human, and fiscal resources to undertake the subsidy project it anticipated. For example, the commission authorized a certificate for Grenada after determining that within a ten-square-mile area around the city there were 277 unemployed laborers between the ages of eighteen and forty-one. Since the proposed hosiery mill would employ 150, this figure insured that the company would find at least one and a half applications for every job, but it also meant that the new plant would not bid up wages by competing with established employers for workers. After determining that Grenada's *ad valorem* tax valuation showed total property value of $2,377,844, the commission approved the issuance of bonds up to $32,000, a figure less than 10 percent of total property assessments. The bonds were to have a maturity period of twenty-one years and bear interest at not more than 6 percent. The certificate specifically authorized construction only of a hosiery and knit-goods plant and stipulated both the size and cost of land and building for the plant. The Grenada facility ultimately housed Grenada Industries, a division of Real Silk Hosiery Mills.[34]

In practice, the granting of the certificate was a mere formality because the commissioners had been involved throughout the city-industry negotiations and their opinions of the proposed project were well known to local officials. The commissioners also made known their reluctance to approve a contract with an industry if there was any significant opposition in a community. For example, the objections of a single lawyer delayed the issuance of Grenada's certificate.[35]

The commission also encouraged communities to strive for the best

33. *Ibid.*; Harry O. Hoffman, "Memorandum for the Crystal Springs, Mississippi, File," June 23, 1938, Mississippi Industrial Commission Records.

34. Hopkins, *Mississippi's BAWI*, 24–25.

35. "Minutes of the Regular Meeting of the Mississippi Industrial Commission," Grenada, Mississippi, March 16, 1937, "Order Granting Certificate of Public Convenience and Necessity after Hearing," both in Mississippi Industrial Commission Records.

possible deal in their negotiations with new industries. Chairman Hoffman was delighted to see Natchez getting a nibble from a prospect like
the Armstrong Tire and Rubber Company, but he expressed concern
about reports that the city would have to issue $300,000 in bonds to get
an annual payroll of the same amount. He informed Natchez officials that
most return ratios on BAWI contracts ran from 2.5 to 5 to 1 in favor of the
community, and he warned against committing the city to "too large a
contribution." Hoffman's concern about the size of the proposed bond issue arose in part from the fact that Natchez already owed $776,000 in
bonds, and the Armstrong deal would virtually exhaust its remaining
bonding capacity. The commission finally granted the certificate, however, after taking into account the depressed economic conditions in
Natchez due to decreased commercial traffic along the Mississippi. As a
result of the commission's efforts to keep in touch with the local situation,
only those petitions likely to be approved were ever submitted. Between
1937 and 1940, the commission issued a total of twenty-one of these certificates although only twelve resulted in the actual construction of new
plants.[36]

After the certificate had been approved, the campaign to gain local
ratification of the bond issue began. In many cases the number of signers
of the initial petition made approval a foregone conclusion, but in some
cities supporters held parades and rallies to boost their cause. Most issues
carried by a large margin. The total vote in seven BAWI referenda favored
approval 5,478 to 397. Only in Cleveland did a bond issue fail to gain the
necessary two-thirds majority. Some opponents in this city apparently objected to the low wage rates projected for the incoming plant, and the
local newspaper editorialized, "we insist that if a factory concern is not
big enough to erect its own building and doesn't want to come to Cleveland that bad, let them stay away."[37]

Citizen approval was less of an obstacle to the early success of the
subsidy program than was the cloud of uncertainty concerning its con-
stitutionality. Few investors were willing to buy the BAWI securities as
long as there seemed to be a chance that the whole program might be

36. Hopkins, *Mississippi's BAWI*, 24–25; Forrest B. Jackson to Messrs. Charles
and Trauernicht, Attorneys-at-Law, March 8, 1937, in Mississippi Industrial Commission
Records.
37. Hoffman to S. A. Laub, September 8, 1937, in Mississippi Industrial Commission
Records; Hopkins, *Mississippi's BAWI*, 40, 46–47, 39. Voting statistics were compiled from
Hopkins, 38–50, and Prince, "History and Development," 324.

scrapped and their bonds become worthless. Durant, the recipient of Certificate Number One, issued $25,000 in bonds paying 6 percent interest. Yet in spite of the relatively high return rate, a buyer could not be found. With the potential industry, the Real Silk Hosiery Mills of Indianapolis, threatening to back out, a wealthy friend of Governor White's bought the entire issue at par. This gave the program a fighting chance, but the reluctance of investors to buy bonds left even supporters of the plan anxious for a test case to prove the constitutionality of BAWI.[38]

The anticipated challenge came in mid-1937 after Certificate of Convenience and Necessity Number 8 allowed the city of Winona to begin successful negotiations with a bedspread plant. The vote on a $35,000 bond issue had been relatively close in Winona (262 to 113) and W. B. Allbritton, a railroad employee, had filed a suit challenging the program's constitutionality. A local chancery court rejected his argument, but he appealed to the state supreme court. If the judges interpreted the state's constitution literally, Allbritton appeared to have a strong case, for the document specifically declared: "No county, city, town or other municipal corporation shall hereafter become a subscriber to the capital stock of any railroad or other corporation or association or make appropriation or loan its credit in aid of such corporation or association."[39]

The decision just a few years earlier that had prevented Booneville from using a bond issue to finance a garment plant provided little reason to hope that the Industrial Act would survive court scrutiny, but the efforts of White's legal advisers to ground the law in the principle of general welfare paid off handsomely. Defense lawyers argued that the expenditure of tax revenue inherent in the program was actually a legitimate use of public money for a public purpose. They cited numerous instances in which the United States Supreme Court had virtually admitted the impossibility of defining *public purpose*. Thus, it seemed reasonable to infer that the term must be construed according to the individual context in which it was used.[40]

The court sustained this argument in a five-to-one decision on February 7, 1937. The majority opinion was a remarkable departure from the tradition of Mississippi jurisprudence. In a bit of logical gymnastics sug-

38. Hopkins, *Mississippi's BAWI*, 38–39; Jackson to Charles and Trauernicht, March 8, 1937, in Mississippi Industrial Commission Records.
39. Hopkins, *Mississippi's BAWI*, 17.
40. Prince, "History and Development," 89–90.

gestive of the manner in which other conservative southern leaders justified federal intervention that benefitted their region, the justices sidestepped the contention that the BAWI program was socialistic:

> But it is said, in effect, that the engaging by a state or its political subdivision in manufacturing enterprises is a complete departure from the concept our forefathers had of the powers and duties of the state and is a step toward socialism. . . .
>
> Every intervention of any consequence by the state and national government in the economic and social life of the citizen has been so branded, beginning in the latter part of the last century with government control or regulation of industries owned and operated by private individuals and which have come to be recognized as public utilities. We must not permit ourselves to be subjected to the tyranny of symbols.[41]

Justice W. D. Anderson, the lone dissenter, vigorously attacked the majority opinion, maintaining that it drove "a steam shovel through our constitution." Ignoring public welfare aspects of the question, he simply cited the constitution's clear prohibition against direct aid to private corporations. In the final analysis, Anderson was surely correct, but like many other normally conservative Mississippians his fellow justices had reached the point where they were willing to stretch their ideological scruples a bit if it meant alleviating some of their state's economic distress. When the United States Supreme Court refused to hear Allbritton's appeal of the Mississippi opinion because no valid federal question was involved, the BAWI program's continued operation was assured.[42]

BAWI bond issues may have been sound investments in the general welfare of Mississippians, but the rental agreements themselves reflected the degree to which incoming employers held the upper hand in their dealings with the Industrial Commission. An occupied BAWI building produced little or no direct revenue for the local government. The program sought new jobs and the resultant cycle of accelerated spending presumed to be of general benefit to the community. None of the BAWI plants established between 1936 and 1940 paid more than $1,000 per year in rent. Durant supplied a $25,000 building for Real Silk Hosiery Mills in exchange for $5 annual rent and a yearly payroll minimum of $60,000. A payroll in excess of stipulated amounts might reduce the rent

41. *Allbritton* v. *City of Winona*, 180 Mississippi 100, 178 So. 799; quoted in Prince, "History and Development," 91.

42. Prince, "History and Development," 93–94; *Allbritton* v. *City of Winona*, 303 U.S. 627 (1938).

by one-half, be applied against future payments, or cause the rent to be waived altogether. On the other hand, if the company failed to make the anticipated payroll, a monthly payment could be required. If all went well, at the end of ten or twenty years the building itself might become company property for little or nothing, as was the case in Natchez' contract with the Armstrong Rubber Company.[43]

By participating in the White plan, a community was actually "buying" a payroll. Pascagoula made the best long-term investment in new jobs of any of the BAWI cities when it voted a $100,000 bond issue to develop a site for the Ingalls Ironworks Company Shipyard. The Mississippi city had originally offered only half as much but found it necessary to double its bid because of competition from Pensacola, Florida, for the Ingalls Plant. At any rate, the onset of World War II spurred expansion of the facility, which soon prided itself on its "250 mile assembly line." At its wartime peak the plant employed approximately twelve thousand workers.[44] Such a contribution to local economic well-being was deemed well worth the two- to five-mill levy normally required to finance a bond issue.

For the most part the early BAWI plants were low-wage, labor-intensive industries that could capitalize on an abundance of unskilled workers. Four of the plants produced hosiery and a number of them sought an exclusively female work force. A typical inquiry concerning a possible plant site in Mississippi came from Fantus Locating Service: "We are still trying to find a spot for the location of the large athletic underwear operation to employ between 750 and 1,000 women. This is simpler than other types of garment production with the result that the girls can learn more speedily and get to better earnings in a shorter space of time. Average wage scales would run about $10.00 per week."[45] Franklin Sweater Mills contemplated a new plant in Mississippi, which would have paid its employees from $800 to $1,000 a year. Mississippi laborers were willing to work for such low wages because the state's annual per capita income in 1938 was only $185 as compared to a national average of $509.[46] To a

43. Prince, "History and Development," 153–55; Hopkins, *Mississippi's BAWI*, 47.
44. Hopkins, *Mississippi's BAWI*, 43–44; Robert F. Couch, "The Ingalls Story in Mississippi, 1938–1958," *Journal of Mississippi History*, XXVI (August, 1964), 201.
45. Felix Fantus to Hoffman, January 20, 1937, in Mississippi Industrial Commission Records.
46. Pfahl to Hoffman, October 10, 1938, in Mississippi Industrial Commission Records; Raymond F. Wallace, *An Analysis of the Balance Agriculture with Industry Program*, State

family struggling to survive under such economically depressed conditions a daughter or wife's extra income of $800 surely seemed more a blessing than an insult.

The affinity of many BAWI employers for cheap female labor led the Industrial Commission to search energetically for plants that would employ males. These operations not only would alleviate male underemployment but would pay a higher average wage than that received by female workers. For example, the commission maintained an active interest in prospects like the Kokomo Sanitary Pottery Company, which was considering a move to Greenville. Of special importance was the fact that this plant would employ 250 men at an average annual wage of $1,200. Natchez leaders were delighted to land the Armstrong Tire and Rubber Plant, because it would employ about 400 men. The Natchez case exemplified the efforts of the commission to tailor industrial growth to local circumstances. Armstrong's need for a male work force meant that it would not compete with a newly established garment plant for female labor.[47]

Incoming companies made it clear that they expected state and local officials to preserve the nonunion climate that helped to keep wages low in Mississippi. When the Real Silk Hosiery Company located in Grenada, the city promised to help preserve the stable labor situation: "The Second Party (Grenada Industries, Inc.) pledges itself to be fair in all of their dealings with employees and to pay fair and reasonable wages, and the First Party (the city) agrees that it will so far as possible prevent any interference from outside sources which may cause or result in labor disputes or trouble and the payroll guarantee hereunder by the Second Party shall be cancelled during the period of any labor disturbance caused by outside interference."[48]

By April, 1940, the expiration date of the Mississippi Industrial Act, the commission had granted twenty-one Certificates of Convenience and Necessity. Seven new plants were in operation and five more had firm plans to begin production in the near future. The twelve BAWI manufacturing facilities included four hosiery plants, three shirt factories, a che-

---

Administration Series, Bureau of Public Administration, IV (University: University of Mississippi Press, 1952), 42.

47. Pfahl to Hoffman, November 17, 1938, Laub to Hoffman, August 21, September 4, 1937, all in Mississippi Industrial Commission Records.

48. Prince, "History and Development," 159.

nille bedspread concern, a woolen mill, a plywood operation, a tire and rubber plant, and a shipyard. Still, many felt the subsidy program had been a failure because it had not yet produced much industrial growth. The seven BAWI plants then in operation employed only 2,691 workers, less than 5 percent of Mississippi's total industrial labor force. Certain developments on the national and international scene also contributed to a slackening of support for BAWI. With the advent of war in Europe and defense preparedness in the United States, prosperity began to return to the nation and even Mississippi shared in the benefits of increased employment. Fewer companies seemed to be interested in relocating by 1940, and the once steady flow of inquiries received by the Industrial Commission had slowed to a trickle. Most communities that were willing and able to subsidize a plant had already done so. In short, BAWI no longer seemed as necessary or appropriate in 1940 as it had in 1936.[49]

The program had also encountered significant criticism both from Mississippians and from financial experts across the nation. One of the state's bankers condemned the BAWI plan, saying, "The thing was outright socialism and should never have been attempted, much less held constitutional." Many fiscal conservatives expressed concern about the risks inherent in the contracts because rental payments were seldom sufficient to amortize the principal of the loan over the life of the bonds. Finally, a few critics charged that the predominance of textile and apparel plants among BAWI industries clearly smacked of exploitation of low-wage labor.[50]

In a broader sense, the BAWI system as it functioned under the tight rein of the Industrial Commission actually perpetuated the economic colonialism that had its critics in every southern state. The commission's reluctance to approve contracts with any but the soundest and best established companies meant that all of the firms that received subsidies probably could have built plants in Mississippi without them. In its efforts to protect small towns and communities from bad investments, the commission's overprotectiveness may have thwarted the establishment of a number of potentially productive enterprises. This caution also led the commission to practice a certain amount of discrimination against projects proposed by Mississippians. Ignoring calls for the establishment of more locally owned plants to process the state's agricultural and mineral

49. Hopkins, *Mississippi's BAWI*, 51–52.
50. *Ibid.*, 61; Prince, "History and Development," 164–76.

resources, BAWI decision-makers did little to stem the flow of the state's raw materials to processing centers located elsewhere. They apparently had doubts about the availability of local capital and the level of managerial expertise in their own state and consequently steered the surer course of courting reputable "foreign" investors whose profits would be siphoned away from Mississippi.[51]

When Governor White had presented his industrial program in 1936, he had emphasized its temporary nature and pointed out that the plan would expire in 1940. Paul B. Johnson, Sr., a bitter foe of White who identified publicly with the "wool hat," anti-big business element in state politics, won the governorship in 1940. Johnson expressed no particular hostility to White's plan, but against the urgings of a number of prominent Mississippians, he took steps to terminate the program. On March 19, 1940, Johnson vetoed a bill to extend the coverage of the Industrial Act, explaining "I believe the Act to be unconstitutional and, in my opinion, it is against the public policy. I do not believe a lien should be voted upon the people's property to assist private individuals or corporations as set forth in this bill."[52] Shortly thereafter, without a kind word being spoken in behalf of what had promised to be the White adminstration's greatest accomplishment, the legislature officially terminated the BAWI industrial subsidy program.

Although BAWI disappeared temporarily in 1940, Mississippi did not abandon industrial promotion altogether. The act that repealed the subsidy plan created the Mississippi Board of Development, which assumed the combined functions of the Advertising, State Planning, and Industrial Commissions. This "practical and wise" merger, as the Jackson *Daily Clarion-Ledger* called it, aimed at the elimination of overlapping functions and promised a savings of $130,000 over the next biennium.[53]

Much of the board's effort went into managing a number of planning and research projects funded by the Work Projects Administration. The Board of Development invested nothing in advertising, largely because it had nothing to invest. Its representatives lobbied for publicity funds in 1942, telling lawmakers, "Mississippi has had a monopoly on misinformation in the nation's mind for more than a 100 years," but the tight-fisted solons refused these advances and the state received favorable ex-

51. Hopkins, *Mississippi's BAWI*, 10.
52. Jackson *Daily News*, March 19, 1940, p. 9.
53. Jackson *Daily Clarion-Ledger*, March 3, 1940, p. 6.

posure in print only when and where newspapers and magazines would donate the space.[54]

Since the only favor that communities could now grant to industry was a local tax exemption, the board had no subsidy contracts to evaluate. It did conduct some direct-mail campaigns and, of course, answered any inquiries that resulted. Yet the Board of Development was by no means as aggressive as the Industrial Commission, nor were its staff members as polished and relaxed in their roles. For example, the assistant director did not beat around the bush when he received an inquiry about an airplane plant interested in locating in Mississippi: "Just what size plant do you want to establish—what are your financial resources and, just to be plain, what do you expect from the locality in which you might establish the plant?"[55] All of the information requested was pertinent, but an industrialist was likely to recoil from so direct a request for a financial report and be no less shocked to confront a point-blank inquiry as to what concessions he hoped to wring from the community where he located.

The Board of Development was also plagued by morale problems among its staff and employees. Office furniture disappeared, employees abused long-distance calling privileges, loitering and even drinking on the job became problems. With its industrial development agency in such a sad state, it was fortunate that the opening of army training centers made a major contribution to the state's economy between 1940 and 1944. Even so, Mississippi attracted only $46 million in federally financed war production plants, the smallest amount awarded any state. Since the state tied with Arkansas for the lowest total investment in privately operated war facilities, Mississippians complained that they had not received their fair share of the profits from the conflict. By 1944 Mississippi still stood last among the states in the value of its manufactured products and the amount of its per capita income.[56]

In view of its failure to keep pace with its southern neighbors dur-

54. "A Presentation to the 1942 Mississippi Legislature in Answer to the Question, Why Mississippi Should Invest in an Aggressive Advertising Program," in Mississippi Board of Development Records, Mississippi State Archives, Jackson.

55. Madison Parker to W. P. Markle, May 31, 1941, in Mississippi Board of Development Records.

56. See Memoranda from Parker, August 13, November 25, 1940, January 20, April 3, 1941, in Mississippi Board of Development Records; Rogers, "The Effort to Industrialize," 234–44; Prince, "History and Development," 69.

ing the war, many journalists and politicians wondered aloud if Mississippi would be left even further behind when peace finally arrived. The Jackson *Daily News* stressed the state's obligation to provide jobs for returning servicemen. In 1943 gubernatorial candidate Mike Conner called for more emphasis on industrial development. His victorious opponent, Thomas L. Bailey, who had led the legislative floor fight for the original BAWI program, agreed, pointing out that almost all other states had drafted postwar industrial plans and that competition for new industry would be intense, "particularly in the South."[57]

Concern about industrialization made the White Industrial Plan look far more successful than it had in 1940. Spurred by the wartime boom, all twelve of the plants were now in progressively expanding operation. During 1942, BAWI plants accounted for 42 percent of the state's gains in manufacturing employment and 47 percent of the growth in manufacturing wages. By April of 1943, these plants employed four times their initial work forces and paid out nine times the original amount of wages. Some, like the Armstrong Tire Plant and the Grenada Hosiery Mill, had responded to wartime shortages of raw materials by converting to munitions productions. The Ingalls Shipyard at Pascagoula provided more jobs than all the other bond-financed plants combined. BAWI factories employed 14 percent of Mississippi's work force and paid 23 percent of its total industrial payroll.[58]

On a dollar-and-cents basis, too, the old program seemed a far better investment in 1943 than it had in 1939. As of mid-1943, the aggregate ratio of wages disbursed to bonds issued was nearly forty-two to one. Even without the largest BAWI employer, the Ingalls Shipyard, the average ratio would have been approximately eleven to one. In 1939 when many plants were still struggling to reach full production levels, the average cost per job to the state had been about $600. Four and a half years later expansion and maturation of the twelve industrial operations had lowered that cost to $90.[59]

When the legislature convened in 1944 there was widespread support for the resurrection of BAWI, and the revived act easily passed both

57. Jackson *Daily News*, March 21, 1940, p. 2, July 22, 1943, p. 1, January 14, 1944, p. 5.
58. Hopkins, *Mississippi's BAWI*, 53–54.
59. Ratios were computed from Hopkins, *Mississippi's BAWI*, 57. These figures do not duplicate those given by Hopkins.

the house and senate. The new program was to be administered by the Agricultural and Industrial Board, a twenty-member panel charged with overseeing industrial promotion. The newly established A and I Board plunged into its work, and the subsidy program took up where it had left off in 1940. In the 1944–1946 biennium eighteen communities received Certificates of Public Convenience and Necessity. Fourteen of these held bond elections, which were approved by an overall ratio of nineteen to one. Estimated annual payroll incomes from industrial expansion in these areas totalled nearly $6 million, approximately four times the amount of the bonds issued.[60]

Procedures under the new program remained much the same except that no petition was required for the granting of a Certificate of Convenience and Necessity. Post-1944 contracts resembled those made under the initial plan, the major difference being that after 1949 the board coerced municipalities to insist on rental payments sufficient to pay off the principal and interest on the bonds that were issued. Even with this new policy, rental costs remained relatively low because of the low interest rates on the tax-exempt bonds, and BAWI industries still benefitted from local property-tax exemptions and from state and federal tax laws that allowed manufacturers to charge off rental payments as operating expenses. With the higher rent requirements, BAWI became less a direct-subsidy plan than one that simply gave industry the benefits of a municipality's borrowing advantages.[61]

Although communities did become more aggressive in their bargaining for new plants under the second BAWI plan, the industries still maintained the upper hand in determining contract details. The Superior Coach Company of Lima, Ohio, exacted a promise that Kosciusko would provide no funds or facilities for any other industrial operation during the first five years after the Superior Plant opened. Baxter Laboratories had a similar agreement with Cleveland.[62] The willingness of the board and local leaders to make such promises no doubt pleased incoming employers, but it also depressed competition for labor that might have bid salaries up closer to the national average.

Several firms, especially garment manufacturers, continued to expect

60. Jackson *Daily Clarion-Ledger*, March 2, 1944, p. 1; Mississippi Agricultural and Industrial Board, *First Biennial Report to the Legislature* (Jackson: n.p., 1945), 15.
61. Prince, "History and Development," 79–82, 163.
62. *Ibid.*, 178.

cities or counties to train their workers for them. Calhoun had to maintain a sewing room at the local high school to provide trained operators for the Calhoun Garment Company. Perhaps the most audacious proposal came from Textron, which hoped to build ten plants in Mississippi, all funded by a single twenty-year issue and all furnished with equipment financed by the bonds. The prospect of announcing ten new plants at once was an attractive one, but the A and I Board refused to cooperate, reminding Textron that the BAWI law made no allowance for using bond revenue to buy equipment. Had the proposal been accepted, Textron would have received ten new and fully equipped plants at no immediate cost while charging off rental payments as operating expenses.[63]

Although there was a certain amount of exploitation inherent in the BAWI program, not every firm that moved to Mississippi acted so opportunistically. In December, 1948, the A and I Board authorized a $300,000 bond issue to assist in the location of an International Paper Company rayon pulp mill at Natchez. A few weeks later voters overwhelmingly approved the bond issue only to have International decline the subsidy. The company's vice-president explained that his firm tried to be a "good citizen" wherever it went, apparently meaning that International paid its own way. He added that the favorable vote on the bond issue was a "magnificent tribute" to his company, "proof positive" of Natchez' desire to have the new plant. BAWI boosters repeatedly pointed to this incident as evidence that a community's willingness to grant a subsidy was often as important to a new industry as the subsidy itself.[64]

By the beginning of 1950 a total of $5,360,000 in BAWI bonds had been issued and the annual interest and amortization cost to the citizens of Mississippi stood at $428,840. In the preceding fiscal year the Agricultural and Industrial Board had operated at an expense of $172,684, overseeing the BAWI program and also promoting tourism and other projects. If the A and I Board's costs were added to the cost of the bonds, however, the entire promotional program in 1949 was operating at an approximate total annual expense of $600,000. In the same year the 10,557 employees of BAWI plants drew $18,117,300 in wages. Therefore, BAWI expenditures represented only 3.32 percent of the wage benefits received. By 1958, plants constructed under the second BAWI program had pro-

63. *Ibid.*, 157, 162.
64. Wallace, *An Analysis*, 32–33.

Table 1 Indicators of Manufacturing Growth, 1935–1960

	Percentage Increase in Value Added by Manufacture	*Increase in Manufacturing Employment*
Tennessee	1,036	191,376
Alabama	1,181	131,290
Arkansas	1,483	73,489
Louisiana	981	70,136
Average	1,170	116,573
Mississippi	1,267	72,148

SOURCE: U.S. Bureau of the Census, *Statistical Abstract of the United States, 1938*, p. 779, *1963*, p. 783 (Washington, D.C.: U.S. Government Printing Office, 1938, 1963).

vided 22,669 new jobs and paid $60,495,799 in wages. These concerns contributed 76 percent of the state's increase in employment and 34 percent of its improvement in earnings in the period 1940–1958. By September, 1959, firms established under both the first and second BAWI programs employed 36,000 workers and dispensed an aggregate annual payroll in excess of $100 million.[65] The percentage of this payroll returned to the state through sales, income, and other taxes made Mississippi's experiment in subsidization look even better.

Although it was impossible to determine conclusively how much of a factor the BAWI plan had been in accelerating industrial growth, the A and I Board took credit for Mississippi's economic achievements. Table 1 reveals that, between 1935 and 1960, value added by manufacture in Mississippi increased by 1,267 percent as compared to an average increase for its four South Central neighbors (Tennessee, Alabama, Arkansas, and Louisiana) of 1,170 percent. Mississippi's economy grew at a faster rate than Louisiana's, but Arkansas, which had no program comparable to BAWI, enjoyed greater gains in both value added and manufacturing employment. Moreover, Tennessee and Alabama's increases in employment during the period were far greater than Mississippi's.

65. William Irvin Scott, "Why Manufacturers Have Located in Mississippi" (M.B.A. thesis, University of Mississippi, 1951), 152–53; Williams, "Financing Industry," 2; Mississippi Agricultural and Industrial Board, *Eighth Biennial Report to the Legislature, 1958–1960* (Jackson: n.p., 1960), 9.

A survey conducted by the Mississippi Power and Light Company showed that industrialists felt the availability of capable, low-wage labor and the existence of a cooperative attitude among local residents had been more important than the BAWI plan in bringing new industry to Mississippi cities. On the other hand, the plant-leasing plan ranked ahead of markets, raw materials, transportation, climate, and public facilities as factors that made the state attractive. A student of the BAWI program up to 1950 concluded that subsidies had probably not attracted any new plants that were not drawn to Mississippi by several other factors. He did note, however, that, in spite of reluctance on the part of some executives to admit it, the subsidy plan had frequently tipped the location-decision scales in Mississippi's favor. Moreover, although only 17 percent of the industrialists polled admitted that they considered special inducements of the BAWI variety "important," 42 percent revealed that they had accepted some special favor, such as free land or buildings or tax exemptions from the community where they located.[66]

An analysis of plant location decisions under the second BAWI program from 1949 to 1958 led the author to conclude that had there been no provisions for publicly financed sites and buildings, seven of the fifty plants he surveyed would have located in the same area, four would have gone elsewhere in Mississippi and twenty-eight elsewhere in the South. The remainder would have moved outside the South or postponed their relocations or expansions. This survey produced a ranking that placed municipal financing second in importance only to labor availability as an incentive for location in Mississippi. The author concluded that without the BAWI program the state would have forfeited 27.9 percent of its gains in employment and 12.7 percent of its progress in payrolls during the period 1940–1958.[67]

However important BAWI subsidies may have been, Mississippi's supply of cheap labor was its greatest asset in attracting new industry. BAWI industries were overwhelmingly labor-intensive. By 1961, apparel, textile, food, and lumber and wood products concerns accounted for 52 percent of all BAWI operations.[68] Critics of the bonding program assailed it

66. Williams, "Financing Industry," 439; Scott, "Why Manufacturers Have Located," 166. See Williams' "adjusted" rankings of Scott's findings, Williams, "Financing Industry," 437–38.

67. Williams, "Financing Industry," 155, 167, 175.

68. Wallace, An Analysis, 45; Prince, "History and Development," 280–81.

for facilitating the exploitation of the Magnolia State's workers and called for guarantees that subsidized plants would pay wages comparable to the national average. The BAWI plan did little to elevate local pay scales, but a labor-surplus, capital-deficient state like Mississippi had little attraction for plants other than those that would employ large numbers of unskilled workers. Also, subsidization amounted to "buying" not a plant, but a pay-roll. The BAWI operations that provided the best return in terms of the ratio of bond issues to jobs produced were the competitive, labor-intensive industries that could best take advantage of both Mississippi's surplus of workers and its provisions for subsidization and tax exemption. Finally, a community that was enough in need of industry to subsidize it would hardly be willing to risk making demands on an incoming plant. This was especially the case because of the number of communities competing for industry and therefore willing to be as generous as necessary to bring new plants their way.

Despite occasional criticism, the subsidy plan seems to have been generally well accepted as the most likely vehicle for pulling Mississippi out of the economic doldrums. Attitudes toward the program varied, for the most part, according to economic and political conditions. The long-run success of the first BAWI projects and the anticipation of unparalleled industrial migration in the postwar period combined to rejuvenate support for the program. Those who objected did so largely because of the economic risks involved for the community. Said one lonely dissenter, "God pity the state when we have to go out and beg for industry by having to have the taxpayers, the homeowners, subsidize them."[69]

Mississippi's pioneering role in state-supervised, publicly subsidized economic development programs was not attributable to greater ideological flexibility among Magnolia State citizens than among southerners in general. Acceptance of such a positive concept of government's responsibilities in a state known for its adherence to laissez-faire can probably be explained by recalling several factors. First, the dubious distinction of being last or near last in every measure of industrial development irked influential Mississippians, many of whom realized that more jobs meant more money to be spent for the goods and services that they sold. Moreover, the BAWI plan surfaced in an era of innovation and experimentation when Mississippi and the rest of the South were receiving the much-

69. Jackson *Daily Clarion-Ledger*, March 17, 1944, p. 2.

needed benefits of federal programs that would never have been implemented, much less accepted, in times of prosperity. Finally, the willingness of ostensibly conservative Mississippians to embrace the BAWI program was far from unique in a nation whose leaders had long preached free-enterprise capitalism while formulating policies that had brought all levels of government into a closer relationship with private business and industry.

Despite their state's well-publicized long-term commitment to state sanctioned and supervised economic development, most Mississippians seemed to accept the practice without the principle, choosing to emphasize the program's benefits rather than confront its implications. Said one banker, "The BAWI plan was socialistic in its teaching, but it worked." A businessman disagreed concerning the nature of the plan. "Municipal ownership of a necessary facility and socialism are two very different things." A mayor allowed that, if "a municipal corporation" leased a building to "another corporation," no "high sounding principle whatever" was involved.[70]

The Magnolia State's role in the defense of the status quo in the South often put its leaders in incongruous positions after the advent of BAWI. For example, as the state sanctioned public ownership of the means of production in many Mississippi cities, development spokesmen charged that the spread of labor unionism threatened free-enterprise capitalism. Frank Everett, chairman of the Mississippi Economic Council, a state chamber of commerce of sorts, warned that anyone who traveled the road toward socialism would "feel the might and muscle of the manhood of Mississippi and come in clash [sic] with the Mississippi Economic Council."[71]

Wilbur J. Cash's observations concerning the tendency of southerners to ignore contradictions in their behavior were borne out by the BAWI experience in Mississippi, and his insights became more credible as the Mississippi plan spread across the South.[72] As other states enacted similar measures and otherwise confirmed or expanded such practices as granting tax exemptions, facilitating loans, or donating free sites, southern de-

70. Hopkins, *Mississippi's BAWI*, 61.
71. Jackson *Daily News*, April 20, 1950, in University of Mississippi Library Clipping File, Oxford.
72. Wilbur J. Cash, *The Mind of the South* (2nd ed.; New York: Vintage Books, 1969), 30–60.

velopment leaders remained staunch defenders of conservative government and the free-enterprise system. Subsidy programs like BAWI and its descendants aimed at enhancing the attractiveness of southern locations as competition for industry intensified after World War II. The emergence of BAWI not only raised the curtain on an era of the competitive use of gifts and gimmickry to attract industry to the South but also pointed to a future wherein state and local governments would become increasingly involved in establishing and maintaining optimum conditions for encouraging new industrial investment.

Chapter 2

BUYING INDUSTRY AFTER
WORLD WAR II

Mississippi's controversial BAWI plan contributed to an atmosphere of heightened interstate competition for new industry after World War II as the use of municipal industrial development bonds spread across the South and much of the rest of the nation. The search for the "edge" needed to win industries away from competing states and communities also reconfirmed the use of tax exemptions and inspired the formation of local organizations committed to providing manufacturers with the capital needed to erect buildings and begin their operations. The proliferation and institutionalization of subsidies revealed the intensity of the South's commitment to industrial growth but did little to alter the traditional pattern of development built around low-wage, labor-intensive industries.

Mississippi's BAWI plan had attracted considerable notice by the early 1950s, but there were other southern states where subsidization was actually more common than in Mississippi. In fact, in the period 1935–1945 industrial bond issues in Tennessee, all of them unconstitutional, involved nearly three times as much money as those authorized by Mississippi's better-known subsidy plan. The exasperated Tennessee State Planning Commission finally suggested that, if subsidization could not be stamped out, it should be legalized. The planners noted that if this approach became lawful it could be regulated and supervised within a framework similar to that provided by the Mississippi program, often the butt of criticism from professional planners all over the nation, including those in Tennessee.[1]

Both Tennessee and Kentucky quickly adopted bonding programs similar to Mississippi's, but no southern state more eagerly embraced industrial bonds than Alabama where the Cater Act of 1949 authorized the formation of municipal industrial development corporations that could issue bonds to finance, build, and equip manufacturing or other industrial plants for lease to private firms. The legislature put another weapon in Alabama's industrial development arsenal in 1951 with the Wallace Act, which allowed cities to enter directly into contracts with prospective industries leading to the construction of industrial plants financed by municipal bonds.[2]

By 1962 nine southern and twelve nonsouthern states had established industrial bonding programs. Six years later all of the southern states except North Carolina offered bonds as an enticement to industry, and all but three nonsouthern states had turned to some form of development bonds as "defensive measures." Socialistic and exploitative as it might be, the BAWI approach to industrial promotion had become a bandwagon, and Mississippi's competitors for industry were jumping on.[3]

Although several states allowed the use of development bonds backed by the "full faith and credit" of state or local governments, most bond subsidies were "revenue" issues secured only by the company's plant rental obligations. Industrial revenue bonds offered the South's poor rural communities with surpluses of farm labor a chance to compete for industry that otherwise might never have given them a second look. Small or medium-sized firms lacking capital and unable to get low-interest loans necessary to build their own facilities would ordinarily have to look to larger, already industrialized cities for sites and buildings. With smaller municipalities empowered to issue revenue bonds to construct plants, however, any community with adequate labor and supporting utilities and services became a bona fide bidder for new industry.

1. Tennessee State Planning Commission, "Subsidies for Industries."
2. Alabama Business Research Council, *Industrial Development Bond Financing: Business and Community Experiences and Opinions*, Center for Business and Economic Research, College of Commerce and Business Administration (University: University of Alabama Press, 1970), 27–29.
3. U. S. Advisory Commission on Intergovernmental Relations, "Industrial Development Bond Financing," June, 1963 (mimeo in Library of Congress, Washington, D.C.); Linda Liston, "The Fifty Legislative Climates Come Under Fire," *Industrial Development*, CXXXVII (November/December, 1968), 17.

The bonding program offered industrialists a number of significant advantages. First, the interest income on municipal bonds was exempt from federal taxation. This meant that such issues could be sold at a significantly lower interest obligation. For example, in 1966 typical municipal revenue bonds were offered at 1 percent below the general interest rate. Although seemingly small, for most industrial offerings this difference could easily amount to a savings of $250,000 or more over a twenty-five-year period.[4] In essence, financing plants with industrial revenue bonds simply transferred the municipality's borrowing advantages to private industry, but low-interest loans were not the plan's only advantages. The industry could deduct rental payments from federal taxes as an operating expense. Moreover, because the municipality actually held the title to the facility, the plant was normally exempt from all state and local *ad valorem* taxes.

The city that issued the bonds enjoyed several benefits. The direct expense to the local taxpayer was minimal because the rental payments were sufficient to amortize both the principal and interest on the securities. The savings enjoyed by industry and the community resulted from the federal government's forfeiture of tax revenue on the interest paid by the municipal bonds. Had the approximately $1 billion in industrial bonds outstanding in mid-1966 not been tax-exempt, they would have paid 5.5 percent interest. Taxed at the 48 percent corporate rate; this interest income would have added $26.4 million to the government's coffers.[5]

The growing reliance of southern states on industrial bonds as development tools quickly provoked criticism from financial experts and political leaders who felt their states were losing industry to the South. Because it represented the premier example of the subsidy bond approach, Mississippi's BAWI program became the target for most of the early opposition. Prior to 1951, Mississippi communities had sold only $15 million in bonds. Kentucky, Tennessee, and Alabama had sold, in much lower amounts, industrial bonds secured only by plant revenue rather than the full faith and credit of a municipality. Up to this point most critics of BAWI had contented themselves with exposés of the exploitation of labor or charges that the program was a step toward socialism. Near the end of 1951, however, Greenville, Mississippi, sold $475 million worth of bonds to build a large carpet mill. Most of these went to no less a buyer

4. "Companies Rush for Cheaper Money," *Business Week*, June 11, 1966, p. 121.
5. *Ibid.*

than J. P. Morgan and Company. In the first half of 1952, voters in Kentucky, Tennessee, Mississippi, and Alabama kept the polls humming on the way to approving $63 million in industrial bonds for projects like a $6 million textile plant for Elizabethton, Tennessee, and a $350,000 garment plant for Hamilton, Alabama.[6]

At this point the Investment Bankers of America stepped into the picture. Out-of-state financiers had long had their doubts about the BAWI plan and in December, 1951, the banking organization went on record as encouraging members to fully acquaint themselves and their clients with the dangers inherent in industrial bond financing. Almost simultaneously, Securities and Exchange Commission Chairman Harry A. McDonald expressed alarm over the spread of municipal subsidies and suggested that Congress might curb the practice by denying tax exemptions to industrial development securities. Moody's Investors Service chimed in, urging readers to avoid all such bonds. Wishful thinkers among Mississippi promoters hoped the criticism was aimed at states where industrial bonds were secured only by a new industry's earning power, but the significance of the IBA's action became clear when Meridian's efforts to sell its $6.5 million issue in behalf of Textron failed to attract a single bid from a major banking house and Textron backed out of Meridian.[7]

In order to market their securities, Mississippi cities turned to local and regional banks and bond houses and the Mississippi Public Employees Retirement Fund, which was a heavy investor in municipal bonds. As Mississippi banks rallied to the support of BAWI, the program then ran afoul of the Federal Deposit Insurance Corporation, which had become concerned that those banks were acquiring too many bonds of questionable rating. In June, 1953, the FDIC put BAWI bonds issued by Indianola, Cleveland, and Kosciusko into Class II, a designation reserved for securities involving "a substantial and unreasonable risk" and therefore not acceptable for member bank portfolios. In response to the FDIC's action, the A and I Board took steps to tighten its control over the program, requiring annual financial statements from participating munici-

6. Lester Tanzer, "Dixie Dilemma: Bond Buyers Frown on Public Money Lure for Southern Plants," *Barron's*, August 18, 1952, pp. 15–16; John D. Garwood, "Are Municipal Subsidies for Industrial Location Sound?" *American City*, LXVIII (May, 1953), 110–11.

7. Jackson *Daily Clarion-Ledger*, December 9, 1951, University of Mississippi Library Clipping File, Oxford; Garwood, "Municipal Subsidies," 11; *Wall Street Journal*, May 7, 1952, p. 1.

palities and prohibiting the use of bond revenue for the purchase of equipment or machinery.[8] BAWI survived these assaults by northern financiers, but the challenges marked the beginning of a lengthy controversy surrounding the South's use of municipal bonds to subsidize its industrial development.

In addition to the criticisms from the North, Mississippians heard complaints from some of their southern neighbors. North Carolina textile manufacturers howled about the unfair competitive advantage that BAWI gave Mississippi. Citing the income tax exemption enjoyed by municipal bonds, these critics pointed out that in 1952 such securities could be sold with interest rates as low as 2 percent, while a privately funded operation could not be financed at less than 4 percent. The municipally financed plant had obvious competitive advantages because it received local tax exemptions and deducted its rent as an operating expense for income tax purposes. One expert concluded that under BAWI an $8 million cotton mill could break even and remain solvent at a 2.4 percent profit while the same plant, financed on a private basis, would have to make 4.36 percent to remain in operation.[9]

Because of the fierce competition in textiles, huge contracts were being won or lost on bids varying only fractions of a cent per yard. Under BAWI, Mississippi textile plants were in a much better position to produce lower-cost goods than their North Carolina rivals. This example provided an important insight into the reasons for the South's attraction for heavily competitive industries. Firms whose major operating costs consisted of employee wages found obvious advantages in a southern location. If these firms were not in highly competitive industries, however, they might simply choose to pass rising labor costs on to consumers. The same would be true of the costs of constructing a new plant facility. In industries like textiles where competition was stiff and profit margins slim, savings in wages, fringe benefits, and initial outlays for new plants could make the difference between red or black ink at the end of the year. Thus, subsidies like bond financing, coupled with the South's cheap labor, helped to confirm the region's already heavy concentration of competitive, wage-sensitive industries.

Although BAWI attracted the earliest and most hostile attention of the

8. Prince, "History and Development," 180–81, 194–96; *Wall Street Journal*, May 7, 1952, p. 1.
9. "The Economic Consequences of BAWI," *Business Week*, April 26, 1952, p. 180.

critics of industrial bonds, the spread of the practice across the South led to more general objections. Opponents had a number of common criticisms of the plan. First, it was a threat to free-enterprise capitalism because it brought public credit into competition with private capital. Historically, periods of widespread local subsidization preceded financial chaos in the United States and resulted in a general weakening of faith in municipal credit. Such chaos promised to bring on increased government regulation, anathema to most conservative economists and financiers, and threatened the tax-exempt status of municipal bonds as well.[10]

The increased size of individual issues raised questions as to whether industry-starved low-income communities possessed the resources to provide the expanded public services that industrial growth seemed to demand. The subsidy plans also created ill feeling not only in competing states but among established local manufacturers who wondered why newcomers were so much more appreciated and favored than they were. Also, massive industrial issues were forcing up interest rates on other municipal securities for schools, roads, sewers, water supplies, and other public projects.[11]

Not only did bond financing give the subsidized plant an advantage over its competitors but some well-heeled firms were apparently buying their own bond issues and collecting tax-free interest that actually originated with their own tax-deductible rental payments. For example, a $500,000 manufacturing plant might be required to pay $32,000 a year for rent. By deducting this payment from federal taxes, the company could reduce the actual cost of occupying the building to $15,360. If the firm purchased the bond issue at 4.75 percent interest, the first year's tax-exempt interest income was $23,750, leaving an "after rent" profit of $8,390.[12]

The proliferation of bonding plans enabled industries to narrow their location choices to a few that met critical requirements like labor, markets, or materials and then bargain among the competing communities for the best possible financing arrangements. This seemed to be the case when United States Rubber, hardly a needy concern, decided to build a new southern plant. Because Atlanta was the company's major distribution center for the region, executives realized that their new facility

10. Garwood, "Municipal Subsidies," 110.
11. "Companies Rush," 114–16.
12. "Hotter Bidding for New Plants," *Business Week*, December 16, 1961, p. 126.

must provide easy access to the Georgia capital. A vigorous and methodical search turned up numerous suitable sites, but the nod went to Opelika, Alabama, a town of sixteen thousand, which obligingly used bonds' to construct a $20 million plant at no initial cost to U.S. Rubber.[13]

Conservative financiers and businessmen who opposed the use of development bonds found themselves in unaccustomed agreement with labor leaders who claimed the practice fostered runaway industry by encouraging migration to low-wage, nonunion areas, mainly in the South. Labor leaders also disliked the fact that bonding programs had federal sanction in the form of tax-exempt status for the interest from securities. They charged that the federal government's fiscal policy actually subsidized the economic development of states where public officials sought to deny labor the right to organize. As a result, at its 1952 convention the American Federation of Labor approved resolutions condemning both direct and indirect subsidies to industry.[14]

Because of its well-publicized BAWI program, Mississippi absorbed a large part of labor organization criticism. The Mississippi giveaways that lured plants away from unionized areas or encouraged expansion in these areas often put union members out of work or denied organized labor the chance to extend its influence within a particular industry. Faced with the threat of a plant move, collective bargainers naturally had less leverage in their dealings with management.

The BAWI program was in the spotlight in 1954 when the Alexander Smith Company, a carpet manufacturer, faced a strike at its plant in Yonkers, New York. The 2,500 workers at Yonkers belonged to Local 122 of the Textile Workers Union, CIO. When the union called for a strike the company responded by announcing it was closing the Yonkers plant and relocating its operations in the South. In January, 1951, Greenville had voted a $4,198,000 bond issue to construct a plant for Alexander Smith. With fifteen acres of floor space, the modern plant soon employed five hundred nonunion workers. The company denied it had closed the Yonkers plant or moved to Mississippi to escape the unions, claiming that a combination of labor troubles, high costs, and out-of-date plant facilities had prompted its relocation.[15] Whether this was true or not, the fact that

13. Eugene Lichtenstein, "Higher and Higher Go the Bids for Industry," *Fortune*, LXIX (April, 1964), 160.
14. Prince, "History and Development," 187.
15. *Ibid.*, 184–85.

Smith Company executives knew they could secure a large, modern plant and a nonunion work force at no expense other than moving costs had left the unionized Yonkers employees in a severely weakened position.

Labor also complained bitterly when the Johnson Lawn Mower Plant closed its unionized operation in Ottumwa, Iowa, in 1952 and moved to a $600,000 BAWI plant in Brookhaven, Mississippi, especially after attempts to organize the workers at the new plant met with hostility from local businessmen and civic leaders. The Brookhaven episode was explained in an American Federation of Labor pamphlet that offered case histories of plant moves encouraged by Dixie giveaways. Arguing that New England bore the brunt of this industrial piracy, the study pointed to companies like Textron, which in 1954 had fifteen plants in the Northeast and nine in the South. Three years later all of the company's production facilities were below the Mason-Dixon Line. The survey also listed forty alleged cases of subsidized migration that weakened local economies outside the South. The losers in the process were the jobless workers whose union affiliations had afforded little protection when their employers took off for greener and nonunion pastures.[16]

The outcries of financiers and labor leaders quickly began to elicit responses from Washington lawmakers who represented areas suffering from the loss of industry to the South. Northeastern congressional leaders, led by Senator John F. Kennedy of Massachusetts, decried southern "raiding," particularly in the textile industry, and they invariably brought up the BAWI plan when they spoke of "unfair competition." Kennedy referred to a news report that the American Bosch Company, "a permanent fixture" in Springfield, Massachusetts, was leaving for a free plant, ten-year tax exemption, and cheap labor in Columbus, Mississippi. Citing a case where the mayor of Woodville, Mississippi, offered a free site and building to a Connecticut manufacturer, Kennedy approvingly quoted the Boston *Record* to his Senate colleagues in 1953, "Instead of utilizing their municipal bonding privileges for public works and the protection of the people from disaster and disease, the southerners put up streamlined mills which various cities and towns rented for almost unbelievably small amounts to bargain-hunting individuals from the North. This naturally

16. American Federation of Labor, *Subsidized Industrial Migration: The Luring of Plants to New Locations* (Washington, D.C.: n.p., 1955), 1–4, 45–46, 49–50, 66–69.

enabled the fugitives to pare down their tax bills and to slash their operating costs so drastically that they could undersell their northern competitors in the domestic and foreign markets."[17] In speeches and articles Kennedy warned that many of the subsidy issues were extremely reckless, telling of one town of ten thousand that proposed to issue $1 million in bonds, thereby incurring additional indebtedness in excess of $4,000 for each resident. "What happens," asked Kennedy, "when their newfound (industrial) benefactors leave for another bargain elsewhere?"[18]

In 1952 Representative George M. Rhodes of Pennsylvania introduced a bill that would have effectively destroyed bonding programs. Attempting to capitalize on cold war anxiety, Rhodes described his measure as an effort "to protect the national defense effort and the normal flow of interstate and foreign commerce from the interference caused by the movements of business enterprises leased from states and political subdivisions of states." Rhodes managed to attach the specter of Communist subversion to southern efforts to attract new plants, warning that the migration of industry and the resultant unemployment in certain areas was "doing more to plant communist seeds of dissension than all of the propaganda of the Kremlin." Rhodes's measure would have banned the shipment in interstate commerce of goods produced in leased buildings financed with public funds.[19]

Congressman Rhodes's unsuccessful bill was the first of many such efforts to restrict the use of industrial development bonds. In 1961, for example, Congressman Robert Griffin of Michigan introduced a proposal to deny tax deductions to plants financed by municipal bonds. By mid-1966, fourteen bills had been introduced in Congress to curtail or abolish the issuance of municipal industrial securities. Typical proposals included removing the tax exemption for the bonds and making rental payments nondeductible, but these pieces of legislation usually attracted support only from representatives of states that were losing industry and encountered opposition from spokesmen for the thirty states that employed bonding by the mid-1960s. The most effective resistance came from seniority-laden southern delegations and prominent individuals like

17. *Congressional Record*, 83rd Cong., 1st Sess., May 1–27, 1953, Vol. 99, Pt. 4, pp. 5, 233–234.
18. John F. Kennedy, "New England and the South: The Struggle for Industry," *Atlantic Monthly*, CXCIII (January, 1954), 36.
19. *Congressional Record*, 82nd Cong., 2nd Sess., Appendix, Vol. 98, Pt. 8, p. A1136.

House Ways and Means Committee Chairman Wilbur Mills of Arkansas, a state that was a leader in the use of development bonds.[20]

Meanwhile, the size of industrial issues grew rapidly, as indicated by the $80 million subsidy provided by Wickliffe, Kentucky, for West Virginia Pulp and Paper and the $75 million sale by Crossett, Arkansas, in behalf of Georgia Pacific. The $1.39 billion in securities issued in 1967 was more than double the 1966 volume and six times that of 1965. This was true primarily because major firms like Cessna, Olin Mathieson, and RCA, to name but a few, began to see bond financing in a different light as interest rates reached new highs in the 1960s. Rubber companies seemed to find bond programs especially attractive; between 1962 and 1967 every tire plant built in the United States was financed by this method. Although the use of industrial development bonds spread rapidly in the 1960s, in the period 1956–1968, Alabama, Arkansas, Georgia, Kentucky, Mississippi, and Tennessee were still responsible for 87 percent of industrial development bond issues and 60 percent of the dollar value of all such bond sales.[21]

Congressional opponents of industrial bonding made no headway until February, 1969, when the Treasury Department announced its intention to remove the tax exemption on industrial development issues larger than $1 million. Senator Abraham Ribicoff of Connecticut, long a critic of industrial piracy, then introduced an amendment to the Revenue and Expenditures Control Act of 1968 that would have given congressional sanction to the Treasury ruling. A contingent of senators and representatives from states with bonding programs countered with a proposal to raise the exemption limit to $5 million. The debate over revenue bonds reflected the growing intensity of interregional competition for new plants. Gaylord Nelson and William Proxmire of Wisconsin and Hugh Scott of Pennsylvania joined Ribicoff in the fight to deny exemptions to industrial issues larger than $1 million, while Senators John Stennis and James Eastland of Mississippi, J. William Fulbright of Arkansas, Howard Baker of Tennessee, and Representative Wilbur Mills of Arkansas defended the use of bonds to promote the development of the South. Representative Speedy Long of Louisiana claimed that industrial bonds

20. Lichtenstein, "Higher and Higher," 164; "Companies Rush," 121.
21. Kenneth J. Crepas and Richard A. Stevenson, "Are Industrial Aid Bonds Fulfilling Their Intended Purpose?" *Financial Analysts Journal*, XXIV (November-December, 1968), 105–106; Alabama Business Research Council, *Industrial Development Bond Financing*, 19–23.

brought $123.3 million in new plant investment to his state in 1967. The southern contingent found unaccustomed allies from the Midwest like Senators Roman Hruska and Kenneth Curtis of the bond-utilizing state of Nebraska who spoke of the desirability of letting "rural America help itself."[22]

The debate over bonds occasionally became heated as southern spokesmen allowed lingering sectional bitterness to creep into their rhetoric. Senator Fulbright of Arkansas responded angrily to charges of industry stealing by Senator Joseph Clark of Pennsylvania by retorting that Clark's state had "no need for capital, having robbed the rest of the country, and particularly the South." Clearly referring to the old charges of colonial exploitation by the North, Fulbright reminded Clark, "We are the ones who buy your automobiles and gadgets many of which are superfluous to good living. . . . It is very shortsighted for you not to allow us to participate in the growth of this country."[23]

Representative Clement J. Zablocki of Wisconsin declared that he and his northern colleagues were tired "of having our pockets picked in extra taxes to pay the way for tax-exempt bonds for building factories in other states."[24] For the most part, however, the antibond forces relied on basic economics, arguing that massive industrial issues had forced up interest rates on more "legitimate" municipal securities, such as those used to build schools and hospitals. They also contended, obviously contradictorily, that although bonds were an ineffective location incentive, competition was pressuring nonbonding states to adopt the practice in self-defense. The increasingly widespread use, or abuse, of bonds was denying the Treasury needed revenue, which could only be recovered through higher income taxes that would fall equally, but unfairly so, on the residents of bonding and nonbonding states. Although Congress eventually placed the exemption limit at $5 million, this action was nonetheless an important step in the direction originally charted by Senator Ribicoff and his allies, for the total value of industrial issues fell from $639.8 million during the first half of 1968 to under $8 million for the same period of 1969.[25]

22. *Congressional Record*, 90th Cong., 2nd Sess., Vol. 114, Pt. 6, pp. 7,336, 7,679–702, Pt. 8, pp. 10,241, 10,297, 26, 418; Alabama Business Research Council, *Industrial Development Bond Financing*, 24–25.

23. *Congressional Record*, 90th Cong., 2nd Sess., Vol. 114, Pt. 6, pp. 7, 686–687.

24. *Congressional Record*, 90th Cong., 2nd Sess., Vol. 114, Pt. 8, p. 10, 241.

25. Daryl A. Hellman, Gregory H. Wassall, and Laurence H. Falk, *State Financial In-*

The restrictions placed on the size of tax-exempt industrial bonds held down the size and total value of such issues for approximately a decade. By the late 1970s, however, lawmakers faced mounting pressure from promoters and industrialists whose expansion plans were threatened by rising interest rates. In 1978 Congress raised the ceiling on tax-exempt issues to $10 million. By 1980, local governments were issuing $8 billion in industrial revenue bonds annually and the once-familiar calls for stripping these securities of their tax-exempt status began to be heard again. Moreover, the limitations on the size of industrial development issues had specifically exempted those intended to finance the purchase of industrial pollution control equipment. Thus, bond financing remained a valuable tool for the southern states as they tried to maintain their growth momentum without running afoul of strengthened federal clean air and water statutes.[26]

The restrictions placed on bond financing at the end of the 1960s fell far short of bringing subsidization to an end in the South, for states and communities offered a number of other concessions to new industry. In 1926 the Arkansas legislature amended the state constitution to provide *ad valorem* tax exemptions for textile mills in the apparent belief that such enterprises were peculiarly suited for the state. The lawmakers subsequently extended the exemptions to all new "manufacturing and processing establishments." Alabama adopted a similar measure in 1935, freeing new industries of all except their school tax obligations for a period of ten years. In many states, new industries seemed to prefer clandestinely arranged low property assessments to publicly announced exemptions. This was the case in Alabama as well as in Arkansas where the constitution set assessments at 50 percent of true value, although in reality they seldom reached more than half that figure. In all states plants built with industrial bonds were considered public property and were therefore exempt from state and local *ad valorem* taxes.[27]

Among the southern states, Louisiana's industrial development program made the most extensive use of tax exemptions for new industries. A 1936 constitutional amendment exempted new manufacturing concerns and all additions to existing plants from state and local *ad valorem*

---

centives to Industry (Lexington, Mass.: Lexington Books, 1976), 11; Alabama Business Research Council, *Industrial Development Bond Financing*, 26.

26. Des Moines *Register*, February 8, 1981, p. 1-c. See also Chapter IX.

27. Ross, "Industrial Promotion," 162–66, 189–90.

taxation. In the same year the legislature created the State Department of Commerce and Industry to administer the exemption program, which required the issuance of contracts to incoming industries. Actually, the Department of Commerce and Industry functioned in much the same way as Mississippi's Agricultural and Industrial Board. The department received preliminary applications from the owners of new plants seeking exemptions. These applications specified the location and nature of the proposed operations and estimates of costs of construction and operation, as well as the number of employees involved in both processes. After examining this information the department would send a field representative for a personal investigation. All pertinent data would then go to the agency's board of directors who made the decision on whether to issue a tax-exemption contract.[28]

Like their Mississippi counterparts, Louisiana development officials tried to encourage diversification rather than industrial competition. Thus, no exemption contract could be granted to a new plant that would produce goods competitive with those already manufactured in a community unless the established concern gave its permission in writing. The original exemption was good for five years but would be renewed automatically if the firm lived up to its contractual obligations. By 1950 a total of 1,059 exemptions had been granted on property valued at $573 million. Some large corporations expanding into the state had received more than one exemption. A paper firm had been freed from tax responsibilities twenty-five times. Assuming that the total property tax rates were approximately thirty dollars per thousand dollars of assessed value, Louisiana denied itself nearly $12 million in revenue in 1948 alone, a figure approximately 20 percent as large as its total property tax collections for that year.[29]

Ironically, relocating industrialists considered Louisiana a "high tax" state relative to its southern neighbors; the state bore an anticorporate stigma that dated back to the Huey Long era. Because new plants in Louisiana were assessed at 100 percent of their actual cash value, rather than the lower percentages found in other southern states, many businessmen surmised that, after the ten-year exemption expired, industries

28. Ronald Isaac Rainey, "A Description and Analysis of the Primary Features of Louisiana's Industry Inducement Program" (M.A. thesis, Louisiana State University, 1967), 8–11.
29. Ross, "Industrial Promotion," 151–52.

would pay dearly for the special favors they had received. Commerce and Industry officials, however, spoke of their exemption program as a means of convincing businessmen that Louisiana was no longer a "soak the-corporations" state. Promoters felt that in addition to making Louisiana seem friendly to new industry, the exemption neutralized the attractiveness of competitive low-tax southern states with reputations for more favorable business climates.[30]

By the mid-1960s five of the seven most active exemptors of taxes were in the South. Alabama, Mississippi, and Louisiana led the way by offering ten-year exemptions on both state and local taxes. South Carolina and Kentucky followed with five-year moratoriums on local taxes. Between 1958 and 1961 these states granted industry valued at $1,472,800,000 exemptions worth $143,840,000. They persisted in this practice in the face of overwhelming opposition from economists, financiers, and industrial location experts. Those who opposed exemptions argued that the tax costs were seldom crucial to a company's location decision. A 1960 study that computed tax loads for a hypothetical corporation in sixteen different locations in Kentucky, Indiana, Ohio, and Tennessee showed that none of the overall tax requirements in any of the states varied sufficiently to change operating costs more than 0.20 percent. Theorists further surmised that competitive tax cutting or exemptions negated the advantages any particular locale might have had in attracting new industry. Moreover, the poorer communities that needed industry most were also in the greatest need of additional tax revenue.[31]

Location experts also warned that progressive industrialists were far more interested in the level of services that a community provided than in saving a few tax dollars. An article in the *American City* cited an instance "where low taxes repelled an industry" because executives did not see how the community "could furnish proper schools, recreation, sewers and city services" for their employees. A planning official reported that a friend whose company had accepted tax concessions now regretted it because the exemption had expired and his firm was being taxed to pay for

30. *Ibid.*, 155–56.

31. William Edward Morgan, "The Effects of State and Local Tax and Financial Inducements on Industrial Location" (Ph.D. dissertation, University of Colorado, 1964), 129; Don M. Soule, "Comparative Total Tax Loads of Selected Manufacturing Corporations with Alternative Tax Loads Computed for a Hypothetical Manufacturing Corporation and Sixteen Variations Thereof," Bureau of Business Research, University of Kentucky, Lexington, Kentucky, 1960 (mimeo in Library of Congress, Washington, D.C.).

community facilities and services that could have been established ten years earlier at a much lower cost. When questioned about their attitudes toward exemptions, industrialists consistently asserted that their company wanted to pay its "fair share."[32]

The most frequently cited empirical study of the effectiveness of tax exemption as a locational inducement was William Ross's survey of executives of the plants that had accepted exemptions in Louisiana in the period 1946–1950. Approximately 60 percent responded to questions concerning the influence of the tax program on their decisions to locate or expand in Louisiana. When asked whether they would have done the same in the absence of the exemption provision, 65 percent replied in the affirmative, 18 percent were uncertain, and 17 percent would have done otherwise. The plants that would have been lost without the tax incentive were valued at $25 million, only 6 percent of the total value of new industry established in the period. Using an estimated average assessment figure Ross concluded that over a ten-year period state and local governments in Louisiana gave up well over $51 million in potential revenues to tax exemptions in order to attract industry valued at only $25 million. Louisiana, he concluded, had made a bad bargain with costs far out of proportion to benefits. Although Ross failed to compare tax losses to payroll gains, planners and theorists, especially those outside the South, pointed triumphantly to his study as proof that tax exemptions were extravagant and inefficient locational incentives.[33]

Ross's conclusions may have influenced some locational experts, but a number of southern states continued to offer tax exemptions as location incentives, and although executives consistently minimized the importance of exemptions, they also continued to take advantage of them. No less a firm than Westinghouse Electric Corporation gratefully accepted a tax exemption granted especially to them by the Mississippi legislature in 1952. Alabama's exemption program continued to function on a grand scale and many new investors quietly insisted that Governor George C.

32. "When Low Taxes Repelled an Industry," *American City*, LXV (August, 1950), 5; "Bargains for Industry," *American Society of Planning Officials Newsletter*, XVIII (August, 1952), 1.

33. William D. Ross, *Louisiana's Industrial Tax Exemption Program*, Division of Research, College of Commerce, Louisiana State University, *Louisiana Business Bulletin*, XV (Baton Rouge: Louisiana State University Press, December, 1955). One of the few critiques of Ross's work appears in John E. Moes, *Local Subsidies for Industry* (Chapel Hill: University of North Carolina Press, 1962), 215–17.

Wallace include "a letter of intent from the Alabama Commissioner of Revenue which is to assure you that your company will be granted the ten-year ad valorem tax exemption, except for school taxes, as provided under Title 51, Section 6, of the Code of Alabama."[34]

Like development bonds, tax exemptions were used to "buy" payrolls. Whereas municipal industrial securities relied on the advantage of federal tax exemptions, however, *ad valorem* exemptions involved the direct forfeiture of tax revenue by state and local governments in exchange for the benefits of increased employment. Critics argued that such tactics surrendered the only universally beneficial result of industrial growth, the increase in tax revenue that might be used to provide the expanded services needed to serve not only the general public but the needs of incoming industry as well. Defenders of the policy cited the positive impact of a new payroll and argued that the forfeiture of tax revenue was not a loss since, had a new plant not been constructed, no new taxable property would have been created. Moreover, once the exemption period expired, the industrial property would be added to the tax rolls. While it cannot be determined whether tax exemption was a justifiable sacrifice on the part of the community, the policy clearly benefited the incoming industry. The protestations of industrialists notwithstanding, in cases where several locations were equally suitable, executives may have chosen the one that offered the most significant exemption.[35]

Not all financial aid to industries offered by southern cities came in the form of bond financing or tax exemptions. At the local level, monetary assistance to new industry often originated with privately supported development corporations. The southern pioneer in this type of endeavor was the Louisville Industrial Foundation, which was incorporated in 1916 in the same manner as any other commercial investment company, except that its charter promised that "its business shall be to advance and develop the city of Louisville and vicinity industrially." The foundation pursued this goal primarily by using monies raised by public subscription to make medium-term loans to manufacturing enterprises. The foundation used its original capital as a revolving fund, lending it, having the

34. Rainey, "A Description and Analysis," 29; Hugh L. White to B. S. Burke, February 7, 1952, in Hugh L. White Correspondence, Mississippi State Archives, Jackson; George C. Wallace to Joseph R. Hager, Jr., July 7, 1964, in George C. Wallace Correspondence, Alabama State Archives, Montgomery.

35. William E. Morgan and Merlin M. Hackbart, "An Analysis of State and Local Industrial Tax Exemption Programs," *Southern Economic Journal*, XLI (October, 1974), 205.

loans repaid, and making new ones, and it became a pivotal institution in Louisville's industrial development because it supplied money to firms that, for various reasons, might have been unable to acquire it otherwise. For the most part, this meant loans to small companies at the current interest rate. Stockholders received no dividend payments, but it was assumed they would share in the general benefits of industrial progress. The foundation's charter required that all loans be made within the Louisville metropolitan area. The standard means of supplying building or expansion capital was a first-term mortgage on land, buildings, and equipment.[36]

In theory, the foundation avoided competition with banks and other lending institutions by refusing to make loans unless an enterprise could not obtain needed capital elsewhere. In fact, the foundation's directors occasionally helped to persuade a local banker or loan official to supply the financing for a new or expanded operation. In other cases, interested bankers referred industries to the foundation. Although its mission of aiding smaller firms entailed certain risks, the organization's directors were conservative businessmen who refused to take chances with their money unless there was a good prospect of success. Some even thought the directors had been too protective of their capital supply, especially during the Depression when jobs had been particularly scarce.[37]

By 1958 the foundation had made loans totalling nearly $6.5 million, almost half of them coming in the period after World War II when competition for new industry became especially heated. Unlike revenue bonding programs, the Louisville organization offered loans at prevailing interest rates, but some of the firms it aided might otherwise have been unable to acquire capital at all. Many of these "long shot" loans paid off more handsomely than the lenders ever dreamed possible. In 1918 a term loan to Reynolds Metal expedited the growth of a firm destined to become world famous for its aluminum products. The foundation's directors proved willing to extend new or supplemental loans to enterprises they had aided initially, thereby making investments in their own investments. In later years the foundation provided consulting services, sent its officials to company board meetings, and generally encouraged local enter-

36. Ernest J. Hopkins, *The Louisville Industrial Foundation: A Study in Community Capitalization of Local Industries* (Atlanta: Federal Reserve Bank of Atlanta, 1945), 1, 4–7, 10, 13–14, 16–18, 54–61.
37. *Ibid.*, 6–7, 30.

prises by helping them to find solutions to the various problems that plagued small businesses.[38]

Local industrial development foundations or corporations (LIDCs) became far more common in the South after 1950. A 1958 study revealed that most active development corporations had been created in the previous five years. The majority of these seemed to be operating in smaller towns with high unemployment and little industrial development. It is difficult to arrive at an accurate estimate of the number of these organizations because they were continually being created, passing out of existence or merging with chambers of commerce or other organizations. In 1958 the South accounted for 25 percent of the nation's development corporations and four years later, 29 percent. Nationwide, during the same period the number of local development corporations increased by 75 percent while the number of such groups in the South grew by 99 percent.[39]

There was much variation in goals and tactics where LIDCs were concerned, but they all provided certain advantages, primarily in the area of financing, for relocating industries. Many local development corporations offered loans or loan guarantees that made it possible for rapidly expanding or distressed companies or those locating in capital-scarce rural areas to obtain financing at or near the prevailing rate. As was the case in Louisville, development corporations often funded higher-risk enterprises, which might not have been able to secure the necessary loan at a feasible rate of interest, if at all. Because they were often nonprofit organizations supported by public subscription or donations from local interest groups, LIDCs could afford to take greater risks than competitive commercial financial institutions.

A 1963 Internal Revenue Service ruling accorded nonprofit industrial development corporations the option of issuing tax-exempt bonds provided the LIDC had the approval of the state or a political subdivision of the state and engaged in activities intended to be of general public benefit. During 1960 and 1961 development corporations in two counties ac-

38. Louisville Industrial Foundation, *Forty-third Annual Report* (Louisville: n.p., January 15, 1959).
39. Victor Roterus, "Community Industrial Development—a Nationwide Survey," in U.S. Congress, Senate Committee on Banking and Currency, 86th Cong., 1st Sess., *Development Corporations and Authorities* (Washington, D.C.: U. S. Government Printing Office, 1959), 124; D. Jeanne Patterson, *The Local Industrial Development Corporation*, Indiana University Bureau of Business Research, Graduate School of Business (Bloomington: Indiana University Press, 1967), 6–7.

counted for half the total volume of industrial revenue bonds issued in Tennessee.[40]

Local industrial development corporations were often vital links between industry-hungry communities and outside funding programs that could assist in promoting industrial expansion. The Small Business Administration provided loans of up to $550,000 to qualified companies with the local organization underwriting as much as 20 percent of the cost of the project. As of mid-1965, 43 percent of SBA loans had gone to southern communities, which were the beneficiaries of 47 percent of all the jobs created by the SBA funds. The Area Redevelopment Administration required first 10 and later 15 percent contributions to industrial loans by a group representing the local community. Forming an LIDC was often the most expedient means of participating in the ARA program. In cases where states provided financial assistance to communities that wanted to participate in these federal programs or where states made direct loans to support industrial development, LIDCs were usually responsible for administration and repayment of the loans.[41]

As was the case in Louisville, many southern communities formed development corporations or took other vigorous actions to promote industrial development in response to a local economic crisis or recession. Augusta, Georgia, was an excellent example. Until the late 1940s, Augusta industry consisted primarily of textile and needle-trade firms, many of which had been in operation since before the turn of the century. Wartime expansion of nearby Camp Gordon provided some stimulation to the local economy, but the biggest boost came with the construction in 1952 of the Savannah River Nuclear facility at nearby Barnwell, South Carolina. At one time more than 35,000 workers took part in the huge plant's construction and both housing demand and retail sales skyrocketed. Just as the Augusta area was taking its prosperity for granted, completion of the plant let most of the air out of the balloon. Rising unemployment and a drastic oversupply of newly constructed homes and buildings slowed economic activity and produced a local recession.[42]

40. Patterson, *The Local Industrial Development Corporation*, 40.
41. *Ibid.*, 33–36, 38–39.
42. Augusta Chamber of Commerce, Augusta, Georgia, "Augusta Industrial Program" (undated typescript in possession of Augusta, Georgia, Chamber of Commerce, Augusta); James C. Cobb, "Politics in a New South City: Augusta, Georgia, 1946–1971" (Ph.D. dissertation, University of Georgia, 1975), 82–83.

With the support of Mayor Millard Beckum, a former chamber of commerce executive, a group of local businessmen formed a "Committee of 100" and immediately swung into vigorous action. Continental Can announced the construction of a $45 million plant with a $2 million payroll after the Committee of 100 had employed a high-pressure campaign to raise $200,000 to purchase a suitable plant site. Also, in 1958 the committee helped to attract an S. H. Kress Company warehouse, a General Electric television tube plant, and a large shirt factory.[43]

Most development corporations offered or were prepared to offer some kind of subsidy. Often these groups could arrange for free or low rent, power, and water, as well as interest-free loans or free sites. Many corporations constructed buildings and made them available to industries at a monthly rental. In some cases, rentals were nominal, but in a larger number of instances, they were sufficient to provide the development corporation's treasury with a return exceeding the original investment. If a locality had the inclination to offer concessions, chances were good that its development organization handled the subsidy. Of 168 new industries that located in fifteen Tennessee cities between 1945 and 1953, 41 plants had been financed by municipal revenue bonds, 50 by local development corporations and only 77 had provided their own funds.[44]

Many southern communities had been offering special inducements to new industry long before they established formal development organizations, and in many cases, the new foundation or commission simply took over supervision of an established practice. Macon County, Tennessee, began an informal subsidy program in order to bail out a local electric cooperative threatened by consumer out-migration. Local leaders contributed $42,500 to induce a garment manufacturer to come to the town of Lafayette. The industrialist used the sum as part payment for a factory large enough to employ 350 people and consume a considerable amount of electricity. This success encouraged further subsidization ventures that led to the establishment of a dairy processing plant in 1946 and a hardwood flooring company a few years later. Hoping to add continuity and direction to industrial promotion efforts, local businessmen subse-

---

43. "Committee of 100 Has Accomplished Much in Augusta Area," *Georgia Magazine*, II (April-May, 1959), 30; Cobb, "Politics in a New South City," 86.
44. "Needed: Investment Capital," *Tennessee Town and City*, VIII (December, 1957), 12.

quently supported formation of the Macon Industrial Corporation, which soon attracted a large shirt factory by erecting a $400,000 building, which was leased to the operators for thirty years at an accumulated rental only slightly less than the purchase price. This project involved private donations, gifts, and loans from the city and county, special bank credit, and a loan from the federal Small Business Administration.[45]

In 1961 newly elected Mayor Joe McCauley oversaw the formation of the Middlesboro, Kentucky, Industrial Commission, headed by a local attorney. The Industrial Commission tried to make Middlesboro more attractive by creating a flat industrial site, a rarity in eastern Kentucky. Actually, the area became a forty-five-acre industrial park financed in part by an $8,000 gift from the Chamber of Commerce, a $60,000 loan from local lending institutions, and a $55,000 loan from the Kentucky Industrial Finance Authority. With this work under way, the commission began a labor survey that attracted ten thousand expressions of interest in industrial employment, many coming from northern Tennessee, western Virginia, or from former area residents who had migrated elsewhere. This effort began to show some results when in 1964 the town attracted a $1 million shirt plant subsidized by revenue bonds and then a much larger plywood plant financed in large part by a grant from the Area Redevelopment Administration.[46]

In 1957 Owensboro, Kentucky, citizens supported the creation of the Owensboro-Daviess County Industrial Foundation, which was financed by the sale of stock. Like their counterparts in Middlesboro, foundation officials tried to make their community more attractive by building an industrial park financed in part by low-interest loans from various government agencies. The Owensboro and Middlesboro cases pointed to the fact that another popular means of subsidization by the late 1950s was the planned industrial district or park. Most of the early parks were sponsored by railroad industrial development divisions seeking new customers, but by 1957 only 29 percent of these districts belonged to railroads, while private investors held 40 percent and community development organizations and local governments accounted for approximately 30 percent of them.[47]

45. Moes, *Local Subsidies*, 57–58.
46. *Wall Street Journal*, January 7, 1966, p. 1.
47. Drewery I. Page, executive vice-president, Owensboro Chamber of Commerce, to

Although companies purchased or leased buildings or plant sites in industrial parks, there was often a subsidy involved. With the proliferation of industrial revenue bonds, it became a simple matter to provide low-cost financing on lease or sale agreements. If the property remained in the city or county's name, the tax advantages were obvious. There were also subsidies in kind such as free access roads, water and sewer lines, and utilities for the new plant. Smaller and medium-sized firms often found the costs of site development crucial, and if industrial parks could provide a location at a reasonable expenditure, then they were logical locations. Moreover, because of economy of scale, utilities or services could be provided more cheaply to industries concentrated in a single area.

Industrial parks multiplied in response to changes in production technology, such as the move to horizontal-line assembly systems requiring large one-story buildings unavailable in central cities. More scientifically managed companies also became aware of the need to escape high city taxes or to provide employees with attractive plants and ample parking lots. By 1970 there were more than 2,400 such parks in operation. This was twice as many as had existed only four years earlier and a sample survey led researchers to conclude that over 75 percent of the industrial parks in operation in 1970 had been completed in the preceding decade. The states with the most industrial parks were located outside the South, but Texas had more than two hundred, both Georgia and Florida had more than fifty, and no southern state had fewer than ten.[48]

Coupled with the South's advantages relative to labor, taxes, construction, and heating expenditures, an industrial park could go a long way toward boosting a local economy. Parks seemed most effective, however, in attracting industries to larger population centers that already had significant industrial bases. Industrial parks in Jacksonville, Florida, for instance, filled rapidly while smaller Florida cities like Lake City and Starke were not as successful in securing new plants. Predominantly rural counties often had even more difficulty. The Madico Industrial Park in

the author, April 8, 1977; Donald R. Gilmore, *Developing the "Little Economies,"* Committee for Economic Development, Supplementary Paper, X (New York: n.p., April, 1960), 134–35.

48. Richard T. Murphy, Jr., and William Lee Baldwin, "Business Moves to the Industrial Park," *Harvard Business Review,* XXXVII (May-June, 1959), 79–88; Linda Liston, "Proliferating Industrial Parks Spark Plant Location Revolution," *Industrial Development,* CXXXIX (March-April, 1970), 7.

Madison County, Georgia, languished amidst cotton and soybeans for a number of years, suffering, no doubt, from its remote location and its ability to provide access only to an unpainted country store.[49]

By the end of the 1960s most southern states relied heavily on subsidies to make themselves more attractive to new industry. The BAWI bonding scheme, often modified by replacing "full faith and credit" securities with the less risky revenue issues, was in use everywhere in the South, except North Carolina. Public subscriptions and industrial funds were available in every state to lighten the expense of setting up new manufacturing operations. Legal and informal agreements afforded tax exemptions and concessions to hundreds of new plants and ambitious communities constructed impressive industrial parks with made-to-order sites and all the necessary supporting services and facilities.

This prodigious array of incentives and gimmicks did not escape the notice of the remainder of the nation. Economic and industrial theorists who for years had shaken their heads in dismay at the South's backward condition now took a critical view of the region's efforts to better itself through industrial subsidies. The classic argument against subsidization had appeared in Glenn E. McLaughlin and Stefan Robock's *Why Industry Moves South*, a study published in 1949 by the National Planning Association's Committee of the South. In the course of their research, McLaughlin and Robock investigated the circumstances surrounding eighty-eight new plant-location decisions made since World War II. The authors relied heavily on information supplied by company executives, most of whom denied that subsidies, even if accepted, played any part whatsoever in their plant location decisions.

McLaughlin and Robock concluded matter-of factly: "Corporate executives are generally convinced that it would be poor business on their part to accept any special concession from a local community." Those who made the final decisions about plant location told the authors that gifts such as free land or cheap buildings actually did little to reduce the overall costs of creating a new plant because the major expenditures were normally made for machinery and equipment. In addition, remarked one executive, "They usually offer inducements when the location doesn't have much to offer." The executives contacted by McLaughlin and Robock

49. Donald E. Agthe, "The Economics of North Florida Industrial Parks" (Ph.D. dissertation, Florida State University, 1970), 177–81.

also seemed to feel that accepting local largesse could damage an industry's relations with the community because it gave townspeople reason to think they should have input into management decisions.[50]

Although they noted that most industries did accept tax concessions when they were offered, McLaughlin and Robock adhered to the principle that "any worthwhile industry ought to row its fair share in the boat." Subsequent commentators on subsidization agreed overwhelmingly, never questioning whether it was reasonable to expect industrialists to admit that their company needed a subsidy or had taken advantage of it simply because it was available. Thus, throughout the 1950s and 60s articles on industrial promotion echoed the conclusion that "the right industry needs no subsidy, the wrong one does."[51] If this assertion was correct, a number of major national firms like Westinghouse and Olin Mathieson had "gone wrong" by the 1960s. Such companies were obviously able to build new plants in the South without special help but nonetheless appreciated the savings that bond financing or tax exemptions offered. Subsidies probably had their greatest influence on the location decision when two or more potential sites were equally attractive otherwise. Given the likelihood that concessions were more effective as development incentives than experts argued, did such enticements represent a good investment for the industry-seeking community?

Many local leaders insisted that subsidization made sense. Boosters who had helped bring new industry to Lafayette, Tennessee, explained their strategy to the state's Municipal League in 1957. The mayor told the group: "The little town that wants industry to stop the flow of young people away from its surrounding rural area does what is called 'buying industry' or it does not get any." For emphasis the mayor added, "I am awfully tired of hearing the fine theorists of industrial development say to the little town desperate for a payroll: 'Only a sick industry wants a subsidy.'" One of his cohorts agreed: "You listen to the experts tell you 'No!' Then if you are wise you do whatever it takes to get the plant, and I mean just that, 'whatever it takes'!" Local promoters believed that, for Lafayette,

50. Glenn E. McLaughlin and Stefan Robock, *Why Industry Moves South: A Study of Factors Influencing the Recent Location of Manufacturing Plants in the South*, NPA Committee of the South Report, III (Kingsport, Tenn.: Kingsport Press, 1949), 112–13.

51. *Ibid.*, 113. See, for example, Richard C. Holmquist, "Gimmies and Gimmicks: A Penetrating Analysis of the Right-and Wrong-Ways to Attract New Industries," *Commonwealth*, XXIX (May, 1962), 17–19.

a town of two thousand, this willingness to "pay the price" had produced in ten years an annual payroll of $1,775,000.[52]

One of the few economists who agreed with the Lafayette boosters was John Moes, who created a stir not only by speaking out in favor of concessions as a means of furthering southern growth but by arguing that depressed areas in the South should be even more aggressive and competitive in offering enticements to new industry. Moes viewed a subsidy as a sound investment in community prosperity, one that he felt produced handsome returns in terms of new payrolls. Taking as an example Natchez, a city that had allegedly made one of the poorer bargains under the first BAWI program, Moes showed that most subsidies were actually quite small relative to the economic gains they produced. The Mississippi city had invested $300,000 in a building for Armstrong Tire and Rubber with the expectation that the company would rapidly achieve a payroll of the same value. Though BAWI officials had been skeptical of this agreement because it promised such a low percentage return to the economically strapped community, Moes argued that the single investment of $300,000 actually brought dividends of 100 percent and more if the impact of the payroll on the spending cycle was considered. Moes also estimated that the $25 million in industrial investment Ross identified as having been attracted to Louisiana by tax exemptions may have also dispensed a ten-year payroll of $10 million.[53]

Moes's argument for the use of subsidies received support from a study conducted by the Chamber of Commerce of the United States, which estimated the benefits of industrialization in eleven counties that experienced significant growth in manufacturing between 1950 and 1960. The results were distributed as inspirational material to local boosters all over the nation. The chamber contended, for example, that a hundred new industrial jobs might increase a county's personal income levels by $710,000 and bank deposits by $229,000. Sixty-five new nonindustrial jobs could be created, three new retail establishments might open, and ninety-seven new automobiles would be purchased. Other chamber studies cited specific southern examples like Front Royal, Virginia, where the coming of American Viscose had created 2,626 jobs in manufactur-

52. "'Buy Industry' or 'You May Not Get It,' Says Lafayette Mayor Who Learned the Hard Way," *Tennessee Town and City*, VIII (July, 1957), 6; Moes, *Local Subsidies*, 57–59.
53. Moes, *Local Subsidies*, 216, 236.

ing between 1935 and 1945 with an apparent spinoff of 795 jobs in other activities.[54]

Lawrenceburg, Tennessee, promoters claimed that within a year after the opening of a new bicycle plant in 1956 there were 1,462 new jobs, building was booming, and land values were rising at 10 percent per year. The precision of such statistics was rightly subjected to some skepticism, but they nonetheless provided significant support for what Moes and others called the "multiplier effect." The theory of multiplication simply argued that an initial increase in income in a community, such as that caused by a new industry, "leads to increased consumption of locally provided goods and services and hence creates additional employment." Thus, the true return on a subsidy investment exceeded the simple differences between the cost of concessions and the new payroll income.[55]

Moes depicted subsidization as a surefire route to higher incomes and general improvement of the local standard of living, but he and many who agreed with him gave little attention to the indirect costs of industrial growth to the community. For example, the same Chamber of Commerce study that extolled the benefits of industrial growth also warned that a new factory might create a need for new streets or roads, expanded utilities, and increased police and fire protection. The costs of extending new services and facilities obviously fell squarely on local governments, which in the South were hardly known for generous expenditures. In 1966 and 1967 no southern state ranked higher than twenty-first in per capita expenditures for highways or twenty-third in per capita spending for local fire protection. Only Florida (thirteenth) ranked higher than twentieth in police protection outlays.[56] Even in communities that offered no exemptions to new plants, property levies were generally minimal, and where an alternative local option sales tax existed, the burden fell disproportionately on the poor. The sales tax took the biggest bite out of the already meager incomes of blacks, many of whom found it difficult to find employment in southern industry. Although the burden of supplying expanded services and facilities for incoming industries fell on all taxpayers, most of the benefits of industrial growth went to employees of the

54. *Ibid.*, 169; "How New Plants Help," *Nation's Business*, L (December, 1962), 88.
55. Moes, *Local Subsidies*, 157–170.
56. U. S. Bureau of the Census, *Compendium of Government Finance*, Vol. 4, No. 5, of *Census of Governments, 1967* (Washington, D.C.: U. S. Government Printing Office, 1969), 71; "How New Plants Help," 88.

new plant and to merchants, professionals, and those associated with local service industries.

Another phenomenon that neither Moes nor the critics of subsidization chose to discuss was the tendency of concessions and special favors to facilitate the dominance of a town by a single employer. Even when no subsidy was involved, a city could easily become dependent on the major local industry's payroll. When a community made an investment in a plant through public financing or a tax exemption, its leaders assumed an even weaker bargaining position relative to the new employer. The willingness of Kosciusko and Cleveland development leaders to withhold support for new firms that might compete with existing BAWI operations was a case in point. A 1964 Mississippi Power and Light Company promotional advertisement illustrated the community's dependent relationship with an industry subsidized by a BAWI bond issue: "After the industry locates the people will cooperate in seeing that a successful operation results, for in reality by voting for such bond financing they have placed a mortgage on their homes to invest in the industrial property."[57]

The textile and apparel manufacturers that chose southern locations were described as footloose industries because their major operating requirements were a supply of cheap labor and an inexpensive plant building. With most southern communities able to supply the former and many the latter, no community could be entirely certain where it stood with local industry. The subsidy investment had to be protected not only by keeping out unions or competing industries but often by the granting of subsequent favors. In 1935 Savannah promised Union Camp not only tax concessions but protection from future pollution suits. A labor publication charged in 1962 that Chester, South Carolina, had shaped itself into a doughnut to provide a tax-free inner-city haven for the Spring Mills Textile Company, which had threatened to move unless such a concession was made.[58]

A number of BAWI plants were obviously footloose enough to seek greener pastures and the A and I Board, apparently hoping at least to keep the industry within the state, occasionally approved the use of bond financing to move plants from one Mississippi city to another. When the'

57. Bill P. Joyner and Jon P. Thames, "Mississippi's Efforts at Industrialization: A Critical Analysis," *Mississippi Law Journal*, XXXVIII (1967), 463.

58. James M. Fallows, *The Water Lords* (New York: Grossman, 1971), 159; "Southern Exposure," *I.U.D. Digest*, VII (Spring, 1962), 105.

board agreed to the move of the Alexander Manufacturing Company from Picayune to Yazoo City, Picayune's mayor and chamber of commerce protested vigorously. The Picayune *Item* editorialized, "No good purpose will ever be served to aid and abet or unify with a bond issue, a move by one Mississippi community to take an industry away from another Mississippi community. If this is permitted the BAWI law is a sham and a mockery and chaos will result in state industrial circles. Some industry might move around every ten years, taking advantage of the benefits offered. No community would ever be safe from a sister community's actions."[59]

Kannapolis, North Carolina, a town of 37,000, remained unincorporated even in the 1970s at the behest of mammoth Cannon Mills, which employed most of the area's labor force. Defenders of the company cited the philanthropic tradition established by Chairman of the Board Charles A. "Mr. Charlie" Cannon, who often made sizable donations to churches, schools, and civic building projects. Yet, by remaining unincorporated, Kannapolis, which would have been the state's tenth largest city otherwise, freed Cannon Mills from municipal tax obligations and allowed the company to become the owner of not only much of the city's housing but the central business district and water supply as well. Cannon also selected and paid the entire police force. Local black residents were frustrated because, even after the Voting Rights Act of 1965 assured their right to register, there were no local elections in which to vote. Finally, Cannon Mills used its control of the water supply and its formidable economic influence to thwart efforts to bring in new industry. Said one Cannon employee, "Mr. Charlie don't want nobody coming in here and running up wages."[60]

Even with a development corporation or a chamber of commerce overseeing subsidization, there were still flagrant abuses. Madisonville, Kentucky, floated a $100,000 bond, constructed a building and leased it for twenty years to an industry that had promised to hire seventy-five people but never employed more than fifteen. The payroll guarantees in Mississippi's BAWI contracts were supposed to be legally binding, and Greenville leaders had apparently expected 186 jobs to be created when their

59. Quoted in Joyner and Thames, "Mississippi's Efforts," 446.
60. *Wall Street Journal*, April 29, 1969, p. 1. See also Ralph R. Triplette, Jr., "One Industry Towns: Their Location, Development, and Economic Character" (Ph.D. dissertation, University of North Carolina, 1974).

city approved a million-dollar bond issue for the Cleaver-Brooks Company. Yet, despite the fact that the firm employed an average of eight workers for the first four years of operation, local leaders chose not to demand compensation from the company. Interviews with Mississippi development officials suggested that Greenville leaders feared that a suit against a BAWI plant would destroy the community's reputation as a haven for industry and impede efforts to recruit other manufacturing operations.[61]

Proponents justified the use of subsidies to attract new industries by arguing that areas that lacked investment capital, consumer demand, or skilled workers needed some special feature to make them more alluring to potential investors. These incentives may have contributed significantly to southern industrial growth, but they also helped to reinforce the region's attraction for competitive, low-wage manufacturers because these were the firms most in need of the extra savings afforded by subsidies or concessions. Shackled with poorly paying, slowly growing industries, the region had little opportunity to experience the rapid, self-sustaining expansion that might have generated the capital and demand needed to attract more desirable firms. In the long run, subsidies helped to perpetuate the deficiencies that, in turn, appeared to justify the continued use of subsidies. Still, there is no evidence that the South's economy would have grown more rapidly had industry not received concessions and tax exemptions. Subsidies or no subsidies, so long as the region lacked adequate financial resources, a significant consumer market, and a well-trained, productive labor force, developers could hope to attract only the same types of low-paying, labor-oriented industries that had done little to impair the South's reputation as the nation's "number one economic problem."

61. H.W. Wells, executive vice-president, Greater Madisonville Area Chamber of Commerce, to the author, May 24, 1977; Joyner and Thames, "Mississippi's Efforts," 448.

Chapter 3

THE SELLERS OF THE SOUTH

The evolution and proliferation of subsidies failed to alter the basic course of southern industrial development, but they did contribute to an accelerated effort to sell the South—and its special incentives—to industrial investors. The crusade for new industry after World War II encouraged a greater emphasis on development efforts by state and local governments and also enlisted the services of key public officials, growth-oriented business leaders, and influential private citizens.

Many of the state-supported organizations that were to play such an active role in the post–World War II South's campaign for economic progress had their roots in the boosterism of the early 1920s. In 1923 Alabama established the Department of Commerce and Industries to promote jointly the advancement of agriculture and manufacturing. Four years later the state created an Industrial Development Board to concentrate solely on bringing new plants to Alabama. When the Florida Bureau of Immigration began operations in 1925, it was charged with attracting not only tourists and new residents but new investors as well. Both South Carolina and Virginia established promotional agencies in the mid-twenties and in 1927 North Carolina's new Department of Conservation and Development defined a major portion of its role as acting "in the nature of a state chamber of commerce."[1]

---

1. Albert Lepawsky, *State Planning and Economic Development in the South* (Kingsport, Tenn.: Kingsport Press, 1949), 8. See also Paul Barnett, *An Analysis of State Industrial Development Programs in the Thirteen Southern States*, Bureau of Research, School of Business Administration, Division of University Extension, University of Tennessee, XIII (Knoxville: University of Tennessee Press, 1944).

The industrial development emphasis never disappeared at the state level, but during the desperate early New Deal years, the southern states were at the vanguard of a national trend toward planning and research aimed at producing even, predictable growth. Although there were numerous examples of state government involvement in economic planning dating well back into the early nineteenth century, state planning activity was at a minimum when Franklin Roosevelt took office in 1932. In July, 1933, Public Works Administrator Harold L. Ickes announced the establishment of the National Planning Board to assist in proposing a comprehensive program of public works projects aimed at promoting recovery. In the interest of coordinating planning throughout the nation, Ickes called for state-level planning agencies and within sixty days thirty-seven states had taken steps in that direction. These agencies conducted public works surveys and studies of transportation, land use, intergovernmental relationships, recreation, zoning, and a host of other questions relating to economic recovery and improvement of the quality of life within their states.[2]

At first glance the rhetoric used by southern state planning officials seemed to reflect a deep commitment to the ethos of the New Deal. The Arkansas Planning Board justified its own existence by explaining that state planning simply meant "the application of that common sense principle of directing the future development of a state in accordance with a comprehensive long-term coordinated plan." An Alabama official treated planning even more reverently: "Democracy is the implementation of Christianity . . . and planning is a broader experience in democracy."[3]

These examples seemed to indicate wholehearted acceptance of the principle of economic planning, but many of the agencies' reports and position papers were actually the work of federal consultants supplied by the Work Projects Administration, which furnished 82 percent of all the employees of state planning agencies. Moreover, because public works projects needed the blessing of planning boards before they could gain official approval, most southern leaders probably saw a viable planning agency as a prerequisite for receiving federal funds. Another reason to suspect that the South's affinity for planning was largely pragmatic was the fact that only the Virginia, Tennessee, and Alabama agencies sur-

2. Lepawsky, *State Planning*, 1–14.
3. *Ibid.*, 16; W. O. Dobbins, Jr., "City Planning" (uncatalogued typescript in Alabama State Planning Commission Records, Alabama State Archives, Montgomery).

Table 2 Southern State Planning Agencies, 1936–1948

Agency, 1938	Date Terminated*	Remaining Development Agency	Date Established
Mississippi Planning Commission	1940	Agricultural and Industrial Board	1944
Georgia Planning Board	1943	Agricultural and Industrial Development Board	1943
South Carolina Planning Board	1945	Research, Planning, and Development Board	1945
Arkansas Planning Board	1945	Research and Development Commission	1945
North Carolina Planning Board	1947	Department of Conservation and Development	1925
Kentucky Planning Board	1936	Agricultural and Industrial Development Board	1947
Florida Planning Board	1945	Florida Improvement Commission	1941
Oklahoma Planning and Resources Board	1939	Reorganized as a development agency under the same name	1947
Louisiana Planning Commission	1940	Department of Commerce and Industry	1936
Texas Planning Board	1939	Texas Postwar Economic Commission	1943
Tennessee Planning Commission	—	(continued unchanged)	1935
Virginia Planning Board	—	Department of Conservation and Development	1948

SOURCE: Albert Lepawsky, *State Planning and Economic Development in the South* (Kingsport, Tenn.: Kingsport Press, 1949). 20.
*Officially, only North Carolina, Kentucky and Texas abolished their planning agencies outright. The Louisiana Planning Commission became part of the Planning Division of the Louisiana Department of Public Works. The rest of the agencies were absorbed into state development agencies.

vived World War II. As Table 2 demonstrates, even before the National Resources Planning Board disappeared in 1944, Georgia, Mississippi, Kentucky, Oklahoma, Louisiana, and Texas had scrapped their planning programs or consolidated them with other activities. Florida, Arkansas, and South Carolina followed suit during 1945, and North Carolina's legislature simply refused to make further appropriations for state planning in 1947. The southern states were actually conforming to a national trend. By mid-1947 half of the forty-five states that had once had planning boards had disbanded them or subordinated them to industrial or economic development agencies with no apparent responsibilities for planning.[4]

Several factors lay behind this return to the original development trend of earlier decades; some of them were also responsible for the abolition of the National Resources Planning Board in 1943. One of the most frequent criticisms of planning was that it produced no tangible benefits, merely a mass of reports and statistics that, unless they could be utilized directly in economic development, were all but useless. Thus, critics charged that planners planned merely to justify their existence and that, therefore, an activity aimed at eliminating waste and facilitating efficient utilization of resources actually resulted in the evils it sought to prevent. In addition, the notion of centralized planning ran against the grain of conservative southerners who had already stretched their tolerance for "big government" to the limit in the interest of receiving badly needed New Deal funding. Not only was planning anti-laissez-faire but it also seemed a crucial step toward the kind of regulation and regimentation that southern politicians felt they no longer had to tolerate in a more prosperous World War II context. There is some debate as to the contributions of the New Deal planning agencies to industrial promotion, but at least these boards provided a niche in the state bureaucracy for their more development-oriented successors.[5]

Although there was some variation in the structure and functioning of development boards in the postwar South, most of them operated according to a similar pattern. For the most part, members were gubernatorial appointees or state officials who held their positions *ex officio*. Membership varied from three in Louisiana to twenty-one in Georgia. In most

4. Lepawsky, *State Planning*, 14–27.
5. *Ibid.*, 27–31.

states members served with little or no pay. Most of the legislation establishing the boards called for the appointment of outstanding individuals
from the areas of business, agriculture, finance, and academe, and some
of these acts stipulated that board members be selected with an eye toward providing balanced representation for all of the state's geographical
areas. In fact, an examination of the membership of state planning and
development boards in the South at the end of the 1940s indicated that
businessmen, bankers, publishers, utility executives, industrialists, and
farmers predominated. On the other hand, labor was conspicuously un-
derrepresented. Governors also saw development commission appoint-
ments as opportunities to reward or at least honor "qualified" supporters.
Thus, more often than not, the boards did little more than echo the chief
executive's development philosophy. Certainly the board members lost no
opportunity to praise the governor's achievements in the area of industrial development. In many states, the terms of members corresponded to
those of the governor who appointed them and in others they often resigned when a new governor took office.[6]

While the development boards made their greatest contributions in
public relations, the day-to-day work of industrial promotion remained in
the hands of the executive director and his staff personnel. Some of the
states, like Tennessee, preferred directors with training and experience
in local and regional planning. Other states, like Mississippi, opted for
people experienced in journalism and public relations. Whatever their
qualifications or background, the directors set the tone for the operations
of staffs that also varied widely in size, resources, and expertise. Tennessee's Planning Commission employed twenty-eight persons in 1947,
Mississippi's Agricultural and Industrial Board only six. The Tennessee
staff was trained in fields as diverse as history and geology. South Carolina's promotional staff had experience in teaching, industry, and government employment. Staff turnover was high in the early postwar years
primarily because of low entrance salaries and personnel policies that indicated higher regard for work experience than for training.[7]

State development agencies played a crucial role in the South's efforts
to hold onto wartime gains and avoid reliving the still vivid memories of
the 1930s. Hence, as the war ended, developers cooperated with political
leaders and public officials to encourage policies and incentives that

6. *Ibid.*, 150–58.
7. *Ibid.*, 158–65.

would facilitate conversion of wartime production operations into peace-time industrial plants. In 1946, for example, Florida's promotion staffers supported the state Chamber of Commerce "Industrial Air Tour" of plants that had become idle since the war. Boosters hoped that the touring executives might find a building suitable for their expansion needs.[8]

State development agencies responded promptly to inquiries from manufacturers like the president of Laury Rich Frocks of New York City, who expressed interest in a location with a large supply of experienced seamstresses and asked for information concerning prevailing wage rates for women, the extent of union activity in a prospective location, and "whether the locality is prepared to offer any inducements to attract plants thereto." Developers also sought out prospects through blanket-mailing techniques and "prospecting" trips to the North. On one such trip in July, 1948, for example, a North Carolina representative tried to persuade an executive interested in moving a plant out of Chester, Pennsylvania, to relocate in Asheville.[9]

Southern industrial promoters in the early postwar period were caught in an accelerating trend toward interregional and interstate competition for new plants. The competitive intensity of industry-hunting necessitated rapid action once a prospect was on the line. The Louisiana Department of Commerce and Industry sent the following "Industry Inquiry" to interested communities:

> A well-rated Louisiana manufacturer of men's clothing wants to establish a branch plant in the state, preferably within four or five hours of New Orleans. They will have approximately 250 white women employees, and their annual payroll will average about $250,000. They do not want to locate in any community where they will have to compete with similar manufacturers for white female labor. . . . They already have two offers from *Arkansas*, two from *Mississippi*, one from *Alabama*, and one from *Louisiana*, under which the community or a group of interested citizens would put up the required building on a ten-year lease, receiving four percent of the building costs as an annual rental. . . . It should be noted that these communities in other states have actually made such an offer, and further, that the company would like to reach a decision within the next ten days.[10]

8. Harold Colee, executive vice-president, State Chamber of Commerce, to Governor Millard Caldwell, "Industrial Air Tour," memorandum, September 5, 1946, in "Governor's Correspondence for 1946," Florida State Archives, Tallahassee.

9. Sam Rosenthal to State Capital (*sic*) Building, Charlotte (*sic*), N.C., July 26, 1946, W. C. Guthrie to Mr. Kelly, memorandum, July 12, 1948, both in North Carolina Division of Commerce and Industry Correspondence, North Carolina State Archives, Raleigh.

10. Lepawsky, *State Planning*, 122–23.

The frantic competition for new industry meant that any new plant, no matter how small, was considered a prize. An investor interested in bringing a wood products concern to North Carolina made a detailed inquiry concerning wage rates and taxes on property, personal and corporate income, and stock dividends. Although he expected to employ only fifteen people, he received a prompt response from the Division of Commerce and Industry. In such a competitive atmosphere, promoters were often reluctant to give up on a prospect. In 1948 a representative of North Carolina's Department of Conservation and Development wrote a drug firm that had chosen Baltimore over Greensboro, "Now that you have moved to Baltimore, is it too much to hope that you might change your mind and come back again?"[11]

Increasingly, state promotional agencies began to emphasize their state's particular advantages and cite the competition by name. In 1955 a Florida development staffer wooed a California manufacturer of aircraft rivets with information on "tax and governmental advantages" and statistics showing that in 1952 the average unemployment compensation tax rate for employers in California was more than two and a half times the rate in Florida. The South Carolina Development Board informed an executive apparently considering both Charleston and Savannah for a new nitrogen plant that average labor costs were twenty-six cents per hour lower in the South Carolina city. The Carolinians also pointed out that, unlike Georgia, their state exempted industrial machinery from the state's sales tax. Finally, the South Carolina propaganda pitch included a copy of the Augusta (Georgia) *Courier*, a right-wing extremist newspaper published by archsegregationist Roy Harris, as evidence of the unstable political and economic climate in the neighboring state.[12]

By the 1960s state industrial promotion agencies were a far cry from the shoestring operations of the early postwar years. Directors and staff members were more likely to be experienced professionals than political cronies. Gone were the blanket mailings and form letters. In their place was a sophisticated system that concentrated only on realistic prospects and offered them only such information as seemed relevant. When a

11. Phillip Schwartz to W. W. Barry, Jr., January 27, 1948, Schwartz to Morris Roseman, July 23, 1948, both in North Carolina Division of Commerce and Industry Correspondence.

12. Stanmore Cawthon to George S. Wing, July 13, 1955, in Leroy Collins Correspondence, Florida State Archives, Tallahassee; S. W. Gable to John R. Riley, May 5, 1955, in South Carolina Development Board Correspondence, South Carolina State Archives, Columbia.

prospect expressed enough interest to reveal specific plans and location criteria, the state agency would turn to its files of pertinent data and compile packages of information about the areas in which the company might be interested. At this point all that state promoters could do was wait and hope or perhaps make a discreet follow-up telephone call. If company executives liked what they saw and expressed an interest in examining prospective locations, the agency staff would then arrange an itinerary for their visit, offer them transportation, and inform local officials that their city was under consideration for a new industry. When the inspection team arrived, the professional developers would answer questions and quietly push the general advantages of the state but otherwise leave the final stage of the selling process to local promoters. At the close of a prospect's visit, which may have included inspections of several locations, state personnel would answer final questions and assure the industrialist that he would find a warm welcome in any of the cities he had toured. If, at the end of a reasonable span of time, the prospect had not been heard from, the staff members who had been working with him would make a low-key inquiry into the status of his deliberations.

It is difficult to make meaningful comparisons among state development agencies as to their effectiveness in attracting new industrial investments into their respective states. However, Table 3 at least presents a comparison of industrial development appropriations of the southern states in 1966. These figures suggest that in that year Kentucky, Georgia, and South Carolina put the greatest emphasis on industrial development. Agency budgets presumably reflected the intensity of a state's commitment to industrial promotion, but such figures may have been misleading. Appropriations for industrial development sometimes changed significantly from year to year as did methods of reporting budgets. State promotional programs obviously received more support when a powerful governor emphasized industrial development and less when the governor was pledged to economy. Also, like local organizations state development offices experienced periodic shake-ups and reorganizations that resulted in changes in agency personnel and duties.

State development agencies bore the major responsibility for bringing in new plants, but they received a great deal of assistance from state officials, other state agencies, utility and construction companies, and influential businessmen and private citizens. Postwar pressure for industrial growth mounted so rapidly that election to a southern governorship soon

Table 3 Industrial Development Appropriations in the South

State	1966 Industrial Development Appropriation
Alabama	$ 140,000
Arkansas	497,000
Florida	660,000
Georgia	1,220,000*
Kentucky	1,530,000
Louisiana	235,000
Mississippi	420,450
North Carolina	578,909
Oklahoma	—
South Carolina	1,160,200*
Tennessee	565,000
Texas	230,000
Virginia	717,315

SOURCES: W. H. Long, "$40,000,000 Being Spent to Lure More Industry and Tourists," *Public Relations*, XXII (August, 1966), 33; William Ronald Thomas, "State Industrial Development Organizations in the Southeast: An Evaluation of Performance by Industrial Executives" (Ph.D. dissertation, Georgia State University, 1971), 116–17.
* 1965–1966 Appropriation

carried with it the responsibility of furthering the state's industrial development. Before 1945 the governor's development responsibilities consisted of giving pep talks to local promoters, presenting and accepting the credit for annual growth statistics, and writing form letters for blanket mailing or an occasional personal note to a particularly "hot" industrial prospect. As competition between the states became more heated, however, the chief executive had no choice but to take a more active role in the day-to-day recruitment of new plants.

Southern governors worked through the Southern Governors' Conference to promote industrial dispersion and to remove the impediments to a more uniform distribution of manufacturing plants. Promotional ads followed the lead of the Governors' Conference promising freight rate equalization and urging decentralization of industry. In the tense early years of the atomic age southern governors reminded industrialists, "Dispersion of industry is considered the most practical solution to the problem of protecting industrial machinery from potential attack." If this was true, Mississippi's remoteness actually became an advantage because it offered "relative strategic safety" from nuclear devastation.[13]

Those involved in efforts to bring in new manufacturing facilities often requested gubernatorial intervention to give "an additional push" to "match the efforts of some of our competing states." In 1948 W. C. Guthrie, who made numerous industrial prospecting forays into the Northeast representing North Carolina, visited Continental Synthetic Textiles in New York City. At the time Continental was considering building somewhere in the South a $30 million to $50 million rayon plant that would employ a thousand workers. When Guthrie learned that the firm's vice-president had been personally wined and dined by the governor of South Carolina, furnished a private plane, and generally entertained in a "lavish manner," he suggested that North Carolina's Governor Cherry also make a personal effort to woo the new plant.[14]

Even a mention of an expansion in the newspaper was unlikely to escape gubernatorial gaze. After reading that International Paper Company anticipated opening another newsprint plant, Governor Leroy Collins fired off a telegram, advising company executives of his willingness to meet with them to discuss the advantages of a Florida site. A state development agency would keep its chief executive apprised of significant inquiries, and the governor would send follow-up letters hoping to impress prospects with his state's earnest desire to have their new plants.[15]

Governors responded to escalated competition for industry by calling attention to the deficiencies of rival states. Fearing that an expanding rubber company might choose Mississippi over North Carolina, Governor Luther Hodges warned, "You may get more immediate benefit in Mississippi or some state south of us, but I can say to you with great honesty that they are ten to fifteen years behind this state in certain of their services, including education, roads, mental hospitals and so forth." As more governors worked closely with industrial development teams, personal letters gave way to telegrams, which were eventually superseded by tele-

13. "Report of Governor Gordon Browning, Chairman, Freight Rate Section, Southern Governors Conference, New Orleans, Louisiana, November 16–18, 1952," in Fuller Warren Correspondence, Florida State Archives, Tallahassee. The quotation is from Mississippi promotional ad, *Business Week*, January 20, 1949, p. 70.

14. Guthrie to Kelly, July 12, 1948, in North Carolina Division of Commerce and Industry Correspondence.

15. Leroy Collins to John H. Hinman, January 26, 1955, in Collins Correspondence.

phone calls. Governor J. Lindsay Almond, Jr., of Virginia tried calls to New York, Toledo, and even Hot Springs before sending a letter wooing Owens Corning.[16]

By the mid-fifties southern governors began to make frequent prospecting trips to the more heavily industrialized areas of the nation. Gubernatorial missions to the North in search of new industry became so common that one writer's facetious dialogue did not seem terribly far-fetched:

SECRETARY: There's a salesman here to see you.
MANAGER: Does he have an appointment?
SECRETARY: No.
MANAGER: What's he selling?
SECRETARY: A state.
MANAGER: A what? Who is he?
SECRETARY: He claims he's the governor.[17]

An industry-seeking tour was a hectic mixture of luncheons, private meetings, and speeches. North Carolina Governor Terry Sanford's six-day swing through the Ohio Valley in 1961 must have left him exhausted. Arriving in Pittsburgh on Sunday night, he received a briefing on the week's activities. On Monday he spent eight hours making personal calls on industrialists before hosting a reception and dinner for prospects at his hotel. The next morning he was on a train to Columbus at 5:45 A.M. At 9:00 A.M. he began another full day of visiting, climaxed by another reception and dinner. By late evening, he was on another train headed for Dayton where he repeated a now familiar routine that would continue until he boarded a plane for home in Cincinnati on Friday evening. Sanford's pace was by no means atypical. During a single day in New York City, Georgia Governor Lester Maddox visited six major national concerns including Allied Chemical, Colt Firearms, International Paper, and Lever Brothers.[18]

16. Luther H. Hodges to Mr. T. W. Smith, Jr., May 23, 1955, in Luther H. Hodges Correspondence, North Carolina State Archives, Raleigh; Lindsay Almond, Jr., to Harold Boeschenstein, October 20, 1959, in Virginia Department of Conservation and Development Correspondence, Virginia State Archives, Richmond.
17. "The Battle for New Industry," *Steel* (December 4, 1957), 61. See also "Governors Help Attract Industry," Richmond *Times Dispatch*, February 10, 1958, University of Virginia Library Clipping File, Charlottesville.
18. "Tentative Program, Ohio Valley Industrial Trip, May 21st–May 26th, 1961" (typescript in Terry Sanford Correspondence, North Carolina State Archives, Raleigh); "Industry Calls, New York City" (typescript in Georgia Department of Industry and Trade Correspondence, Georgia State Archives, Atlanta).

Insofar as possible, industrial developers attempted to provide the governor with enough information to make him appear knowledgeable about each individual company's prospects and interests. Using information supplied by local developers and utility companies, the Alabama Planning and Industrial Development Board prepared capsule briefing memoranda for all of Governor George Wallace's calls on northern industries in 1964. When Wallace visited Charles Taylor and Sons in New York, he knew that the company produced processed aluminum and paint pigments. He also knew that the firm had expressed interest in an Alabama location that could provide access to kaolin and silicates. Wallace's briefing book further advised that Taylor and Sons were not contemplating an immediate decision and should be considered a long-range prospect.[19]

Such personal salesmanship reminded voters that the governor was hard at work to bring more industries into his state. Back home, newspapers presented daily accounts of the chief executive's activities, and rare was the governor who returned from such a safari without claiming to have "bagged" at least one or two new plants. It is difficult to evaluate the effectiveness of governors in dealing with industrialists, but many executives were clearly flattered to be contacted by a state's highest ranking official. Weyerhauser spokesmen expressed great pleasure over the visit of Governor Wallace of Alabama, and RCA executives credited the "hospitable" attitude of Governor Farris Bryant with changing their minds after they had already written off a Florida site for a new computer plant. Georgia Governor Ernest Vandiver explained the rationale for making the governor a supersalesman: "If you send an industrial representative to these places, he talks to his counterpart in the business, but a governor— any governor—gets to the president and chairman of the board where the final decisions are made."[20]

These well-planned, highly visible, and energetically executed gubernatorial forays naturally provoked consternation and anger among northern chief executives who felt their states were being "pirated." During the early 1950s, as the clouds of the civil rights conflict gathered, the battle for prospective new industries took on even greater sectional over-

19. "Industrial Prospects—North Central U.S." (typescript in Alabama Planning and Industrial Development Board Correspondence, Alabama State Archives, Montgomery).

20. Peter C. Mohr to George C. Wallace, January 22, 1964, in Alabama Planning and Industrial Development Board Correspondence; Ocala *Star Banner*, August 21, 1960, Florida State University Library Clipping File, Tallahassee; Atlanta *Constitution*, June 2, 1961, pp. 1, 20.

tones. When the governor of Rhode Island leveled the charge of "raiding," Georgia Governor Herman Talmadge responded with a threat: "If he wants war, we'll give him war." Talmadge then unveiled plans to cut Georgia property taxes to a fraction of their already low levels, a move apparently designed to make the state even more attractive to relocating industry.[21]

In 1955 Connecticut Governor Abraham Ribicoff made himself enormously unpopular in the South by denouncing industry-seekers and suggesting they were unwelcome in his state. Ribicoff was angered by a wave of visits by southern developers after the floods of 1955 had done considerable damage to many New England industries. Governor George Bell Timmerman, Jr., of South Carolina responded with a telegram expressing dismay at Ribicoff's harsh words: "I am shocked that you would issue such a statement. The implications are false. . . . You have been misinformed and I assure you that South Carolina's industrial development has never been, nor will it ever be, based on the misfortune of others." Timmerman reminded Ribicoff of the recent hurricanes that had pounded South Carolina and, perhaps with tongue in cheek, promised contributions through the Red Cross to relieve the distress in the New England states. Many southern leaders saw recruitment of northern plants in terms of symbolic revenge for the Civil War. In Oxford, Mississippi, the editor of the Oxford *Eagle* made little effort to conceal his contempt for New Englanders' complaints when he argued, "It is nothing but good neighborliness to help a stricken acquaintance rebuild by advising him where the sump holes are and which is the high ground."[22] Objections to industrial prospecting by southern governors were closely related to the opposition of northern leaders to the use of industrial bond subsidies to bring new plants southward. Although the impact of such "piracy" was exaggerated, highly publicized industry-seeking treks by southern governors contributed to the emergence of a new sectional conflict, this one centered around jobs and new plant investments.

The governor was expected to shoulder a great deal of the responsibility for his state's development, but he could and did enlist the aid of other state officials. State legislators were generally cooperative in making or

21. Atlanta *Journal*, January 3, 1952, p. 1.
22. New York *Times*, August 25, 1955, p. 16; George Bell Timmerman, Jr., to Abraham Ribicoff, August 25, 1955, in South Carolina Development Board Correspondence; Oxford (Mississippi) *Eagle*, November 3, 1955, University of Mississippi Library Clipping File, Oxford.

remaking laws in order to attract new industry. South Carolina's law-makers proved willing to alter state tax regulations to make them more pleasing to potential investors. Palmetto State solons gave further demonstration of their support for industrial development in June, 1956, when they convened in special session, at a cost of $30,000 to the taxpayers, to make it possible for the Bowater Paper Corporation, an English firm, to build a plant in York County near Rock Hill. The business at hand was rewriting the state's alien ownership law, which prevented foreigners from holding title to more than five hundred acres of land.

Governor Timmerman came before the General Assembly to ask that this impediment to progress be removed. He noted that the previous year had been a banner one for the state economically because of the $230 million invested in new plant expansions. Previously, annual investments had not exceeded $95 million. Timmerman argued that, given the state's momentum in development, it would be a shame to lose a plant expected to make long-term expenditures in excess of $100 million. The Bowater Plant would start with a work force of 400, gradually increase it to 4,200 and eventually dispense an annual payroll of $2 million. In addition, the company would buy $4.5 million worth of wood annually, thereby encouraging expansion of South Carolina's underdeveloped timber industry.[23]

To secure the blessings Bowater could bring, Timmerman recommended that the state's sixty-year-old restriction on alien ownership be scrapped in favor of a more liberal one that would allow Bowater, and any other foreign company, to acquire up to 500,000 acres. Mindful of prevailing sentiment in the mid-1950s, the governor explained that the old law was a bad one because it did not "prevent the Communist Party or subversive organizations, or other undesirables" from "doing business" in South Carolina, but it did penalize the good people of South Carolina and a group of "reputable Britishmen." The thrust of Timmerman's appeal, however, was that failure to act would mean the loss of the "best industrial prospect" in the state's history.[24]

Legislative approval of a new ownership bill was not the only hurdle to be cleared, but there was little problem in getting the Water Pollution Control Authority to grant Bowater an exemption that freed the company from certain recently imposed pollution control standards. Despite some

23. "Address by Governor George Bell Timmerman, Jr.," *South Carolina House Journal*, Extra Session, Beginning Monday, June 4, 1956, pp. 7–9.

24. *Ibid.*, 10–11.

criticism from environmentalists, the actions of the governor and legislature were generally well received and the Bowater story quickly became part of South Carolina's industrial advertising campaign, providing indisputable evidence of the cooperative attitude of state government toward industrial development.[25]

In addition to their legislatures, southern governors attempted to marshal the entire state bureaucracy behind their promotional efforts. In 1954 Governor Luther Hodges called on all state officials to give their "full support and cooperation to the Department of Conservation and Development." Should they make contact with any sort of industrial prospect, Hodges urged them to employ a "smile and a warm welcome" to keep "selling" North Carolina.[26]

A governor's influence over the highway department was often of great importance in granting special favors to new industry. In 1948 Arkansas's Sid McMath wrote a Texarkana business leader authorizing him to promise representatives of the Eastman Corporation a four-lane highway to their factory if they located near Texarkana. Alabama's George Wallace wooed the Hammermill Paper Company to racially tense Selma in 1965 with promises of a new bridge designed to make the plant site more accessible.[27]

In Tennessee the Division for Industrial Development attempted to enlist both federal and state agencies in the promotional effort. The Tennessee Valley Authority had long been a boon to the state's development program. TVA's lakes supplied low-cost power, and its staff researchers provided information about raw materials, markets, and potential industrial sites. Such assistance facilitated the conversion of abandoned Stewart Air Force Base into an industrial center. In cooperation with TVA, the Division for Industrial Development asked that a new industry be supplied with water from Cave Lake State Park. In August, 1967, the chief geologist of the State Department of Conservation accompanied Indus-

25. For criticism of allowing Bowater to come to South Carolina, see Charles L. Knight to Timmerman, telegram, May 29, 1956, and J. Roy Pennell to Timmerman, May 26, 1956, both in George Bell Timmerman, Jr., Correspondence, South Carolina State Archives, Columbia. For use of the Bowater episode as an advertisement, see "Statement by George Bell Timmerman, Jr., for use in January Industrial Advertisement," in Timmerman Correspondence.

26. Hodges to ———, December 1, 1954, form letter, in Hodges Correspondence.

27. James E. Lester, Jr., *A Man for Arkansas: Sid McMath and the Southern Reform Tradition* (Little Rock: Rose, 1976), 138; Wallace to Herman Nelson, memorandum, October 20, 1964, in Alabama Planning and Industrial Development Board Correspondence.

trial Development staffers on a trip to New Orleans to make a presentation to an industrial prospect.[28]

Influential private citizens often participated in efforts to bring a new industry into the state. In 1969 the bishops of three Mississippi denominations joined a leading industrialist at a luncheon with General Motors officials in Jackson. The bishops did their best to impress the executives with Jackson's and Mississippi's need for more payrolls. Tennessee enlisted singer Eddy Arnold, one of its more famous citizens, in the industry-seeking brigade by naming him as a member of its Agricultural and Industrial Development Commission. Meanwhile, despite his Republican politics, wealthy, influential Winthrop Rockefeller agreed to become head of the Arkansas Industrial Development Commission.[29]

Governors and their development staffs could also call on utility companies and private businessmen and financiers who stood to profit from industrial development. Mississippi Power and Light was a tireless booster for the Magnolia State. In Georgia the promotional staffs of the Georgia Power Company and the Citizens and Southern National Bank worked closely and effectively with the state agency staff. Several southern railroads conducted industrial development programs.[30]

Growth-minded businessmen like Charles E. Daniel of South Carolina's massive Daniel Construction Company played a leading role in development and urged their colleagues and competitors to join them. Daniel Construction spent $100,000 on advertising and promotion in 1954 alone and sent a representative on thirty-three industrial prospecting trips in the Northeast. Daniel was particularly distressed because several of the state's influential bankers declined to become involved in trying to bring more industry to South Carolina. The staff director of Tennessee's Industrial Development Division asked bankers to pass along any news of prospective expansions into the Southeast, promising, "you

28. "Assistance TVA Can Provide to the State Staff Division for Industrial Development," Dwight O. Nichols to James H. Alexander, April 2, 1969, Walter L. Criley to Nichols, December 17, 1968, Jim Alexander to Boyd E. Garrett, memorandum, August 11, 1967, all in Tennessee Division for Industrial Development Correspondence, Tennessee State Archives, Nashville.

29. William E. Barksdale, "The Saga of a Shoestring Operation," in American Industrial Development Council, Inc., "Practitioner's Notes," March, 1973 (mimeo in possession of the author), 3. For correspondence with Eddy Arnold, see Tennessee Division for Industrial Development Correspondence; "Arkansas: Opportunity Regained," *Time*, December 2, 1966, pp. 24–28.

30. C. E. Wright, "Area Development by Utilities," *Public Utilities Fortnightly*, LXIV (November 5, 1959), 766–73.

may be assured that we would not betray your confidence to your competitors and would keep you advised of any future developments with this particular firm."[31]

Existing industries could also be called into service when there was particular need. Governor Hugh White asked an industrial executive to help him secure a Ford Motor Company glass plant for Mississippi. The result was a letter so positive that it might as well have been drafted in the A and I Board office:

> We built a plant down in Tupelo and we have never found any community where we made friends so quickly who were so eager and willing to aid us in every possible way.
>
> Governor White has done a wonderful job in promoting and protecting industry in the state, and his efforts have drawn many new industries in the area. You undoubtedly know that the state has low living costs, low taxes, and low cost natural gas and electric power; and we can assure you that they have a supply of workers who quickly adapt themselves to factory work and truly appreciate a good job.[32]

In 1967 Robert G. Worden, the director of the Industry Division of Georgia's Department of Industry and Trade, reported to Governor Lester Maddox concerning his efforts to lure a Colt firearms plant from Hartford, Connecticut, to Georgia. Because a major reservation on the part of Colt was the "emotional attachment" of key personnel to New England, Worden suggested that Maddox might want to borrow a Lockheed Jetstar from that company's Marietta facility in order to fly some of the Colt executives down for a first-hand look at the state's attractions. Capital Automobile Company of Atlanta put two Cadillacs at the department's disposal during the visit of a major prospect, and Executive Director Louis W. Truman conveyed his thanks, assuring the car dealer that his help "may have been instrumental in getting Georgia a major new industry."[33]

Representatives of prospective industries occasionally tried to capitalize on a congressional delegation's commitment to its state's economic development. In 1967 Kaiser Industries had acquired an option on a building in Ashburn, Georgia. A Kaiser vice-president contacted General

31. Charles E. Daniel to Edgar A. Brown, January 21, 1955, in Timmerman Correspondence; Jim Alexander to Ridley Alexander, John P. Wright, March 20, 1967, in Tennessee Division for Industrial Development Correspondence.

32. Willard F. Rockwell to D. S. Harder, March 25, 1965, in White Correspondence.

33. Robert G. Worden to Lester G. Maddox, memorandum, September 1, 1967, Louis W. Truman to Elwyn C. Tomlinson, November 14, 1967, both in Georgia Department of Industry and Trade Correspondence.

Louis W. Truman, executive director of the Georgia Department of Industry and Trade, to inform him that Ford Motor Company rather than Kaiser had received a $300 million bid to construct thirty-three thousand military vehicles. Because Ford workers were on strike, the Kaiser representative suggested to Truman that the Georgia congressional delegation might use its influence to have some of the new contract switched over to Kaiser from Ford. As interpreted by Truman, the Kaiser executive's call implied that his firm's interest in opening a Georgia facility was related to its ability to get part of the new Defense Department contract.[34]

Most southern political aspirants expressed strong commitments to economic growth. In Mississippi candidates for governor and lieutenant governor mutually agreed to muzzle themselves in the interest of the state's industrial development. In 1967 Litton Industries' proposed expansion of the Ingalls Shipyard at Pascagoula entailed a $130 million bond issue to be paid off under a lease-purchase arrangement at only 5 percent interest. Litton's own investment was to be only $3 million. This bold request won the support of Governor Paul B. Johnson because it promised twelve thousand new jobs for Mississippi. Johnson called every candidate for governor and lieutenant governor into his office for a meeting with Ellis Gardner, then head of Litton's Pascagoula facility. Gardner described this unusual meeting: "I said, 'We will drop this whole subject like a hot potato, right now unless we have your assurances, gentlemen, that this matter will not become a political football in the coming campaign.' The tape recorder was whirring away and each man got up and identified himself by name and said, 'I will keep this out of politics.' The result: Not once during that year's election campaign did the bond issue become a political issue."[35]

Once state developers and their numerous allies succeeded in cultivating an investor's interest in a particular area within the state, the task of landing the prospect fell to a community's promotional leaders. Because there is relatively little survey material on the subject, it is difficult to sketch any group portrait of local promoters, but the two most active proponents of industrial expansion in any southern city were likely to be the mayor and the head of the chamber of commerce. One Georgia survey, which involved fifty mayors and sixty-nine chamber heads, showed

34. Truman to Maddox, memorandum, September 14, 1967, *ibid.*
35. Neal R. Peirce, *The Deep South States of America: People, Politics, and Power in the Seven Deep South States* (New York: W. W. Norton, 1974), 209–210.

that nearly half of this sample had college degrees and 40 percent had majored in business.[36] Information about other members of local development teams is less specific, but a survey of the accounts of community promotional efforts and techniques suggests that professionals in the legal, insurance, real estate, banking, and journalism fields were heavily involved, probably because they realized that industrial growth was likely to increase demand for their services. The same was true of small businessmen and merchants, who always welcomed an increase in consumer spending.

Most cities or counties had development organizations, although it is difficult to state with precision the number and distribution of these groups in the South at any one time. Local development corporations or "committees of 100" were often formed for the purpose of combatting an economic crisis or wooing a specific industry, and they often disappeared when their missions were accomplished or abandoned. Even chambers of commerce occasionally ceased to function. There have been several efforts to identify local development agencies, but one of the most thorough was published in 1966 by *Industrial Development*, an industrial promotion magazine. This survey revealed that at least 1,811 communities in the southern states had active development organizations. Nearly 81 percent had chambers of commerce, nearly 25 percent had local development corporations, and more than 44 percent had more than one local booster group. If the latter category was an indication of the degree of commitment to industrialization, Table 4 suggests that Arkansas may have had more plant-hungry communities than any southern state.

Although they had to sell the prospect on a specific community rather than a list of potential locations within the state, local promoters utilized many of the techniques employed by state development agencies. In 1959 the Fort Smith, Arkansas, Chamber of Commerce organized teams of "minutemen" who reacted to even the faintest rumor of investor interest with a solicitous inquiry and unsolicited information. When local boosters learned that the Norge Division of Borg-Warner hoped to locate a refrigerator plant in the Missouri-Arkansas area, the minutemen armed themselves with labor and wage-scale information and assaulted the company. Local utilities joined the crusade as did Arkansas Governor Orval

36. William Lee Ellis, "A Survey of Georgia Industrial Developers Operating at the Local Level in 1969" (M.A. thesis, University of Georgia, 1972), 24–26.

Table 4   Percentage of Communities with Industrial Development
Organizations

State	Number of Communities with at Least One Development Organization	Chamber of Commerce	Local Development Corporation	More Than One
		(N)	(N)	(N)
Alabama	124	(80) 64.52	(2) 1.61	(25) 20.16
Arkansas	151	(130) 86.09	(136) 90.07	(102) 67.55
Florida	227	(223) 98.24	(11) 4.84	(74) 32.60
Georgia	150	(148) 98.66	(65) 43.33	(87) 58.0
Kentucky	146	(127) 86.98	(20) 13.70	(79) 54.11
Louisiana	78	(48) 61.54	(4) 5.13	(29) 37.18
Mississippi	56	(44) 78.57	(6) 10.71	(22) 39.28
North Carolina	211	(135) 63.98	(112) 53.08	(112) 53.08
Oklahoma	171	(165) 96.49	(8) 4.68	(67) 39.18
South Carolina	101	(72) 71.29	(12) 11.88	(32) 31.68
Tennessee	124	(62) 50.00	(24) 19.35	(50) 40.32
Texas	174	(170) 97.70	(4) 2.35	(84) 48.28
Virginia	98	(62) 63.26	(44) 44.90	(40) 40.82
Totals	1,811	(1,466) 80.95	(448) 24.74	(803) 44.34

SOURCE: H. McKinley Conway, *Area Development Organizations* (Atlanta: Conway Research, 1966), 113–15, 117–20, 138–40, 164–69, 190–92, 217–22, 231–35, 249–61, 263–65.

Faubus. The Fort Smith Development Corporation encouraged Green-wood, a suburban community, to agree to a $7.5 million bond issue to build the plant and led the campaign to construct new streets and sewers and initiate a new training program at the local junior college. After sniffing out the industry and recruiting it, the Chamber of Commerce drummed up public support for $230,000 in improvements in order to show the community's "warm feelings for Norge."[37]

A local development group's discovery of a likely candidate for relocation might result from the efforts of self-interested businessmen. Late in 1959, a local mobile home sales firm representative helped put the Cham-

37. "The Go-Getters of Fort Smith, Arkansas," *Fortune*, LXIX (April, 1964), 121.

ber of Commerce of Marianna, Florida, in contact with a Pennsylvania manufacturer of mobile homes who might be interested in expanding into the area. The chamber president assured the industrialist, "Our city recently has become very alert to the advantages to be gained from industrial development and is prepared at this time to enter attractively [*sic*] into arrangements with you, making your coming here mutually advantageous." The chamber worked closely with the Jackson County Improvement Corporation, a businessman's group, which promised the new prospect any information or assistance he desired.[38]

The prospect, once smelled out, had to be prodded occasionally in much the same manner as state developers made their follow-up contacts. In this case, after the mobile home producer had made no response for nearly a month, the Marianna Chamber made a second inquiry, assuring the prospect of the enthusiasm with which he would be welcomed to Marianna and Jackson County. Most local developers felt that the key to landing a new industry was getting company officials to visit. To this end Marianna's promoters assured the executive that they were willing to answer "any special questions you may wish to ask which promises to encourage you to come to Marianna to look over the facilities here."[39]

Included in the information sent to the prospect was an annotated list of the advantages Marianna could offer a mobile home manufacturer. These included a "unique" location offering access to major southeastern cities, especially the "thickly populous, glamorous, luxury cities east and south to Miami." Excellent sites were available under a policy whereby the Jackson County Improvement Corporation would either provide free land or retain the land and construct a specified building under a lease-purchase arrangement. Local taxes were low and officials were willing to make long-term commitments to keep them that way if an industry desired. An abundance of workers, many drawn to Florida by attractive living conditions and therefore willing to accept lower wages, awaited the incoming industry. Other information included testimonials from managers of local plants attesting to the market accessibility, labor supply, and governmental cooperativeness that the Marianna area could offer.[40]

38. W. T. Lyford to Robert A. Derose, December 21, 1959, letter in possession of Marianna, Florida, Chamber of Commerce.

39. J. M. Sims, Jr., to Derose, January 15, 1960, letter in possession of Marianna, Florida, Chamber of Commerce.

40. Typescript and copies of industrialists' testimonials are in possession of Marianna, Florida, Chamber of Commerce.

When a prospective industry narrowed its choices, the final selection often depended on the persuasive abilities of competing chambers of commerce. In 1962 the Athens, Georgia, Area Chamber of Commerce learned that an electric products plant would locate either in Athens or Wheeling, West Virginia. Working closely with the Industrial Development Division of the Georgia Power Company, the chamber helped to produce a concise argument for putting the new plant in Athens. In addition to the assurances of the cooperativeness of local government, the chamber and the Georgia Power staff put together figures promising a total annual savings of $447,900 if the proposed plant were located in Athens. Most of the savings came from lower wages and fringe benefits as well as the ability to scale down salaries by readjusting job classifications. The former tactic would be possible presumably because of the Georgia city's nonunion climate. Under a 1960 legislative provision, there was also the prospect of industrial revenue bond financing leading to a twenty- to thirty-year lease-purchase arrangement with an annual rental sufficient to amortize principal and interest. Other information about the superlative quality of local facilities and institutions rounded out the package.[41]

Investors usually wanted to learn as much as possible about sites, local labor, and business conditions. An aggressive, well-supported chamber often prepared descriptive booklets for each available site in the community. These pamphlets would give detailed information on size, topography, drainage, railroad and highway accessibility, zoning, and utility connections, as well as cost estimates for preparing the site. Some, like the Fort Smith Chamber, even provided soil borings and contour maps.[42]

After inspecting sites, the prospect usually toured housing developments, the downtown business district, and local facilities and institutions. He often expressed an interest in talking with a local industrialist, and if community leaders were well prepared, they could grant his wish without concern. One local developer from Harrisonburg, Virginia, told a group of colleagues in a seminar on industrial promotion: "Certain key people in our area are appraised [sic] of our undertakings and we know in

41. Georgia Power Company and the Georgia Institute of Technology, Atlanta (comps.), "A Comparative Cost Analysis: Cost of Operating a Lighting Fixture Plant in Wheeling, West Virginia, v. Athens, Georgia" (mimeo, September 19, 1962, Athens, Georgia, Area Chamber of Commerce).

42. Fort Smith Chamber of Commerce, "Site #9, Fort Smith Chamber of Commerce, Fort Smith, Arkansas" (undated mimeo in possession of Fort Smith, Arkansas, Chamber of Commerce, Fort Smith).

advance that we can count on their help and that they will say and do just what we will want them to say or do." He then told of a prospect who expressed a desire to talk "labor" and "union" with the area's largest employer. This was arranged; the employer just "happened" to have his labor contract on his desk and the prospect came away happy. Later that evening, the local executive called the developers to determine whether what he said was satisfactory. Harrisonburg's development team was also prepared to field questions about the community's social and religious climate: "Adrian Sonn, a leading merchant of the valley helps if we have a Jewish visitor. Ham Shea, owner of the radio and television station, is an expert salesman, and he takes over on the questions about Catholicism."[43]

To prepare cities for an industrial prospect's visit, most state development agencies devised programs intended to help local boosters put their best foot forward. The Arkansas Industrial Development Commission sponsored a "Six Point Preparedness Program" designed to insure that industry-hungry towns did not bungle their chances to impress a visiting industrialist. Each participating community received a "preparedness kit" that guided them toward completion of the program. After conducting labor and resource inventories and preparing assessments of planning and zoning statutes, the city received a plaque recognizing its achievement. In essence, the plan encouraged local leaders to gather the kind of information a prospect would desire. State development officials hoped this approach would supplant less formal promotional techniques like the mayor's wife's entertaining the visitors with a piano concert. The AIDC sold its preparedness program to cities with a series of ads, one of which warned, "sometimes your best friend won't tell you when an industrial prospect will be in town."[44]

Local developers went to such lengths to prepare themselves to deal with prospects because of the competitive atmosphere that had developed so quickly in the postwar period. Landing a new plant was a victory not only for one's community but for one's state. An Asheville, North Carolina, booster hinted to Governor Luther Hodges that he and his associ-

43. D. P. Davis, "Entertaining the Prospect," in Virginia Division of Industrial Development and Planning, "Community Development Seminar, November 14–16, 1962" (mimeo in Library of Congress, Washington, D.C.), 81–82.

44. Quotation is from a series of advertisements used to promote the Arkansas Industrial Development Commission's "Community Accomplishment Contest" during 1959, in Arkansas Industrial Development Commission pamphlet.

ates might not be above sabotaging efforts by Greenville, South Carolina, to land a new plant, in the hope that the facility would then be built in Asheville: "I believe that our best hope is for a last minute break, which might appear in the form of some objection by certain textile interests in the Greenville area. I do know that there is some resistance to their coming in and we are going to try to activate this if at all possible."[45]

Within a state, intercity or even intracounty rivalries were often intense. Early in 1968, leaders in Cleveland and Bradley County, Tennessee, began a campaign to organize a local committee of 100. At a rally on January 22, they appealed to local patriotism, citing the "Econo-Civic Mission of all good citizens." The organizers portrayed the crusade for industrial development as a contest between communities. Therefore, it was crucial that Cleveland not let others get too much of a head start: "Our neighboring communities are putting twice as much financial support behind their development efforts as we are. The result of failure to respond to this kind of competition eventually will be just what you'd expect: Cleveland and Bradley County, a leading East Tennessee area today—will be left behind as others pull ahead tomorrow."[46]

Local development leaders also appealed to civic pride as they attempted to drum up support for industrial bond issues or fund-raising campaigns. The Mississippi Agricultural and Industrial Board left little to chance when it put together a BAWI Action Kit to help local leadership sell bond issues to their communities. The kit included a set of prepared news stories, editorials, cartoons, and advertisements to be utilized by cooperative local newspaper editors and radio stations. Such materials were helpful, but if a community really needed selling on a bond issue, the job had to be done by the local chamber of commerce or committee of 100. If they could not rely on community spirit to assure that the issue would be approved, boosters also provided impressive and often exaggerated estimates of the benefits of new industry. It was much easier to mold public opinion in this fashion if the local media were cooperative, and more often than not, they were. In Augusta, Georgia, the newspapers had contributed heavily to the fund-raising drive for the Committee of 100 and they encouraged others to follow suit. In addition, both of the city's news-

45. Frank Coxe to Hodges, April 27, 1955, in Hodges Correspondence.
46. "Our Econo-Civic Mission" (mimeo, in Tennessee Division for Industrial Development Correspondence).

papers as well as its seven radio stations and two television outlets declined to air behind-the-scenes information about the committee's dealings with prospects. With the media enlisted as part of the promotion team, it became easier to suppress premature speculations about new plants or details of the maneuvers and concessions made to land a new industry.[47]

Although state promotional agencies were supposed to show no favoritism among communities, local development officials still felt it necessary to remind the state staffers of their cities' needs and the advantages they offered to new industry. Most small towns relied on the same locational appeal: good climate, low taxes, cooperative government, and an abundance of eager, nonunion labor. Because they sensed that labor remained the key factor in most relocation decisions, local boosters painted portraits of endless masses of willing workers. Late in 1950 when the North Carolina Division of Commerce and Industry contacted the Wilkes County Chamber of Commerce about a sewing plant seeking a new home, the chamber manager replied enthusiastically, "If there were any prospect of additional employment at average wages, we could secure an almost unlimited supply of workers—in my opinion, easily 5,000 men and women combined."[48]

Realizing the central importance of labor information in landing a new industry, local promoters gradually became more precise in their presentation of such data. In 1969 with Chattanooga in line for a plant employing fifteen hundred women, Bill Teuton, the director of the local committee of 100, sent a detailed labor analysis to the state's Industrial Development Division, pointing out that 36 percent of Chattanooga's nonagricultural work force was female. Department of Employment Security estimates put the eligible female work force within a twenty-five-mile radius at 5,600. Teuton also reminded the state developers that Chattanooga had an excellent worker training program and that, although 35 percent of the area's labor force was unionized, the percentage was much lower among women.[49]

Local developers believed that it paid to keep in touch not only with

47. Mississippi Agricultural and Industrial Board, *First Biennial Report*, 14–15; Louis C. Harris, "Don't Overlook the Newspaper's Role," *Industrial Development*, CXXXVI (March-April, 1967), 21–23.

48. Tom S. Jenrette to H. P. Cotton, November 17, 1950, in North Carolina Division of Commerce and Industry Correspondence.

49. Bill L. Teuton to James H. Alexander, May 29, 1969, in Tennessee Division for Industrial Development Correspondence.

the state development office but with the state's supersalesman, the governor. When a prospect was showing interest, the chief executive's intervention could be crucial. Thus it was that boosters in Cordova, Alabama, enlisted the aid of Governor George C. Wallace in landing a new industry. Wallace, whose popularity rested in part on his ability to communicate with local politicians and leaders, worked hard to support industry-seeking efforts and thereby further ingratiate himself with local promoters. Wallace called a Cordova prospect, invited him down for a personal visit and then reported to the community's leaders, "It was a pleasure to call this fine prospect. I am always happy to try to help you folks in Cordova and Walker County."[50]

When a chamber of commerce ventured north to visit an industrialist, a letter of introduction from their governor seemed a nice way to break the ice. Hugh White, back for another term as governor in 1954, wrote Lowenstein and Sons in New York boosting the delegation from Kosciusko, Mississippi, that would soon be visiting them. After a general explanation of the BAWI plan, White concluded with the assurance that "no representation will be made to you by the citizens of that city that the state cannot endorse."[51]

Because migrating industry chose not only a state but a community, the successful attraction of a prospect normally entailed a significant degree of cooperation between state and local promotional leaders. Insofar as promotional efforts seemed to influence location decisions, the better coordinated state and local efforts were, the greater the chances that development leaders at both levels would be able to claim credit for any community's new industry.

An area where state and local efforts overlapped was that of industrial development advertising. Accurate estimates of expenditures for promotional publicity were difficult to formulate because some organizations were reluctant to divulge their expenditures, others had no specific amount stipulated for advertising, and still others made no distinction between expenses for industrial recruitment and those to promote travel and tourism. Yet, a few approximate figures are available. The New York *Times* sold a total of $46,000 in state advertising space in 1949, but that amount had increased to $520,000 by 1961. The 295 state and local groups

50. Wallace to Roland J. Richardson, September 28, 1964, in Wallace Correspondence.
51. White to Leon Lowenstein, May 17, 1954, in White Correspondence.

that responded to a Curtis Publishing Company survey in 1961 anticipated a twelve-month investment in advertising of $3,287,330 with state appropriations representing approximately 79 percent of this figure.[52]

Among the southern states, Florida was a consistent leader in advertising expenditures as the state's promoters tried to sell fresh air and sunshine to tourists and industrialists alike. Cities in the Sunshine State also invested heavily in publicity. With annual expenditures of $65,000, the Greater Tampa Chamber of Commerce ranked as the second most energetic advertiser among local development groups surveyed in 1961.[53]

Although locational theorists consistently minimized the impact of advertising and surveys of industrialists appeared to bear them out, many southern developers swore by the ads they placed in major national magazines. South Carolina promoters linked an aggressive advertising campaign that began in 1945 to the six hundred new businesses that came into the state during the following two years. They also credited a twenty-page supplement to the New York *Times* in 1953 for at least thirty-five new factory openings. The "Forward Atlanta" movement launched at the beginning of the 1960s aimed at making the Georgia capital more competitive with faster-growing southeastern rivals. The campaign raised about $1.6 million through private donations, approximately one-half of which went for advertising. Within the next two years, nonagricultural employment increased by nineteen thousand, double the "Forward Atlanta" goal, while the city moved from twenty-first to sixth in a ranking of housing construction in major urban areas. There was no proof that advertising had any relationship to the success enjoyed by either South Carolina or Atlanta, but many promoters nonetheless insisted on seeing a direct link between the two.[54]

Developers in the South appeared to believe more strongly in advertising than their counterparts elsewhere. As Table 5 demonstrates, seven of the nine southern states for which advertising budgets were available ranked in the nation's top ten spenders for promotional publicity with the remaining two not far behind. The southern states listed in the table averaged an annual budget for advertising in 1964 that was more than

52. "How Ads Relocate U.S. Industry," *Printer's Ink*, CCLXXVIII (March 9, 1962), 23.
53. *Ibid.*, 28.
54. *Ibid.*; Robin C. Nelson, "Ads and 007's Lure Industry," *Printer's Ink*, CCXCIV (February 24, 1967), 39.

Table 5   Print/Broadcast Advertising and Preparation as of August 15, 1964

	Amount	National Rank
Arkansas	$ 160,000	4
Florida	325,000	2
Georgia	55,000	13
Kentucky	125,000	7
Louisiana	90,000	9
Mississippi	161,265	3
North Carolina	140,000	5
South Carolina	71,181	11
Tennessee	90,000	9
Total	$1,217,446	
Average of thirty-one states reporting	$73,201.58	
Average of nine southern states reporting	$135,271.77	

SOURCE: "Corporate Advertising Picture of the 50 States' Development Programs," *Public Relations Journal*, XX (October, 1964), 28.

170 percent of the average for the thirty-one states that reported their advertising budgets.

Advertising contracts were allocated and structured according to political as well as economic considerations. Often the agency that handled the state's advertising had been active in the governor's most recent election campaigns. A firm involved in promotional publicity would also have the opportunity to advertise its own effectiveness and, hence, would be happy to cooperate with the governor's office in distributing literature that spotlighted the current administration's success in attracting new plants.[55]

Development advertisements focused on the South's major attraction—a surplus of nonunion workers needing employment. A survey of promotional advertisements indicates that southern boosters put a great deal of stock in "Anglo-Saxonism." Their positive emphasis on their state's

55. W. H. Long, "Why States Are Budgeting Too Little," *Public Relations Journal*, XX (October, 1964), 25.

native-born population was an attempt to capitalize on a long-standing prejudice against foreigners and their alleged propensity for joining collective organizations like labor unions. Any reader of any state's promotional material was certain to be informed of a "pool of labor drawn almost entirely from pure American stock." Not satisfied with labor only 96.6 percent native born, Mississippi raised the percentage to 99.6 a few months later. An advertisement lauding Louisville was even more blunt. It pictured a worker with the descriptive caption—"He speaks English!"—and assured readers, "Labor in Louisville doesn't require foremen who speak half a dozen different languages. Our workers are *Americans*. They talk and think American."[56]

Although southern promotional ads became less blatant in their appeals to nativist sentiment after World War II, they continued to emphasize an abundance of docile laborers more than willing to work for wages well below the national average. Typical advertisements illustrated this point by pay scale comparisons between a southern state's workers and those in the Northeast. A 1964 Mississippi Power and Light pamphlet used boldface type to highlight Mississippi's figures, which were 20 percent lower than Alabama's and 30 percent lower than Louisiana's. Another piece of promotional material urged executives, "Don't look at the Mississippi laborer in terms of production per man hour; consider him instead in terms of production per dollar spent."[57]

Apparently fearing that such a sales pitch might backfire by giving industrialists the idea that southern workers were incapable of performing industrial tasks, promoters began to publish testimonials from satisfied employers. Officials of established industries appreciated the fact that the South's workers were both productive and willing to work for less than their counterparts elsewhere. An R. G. Letourneau Company representative provided this revealing testimonial: "While southern labor is capable of learning quite as rapidly as that fact from other sections, we find Mississippi labor reasonably acceptable to working at 'trainee' wages until they reach proficiency . . . it is with pride that I can report that many of our men are approaching the capabilities of any to be found in the industrial sections of the country." The Letourneau Company had been in Mississippi for a number of years when this advertisement appeared.[58]

56. *Business Week*, July 17, 1937, p. 52, October 16, 1937, p. 28.
57. Joyner and Thames, "Mississippi's Efforts," 461–62.
58. *Ibid.*, 465.

The cheap labor thrust of the South's promotional ads confirmed the region's ongoing courtship of low-wage, labor-intensive industries, and there was also little chance that an industrialist would be allowed to forget the many subsidies and concessions available if he chose a Dixie location. An Alabama advertisement boasted, "Alabama has got what industry looks for. Our Cater and Wallace Acts finance $50 million plants as easily as $50 thousand plants." [59]

Cheap raw materials and resources remained important elements of the southern sales pitch. Because only 4 percent of the state's water supply was being used, a Georgia Power promotional message declared: "We've got H_2O running out of our ears in GA." "Big Things" happened in Kentucky because of electric power, natural gas, coal reserves, and other raw materials. [60] As competition became increasingly heated in the fifties and sixties, many states tried to make their promotional advertisements distinctive by the use of puns or other attention-getting devices. "Long Johns, Who's That?" asked a piece boosting Pinellas County, Florida. The ad explained, "People down here hardly know what long johns are . . . little folks have never found out . . . newcomers have almost forgotten . . . just as they have forgotten the cold weather, illnesses and the driving hazards formerly involved in getting to the plant." Florida also offered room to expand, as an Orlando message suggested by captioning a bottle of olives with the observation, "Industries all stuffed together tend to get bottled up," and a healthy orange with the assurance, "But there's profitable growing room in Orlando." [61]

An important initial obstacle to effectively advertising a southern state or community was the persistent stereotype of the South as a backward, degenerate region. No state suffered more in this regard than Mississippi whose Agricultural and Industrial Board began working early in the period after World War II to transform citizens into boosters and encourage them to spread the good word about their state: "People who live in Mississippi know that it is not a Congo-like wilderness of unpenetratable [sic] jungle growth inhabited by half-savage natives who live shoeless in trees to escape the flood, but still these misconceptions exist in the minds of thousands of people throughout the nation. As long as they do exist they

59. See *Business Week*, March 5, 1966, p. 126.
60. *Ibid.*, March 8, 1958, p. 124, March 3, 1962, p. 66.
61. "Area Development Ads: Some Good and Bad Attempts to Blight Our Countryside Further," *Industrial Marketing*, LIII (May, 1968), 72–73.

might as well be true as far as our standing in the national spotlight is concerned."[62]

Some states tried to capitalize on their histories. A Virginia advertisement reminded readers that "Virginia was the first corporation in America." Another claimed, "Virginia Brought Profit to America." Georgia tried to overcome its past, but risked the revival of negative stereotypes in the process. One ad asked, "Hillbillies?" and then retorted, "You won't find them dining in a revolving restaurant-lounge atop the breathtaking Atlanta Skyline." Another mentioned "Tobacco Road" but depicted a modern superhighway, which indicated that the "rutty dirt road is fast coming to an end." A cynical observer suggested other ads might feature chain gangs or signs pointing to the back of the bus. The tumultuous years of the late 1960s had marred the images of several southern communities. Monroe, Louisiana, boosters reminded industrialists that their city had experienced "no riots . . . no marches . . . no demonstrations . . . no teacher strikes." The ad went further—in fact, too far—by claiming that Monroe was "unique" in the nation because "every resident" enjoyed "equal opportunities and facilities."[63]

Industrial ads also promised industrialists that state and local leaders in Dixie were cooperative to the point of subservience. Southern governors seemed ready to don work clothes and help build the new plant if necessary. Mississippi Governor James P. Coleman issued "personal invitations" for businessmen to visit his state. Kentucky's Wilson Wyatt asked industrialists to write him, and George Wallace gave them his office phone number.[64]

Hoping to create a bandwagon effect that would attract an increasing number of market-conscious industries, most states found impressive but often confusing ways of highlighting their own growth. Kentucky claimed to have received a "multimillion dollar vote of confidence" from industry. Alabama hoped to impress investors by revealing that the impressive statistics in its February, 1965, ads had actually understated the value of recent plant investments by $122 million.[65]

Not surprisingly, larger cities and metropolitan areas did most of the

62. Mississippi Agricultural and Industrial Board, *First Biennial Report*, 27.
63. "Area Development Ads," 62, 64, 69–70, 76.
64. *Fortune*, LV (March, 1957), 236; *Business Week*, March 3, 1962, p. 66, March 5, 1966, p. 146.
65. *Business Week*, March 3, 1962, p. 66, March 5, 1966, p. 146.

advertising for specific locations for industries within a state. For the most part, these advertisements merely repeated the various advantages stressed by the state in its promotional messages. Every city bragged about abundant labor, cooperative government, and low taxes. As they began to experience rapid growth, some urban areas like Atlanta could emphasize the buying power of their residents: "You've Got to Be Here to Compete for This 28 Million People Market."[66] Despite questions concerning the effectiveness of industrial promotion publicity and the political ramifications involved, southern states and communities kept spreading the good word. Advertising may have provided little useful technical information, but like subsidies and right-to-work laws, it sent the message that industry could expect a warm welcome in the South.

A new industry relocating in a southern community was likely to come into contact with at least one and often more of the industrial promotion organizations supported by state government, local communities, or service industries. Although it may have been true, as locational theorists insisted, that labor costs, markets, raw materials, and a host of other economic, technical, or physical factors were still the basic site-selection determinants, many communities in several states could satisfy most of these criteria almost equally well. Because the industrialist could choose from a number of potentially acceptable locations, attractive advertising or tactful persuasive assistance could mean the difference for a southern town between a much needed new payroll and the loss of a plant to a community that had been more effectively "sold" to the prospect.

66. *Ibid.*, March 6, 1954, p. 48.

Chapter 4

WITH LABOR THROWN IN

After World War II the South greatly expanded both its public and its private industry-seeking efforts. An obsession with new plants and payrolls doubtless made the region more attractive to industrial investors, but the rabid boosterism of the postwar decades did nothing to strengthen the South's hand in dealing with incoming industrialists, most of whom continued to choose southern locations because of the savings they offered, particularly in the area of labor costs. In order to capitalize on this advantage, state and local developers often had to enlist the aid of lawmakers, public officials, and private citizens to maintain the stable labor conditions that manufacturers seemed to want. Thus, government and the community moved into an even closer partnership with industry, one that promised continued growth but confirmed the established pattern of low wages for southern workers.

In the 1880s when Henry Grady breathed new life into the dormant dream of southern industrial progress, he placed at the center of his appeal for northern capital the South's most abundant resource, its surplus labor. New South crusaders of the late nineteenth century and urban boosters of the early twentieth promised investors an inexhaustible supply of "100 percent Anglo Saxon" workers so grateful for any sort of payroll that they would work cheerfully for the meagerest of wages and resist emphatically the entreaties of labor organizers. Grady and his disciples cast their lot politically with the industrialists who had accepted the cheap labor sales pitch, and for many decades after the New South movement began the region remained most barren ground for those who sought to cultivate class consciousness among workers.

The whiplash effect resulting from the end of World War I and the economic collapse of the late 1920s did cause southern labor to stir at the close of the decade. Violence in textile towns like Gastonia forced some of the region's more enlightened observers to speculate about the need for improvements in wages and working conditions, but it was not until the New Deal era that organized labor gained even the beginnings of a foothold in Dixie. The National Industrial Recovery Act, a keystone of Roosevelt's Hundred Days response to the Depression, helped to encourage union membership in the South. Organizers interpreted NIRA's Section 7A as a sign of the president's desire to have all labor organized, and intimidated workers saw the guarantee of the right to bargain collectively as a promise of protection if they did organize. The disappointing results of a general textile strike in 1934 and the Supreme Court's invalidation of NIRA a short time later put a damper on union activity temporarily, but labor also received some encouragement in 1935 when the National Labor Relations Act outlawed intimidation and other "unfair labor practices," provided machinery for democratic selection of bargaining agents by majority vote, and set up the National Labor Relations Board to enforce its other provisions. The NLRA offered significant psychological support for embattled organizers and cowed workers.[1]

Union leaders realized that if organized labor were to gain a foothold in the South, it would have to overcome the determined resistance of textile and garment employers. By 1938 the Amalgamated Clothing Workers of America had 4,500 southern members, but in the same year the International Ladies' Garment Workers' Union, which had a large pool of prospective supporters in scattered apparel plants all over the region, could claim only 678 converts. In the textile field, the Textile Workers' Union of America, a CIO affiliate, established a beachhead, but its overall progress was slow. Between 1939 and 1953 the South experienced an increase in union membership of 185 percent, a figure 37 points above the average for the period outside the South. In terms of the percentage of all manufacturing employees belonging to labor organizations, however, unions grew only half as fast in the South between 1939 and 1953 as in the rest of the nation. The 1950s produced no major gains for organized labor in

1. For a survey of the development of labor unions in the South before 1932, see F. Ray Marshall, *Labor in the South* (Cambridge, Mass.: Harvard University Press, 1967), 41–133. See also George B. Tindall, *The Emergence of the New South, 1913–1945* (Baton Rouge: Louisiana State University Press, 1967), 318–53, 505–513.

Dixie, and as the next decade began, the region remained almost an uncharted frontier for organizers, a frontier that they failed to conquer. Although absolute union membership in the South increased by approximately 173,000 between 1953 and 1964, the percentage of the region's nonagricultural work force belonging to labor organizations stood in 1964 about where it had been in 1939, at 50 percent of the nonsouthern average.[2]

Because cheap, nonunion labor remained the key element in the South's appeal to new industry, in the early postwar years southern promotional ads made sure industrialists knew what a minimal percentage of any particular state's work force was unionized. Statistics were not always necessary to get the point across. Clanton, Alabama, simply promised industries: "No Hostile Union Here and None Desired." Williamsburg County, South Carolina, promoters were proud that there were "no unions or union activity in the area" and that "the appreciation of fair play and genuine spirit of cooperation inherent in the people make such activities an extremely remote possibility." Other advertisements stressed individualism, suspicion of outsiders, and willingness to give "a day's work for a day's pay." Mississippi fairly begged for someone to come down and take advantage of a labor surplus ripe for the exploiting. The mayor of Pelahatchie, Mississippi, assured a Connecticut manufacturer that Pelahatchie was a "veritable Industrial Paradise" where "our wonderful labor, 98% native born, mostly high school graduates, will lower average hourly industrial wage rates 5¢ to 49¢ below other southern states and from 50¢ to 95¢ below northern states."[3]

Even the supposedly scientific, planned approach to industrial development often involved oblique references to nonunionism and cheap labor, such as "native born workers" and "a day's work for a day's pay." The South Carolina State Planning Board assured investors that the average laborer in the Palmetto State "has never heard of one loom to a weaver in cotton mills, he doesn't know anything about two sides of spinning to the operative, and he is willing to run his job to the best of his ability and capacity."[4]

2. Tindall, *The Emergence*, 516–19; Marshall, *Labor*, 299.
3. Stetson Kennedy, *Southern Exposure* (Garden City, N.Y.: Doubleday, 1946), 228; Williamsburg County Legislative Delegation, County Commission, Industrial Commission, Superintendent of Schools, "Williamsburg County—Industrial Data—1957" (mimeo in South Carolina State Archives, Columbia), 19; H. C. Rhodes to Hobart J. Hendrick, June 10, 1954, in American Federation of Labor, *Subsidized Industrial Migration*, Appendix IV.
4. South Carolina State Planning Board, "An Opportunity for the Woolen and Worsted

Many migrating industries were determined to select a new location that would guarantee them peaceful labor relations. Although plant executives apparently realized that they could not elude organizers forever, settling in a nonunion climate assured freedom from harassment during the critical early phases of operation. Said one manufacturer, "There is no doubt that by moving South we only escape trade unionism for the moment. . . . But it is supremely important to me that in the years during which I am organizing this new industry and training labor in the plant that I should not have to operate within the straight-jacket of union rules with respect to seniority, featherbedding practices and the like."[5]

Whenever a prospect made it clear that he desired to move into a nonunion environment, state development officials did their best to accommodate him. If the industry was "footloose" and needed only to be near its labor, there was little problem in finding the right location. Even if a firm needed to be near markets and raw materials, developers usually managed to find several suitable sites. In October, 1958, Stiles, McKinley, Watson, and Company expressed an interest in moving to a small nonunion town near Charleston, South Carolina. The State Development Board replied promptly with a list of eleven cities that fit the bill. In later years industrialists began to specify locations at least a hundred miles from areas of union strength. This distance stipulation would have created more headaches for developers when antiunion industries also needed access to major distribution centers like Atlanta had it not been for the proliferation of interstate highways in the region. State developers also had to respect the wishes of local entrepreneurs and developers who revealed their distaste for organized labor. Wrote one, "I am desperately afraid of unions and am interested only in a business that is not so conducive to union activities."[6]

The language of avoiding labor unions was often euphemistic, but both promoter and prospect understood that language well. When Governor Fielding Wright of Mississippi courted the Whirlpool Corporation, he assured executives, "The particular area you have in mind has an abun-

Industry in South Carolina," Bulletin No. 10, n.d. (in South Carolina State Archives, Columbia), 19.

5. Calvin B. Hoover and B. U. Ratchford, *Economic Resources and Policies of the South* (New York: Macmillan, 1951), 413.

6. S. W. Gable to Ned L. Threatt, October 2, 1958, Gable to "Stiles, McKinley and Watson," October 2, 1958, both in Timmerman Correspondence; J. B. Benton to Phillip Schwartz, January 5, 1946, in North Carolina Division of Commerce and Industry Correspondence.

dance of intelligent native labor and is entirely free of those conditions that tend to impair employer-employee relations." With this cryptic description of the nonunion climate in Mississippi came the implicit promise that no conditions that were likely to "impair employer-employee relations" would be allowed to develop. Developers persisted in speaking in code about the absence of unions, even among themselves. The executive director of Tennessee's Department of Commerce and Industry explained to a Louisiana counterpart that one of the factors that brought Goodyear Tire and Rubber Company to Union City, Tennessee, was the fact that Union City was a "prime farming area." It seemed to him that Goodyear felt that "farm acclimated" labor could do the best job in its new plant, and he failed to mention that "farm acclimated" labor was likely to prove amenable to lower wages and resistant to the entreaties of union organizers.[7]

Because they felt that the weakness of organized labor was conducive to industrial growth, southern political leaders at all levels could be counted on to oppose any proposed changes in federal policies that would create a more favorable climate for unionism in the region. In 1935 Representative Eugene Cox of Georgia and a number of his southern colleagues opposed the Wagner Act's assault on "state sovereignty," but the bill passed with some southern support coming from those who felt the bill would eventually die at the hands of the Supreme Court. Although the Court ultimately upheld the legislation, Representative Robert Ramspeck of Georgia did succeed in attaching an amendment banning compulsory industry-wide bargaining, thereby requiring that each isolated textile plant in the South be organized separately.[8]

In 1937 many southern congressmen rallied in opposition to the Fair Labor Standards Act, which set minimum wages and maximum hours. Senator Ellison D. "Cotton Ed" Smith of South Carolina called the bill an attempt "by human legislation to overcome the splendid gifts of God to the South." Sam F. Hobbs of Alabama saw it as an effort "to drive western and southern businessmen and industrialists back between the plow-handles—looking at the east end of a west bound mule." Only after opinion polls and special congressional elections pointed to substantial public

7. Fielding Wright to Whirlpool Corporation, February 16, 1951, in Fielding Wright Correspondence, Mississippi State Archives, Jackson; James H. Alexander to William T. Hackett, April 4, 1968, in Tennessee Division for Industrial Development Correspondence.
8. Tindall, *The Emergence*, 513.

support for the minimum wage bill in the South did it escape the clutches of conservative southerners and win congressional approval.[9]

As might be expected, southern politicians were among the most vociferous supporters of the 1947 Taft-Hartley Act, a measure that gave several advantages to companies resisting collective bargaining, including the right to file charges of unfair labor practices against unions. In addition the act initiated a number of procedural changes that lengthened the time required to hear labor complaint cases. Taft-Hartley also encouraged southern legislatures to pass right-to-work laws banning the closed shop. Under such a law, even when employees of a particular plant approved unionization, no worker could be forced to pay union dues. In such circumstances a union might win acceptance only to see its membership slip away because dues payers realized that nonmembers, and therefore nonpayers, received the same benefits as they did.[10]

Arkansas and Florida had led the right-to-work crusade with constitutional amendments in 1944. Either by amendment or statute or both all of the other states included in this study, except Kentucky and Oklahoma, followed suit between 1947 and 1954. Although right-to-work laws ostensibly offered protection to unions as well as their opponents, the promanagement sentiments of the measures were unmistakable. Arkansas's right-to-work guarantee was typical: "No person should be denied employment because of membership in, or affiliation with, a labor union; nor shall any person be denied employment because of failure or refusal to join or affiliate with a labor union; nor shall any person, unless he shall voluntarily consent in writing to do so, be compelled to pay dues, or any other monetary consideration to any labor organization as a prerequisite to, or condition of or continuance of, employment."[11]

Southern development officials lost no time in incorporating their right-to-work statutes into their promotional arsenals. William P. Rock of Arkansas's Industrial Development Commission felt that his state's growth in population, personal income, and job opportunities was directly related to its right-to-work law. When Mississippi wrote its version

9. *Ibid.*, 533.
10. Marshall, *Labor*, 323–31.
11. U.S. Department of Labor, *Growth of Labor Law in the United States* (Washington, D.C.: U.S. Government Printing Office, 1962), 249. Louisiana repealed its right-to-work law in 1956 but enacted a new one in 1976. "Arkansas's Right to Work Laws" (typescript supplied to industrial prospects by the Arkansas Industrial Development Commission, Little Rock).

of the law into its constitution, the state's growth accelerated rapidly, according to Governor Ross Barnett, who cited an increase in capital investment "three and a half times more than the average in any one of the last ten years."[12]

Despite the contentions of promoters that right-to-work laws had been invaluable to them, experts consistently rejected the notion that such measures significantly influenced plant location. A study of the industrial development experiences of several central and western agricultural states concluded that right-to-work laws could not be expected "to foster industrialization" or even to retard unionization. A poll of one hundred plant executives in Indiana produced only one response indicating that the employer, in this case of only sixty people, felt the state's right-to-work law had been a major location factor and only seven cited it as a secondary consideration. A Texas survey resulted in similar findings, and the researcher concluded that the right-to-work provision's importance was largely symbolic.[13] The major problem with such surveys was that they were based on the response of industrial management to items that asked them, in essence, if they had chosen a particular state as a location in order to avoid unions, a response that they might be reluctant to make because it would cast their firms in a negative light.

If right-to-work laws were not crucial to regional growth, why did so many southern promotional advertisements spotlight these measures? The Texas study touched on the true importance of these laws as promotional tools—the fact that they sent an unsubtle but at least not bluntly specific message to new industry that the state in question offered a climate in which unionization of a new plant, if not impossible, was unlikely. The right-to-work law also became associated in the mind of the industrialist with antipicketing laws, permissive attitudes toward the use of strikebreakers, cooperative police, and the absence of widespread sympathy for dissident workers. In other words, such laws provided statutory evidence of deep-seated antiunion sentiments.

A number of local development leaders were willing to make a written commitment to the protection of incoming industry from organized labor. Elizabethton, Tennessee, leaders signed an agreement with a rayon com-

12. Marshall, *Labor*, 320–21.
13. Benson Soffer and Michael Korenich, "'Right to Work' Laws as a Location Factor: The Industrialization Experience of Agricultural States," *Journal of Regional Science*, III (1961), 55.

pany promising to keep unions out of the community and gave the added assurance that local workers would not demand more than ten dollars per week in wages. The written promise from Grenada, Mississippi, to discourage union organizers reflected the same concern about labor stability that inspired several BAWI contract clauses giving executives of a subsidized plant the right to screen future prospects with an eye toward their potential impact on local wage scales and their susceptibility to unionization. More commonly, industrialists and local developers handled such matters through informal "gentlemen's agreements." [14]

Many southern communities tried to discourage union organizers with restrictive local ordinances. The Macon, Georgia, City Council voted to prohibit the distribution of any kind of literature. Three times during 1940, Birmingham officials invoked a city ordinance allowing them to hold a person indefinitely without filing a formal charge. Baxley, Georgia, required that unions pay a $2,000 license fee and $500 for each member secured. The license was to be granted only after disclosure of the union's assets, as well as the salaries and backgrounds of the organizers. Even then, the mayor and city council were given the authority to withhold the license if they felt such action would be in the best interest of the "general welfare" of Baxley. A court battle following the 1954 arrest of two International Ladies' Garment Workers' Union organizers for violating the Baxley law led ultimately to invalidation of the statute as a violation of free speech. Although patently unconstitutional, such ordinances were valuable for purposes of intimidation and they appeared in a number of small towns across the South. In November, 1955, for example, Sandersville, Georgia, adopted an ordinance to regulate the solicitation of membership for "any organization, union or society." This measure required a union to pay $2,000 for a permit and $500 per new member obtained. [15]

After voters in Star City, Arkansas, approved a $150,000 bond issue for a new garment plant, the city council passed an ordinance requiring union organizers to pay a daily license fee of a thousand dollars. The mayor explained that the manufacturers had made it clear that "if the

14. John Fred Holley, "Elizabethton, Tennessee: A Case Study of Southern Industrialization" (Ph.D. dissertation, Clark University, 1949), 306; Joyner and Thames, "Mississippi's Efforts," 472.

15. Virginius Dabney, *Below the Potomac: A Book About the South* (New York: D. Appleton Century, 1942), 129; Marshall, *Labor*, 330–31; Robert B. Cassell, "An Industrial Ap-

union ever got into the plant here, they might have to close up. We've got too big a stake in this to let anything like that happen."[16] The subsidy had thus encouraged local government officials to play a more active role in suppressing unions in order to insure that the community's investment was safe.

Occasionally, company executives made good on their threats to close down if a plant's work force voted to organize. An admiring textile magazine reporter was delighted that Deering-Milliken had "licked the everlasting daylights out of the union" by liquidating the Dallas Manufacturing Company of Huntsville, Alabama. The company took similar action in Darlington, South Carolina. On September 6, 1956, Darlington Manufacturing Company employees voted in the Textile Workers' Union of America as their bargaining agent. Six days later a stockholders' meeting produced a resolution to liquidate the company. By the end of the year all of the plant machinery had been sold or moved elsewhere. Company head Roger Milliken ignored a plea from the mayor of Darlington and a petition signed by four hundred employees who wished to retract their votes for the union. The TWUA's subsequent charge of unfair labor practices set off twelve years of NLRB hearings and litigation, which finally brought a court decision that the plant had been closed illegally and that Milliken owed back pay to the laid-off workers. Instead of ending the matter, the decision provoked a lengthy legal controversy as Milliken filed an appeal to have its restitution obligations reduced.[17]

Development leaders placed the responsibility for these factory closings not with management, but with "labor agitators." Local boosters utilized newspaper or radio ads, appeals to local pride and warnings of economic disaster if unions won acceptance in the community. Such tactics were so effective that one Danville, Virginia, textile worker joked in the early days of World War II, "I'm not worried a-tall about the Japs movin' in on us; the Chamber of Commerce has kept the unions out, and I reckon as how they can keep the Japs out, too." Early in the postwar period, development advocates predicted that the spread of unionism could cost the South its recent gains. An Associated Industries of Georgia pamphlet

---

praisal of Sandersville and Tennille, Georgia," Sandersville-Washington County Chamber of Commerce, June, 1962 (typescript in University of Georgia Library, Athens).

16. Marshall, *Labor*, 320; *Wall Street Journal*, July 12, 1962, pp. 1, 22.

17. Marshall, *Labor*, 276–78. Laid-off Milliken workers had yet to receive a penny in 1976. Frye Gaillard, "I'll Be Dead . . . Before They Pay," *Progressive*, XL (June, 1976), 22.

warned that tolerating unionism amounted to "throwing banana peels on the pavement of the road to industrial progress."[18]

As time passed, development leaders projected an increasingly sophisticated image, but they remained steadfast in their opposition to organized labor. In 1965 the Georgia State Chamber of Commerce distributed a pamphlet, entitled "Take a Tip from the Beaver, Mr. Businessman," that urged employers to team up to resist unionization in the interest of the state's industrial progress. The chamber reminded growth-oriented capitalists that a major concern for site-seeking industries was the question "How many unions are nearby?" The pamphlet also contained a copy of a letter from Fantus Location Consultants, explaining to a local development official that his city had lost a prospect because of the recent success of the United Mine Workers in the area.[19]

Development groups marshaled every resource at their disposal when a union assault threatened. Law enforcement officials, influential citizens, and the local news media closed ranks to preserve jobs and the community's nonunion reputation. Peace officers in some southern communities often looked the other way when promises to protect incoming industries from unions led to intimidation and, occasionally, criminal acts against union organizers. This was the case in 1938 when an ILGWU worker was kidnapped in Barnesville, Georgia, taken sixty miles away, and ordered never to return by a mob led by businessmen who had guaranteed local industry that the community would remain union free. Such tactics became increasingly rare in the postwar period, although they did not disappear altogether. Union-weary industrialists expected a southern location to provide sympathetic law enforcement officials. In 1967 the mayor of Sneedville, Tennessee, complained to the governor's office about the transfer of a state trooper who had been stationed in Sneedville. According to the mayor, development leaders in his town had three industrial prospects on the line but all three had been the victims of "labor troubles" in the North and were pressing hard for "local law enforcement." The Sneedville leader, therefore, asked that a new trooper be reassigned to his area in the interest of the town's industrial progress.[20]

18. Kennedy, *Southern Exposure*, 289; Savannah *Morning News*, October 2, 1947, in University of Georgia Library Clipping File, Athens.
19. Georgia State Chamber of Commerce, "Take A Tip from the Beaver, Mr. Businessman," Atlanta, 1965 (in University of Georgia Library, Athens).
20. Tindall, *The Emergence*, 525; Charles W. Turner to James H. Alexander, August 29, 1967, in Tennessee Division for Industrial Development Correspondence.

Local clergymen often tried to convince their congregations that God was on the side of the antiunion forces. Lucy Randolph Mason, a CIO organizer in the 1946 Operation Dixie, recalled this incident: "One morning after a Sunday Service, the preacher said he had a special message for union members and requested them to stay after the service. He first made a vicious attack on the CIO, calling it all the bad names he could think of, and finished with a declaration that no CIO members could be 'saved' and that the people would have to decide between the church and the union. Union members were not welcome and would not be accepted in the church, he declared. As a result there was a large withdrawal from the union." Another evangelist told his flock that the letters "CIO" meant "Christ Is Out."[21]

Antiunionism was not confined to clergymen who served a working-class congregation. In March, 1953, the pastor of the First Methodist Church of Brookhaven, Mississippi, wrote a union organizer to let him know "that as pastor of this church, and pastor of many of the leading business and influential people of this town as well as many of the working people, I am opposed to your presence in Brookhaven so long as it is for union organizing. And I shall do everything that I possibly can to prevent any such organization in our midst."[22]

The press was also a valuable ally to local leaders pledged to keep the unions at bay. Editors often portrayed unions as the enemies of economic progress in the South. In 1937 a Tupelo writer warned, "If you join the CIO, you will be endorsing the closing of a factory." Lest such subtlety be lost on the reader, an editor might be more blunt: "The Mississippi National Guard has been mustered up to 2,300 guns . . . and are not afraid to do it when the command to fire is given." In response to an organizing campaign, the Huntsville, Alabama, *Times* warned employees that the mills would move away and union members would be blacklisted: "You may go to Chattanooga or Birmingham, New York or Chicago, BUT THERE ARE NO JOBS THERE FOR YOU. . . . If application is made to another mill elsewhere, the story of this city will be familiar until your dying days!" Editorial columns in southern newspapers regularly featured antiunion pieces, but not all of the editorializing appeared on the proper page. On

21. Lucy Randolph Mason, *To Win These Rights: A Personal Story of the CIO in the South* (Westport, Conn.: Greenwood Press, 1970), 183; Tindall, *The Emergence*, 524.
22. J. Melvin Jones to Willis D. Christy, March 4, 1953, in American Federation of Labor, *Subsidized Industrial Migration*, 84.

March 2, 1944, the Jackson *Daily News* ran a front page article revealingly entitled "CIO Sends Ex-Con to Organize in Jackson—Would Crush Industry." Development-oriented papers like the *Daily News* opposed most measures that promised more protection to the worker. In response to the campaign to create a State Department of Labor, the editor snorted, "Mississippi has about as much need for a Department of Labor as we would have for a pet hippopotamus."[23]

Although the Anderson, South Carolina, *Independent* supported minimum wage laws and other benefits for workers, it bitterly opposed unionization. Writing from the heart of the textile belt, the *Independent*'s editors saw a direct relationship between the Civil Rights Movement and efforts to organize southern workers and charged that the agitation for integration and unionization was part of a plot to halt the southward flow of industry: "In the 1850s there were the abolitionists. In the 1950s there is the NAACP. In the 1850s the South's economy was becoming too strong to suit New England's interests. In the 1950s the migration of industry poses the same challenge to the North and East." Down in the low country of South Carolina, the Charleston *News and Courier* reminded workers that they must consider their regional heritage before they decided to throw in with "union officials who are brainwashed with the popular creed of mixing the races." As a final warning, the *News and Courier* declared "the white man who wishes to preserve his culture, his civilization as he and his fathers knew it, is in the minority as the national labor leaders count noses." National labor union officials who took a prointegration stand doubtless weakened their organizations in the South. One South Carolinian wrote George Meany to inform him that "any southerner who would go along with you on such things is not worth his salt and could not be elected dogcatcher."[24]

In addition to concern about the future of white supremacy, a number of other cultural factors helped to impede union growth in the South. Boosters, politicians, and employers blocked large-scale unionization by capitalizing on the psychological characteristics of southern workers. For the most part, union organizers were "Yankees"; some had "names that even a high school teacher couldn't pronounce," and their inability to

23. Tindall, *The Emergence*, 523–25; Mason, *To Win*, 55; Jackson *Daily News*, March 2, 1944, p. 1, January 19, 1950.

24. Howard H. Quint, *Profile in Black and White* (Westport, Conn.: Greenwood Press, 1958), 163–64.

speak the literal or cultural language of the South created important communications difficulties. Politicians, editors or employers emphasized these differences when they inveighed against unions: "Who are the men who run this union anyway? . . . Baldenzi, Rieve, Cheepka, Genis, Jabor, Knapik, and Rosenburg. Where do you think these men come from and where do they live? Are their background [sic], upbringing, viewpoints, beliefs and principles anything like yours and mine?"[25]

The triple bugaboo of Yankeeism, race-mixing, and communism was easily attached to unionism, especially in the late 1950s when the major unions began to state publicly their opposition to job discrimination or loyalty oaths: "This outside influence is just a bunch of pot-bellied Yankees with big cigars in their mouths and the dues they collect will just go up North. . . . If they come in you will share the same restroom with Negroes and work side by side with them. It comes right out of Russia and is pure communism and nothing else."[26]

Union organizers also found their work difficult because the inbred humility and low expectations of southern workers made them suspicious of lavish promises of bigger paychecks and smaller work loads. Fundamentalist religious training, which stressed acceptance of one's lot in life, interacted with regional mores that stigmatized ambition or any attempt to "get above" one's "raising." At the same time, the individualism bred by a farm upbringing militated against the kind of collective action described by the organizers. Finally, in small plants close social and religious ties among workers, foremen, and even higher level management discouraged employees from taking actions that implied distrust of or ingratitude toward those for whom they worked. The Georgia Chamber of Commerce assured industrialists, "It is difficult to arouse animosity between employers and employees who work closely together in their church and Sunday School."[27]

For all of the major psychological or emotional factors underlying re-

25. Jean Gottman, *Virginia at Mid-Century* (New York: Henry Holt, 1955), 435. The antiunion propaganda was introduced into the *Congressional Record* by Senator John F. Kennedy, *Congressional Record*, 83rd Cong., 1st Sess., 1953, Vol. 99, Pt. 4, p. 5,230.

26. *Congressional Record*, 83rd Cong., 1st Sess., 1953, Vol. 99, Pt. 4, p. 5,230.

27. Glenn Gilman, *Human Relations in the Industrial Southeast: A Study of the Textile Industry* (Chapel Hill: University of North Carolina Press, 1956), 303–310. For an overview of the factors retarding union growth in the South, see F. Ray Marshall, "Impediments to Labor Union Organization in the South," *South Atlantic Quarterly*, LXVII (Autumn, 1958), 409–418; Georgia State Chamber of Commerce, *Industrial Survey of Georgia, 1970* (Atlanta: n.p., 1970), 29.

sistance to unionism, a number of economic forces were at least equally important. First, a great many southern workers had been born into poor farm families that had barely managed to scrape together enough cash to make ends meet. Now, the offspring were enjoying material pleasures the parents had never experienced as children. Union organizers might talk incessantly about wage differentials and show workers in a southern plant check stubs indicating that their own company paid a northern laborer as much as two dollars more per hour for performing similar tasks. The nonunion southern workers were likely to respond that they were making "good money," and that they had made down payments on new cars or new houses or mobile homes. As of 1954, for example, 68 percent of the employees of American Viscose in Warren County, Virginia, had purchased homes since they had been hired. When an outsider urged workers who felt they were prospering to be greedy, to try to get even more, their cool or even hostile response was understandable. One worker explained why his co-workers had voted against collective bargaining: "For some folks this was their first job ever. They was farmers and kept on farming while they worked at the plant—this was the first time they had ever seen a paycheck in their lives and they didn't want to do anything to lose it."[28]

Had southern laborers wanted to respond to an organizer's entreaties, they would have found it difficult. First the plant might, as management occasionally suggested, close rather than employ union workers. Second, union sympathizers might be discharged and replaced with union opponents drawn from the region's surplus of underemployed labor. A small-town worker discharged for his union proclivities was certain to find himself effectively blacklisted. What then? By the 1960s the family farm might have ceased its unprofitable operations. The estranged worker could only leave, a painful move for many; or accept whatever temporary, menial jobs happened to be available.

Social, cultural, and political pressure often stymied the efforts of union organizers, but the structure of the South's industrial economy was also a barrier to union growth. Before the New Deal, large, oligopolistic industries had been in a position to resist unionization, but increased fed-

28. Alexander H. Morrison, "The Impact of Industry on a Rural Area: A Case Study of Development in Warren and Surrounding Counties, 1930–1954" (Ph.D. dissertation, University of Virginia, 1958), 299; Don Stillman, "Runaways—a Call to Action," *Southern Exposure*, IV (Spring, 1976), 53.

eral support for collective bargaining and a perceptible shift of popular opinion in the same direction had their effect on these highly visible firms whose executives feared a loss of prestige if they resisted too strongly. Moreover, manufacturers who faced relatively little competition and those for whom labor represented only a modest percentage of total costs would suffer least by having their work forces organized. Increased labor costs could be passed on to consumers with little fear of diminished profits.[29]

Unfortunately for labor organizers, the South's industrial base rested on a heavy concentration of highly competitive, labor-intensive operations whose profits might be sensitive to the slightest rise in labor costs. Thus, there was little room for compromise with demands for higher wages. In addition, low levels of unionization in the South were directly related to the general weakness of organized labor in nonsouthern plants of industries centered in the South. If most operations in a particular industry were located outside the region, there was far greater likelihood of significant union activity among this industry's southern workers. This was the case, for example, in the automobile, rubber, and steel industries.[30]

The textile industry was one where unions were relatively weak even outside the South. Writing in 1967, F. Ray Marshall found that areas with heavy concentrations of textile operations also exhibited low levels of unionism. Marshall's calculations yielded a strong negative rank correlation ($-.96$) between the percentage of an industry's population concentrated in the South and the extent of collective bargaining in that industry. Marshall also concluded that the tendency of southbound companies to choose rural plant locations retarded the growth of unions. Other scholars believed that the region's heavy concentration of industries with predominantly female work forces was a key factor in explaining the weakness of organized labor in the South.[31]

Although resistance to unionization seemed to deny workers the full financial benefits of industrialization, promoters claimed that the maintenance of a nonunion climate had created many new jobs. Between 1939 and 1954 the number of manufacturing establishments in the South had increased by 80 percent, and between 1940 and 1960 average per capita

29. Marshall, *Labor*, 314–15.
30. *Ibid.*, 315–16.
31. *Ibid.*, 318.

personal income rose by 358 percent.[32] Small plants dotted the rural land-scape, and many southerners, both male and female, whose ancestors had cultivated the soil for generations, were now full-time factory hands and part-time farmers. Apparel or textile plants employed farm wives and daughters and provided paychecks that not only augmented but often surpassed the family's dwindling agricultural income. The South was not yet an industrial giant, but it was making progress and doing it so rapidly that the more heavily industrialized states had not only begun to feel threatened but had taken action to slow the southward flow of industry.

The South's gains were significant evidence that cheap labor attracted industry, but the conditions under which many southerners lived and worked provided a less cheerful perspective from which to view the re-gion's industrialization. Perhaps the worst examples of wage exploitation came in the 1930s when industry-hungry communities were anxious to get any kind of plant that paid any kind of wages. An exposé of southern textile mills produced pay vouchers indicating that some workers brought home no cash whatsoever. This phenomenon was most common in mill villages where the companies operated their own stores and deducted pur-chases from employee paychecks.[33]

Elsewhere during the Depression other workers brought home less than six dollars per week, exactly half the minimum set by the National Recovery Administration before it was squashed by the Supreme Court in 1935. In Georgia one widowed mother of five children, claimed to have worked 182.5 hours over an eight-week span and received only $37.08, an average of slightly less than $0.21 per hour. Although textile execu-tives denied that their pay scales were as low as some prounion writers claimed, manufacturers did find several means of getting more produc-tion from their workers without raising wages. Whether they were called the "Bedeaux," "stretch out" or "production" systems, these policies re-quired employers to pay the stipulated wage only if the individual worker achieved a certain level of productivity. When these systems were intro-duced, bewildered employees often found themselves working harder and longer for the same or less pay. One report concerning a mill in Hat-

32. Percentages computed from U.S. Bureau of the Census, *Statistical Abstract of the United States, 1942*, p. 920, *1960*, pp. 788–89, *1963*, p. 329 (Washington, D.C.: U.S. Gov-ernment Printing Office, 1942, 1960, 1963).

33. Walter Davenport, "All Work and No Pay," *Colliers*, C (November 13, 1937), 10.

tiesburg, Mississippi, told of experienced workers toiling nine hours for five hours' pay and of one young woman who was on the job for two weeks but received credit for only 3.24 standard hours' pay—ninety-seven cents for two weeks' work.[34]

By the end of World War II migrating industries had moved away from the practice of creating a factory or mill village and were instead choosing sites that would allow them to draw from a rural area's farm-based labor surplus. Promoters courted low-wage industries with descriptions of sturdy folk who were willing to work for less because they supplemented their incomes and food supplies by farming. A typical Mississippi ad noted "with plenty of space gardens will be found at practically every home, supplementing cash income." In addition to the fact that they grew their own vegetables, Mississippi workers also had less need for cash income because, typically, they were "wives, sons and daughters and farmers living on the farm." Therefore their wages, even if meager, would nonetheless "mean extra dollars over and above the accustomed existence."[35]

Laborers who grew some of their own food and lived on their own land doubtless had lower living expenses, but farm dwellers who took factory jobs also had to make certain sacrifices. For example, many of them commuted substantial distances to their jobs. At the end of the thirties some of the girls who worked in the Columbia, Mississippi, subsidized factory were paying $1.50 a week from a $7.50 paycheck for transportation. One farm father complained that rural girls were away from home "from sunrise until sunset and they don't have much to show for it when the week is over." As of 1950, 39 percent of a Virginia plant's work force commuted fifteen miles or more to work. In 1967 a typical low-wage plant in rural Tennessee drew 36 percent of its employees from outside a ten-mile radius and 21 percent from as far as fifteen miles.[36]

Although wives and daughters might contribute significantly to a meager farm income, when they took factory work, they denied the farmer part of his labor supply. Thus, he had to work harder or hire help. If the

34. *Ibid.*, 72: Stokes, *Carpetbaggers*, 28.
35. Joyner and Thames, "A Critical Analysis," 462–63.
36. Stokes, *Carpetbaggers*, 31–32; Paul Pence Wisman, "The Nature of the Labor Force of a Rural Industry in Virginia: A Case Study of the Stonewall Plant of Merck and Company, Inc." (M.S. thesis, University of Virginia, 1950), 49; Jonas Boyd Crooke, "The Labor Characteristics of Low-Wage Manufacturing Industries in East Tennessee: The Berkline Corporation" (M.S. thesis, University of Tennessee, 1967), 26.

farmer himself took a job in industry, he might continue to have a garden without much difficulty, but planting and harvesting on his accustomed scale was another matter. Again, he might employ a helper or simply work harder, laboring in the factory by day and in the fields during the late afternoons, evenings, early mornings, and weekends. Thus, the special advantage offered to industry by farm-based labor resulted from the sacrifices of the laborers themselves. Yet, promoters and the industrialists they courted used the willingness of southern workers to attempt to earn two incomes as a rationale for keeping one of those incomes low.

The argument that farm residents could afford to labor for less was closely related to the more general observation that wage differentials were justified in view of the lower living costs in the South. Promoters failed to consider the fact that lower living costs in the South were directly related to a generally lower standard of living. The repression of black southerners made possible some of the cheaper services utilized by white workers and lower tax collections were clearly reflected in the level of public services provided in the South.

Experts argued that wage gaps were inevitable in view of the South's industrial mix which was heavily imbalanced in favor of slow-growth, low-wage, labor-intensive operations. In the early sixties, for example, more than 75 percent of the work forces in 76 of Georgia's 159 counties were still employed in the textile, apparel, and lumber and wood industries. Although the chemical industry continued to expand in Tennessee, chemical plants employed relatively few workers compared to the apparel mills, which created more new jobs than any other industry in the state during the 1950s. Apparel employment was seasonal to some extent, and layoffs in this industry often coincided with periodic unemployment in agriculture. Apparel plants also hired a predominantly female work force, leaving male heads of households the option to migrate elsewhere or accept, at least temporarily, the status of a "go-getter" who sat idle every day until five o'clock when his wife's work day ended, and it was time to "go get 'er."[37]

Many young southerners were understandably reluctant to commit

37. Victor R. Fuchs and Richard Perlman, "Recent Trends in Southern Wage Differentials," *Review of Economics and Statistics*, XLII (August, 1960), 292–300; Amy Collins, "Industrial Development in Georgia, 1958–1965," Industrial Development Division, Engineering Experiment Station, Georgia Institute of Technology, 1967 (mimeo in Library of Congress, Washington, D.C.), 27, 53; "Industrial Growth: But Not the Most Profitable Kind," *Business Week*, November 28, 1959, pp. 130–33.

themselves to careers of drudgery in low-reward, limited-opportunity pursuits such as those most readily available in the South. Between 1939 and 1958 eight southeastern states trailed the rest of the nation by wide margins in surveys of population and employment growth.[38] This exodus began to slow in the 1950s as absolute numbers of out-migrants decreased, but the fact that those who left were likely to be more capable and well trained than those who remained contributed to a "brain drain," which in turn helped to condemn the South to continued dependence on low-wage industry.

Promoters responded to charges that they were facilitating the exploitation of southern labor by arguing that industrial expansion would inevitably bring the paychecks of southern workers up to national norms. Not all economists agreed, however. Between 1907 and 1946 there had been no apparent shrinkage of the wage gap between the South and the Northeast or between the South and the rest of the nation, for that matter. Actually, the differential had widened during the 1930s and had only narrowed because of the spurt of wartime prosperity between 1940 and 1945. The average southern wage stood at 86 percent of the northeastern average in 1907, 74 percent in 1932 and 85 percent in 1946.[39]

Between 1947 and 1954 the incomes of southern workers remained relatively steady at 20 to 25 percent below the national average. Average hourly earnings for production workers in 1959 stood at $2.24 in Pennsylvania and $2.29 in New Jersey, but in North Carolina such workers made only $1.50 per hour and in Mississippi only $1.49. Average weekly wages for the nation as a whole in 1958 were $89.47, but workers in Arkansas, Mississippi, and North and South Carolina received at least $27.00 less each payday. In some areas dominated by low-paying industries, wage differentials were actually widening. In eighteen East Tennessee counties, for example, average annual wages fell from 80 to 77 percent of the national average between 1958 and 1963.[40]

Not only did they work for less, but southern workers were also denied

38. Edgar S. Dunn, *Recent Southern Economic Development: As Revealed by the Changing Structure of Employment*, University of Florida Monographs in the Social Sciences, XIV (Gainesville: University of Florida Press, 1962), 3.

39. Joseph Block, "Regional Wage Differentials, 1907–1946," *Monthly Labor Review*, LXVI (April, 1948), 375.

40. Fuchs and Perlman, "Recent Trends," 292; U.S. Bureau of the Census, *Statistical Abstract of the United States: 1960* (Washington, D.C.: U.S. Government Printing Office, 1960), 227; Crooke, "The Labor Characteristics," 15.

the benefits and security accorded labor outside the region. Disabled workers received lower average weekly payments over a shorter span of time than in the nation at large. In 1950, for example, the average period allowed for drawing disability was 585 weeks in the northern states as opposed to 456 weeks in the South. The average minimum weekly payment in the South was only $6.64 as compared to a northern average of $14.41. Nationwide, in 1959 manufacturers paid out eight cents per work hour for employee vacations, but southern employers contributed less than six cents per hour. Southern workers also received significantly lower unemployment compensation and insurance benefits.[41]

As they faced mounting criticism for allegedly selling southern labor short, promoters denied that cheap labor was a key to continued success in attracting new industry. Yet even in 1968 a local development leader in Tennessee wrote one of his state-level counterparts: "I don't believe I have ever talked with a prospect that didn't almost immediately want to know the employment breakdown in the community along with the wage scale in the community."[42]

Most southern workers obviously enjoyed fewer benefits from their jobs than did workers elsewhere, but the situation of blacks who sought industrial employment was even more frustrating. State development agencies and the subsidy programs they administered ostensibly operated to serve the general welfare by helping to create jobs for *all* of the citizens of the state. In practice, however, prior to the mid-1960s development officials apparently felt a responsibility to provide expanded employment opportunities only for whites. When state promotional messages referred to a surplus of Anglo-Saxon labor, the assumption was clear that unemployment or underemployment of blacks was a natural condition and required no remedy. In fact, such a condition was essential to the functioning of the caste system because it meant a ready supply of agricultural and domestic labor. Farm workers or house servants were easily replaced if they asked for more money, and if replaced they stood little chance of finding more attractive employment as long as incoming industries adhered to discriminatory local customs.

41. Frank T. DeVyer, "Labor Factors in the Industrial Development of the South," *Southern Economic Journal*, XVIII (1951), 197; National Industrial Conference Board, *The Economic Almanac, 1962* (New York: Newsweek, 1962), 71.
42. Wilson Borden to James Alexander, January 25, 1968, in Tennessee Division for Industrial Development Correspondence.

Examples from two Mississippi cities illustrated the concern on the part of southern whites that black employment in industry posed a threat to the caste system. A Yazoo City development leader admitted in 1966 that he and his colleagues were not seeking employment opportunities for blacks. Yazoo County had approximately five thousand more blacks than whites in its population at the time, and white leaders feared a black political takeover if a chance for industrial employment should stem the tide of black out-migration. In McComb, Mississippi, a local investor found the chamber of commerce opposed to his plan to open a garment factory staffed by black women.[43]

Developers generally assumed that incoming plants would hire no blacks unless all or parts of their operations required labor so arduous, distasteful, and low-paying as to be unappealing to most whites. Hence, when the Armstrong Tire and Rubber Company announced plans to move to Natchez in 1937, executives assured BAWI officials the plant would hire "only a few colored for porters and mixing carbon black." Similarly, a chicken-processing plant chose a North Georgia location because of an abundant supply of black female labor. This phenomenon was so pronounced that communities often advertised their labor surpluses with figures broken down by both race and sex.[44]

Some industries showed a higher representation of black workers than others. As of 1964, 50 percent of southern lumber industry employees were black. Employment in the lumber industry entailed arduous labor, usually outdoors, and often under less than desirable conditions. Unless there was no other work available, whites were normally content to concede that many of the jobs in lumbering were "nigger work." Conditions in the textile industry were far from ideal, but prior to the 1960s a southern mill was likely to be almost totally staffed by whites. A study of the impact of the textile industry on the South in the period 1900–1940 found that the discriminatory hiring practices "lowered extraagricultural employment opportunities for Negroes to a substantial degree." In other words, there was a significant correlation between the concentration of

43. Joyner and Thames, "A Critical Analysis," 476–77.
44. S. G. Laub to Harry O. Hoffman, September 4, 1937, in Mississippi Industrial Commission Records; Raymond Mervyn Northam, "An Analysis of Recent Industrialization in Northeastern Georgia" (Ph.D. dissertation, Northwestern University, 1960), 122–23. For an example of labor force statistics broken down by race, see Georgia State Chamber of Commerce, "Summary of Industrial Advantages of Edison, Georgia" (1953, typescript in University of Georgia Library, Athens).

textile plants in any county and that county's rate of black out-migration. Only as the South began to attract industries that offered more attractive employment opportunities for whites, did textile mills begin to employ blacks on a significant scale.[45]

Neither mechanization nor unionization significantly improved the status or prospects of blacks in southern industry. Blacks were normally lacking the skills necessary to capitalize on the new jobs created by advancing technology and were most likely to occupy the positions that fell prey to automation. All too often unions, like employers, accommodated themselves to discriminatory local customs. Even in the mid-1960s the white union local in Bogalusa, Louisiana, opposed any equalization of job opportunities among employees of the Crown-Zellerbach Corporation. At the same time union emphasis on seniority and rank did little to enhance the upward mobility of newly hired blacks. Insofar as unions exerted pressure for higher wages, they actually encouraged some of the mechanization that cost black workers their jobs.[46]

Blacks who did find industrial employment in plants that also hired whites faced a number of frustrations. A 1955 profile of Mississippi industrial workers showed that Negro employees were less likely to be absent or quit their jobs than whites. Yet, almost no Negroes advanced to better-paying positions. If there were layoffs, seniority, experience, and expertise were of little benefit to blacks. A 1958 study of industrialization in rural Louisiana and Mississippi found 35 percent of all white workers making more than forty-five dollars per week while only 2 percent of all black workers' paychecks exceeded this figure. A 1965 survey of black participation in manufacturing in North Carolina found that of the 25,717 foremen in the plants surveyed only 347 were blacks.[47]

Table 6 presents black employment figures in selected southern industries as of 1966 and therefore reflects little, if any, of the effects of fed-

45. Herbert R. Northrup and Richard L. Rowan, *Negro Employment in Southern Industry*, Industrial Research Unit, Wharton School of Finance and Commerce, University of Pennsylvania (Philadelphia: University of Pennsylvania Press, 1970), 1–30; Mary J. Oates, *The Role of the Cotton Textile Industry in the Economic Development of the American Southeast: 1900–1940* (New York: Arno Press, 1975), 121–37.

46. Northrup and Rowan, *Negro Employment*, 95–104.

47. B. M. Wofford and T. A. Kelly, *Mississippi Workers: Where They Come From and How They Perform* (University: University of Alabama Press, 1955), 3, 81; Sheridan Maitland and James Cowhig, "Research on the Effects of Industrialization in Rural Areas," *Monthly Labor Review*, LXXXI (October, 1958), 1,121–124; Larry Wayne Shiffler, "Negro Participation in Manufacturing: A Geographical Appraisal of North Carolina" (M.A. thesis, University of North Carolina, 1965), 69.

Table 6 Percentage of Negro Employment in Selected Southern Industries, 1966

	Paper, Pulp, and Paper Board Mills	Lumber	Textiles	Automobile	Aerospace	Steel	Chemicals	Rubber Tires
White-collar	.9	1.6	.6	1.9	1.4	.7	.5	.6
Blue-collar	13.9	47.8	10.7	12.2	6.9	28.4	9.1	13.5
Craftsmen	1.6	17.0	1.6	.4	2.3	7.4	1.3	2.1
Operatives	12.5	42.4	7.8	12.4	8.3	31.9	8.5	12.6
Laborers	37.6	61.3	33.0	14.9	42.1	62.8	46.9	40.7
Service workers	45.4	37.3	37.1	24.4	35.5	28.2	33.4	66.9
Total employment	11.2	42.1	9.5	3.7		22.5	6.3	11.4

Source: Northrup and Rowan, "Concluding Analysis," in Northrup and Rowan, *Negro Employment*, 9, 1, 19.

eral pressure for equal employment opportunities. The table's figures show that only the lumber and steel industries employed a work force that was more than 11.5 percent black. These percentages also show that blacks held relatively few supervisory positions. What opportunities there were for blacks were concentrated in the blue-collar categories and even there blacks were concentrated in the lowest-paying, least prestigious categories of "laborer" and "service worker" (janitors, maids, and security personnel, for example). The table suggests that the less labor-intensive the operations, the fewer blacks employed.

As bleak as the overall picture of black employment in southern industry seemed, the status of black females was even more distressing. As of 1966 black women appeared to do little in southern industries except clean and maintain plant buildings. Black female employment in the service worker category ranged from a low of 42 percent in textiles (where black employment was still relatively new) to 85 percent in the lumber industry.[48]

By failing to hire blacks for any but the most menial, exploitive jobs, employers forfeited the chance to take advantage of the South's cheapest labor, but the maintenance of a large pool of underemployed blacks also helped to keep white workers in line. Job discrimination against blacks was hardly confined to the South, but the extreme rigidity of the region's caste system greatly reinforced the historic role of unemployment as a potent influence for labor docility in capitalist societies. Unskilled white laborers who objected to wage cuts or refused to perform menial tasks could always be replaced by eager and even cheaper black workers desperate to escape the bonds of agricultural serfdom. Failure to give blacks a fair share of the already restricted benefits of employment in southern industry not only confirmed the income disparities within the South's stunted economy but reinforced the principle that the full productive capacities of black southerners should remain untapped. Inefficient employment of human resources, coupled with the acceptance of wage and benefit discrimination against all southern industrial employees, helped to hold southern economic growth in check.

Although criticisms were often raised against their policies, southern developers doubtless felt they were correct in supporting incoming employers who paid low wages, opposed unionization, and tailored their hir-

48. Northrup and Rowan, "Concluding Analysis," in Northrup and Rowan, *Negro Employment*, 13.

ing practices to the caste system. Along with certain plentiful raw materials, cheap, docile labor was about all the South had to offer new industry. At any time, promoters could look about them and realize that labor cost savings were largely responsible for the new plants coming into their states. Given the South's attraction for industries that could operate almost anywhere there was a supply of cheap labor and an inexpensive building, pressure for higher wages could not only discourage new industry from coming in but encourage existing industry to move out. Thus, as far as promoters and, apparently, a large number of workers were concerned, low wages were better than none. It was small wonder that most businessmen and many workers feared unions. The mere hint of labor trouble or union activity in an area might cost a community a prized prospect and blemish its reputation as a potential site for years to come. A successful organizing campaign might mean a personal and professional victory for a union representative, but for a southern worker it could mean the loss of a job and the possible forfeiture of future opportunities to reenter the industrial work force.

Despite the fears and threats of established employers, many less industrialized communities probably would have noticed little change in labor and employment conditions had a few higher-wage, unionized industries moved in. Such was the case in an eight-county area of Arkansas studied in 1959. Aluminum, chemical, paper and pulp, and petroleum plants employed from 34 to 47 percent of the workers in these counties at higher than average wages, but in none of the counties did manufacturing account for as much as 30 percent of the employment. The result was a surplus of marginally employed farm labor ready to work in even poorly paying jobs. Established employers who seemed apprehensive about high-wage competition failed to consider that many such plants were more technology-intensive than labor-intensive and therefore might hire relatively few workers and expand their work forces little if at all. As a result, few workers would be able to leave their old jobs and find better ones, and low-wage plants would have little need to boost their pay scales in order to hold on to their workers.[49]

If developers suspected that local industries might be able to tolerate a few better-paying neighbors, for the most part, they dared not take the

49. Ethel B. Jones, *Effect of High-Wage Unionized Industries on Neighboring Industries*, College of Business Administration, Industrial Research and Extension Center, University of Arkansas (Little Rock: University of Arkansas Press, June, 1962), 16–18.

risk. Thus, though pledged to economic progress, they cooperated with efforts to keep wages low. In the long run, their policies helped to establish a self-perpetuating pattern of slow growth. The more low-wage industries the South attracted the more committed its leaders became to maintaining policies that helped to keep wages low. As a result, the region's industrial development not only failed to produce a pool of skilled, highly productive workers but also kept wages and, consequently, per capita incomes from rising rapidly enough to make the South attractive to firms that catered to large consumer markets. Unable to offer skilled workers or affluent consumers, promoters had little choice but to continue to sell the South's labor to any and all bidders. Cheap labor promotional policies had been devised as a response to the desperate economic conditions of the early post-Reconstruction period, but like subsidies, these policies had helped to confirm the economic deficiencies they were supposed to remedy.

Chapter 5

TOO BUSY TO HATE

Until shortly after the middle of the twentieth century incoming industries readily accommodated themselves to the South's racial hierarchy. In their zeal to gloss over deficiencies the business progressives of the 1920s had followed in the footsteps of Henry Grady by offering assurances that southern racial problems had been resolved. Boosters persisted in this tactic until the civil rights pressures of the mid-1950s began to focus national attention on the rigid biracialism that, of all the South's traditions, seemed most inconsistent with the goal of a modernized, progressive industrial society. As civil rights concerns mounted, it seemed reasonable to conclude that most image-conscious, nationally known firms would shy away from an area whose racial policies were becoming so offensive to mass society values. Thus, in the interest of continued growth, many of those responsible for recruiting new industry became the reluctant advocates of a peaceful transition to token desegregation.

Optimistic liberals believed that a breakdown of racial barriers must be both a precursor to and a concomitant of industrial growth.[1] The 1954 *Brown* v. *Board of Education* decision seemed destined to put this theory to the test, and it raised the fear on the part of southern promoters that racial tensions might dampen or even defuse the South's postwar boom. Within a year after the Court issued its "all deliberate speed" order in the second Brown decision in 1955, there were ominous reports that industrialists were reconsidering their plans to open new plants in Dixie. A

1. Nicholls, *Southern Tradition*, 114–23; Yinger and Simpson, "Can Segregation Survive?", 15–24.

large manufacturer of electrical equipment refused to construct a new facility in Georgia after engineering and technical personnel expressed concern about moving to the South. A spokesman explained, "They all have families and while they liked the area, they didn't want to move into a mess about schools, social segregation, etc." Explaining that they could not expect employees to accept Kentucky's racial customs, executives of a business machines firm decided to put its new plant in New York instead. A pencil company claimed to have stayed out of North Carolina because the expense of a dual school system threatened to raise taxes to unattractive levels. Fantus Factory Locating Service reported in May, 1956, that at least twenty major factory moving projects were being "seriously reconsidered in light of the situation in the South." Fearing that their dreams of smokestacks and payrolls might be shattered, southern development leaders angrily accused their northern counterparts of manipulating the race issue to halt the South's industrial advance.[2]

Other industry-minded leaders tried to assuage industrialists' fears about racial difficulties in the South. When North Carolina Governor Luther Hodges visited the Radio Corporation of America on an industrial prospecting trip to New York in 1956, advisers cautioned him to "please remember that these people are very liberal when it comes to the segregation problem." Development staffers suggested that Hodges might call RCA's attention to a Western Electric plant in North Carolina where blacks and whites worked "side by side." Hodges and Florida Governor Leroy Collins, both known as ardent crusaders for new industry, were the most prominent advocates of moderation at the 1957 Southern Governors' Conference. In Arkansas, Winthrop Rockefeller, chairman of the state's Industrial Development Commission, warned that if a state or community developed an "unhealthy reputation" in regard to race relations, industry would be scared away.[3]

Ironically, Rockefeller's state would provide the first significant test of the theory that turmoil over integration could blight an area's economic

2. "Writer Says Racial Crisis May Hurt Growth of South," Raleigh *News and Observer*, March 25, 1956, "Integration Scares Industry Rockefeller Says," Arkansas *Gazette*, April 23, 1956 (These clippings are from the Southern Educational Reporting Service, "Facts on File." Page numbers for these clippings are often not available. When this is the case, titles of the articles have been included in the citation.)

3. "New York Prospects," in Hodges Correspondence; "Integration Scares Industry Rockefeller Says," Arkansas *Gazette*, April 23, 1956, "Integration's Secret Weapon," Raleigh *News and Observer*, October 1, 1957 (SERS clippings).

future. Little Rock had established a modest reputation for racial tolerance and the efforts of the Chamber of Commerce had created the basis for optimistic expectations of industrial growth. Then, in a surprise move, on the eve of the opening of school in 1957, Arkansas Governor Orval Faubus used National Guardsmen to block integration of Little Rock's Central High School. By his actions, Faubus had adhered to the doctrine of "massive resistance" to school integration by interposing the sovereignty of the state between its citizens and the authority of the federal government. Although Faubus, who had previously been noncommittal on the race issue, became an instant hero for many southerners, his decision led to considerable damage to Little Rock's image.[4]

Several weeks of torrid rhetoric ensued, followed by a court order for desegregation. The outbreak of violence led a reluctant President Dwight D. Eisenhower to send in troops from the 101st Airborne Division. Meetings of boosters and civic officials in the fall of 1957 produced only a lukewarm plea for compliance with the court order, although the efforts of these growth-minded citizens foreshadowed the successful effort to lead the city back to reason more than a year later. In the fall of 1958, Governor Faubus used the power newly vested in him by the legislature to close the Little Rock schools rather than submit to desegregation. Industrial recruiters from the Chamber of Commerce soon discovered what the crisis had done to their city's image when they could stir up no interest among industrialists in moving to Little Rock, cheap labor and tax concessions notwithstanding. This realization sent a jolt through the ranks of development crusaders, and after the school board resigned in 1958, William Rector, a member of the chamber's industrial committee, organized a businessmen's slate to fill the vacancies. The election of three moderates was offset, however, by the victories of a trio of diehard segregationists, the result being a stalemate as far as an effort to reopen the schools was concerned.[5]

As 1959 opened, E. Grainger Williams, the chamber's incoming president, called for an end to the crisis. Mounting opposition to Faubus' policies crystallized around a campaign to retain forty-four teachers and ad-

4. Numan V. Bartley, *The Rise of Massive Resistance* (Baton Rouge: Louisiana State University Press, 1969), 261–65.
5. *Ibid.*, 328; Elizabeth Jacoway, "Little Rock Businessmen and Desegregation: Some Preliminary Findings," unpublished paper delivered at the April, 1978, meeting of the Organization of American Historians.

ministrators who had been fired after the moderates had walked out of a
school board meeting. Organized by some of the city's most affluent citizens the STOP movement (Stop This Outrageous Purge) succeeded in
recalling the board's segregationists and replacing them with moderates.
The new president of the board, Everett Tucker, Jr., was also the Chamber of Commerce's industrial director. Tucker warned that the desegregation crisis would have disastrous implications for the city's economic
future, and a secret committee of merchants, bankers, chamber representatives, and selected black leaders began to work to desegregate all
public facilities in Little Rock. When the schools opened in August, six
black children enrolled and attended without major incident.[6]

Many of those who counseled moderation in Little Rock argued that
the crisis had crippled industrialization efforts, but William P. Rock, the
executive secretary of the Arkansas Industrial Development Commission, denied that the controversy had done any damage to Arkansas's economic future. Growth statistics did not support Rock's pronouncement.
Across the state in 1958 new industrial investment created almost fourteen hundred fewer jobs than in the previous year. Meanwhile, Little
Rock, which had attracted eight plants in 1957, failed to capture a single
new industry for the next four years. The coming of Jacuzzi Brothers of
Richmond, California, in 1962 was cause for great celebration in the
Arkansas capital not because the plant represented a huge investment or
promised to create a large number of new jobs, but simply because Jacuzzi had ended the four-year drought.[7]

Convinced that there was a lesson to be learned from the Arkansas experience, groups that supported peaceful desegregation and open schools
invited Boyd Ridgeway and Everett Tucker from the Little Rock Chamber
of Commerce to come to their cities and counsel peaceful acquiescence.
Tucker showed audiences in Atlanta and Athens, Georgia, a letter written
by an industrial prospect who had been considering an Arkansas location: "You may dismiss ——— from consideration. Our contacts with
Arkansas have given us an unfavorable opinion of that state in comparison with Tennessee, Mississippi, or Missouri. We have no desire to be

6. Bartley, *Massive Resistance*, 329–32; Jacoway, "Little Rock Businessmen," 11–14.
7. "Racial Problems No Bar to Industrializing South," Memphis *Commercial Appeal*,
January 4, 1958, "Dixie Thrives Under Segregation," Richmond *Times Dispatch*, December
4, 1959; "Little Rock Cont'd," Oklahoma City *Times*, January 27, 1962 (SERS clippings);
"The Price of Defiance," *Business Week*, October 6, 1962, p. 31.

involved in the segregation problems current in that state." Tucker informed a national television audience that instead of receiving such direct evidence of the impact of the Little Rock crisis, industrial promoters in the city often simply failed to hear from "the XYZ Company that it's on the prowl for a new plant location." Tucker closed his talks by admonishing local audiences: "Keep your public schools open. You will never regret it."[8]

As contemporary southern leaders faced racial crises in their own states and communities, it remained to be seen whether they had learned the "lesson of Little Rock." Initially, Virginia's leaders appeared intent on responding to the threat of integration by following the plan of massive resistance outlined by the domineering Senator Harry Flood Byrd. In early 1959 Governor J. Lindsay Almond, Jr., promised to save Virginia from the "livid stench of sadism, sex, immorality and juvenile pregnancy infesting the mixed schools of the District of Columbia and elsewhere." Almond's protectiveness forced several local schools facing court-ordered desegregation to close, alarming businessmen and industrial promoters who feared that the prospect of closed schools might scare away desirable new industries and the executive and technical personnel required to staff them.[9]

Almond received a number of letters from critical citizens like the couple who warned, "Industry surely will not come to a state where education is in the fix it is in Va." Public pressure, especially from the ranks of businessmen and industrialists, began to tell on Almond, and six months after his pledge to resist the cancer of integration, he told an audience, "No error could be more grave, no mistake more costly, no travesty more tragic, no curse more productive of woe than to succumb to the blandishments of those who would have Virginia abandon public education and thereby consign a generation of children to darkness and illiteracy, the pits of indolence and dependency, and the dungeons of delinquency." The state legislature also responded to the pressure from the business community with a narrow vote in favor of a local option plan that allowed individual communities "freedom of choice" between token desegregation and school closing. As Virginia's more moderate political leaders attempted to chart a new course for the state, a grateful promoter wrote Governor

8. Helen Hill Miller, "Private Business and Public Education in the South," *Harvard Business Review*, XXXVIII (July–August, 1960), 77–78.
9. Helen Hill Miller, "Private Business," 80–84, 88.

Almond commending him for choosing a realistic course consistent with the best interests of Virginia.[10]

Events surrounding Georgia's agonizing decision on school desegregation paralleled those in Virginia. In 1958 Ernest Vandiver had won the governorship vowing "No Not One!" black would attend school with whites during his term as governor. Georgia had enacted massive resistance laws similar to Virginia's, and rural counties dominated the legislature. As Atlanta came under court order in 1959 to prepare a plan for desegregation, the legislature confronted the question of whether the schools should be closed or whether the state should enact a plan for local option on the matter, an alternative preferred by influential businessmen in the Georgia capital. Rather than deciding on a course of action in 1960, the legislature created the General Assembly Committee on Schools to hold hearings on the school issue and report back in 1961. Chaired by Atlanta banker John A. Sibley, the committee heard testimony in each of the state's ten congressional districts from eighteen hundred witnesses (sixteen hundred white and two hundred black) and received six hundred letters, as well as petitions with six hundred signatures. Although a minority of the members claimed that 55 percent of those heard from preferred closed schools to integration, Sibley and the majority of the committee's members recommended the local option plan for determining whether a community's schools would operate on a desegregated basis or be closed.[11]

Georgia's solons accepted the committee's recommendation, but they might not have done so had it not been for the long reach of influential Atlanta business and civic leaders. The city's major spokesman for moderation was longtime mayor William B. Hartsfield. Though he had been raised in the segregationist tradition, Hartsfield believed and persuaded others to believe that as a bustling metropolis intent on continuing its commercial and industrial growth, Atlanta had to maintain racial peace. When a court order for golf course desegregation was imminent in 1955, Hartsfield arranged to have the order issued during the Christmas season, hoping to capitalize on holiday good will. The ploy succeeded, and

10. Mr. and Mrs. E. R. Albergotti to J. Lindsay Almond, Jr., January 28, 1959, W. D. Rhoads, Jr., to Almond, February 25, 1959, both in J. Lindsay Almond, Jr., Correspondence, Virginia State Archives, Richmond; Helen Hill Miller, "Private Business," 88.
11. Kenneth Coleman (ed.), *A History of Georgia* (Athens: University of Georgia Press, 1977), 369–70; General Assembly Committee on Schools, "Majority and Minority Reports," Atlanta, April 28, 1960 (mimeo in University of Georgia Library, Athens).

Atlanta maintained its golf courses and enhanced its progressive reputation while Hartsfield began to serve notice to all who would listen that his city was "too busy to hate."[12]

The mayor's efforts to mold and preserve a reputation for stability and moderation in Atlanta received invaluable support from powerful businessmen in the city. A thriving commercial and industrial center, Atlanta had its share of high-ranking executives from firms like Coca-Cola and Lockheed Aircraft, as well as influential bankers like Mills B. Lane, president of the Citizens and Southern Bank, who admitted, "I am just as much in disagreement with the Supreme Court decision as anyone, for I view it as an invasion of state's rights. Yet you cannot look at the experience of our other Southern neighbors in any but a practical way." In 1960 twenty-five prominent Atlanta businessmen, including Chamber of Commerce President Ivan Allen, Jr., petitioned against closing the schools, warning politicians that "next to our children, the Georgia business community has the most at stake in the present school crisis."[13] Atlanta's newspapers, the *Journal* and especially the *Constitution*, edited by Ralph McGill, a tireless spokesman for change, cautioned against rash actions. The newspapers gave prominent coverage to theorists who predicted that racial turmoil would slow industrial growth. The *Journal* warned editorially that actions like closing the schools could cause Georgia to lose its leadership in industrial growth "to states like Florida, North Carolina, and Tennessee where school closings have been firmly rejected." In 1958 the *Constitution*'s business editor conducted a survey concerning the effects of closed schools and reported that "17.1 percent of those in key industrial and university positions" said they planned to leave Georgia if public schools were closed.[14]

Atlanta's reputation as a citadel of moderation in a still-angry and defiant state grew rapidly after the city made its transition to token desegregation in 1961. When reporters poured into the Georgia capital to chronicle the events of the first day of integrated classes, Mayor Hartsfield turned the city council chambers into a press room, arranged for remote

12. Fred Powledge, "Black Man, Go South—Specifically, as Far as Atlanta, for Old Times There Are Now Forgotten," *Esquire*, LX (August, 1965), 72–74, 120–21.

13. Helen Hill Miller, "Private Business," 87; "Business Citizenship in the Deep South," *Business Horizons*, V (Spring, 1962), 63.

14. Helen Fuller, "Atlanta Is Different," *New Republic*, CXL (February 2, 1959), 10; Atlanta *Journal*, June 1, 1960, p. 26; Southern Regional Council, "Leadership Report #3, May 11, 1959," p. 1, in "Leadership Project" Files, Southern Regional Council, Atlanta.

telephone reports from the schools, and supplied typewriters and, of course, plenty of Coca-Cola. There was little to report as it turned out, because desegregation was so peaceful and Hartsfield, anxious to use the presence of these reporters to good advantage, hastily arranged for a trio of buses to conduct a tour of the city emphasizing points of pride such as the "fine Negro homes." That evening the mayor hosted a cocktail party for the visiting press, including black reporter Charlayne Hunter, who only months before had been one of the first two blacks to attend the University of Georgia.[15]

Atlanta's leadership had played a major role in steering the city and the state of Georgia along a more moderate course, but not all Georgians felt desegregation would insure continued growth. One suburban editor, writing in the shadow of the city's skyscrapers, scoffed at the insistence of Atlanta officials that "acceptance of desegregation would be good for industry and business growth. We'll see, as time goes on, how wrong they are. It will have nothing whatever to do with location of plants or growth of business. You can mark these words well. See for yourself."[16]

Such skepticism notwithstanding, the effectiveness of the desire for new industry in encouraging moderation in Atlanta reinforced the efforts of the Southern Regional Council, an Atlanta-based organization committed to social progress in the South. The SRC's Southern Leadership Project aimed at encouraging businessmen to assume responsibility for bringing a speedy and nonviolent end to segregation and discrimination in their cities. The council periodically issued "L Reports," which were sent to a thousand selected decision-makers across the South between 1959 and 1961. These reports presented the recipients with an appeal couched in phraseology calculated to convince a local businessman that in helping his city desegregate peacefully he was providing economic as well as moral leadership.[17]

L Reports contained data concerning the damaging impact of racial disturbances on industrial growth as well as prominent examples of business organizations that had helped to chart a moderate course for their communities. One report quoted Malcolm Bryan, president of the Federal

15. Powledge, "Black Man," 73–74.
16. Forest Park (Georgia) *Free Press*, September 9, 1961.
17. Edwin Lee Plowman, "An Analysis of Selected Strategies Used by the Southern Regional Council in Effecting Social Change in the South" (Ph.D. dissertation, Boston University, 1976), 189.

Reserve Bank of Atlanta, who told a Rotary Club audience, "If we behave like a banana republic, we shall get and deserve the economic rewards characteristic of a banana republic." Another report, "Businessmen Point the Way," quoted public statements by business and booster groups from several southern cities, such as Raleigh where the directors of the Merchants Bureau warned that "the overriding challenge now confronting every Raleigh business person is to do these things that would further human relations and the continued growth of Raleigh." The report also referred to a statement circulated by the Knoxville Chamber of Commerce that affirmed a belief that "what is morally right is economically sound."[18]

In addition to issuing the L Reports, the council sponsored field trips by Benjamin Muse, who visited with officials and community leaders across the South. Between 1959 and 1961, Muse conferred with five southern governors, more than forty newspaper editors, and a number of other local leaders. He offered advice and encouragement and in his reports managed to depict a flurry of behind-the-scenes activities by progressive businessmen who were intent on making their city's transition to desegregation as peaceful as possible. Even though Muse conceded the situation was "dangerous" in Birmingham, he described a massive campaign by chamber of commerce and business leaders to "encourage the location of new enterprises by maintaining recreational advantages and wholesome conditions."[19]

It is difficult to determine the effectiveness of efforts to steer southern cities down the course taken by Atlanta rather than the one taken by Little Rock, although concerned advocates of industrial growth in several cities clearly considered the potential cost of defiance before they decided to acquiesce to desegregation. In 1960 the Dallas Citizens Council, an organization of 250 businessmen, launched a campaign to prepare the city's white residents for desegregation not only of schools but of local restaurants and hotels.[20]

As Charlotte faced the prospect of integration in 1963, local leaders reflected on the experience of Little Rock as well as their city's newly won

18. "Leadership Report #24," February 16, 1961, "#42," June 6, 1963, in "Leadership Project" Files.
19. Plowman, "An Analysis," 189; Benjamin Muse, "Confidential Memorandum," January 11, 1962, in "Leadership Project" Files.
20. Steven M. Gelber, *Black Men and Businessman: The Growing Awareness of a Social Responsibility* (Port Washington, N.Y.: Kennikat Press, 1974), 148.

listing as one of the top forty trade areas in the nation. They also considered the promotional record of the Chamber of Commerce, which claimed to have brought fifty new companies to Charlotte in 1962. The consensus among the city's economic elite was that "this was too good a town to have it ruined," and they joined the Chamber of Commerce in urging peaceful desegregation of businesses catering to the general public. Charlotte's leaders were proud to hear their city referred to as "a little Atlanta," and their pride increased when an executive vice-president of Eastern Airlines announced that one reason his company had chosen the city as the site of a new $6 million computer center was the admirable way race relations had been handled in Charlotte.[21]

By the early 1960s Augusta, Georgia, had earned a reputation as a "go-getter" city. Mayor Millard Beckum, a former chamber of commerce executive, led Augusta's vigorous drive for new industry. In the spring of 1962 as black students from Paine College and local high schools were being organized to demand desegregation of public accommodations, Beckum held a meeting with black leaders. The mayor faced the threat of protests during the upcoming Masters golf tournament, which not only boosted the local economy but normally produced a flood of favorable free publicity. Rather than have the city's image tarnished in a futile resistance effort that might attract Martin Luther King to Augusta, Beckum quietly arranged for the young blacks to desegregate local lunch counters and theaters. In each case, the demonstrations were peaceful and orderly with police out of sight but standing by if needed. In July, 1963, when the *Chronicle*, the local daily, decided "The Time Has Come" for school desegregation in Augusta, the editor reminded readers that new industry would be scared away if Augusta became the scene of protests and violence.[22]

If Atlanta, Dallas, Charlotte, and Augusta provided examples of the crucial role that development leaders could play in facilitating integration, the desegregation crises in New Orleans and Birmingham, as well as the uproar over integration of the University of Mississippi, demonstrated what could happen when influential economic spokesmen remained silent too long. At first glance New Orleans seemed a weak link in the South's chain of resistance to integration. The city had a long history

21. Damonia Etta Brown Leach, "Progress Under Pressure: Changes in Charlotte Race Relations, 1955–1965" (M.A. thesis, University of North Carolina, 1976), 171–72, 186–87.
22. Cobb, "Politics in a New South City," 109–11.

of racial mixing, relatively loose patterns of residential segregation, and a culture shaped more by Catholicism than fundamentalist Protestantism. Moreover, New Orleans had a seemingly progressive mayor in deLesseps S. Morrison, who had been in office for thirteen years. The image-conscious Morrison, along with his chief of police and school superintendent, had affirmed a determination to avoid "mob rule." Yet in February, 1959, eighteen months before the city faced its first desegregation crisis, no local leaders had made any apparent attempt to prepare white residents for what was to come. The press, the clergy, and perhaps most significantly, the business community were silent.[23]

One reason for the silence of local economic leaders was the peculiar, almost unique style of New Orleans—"No Atlanta, no city of southern go-getters, she is still the place of good food, good times, good manners of living." The booster spirit that at times seemed to dominate Atlanta was all but invisible in New Orleans, which had no well-organized, influential industry-seeking organizations in 1960. In fact, many conservative residents of the Crescent City saw new industry as a threatening carrier of a contagion of new ideas, and the local chamber of commerce, an organization associated in Atlanta and elsewhere with moderation, had fired its press agent for defending the Warren Court's decision.[24]

As a court-ordered confrontation over desegregation approached in 1960, the dominant voice was that of political boss Leander Perez, who inveighed against "zionist Jews" and the NAACP and urged his listeners, "Don't wait for your daughter to be raped by these Congolese. Don't wait until the burr-heads are forced into your schools. Do something about it now!" The day after Perez's oration a mob swept through the downtown area and stormed the school board offices. Mayor Morrison, who had cultivated a reputation as a reformer, made a public statement on the night of the riot stressing his concern that "ugly, irresponsible incidents" could mar the image of New Orleans as "a thriving center of commerce and industry." Morrison ended his at best low-key plea for calm with a reminder that he continued to oppose court-ordered integration.[25]

23. Helen Fuller, "New Orleans Knows Better," *New Republic*, CXL (February 16, 1959), 14–17.
24. *Ibid.*, 15–16.
25. Edward F. Haas, *DeLesseps S. Morrison and the Image of Reform: New Orleans Politics, 1946–1961* (Baton Rouge: Louisiana State University Press, 1974), 270; Robert L. Crain, *The Politics of School Desegregation: Comparative Case Studies of Community Structure and Policy Making* (Chicago: Aldine, 1968), 276–77.

To complicate matters, the school board erred in its decision as to which schools should be integrated. Because most members apparently believed that New Orleans blacks were scholastically unprepared for integration, officials placed them in schools where their test scores would be compatible with those of their new fellow pupils. This approach meant that the two downtown schools targeted for integration were in low-income areas where whites felt economic pressure from blacks. Already frustrated and bitter, the white residents were easy marks for segregationist agitators. The result was weeks of ugly confrontations, centering on the activities of "the cheerleaders," a group of women who gathered daily in front of national television cameras to shout obscenities and threats at the black children and their escorts.[26]

New Orleans provided an epic-length drama more shocking than Little Rock in the intensity of hate it portrayed. A Little Rock businessman had come to the Crescent City to warn his counterparts of the potentially disastrous impact of diehard resistance on New Orleans' image, but many local businessmen had refused to talk about the subject and some even crudely rebuffed the ambassador of moderation. Even the efforts of two local groups, Save Our Schools and the Committee of Public Education, failed to elicit significant support from local businessmen. Before the crisis Mayor Morrison had quietly made overtures to members of the economic elite about a call for peaceful acceptance of the court decision, but having received little or no support, he allegedly declared, "if those s.o.b.'s aren't going to do anything, I'll be damned if I'm going to stick my neck out!"[27]

Rather than taking a stand for law and order, as he had earlier indicated he would, Morrison blamed the press for creating a negative image of New Orleans: "We are suffering completely without fault on our part." Economic leaders chimed in, charging that a *Time* reporter and a television cameraman had led a crowd in a rehearsed outburst. These charges reflected local leadership's concern over the economic slump that had set in during the prolonged crisis. Tourist spending and retail trade had dropped precipitously. Finally on December 14, 1960, the business and professional leaders of the community gave in; 105 of them signed a large advertisement in the *Times-Picayune*, calling for order and support for

26. Haas, *DeLesseps S. Morrison*, 267–69, 272–79.
27. *Ibid.*, 257, 262, 276, 278–79.

the school board. The New Orleans crisis did not disappear until the end of the school year in June, 1961, but the belated action of the business leaders in making a public stand for moderation proved to be a crucial turning point.[28]

A leadership vacuum like the one that contributed to the ugly scenes in New Orleans produced a similar result in Mississippi. As the University of Mississippi faced its integration crisis in 1962, Governor Ross Barnett bellowed defiance without encountering significant opposition from business and industrial leaders. The violence that subsequently exploded at Oxford reinforced popular images of Mississippi as the most savage and backward of the southern states and seemed certain to undermine the state's efforts to attract industry. Development leaders showed little initial concern about the repercussions of the Oxford outbreak, however, possibly because they believed that their BAWI program and the state's right-to-work law insured continued growth even if white Mississippians held doggedly to their belief in rigid segregation. In 1961 industrial developers took credit for eighty-three new plants and sixty-eight expansions. Among the well-known firms involved were General Cable Corporation and the General Tire and Rubber Company.[29]

Governor Barnett worked hard to convince white citizens that his obstructionism had not hampered his efforts to sell Mississippi to new industries. He made an average of approximately one out-of-state "prospecting" trek each month. With federal troops still on the Oxford campus, he braved hostile demonstrations to attend a luncheon with industrialists in Chicago. After the meeting he proudly announced that a $2.5 million woodworking plant was coming to Gulfport. Barnett claimed that in the twelve months after the Ole Miss riot, Mississippi could boast of eighty-three new or expanded industries. Near the end of his administration he claimed credit for 555 new plants and forty thousand new jobs although Mississippi Employment Commission figures showed an increase of only thirteen thousand in manufacturing employment between 1960 and late 1963.[30]

28. *Ibid.*, 283–88. For an analysis of the New Orleans crisis emphasizing not only Morrison's failures but those of the city's economic elite, see Crain, *The Politics of School Desegregation*, 292–305.

29. "The Price of Defiance," 31–32.

30. Jackson *Daily News*, September 22, 1963, p. 2F; James W. Silver, *Mississippi: The Closed Society* (New enlarged edition; New York: Harcourt Brace and World, 1966), 73.

Few who were seriously involved in the crusade for new industry accepted Barnett's reassurances, but Mississippi's leading advocates of economic growth were nonetheless slow to act. Seventy business leaders did meet a few days before the Oxford violence in an attempt to draft a "law and order" resolution, but they failed to agree on the wording of the statement. Shortly after the riot, a group of 127 business leaders called for adherence to the law, although they took great pains to condemn the law itself. While valuable, these gestures came too late to save the state from the stigma of Oxford, a burden that would be borne for a long time to come.[31]

As the Magnolia State faced the "Freedom Summer" onslaught of civil rights workers in 1964, the Mississippi Economic Council half-heartedly called for citizens to respond to the "unfriendly activities of many outside students and adults" by conducting themselves "with dignity and, if possible, even good humor." The occasionally violent response of Mississippi whites to the Freedom Summer activities indicated that the MEC's statement had only limited impact. When the bodies of three slain civil rights workers were uncovered on August 4, 1964, Mississippians heard again a refrain that had scarcely waned since the Oxford conflict. Industrial promoters reported that in the last months of 1964 at least a dozen firms "seriously considering a location in Mississippi" had chosen to go elsewhere. An executive of Work Wear of Cleveland, Ohio, wrote a developer, "We won't consider expanding in Mississippi again until the state and its people join the Union again," and a New York *Times* report claimed that one small factory had been moved across the state line into Louisiana in order to avoid having a Mississippi mailing address.[32]

The absence of development-oriented leadership that left Mississippi unprepared for any kind of initial moderate response to integration also kept Birmingham, Alabama, shackled by fear and frustration. With the business community unwilling to speak out for orderly acquiescence, the mayor and city commissioners flinched not a whit as they voted to close the city's white parks, playgrounds, and golf courses rather than accept desegregation. Birmingham also surrendered its minor league baseball

31. Robert Massie, "What Next in Mississippi?" *Saturday Evening Post*, CCXXXV (November 10, 1962), 23.

32. Muse, "Confidential Memo," June 18, 1964; *Wall Street Journal*, February 2, 1965, p. 1; New York *Times*, December 20, 1964, p. 1.

teams and allowed itself to be bypassed on tours by the Metropolitan Opera and travelling theatrical groups. Observers consistently linked Birmingham's reputation for racial backwardness to its economic stagnation. Between 1950 and 1960, the population of metropolitan Birmingham increased by only 14 percent while Atlanta's grew by 40 percent. The United States Steel Corporation dominated the local economy, and company executives provided little encouragement for efforts to attract competitive employers. Without significant new industries, automation in the steel industry resulted in unemployment that went largely unrelieved.[33]

In May, 1961, a chamber of commerce hard-sell campaign and a number of concessions put the city close to landing a major steel products plant. Negotiations with the company were under way when a busload of "freedom riders" bent on testing segregation practices in the local terminal arrived in town. The freedom riders had been attracting a great deal of attention—some of it violent—since they entered Alabama, and they had even telegraphed city officials as to their time of arrival in Birmingham. When they reached the city, however, they saw no police, only a mob wielding blackjacks and steel pipe. The ensuing attack received national media coverage, and the steel company quickly withdrew from negotiations and located its plant in Tennessee even though it had to ship its steel from Birmingham. The president of the local chamber of commerce lamented the fact that his city now had "a black eye we'll be a long time trying to forget." A businessman put it more bluntly: "We let twenty-one college kids looking for trouble come into our town and make a half a million of us look like damn red-necks—besides losing us a lot of money, time and jobs." An explosion at a black church shortly before Christmas in 1962 marked the seventeenth bombing of black churches and homes in Birmingham since 1957. A chamber of commerce official expressed his disgust: "Let a carload of riffraff throw a stick of dynamite and— boom—we're set back another five years."[34]

Hoping to give their city a more progressive image, a group of business and financial leaders succeeded in getting the electorate to scrap the city's three-man commission government for a mayor-council set-up, and in April, 1963, the first mayoral election produced a victory for the moderate segregationist Albert Boutwell over the rabid segregationist city com-

33. Joe David Brown, "Birmingham, Alabama: A City in Fear," *Saturday Evening Post*, CCXXXVI (March 2, 1963), 17.
34. *Ibid.*, 13, 17–18.

missioner Eugene "Bull" Connor. The election did the city's image little immediate good, however, because the embittered Connor filed suit to preserve the city commission's authority, and while the courts mulled over the matter, two sets of officials claimed to be the duly constituted governmental authority. Meanwhile, Dr. Martin Luther King, Jr., arrived in Birmingham to lead an assault on jim crow practices in the city's businesses.[35]

When demonstrations resulted in the use of police dogs and firehoses to disperse protesters, Birmingham's image absorbed another body blow. Commissioner Connor presided over the abusive treatment of young, in some cases, preteen blacks, and television cameras captured the brutality for national audiences. With a divided government, one side vowing defiance and the other unenthusiastic about compliance, the city's "Big Mules," the economic and industrial elite, were the only group that could provide effective leadership. After some crucial hesitation, on May 7, 1963, as the demonstrations became particularly intense, more than fifty white Birmingham businessmen finally met with federal civil rights mediator Burke Marshall, Mayor-Elect Boutwell, and black leaders. The influential whites, who allegedly represented about 80 percent of the hiring power in the area, agreed to a timetable for desegregation, as well as a plan to combat economic discrimination. When the final agreement was announced an emotional Martin Luther King told reporters, "Birmingham now stands on the threshold of becoming a great, enlightened symbol, shedding the radiance of its example throughout the entire nation." Despite King's optimism, before the agreement was made public even the moderate Boutwell government had denied any participation in the settlement and within thirty-six hours more bombs were going off.[36]

The following September, as resentment mounted over court-ordered desegregation of the University of Alabama, more bombs exploded, this time killing four black children. Birmingham's industrial boosters immediately felt the shock waves from the bombings, for they lost a "hot prospect" who called to say "he just didn't want any part of Alabama."[37]

Some Alabama promoters felt their efforts were being undermined by the controversy surrounding segregationist governor George C. Wallace.

35. Vincent Harding, "A Beginning in Birmingham," *Reporter*, XXVIII (June 6, 1963), 14.
36. *Ibid.*, 15, 17–18.
37. "The Economic Fallout over Alabama," Louisville *Courier Journal*, September 22, 1963 (SERS clippings).

Although Wallace was a tireless promoter of industrial expansion in his state, he took a defiant "segregation forever" position in his 1963 inaugural address. Shortly after the governor's speech he received a letter from Henry C. Goodrich, the vice-president of the Birmingham Rotary Club. Goodrich's firm was heavily involved in location engineering, and he was concerned that statements such as Wallace's would impair the state's industrial growth. Goodrich assured Wallace that he and his associates in the Birmingham business and professional community were segregationists, but he warned, "We do think the course you have chosen will lead to economic disaster. I cannot emphasize this too strongly because I have already had many such reactions from prospects in the North who might have considered Alabama. Their files are now closed." Goodrich concluded by urging the governor to adopt a more moderate posture, one that would be "much, much better than the one you have chosen."[38]

Wallace responded by reminding Goodrich of the importance of maintaining constitutional government and state sovereignty: "In the long run, if we are not willing to sacrifice for those objectives, neither you nor I nor the people will have any problems for we will have degenerated to a complete welfare state and Washington will be taking care of all of us." The governor assured his critic that comments received from other parts of the country as he sought new industry indicated there would be "no major problem in bringing industry into the state of Alabama."[39]

Wallace did receive reinforcement from businessmen for his stand on segregation. In May, 1963, the president of the Birmingham Chamber of Commerce informed George Wallace that he was "unalterably opposed to desegregation." One supporter hoped that a means could be found to "stop these Yankee corporations from putting pressure on these third-rate Babbits in these Chambers of Commerce to surrender to these Negroes." When Wallace contacted a New York industrialist in 1964 about locating a plant in Alabama, he received a pleasant reply congratulating him on his showing in the Wisconsin Democratic presidential primary and offering the opinion that 80 percent of the citizens of the United States opposed forced integration. The executive also enclosed a twenty-five-dollar contribution to the governor's upcoming primary campaigns in Indiana and Maryland. Wallace also received a note of support from Texas multimillionaire H. L. Hunt, who expressed the hope that Alabama's problems

38. Henry C. Goodrich to Wallace, January 31, 1963, in Wallace Correspondence.
39. Wallace to Goodrich, February 7, 1963, in Wallace Correspondence.

would not "'bail out' the states outside the South which are having their troubles."[40]

Despite Wallace's claims that his segregationist politics were not an impediment to his industry hunting, executives of an Ohio firm that had expressed interest in Mobile as a site for a kaolin-processing plant obviously began having second thoughts about being associated publicly with Wallace. As the governor prepared to travel north to make a sales pitch in February, 1964, an official called to indicate that along with labor union reaction, "adverse public opinion" was troubling company executives. The firm's representatives requested that the proposed meeting be switched to Wallace's hotel room and that no information be released linking them with the governor's visit.[41]

A year later the decision of the Hammermill Paper Company to locate a pulp mill in Selma, Alabama, escalated the controversy over the impact of diehard segregationism on industrial growth. Hammermill announced plans to come to Selma as that city provided some of the most striking examples of police abuse of demonstrators that occurred during the entire Civil Rights Movement. On the eve of the Hammermill announcement Dr. Martin Luther King, Jr., and 270 protesters were jailed in Selma and 500 more were arrested on the day that plans for the new plant were made public. At the center of the controversy over Hammermill's move to Selma was Dr. Robert W. Spike, director of the National Council of Churches' Commission on Religion and Race. Spike called on Hammermill to reconsider, threatening to organize an interdenominational boycott if the company refused. King joined in the campaign to stop the move and northern college students picketed Hammermill plants. Hammermill responded by promising that it would not discriminate in its hiring practices at Selma and arguing that "by providing job opportunities for the economically depressed central Alabama area, we will be making a positive contribution to the pressing national problems of race relations."[42]

Hammermill received the backing of leaders in the paper industry,

40. William M. Spencer to Wallace, May 22, 1963, George E. Ford to Wallace, April 9, 1964, H. L. Hunt to Wallace, August 21, 1965, all in Wallace Correspondence.
41. "Industrial Prospects—North Central U.S." in Alabama Planning and Development Correspondence.
42. "Company Scored on Selma Plant," New York *Times*, February 7, 1965, Donald S. Leslie (chairman of the board, Hammermill Paper Company) to Albert P. Bailey, February 12, 1965, both in Wallace Correspondence.

and some angry southern whites even suggested a boycott of the National Council of Churches. Although the company went ahead with plant construction, it had been severely embarrassed. Executives explained that they had made the location decision long before the turmoil at Selma and claimed that they had thoroughly investigated the local situation beforehand. If they had, in fact, investigated it, they had obviously given little weight to the discrepancy between a fifty-fifty population mix and a voter registration imbalance of ninety-nine to one.[43]

Actually, Hammermill probably based its decision on economic factors, choosing Selma as a site because it offered purchasable land, softwood timber, and adequate water. Although it seemed on the surface that the company's actions vindicated Wallace's claims that his segregationist philosophy would not hamper industrial development efforts, the Wallace administration was obviously fearful that the company would back out at the last minute. Company executives had apparently felt that a new bridge would be necessary to handle the expanded traffic flow they felt the plant would create. Wallace informed his state highway department director that he had promised Hammermill officials that "if they would announce this industry we would simultaneously announce that we would begin programming a bridge." Hammermill had encountered nothing but cooperation from state and local promoters. The Selma Industrial Development Board had floated a bond issue to build the plant. State officials had sweetened the deal by offering a 50 percent property tax deduction, and the State Water Board had speedily inspected and approved waste disposal plans.[44]

Except for Alabama's Wallace, gubernatorial candidates who expressed the strongest commitment to industrial promotion tended to take a less than extreme position on preserving segregation. In the mid-1950s Leroy Collins of Florida and Luther Hodges of North Carolina expressed their opposition to desegregation, promising to resist it "legally" but stopping short of urging diehard resistance. Collins won reelection in 1956 after a flood of national magazine articles praised his industrial development efforts and Howard Hughes announced he was locating a huge

43. "Hammermill and Race-Troubled Selma Point Up Negro's Basic Problem," *Pulp and Paper* (March 1, 1965), 52; "A Big Johnny Reb Special Editorial," February 23, 1965, in Wallace Correspondence.
44. Wallace to Herman Nelson (Alabama State Highway Director), October 20, 1964, in Wallace Correspondence; *Wall Street Journal*, April 9, 1965, p. 12.

new aircraft construction facility in Florida. Hodges came to office in 1956 pledging to lure new industry and not to "mix the races" but showed no inclination to defy court-ordered integration in 1957 and pridefully cited peaceful desegregation as the best example of the "North Carolina way."[45]

Ernest F. Hollings apparently successfully "out-segged" University of South Carolina President Donald Russell in 1958 and entered the governor's office promising to resist the tyranny of a "power-happy federal government." By the end of his term, however, the industry-conscious Hollings had presided over the peaceful integration of Clemson University and was asking the news media to help prepare the way for desegregation. Russell managed to succeed Hollings in 1962 after segregation was obviously on its last legs. Though he still maintained that he was firmly and irrevocably committed to the "segregated way of life," Russell gave more emphasis to the need for new industry: "A job . . . that's the problem, that's the real campaign issue."[46]

In Georgia the 1962 gubernatorial primary pitted colorful archsegregationist former governor Marvin Griffin against handsome attorney Carl Sanders, also a segregationist, "but not a damn fool." Griffin promised to "put Martin Luther King so far back in the jail you will have to pipe air back to him" and suggested that the best way to handle integrationists was to "brain 'em" with a "black jack sapling." As governor from 1955 to 1958, Griffin had established a reputation for demagoguery and political corruption, a reputation that came back to haunt him in 1962. Although he opposed desegregation, Sanders promised to govern with dignity: "I won't cause you and your state to be spread across the headlines all over the nation and cause you embarrassment." Sanders' promise implied that his opponent's reckless words and questionable ethics would make Griffin an ineffective salesman for the state.[47]

Griffin tried to counter Sanders' strategy by claiming that industry respected a strong stand against integration and pointed to the recent de-

45. Charlton W. Tebeau, *A History of Florida* (Coral Gables: University of Miami Press, 1971), 441–43; Earl Black, *Southern Governors and Civil Rights* (Cambridge, Mass.: Harvard University Press, 1976), 93, 106.

46. Black, *Southern Governors*, 82–83; George McMillan, "Integration with Dignity: The Inside Story of How South Carolina Kept the Peace," *Saturday Evening Post*, CCXXXVI (March 16, 1963), 16–21.

47. Black, *Southern Governors*, 68, 177–81; Ben Hibbs, "Progress Goes Marching Through Georgia," *Saturday Evening Post*, CCXXXVI (February 16, 1963), 69–73.

cision of United States Rubber to locate a new plant in Opelika, Alabama, instead of Macon or another Georgia city. Griffin cited the election of George Wallace as a positive factor in the company's decision. Obviously, Wallace's election had not offended those who made the location decision for United States Rubber enough to make them change their minds, but most Georgians were unwilling to trust Griffin with the governorship again. Sanders received 58 percent of the vote statewide and 72 percent in the Atlanta metropolitan area. Sanders was doubtless encouraged to adopt his moderate, "good government–economic growth" stance by the fact that the recent demise of the state's antiurban county unit electoral system had given populous metropolitan areas the political clout they had been denied for so long.[48]

A survey of the impact of the desire for new industry on gubernatorial politics in the post–Brown decision South confirms the judgment of a recent observer: "Generational considerations aside, the commitment of important segments of southern business to economic development has contributed to the decline of segregationist campaigning. Business-oriented candidates and their financial supporters in the business community *when forced by the national government* to make a choice generally valued economic stability and growth over the principle of racial segregation."[49]

Although an accurate general assessment, this conclusion does little to explain variations in the speed and intensity with which development-oriented businessmen and politicians threw their support to peaceful desegregation. The contrast between the Atlanta experience and the violence and bitterness surrounding Oxford and Birmingham was too stark to be ignored even though it could not be explained completely. All three states involved were committed to industrial development, but Atlanta's leaders had dedicated themselves to this goal to a far greater extent than was true in either other case. Atlanta promoters, influenced by Mayor Hartsfield's ostentatious moderation, were far more agreeable to desegregation than boosters in Alabama or Mississippi. Moreover, Atlanta businessmen wielded considerably more clout than did their Mississippi and Alabama counterparts. It is difficult to imagine a Georgia governor rebuff-

48. "Loss of Rubber Company Still Issue," Macon *Telegraph*, August 6, 1962, in University of Georgia Library Clipping File, Athens; Black, *Southern Governors*, 180.
49. Black, *Southern Governors*, 338 (my italics).

ing the president of the Atlanta Rotary Club. Yet, George Wallace coldly informed Birmingham Rotary leader Henry Goodrich that his call for moderation had been rejected.

Not only were they less influential than Atlanta's economic elite but Alabama's businessmen seemed to be less concerned about the economic implications of a desegregation crisis. Mississippi development leaders were no more prepared for push to come to shove and also showed little initial inclination to create a climate of moderation in their state. As a result, in neither Alabama nor Mississippi did industrial promoters step forward forcefully until much damage had been done. Only after the violence and death accompanying the Selma protests did the Alabama State Chamber of Commerce, the Alabama Bankers' Association, and other state and local promotional groups sponsor a *Wall Street Journal* advertisement calling for "fair and just treatment" of all Alabamians and affirming their intention "to continue working for full development of Alabama, the welfare of its people and the maintenance of conditions favorable to the creation of an economy which will benefit every citizen." Even then, these development leaders could not refrain from noting that many Alabama citizens felt the Civil Rights Act of 1964 contained a number of "unjust and improper provisions."[50]

Mississippi industrial promoters also declined to issue a forceful general call for compliance until the handwriting had been on the wall for a long time. On February 3, 1965, the board of directors of the Mississippi Economic Council adopted a resolution calling for law and order, voting reform, and support for public education "for the purpose of furthering justice, harmony and continued development in Mississippi." The fact that this statement was read into the *Congressional Record* by the state's conservative Senator John Stennis indicated that Mississippi business and political leaders at last realized that they preferred a stable future to continued defense of the indefensible.[51] As significant as it may have been within the climate of opinion in Mississippi, the fact that the MEC statement came only after Oxford, the Philadelphia murders, and countless other ugly scenes suggested that the desire for new industry had obviously been a slower-acting, less pervasive influence for racial progress in some states and communities than in others.

50. *Wall Street Journal*, April 15, 1965, p. 13.
51. *Congressional Record*, 89th Cong., 1st Sess., Vol. 111, Pt. 2, pp. 2,014–2,015.

Judging from the number of cases cited wherein racial troubles in various southern states were said to have caused certain communities to lose prospective industries, it seems reasonable to suppose that those states that made the most peaceful transitions to desegregated facilities would also be those that attracted the most industry during the Civil Rights era. On the other hand, states where well-publicized defiance flared into violence could be expected to have enjoyed little success in attracting new plants. When growth statistics are examined, however, the impact of resistance to desegregation on a state's industrial growth is difficult to assess. Developers in Arkansas and Mississippi pointed defiantly to what they felt was impressive percentage growth in manufacturing employment in their states and boasted that this trend continued through the tumultuous Civil Rights years. Table 7 shows that Arkansas's percentage gains placed it second among the southern states in the period 1954–1960 and third in the years between 1960 and 1967. Similarly, Mississippi stood second in percentage growth between 1960 and 1967, Oxford and Philadelphia notwithstanding. Such figures were probably less representative of the impact of racial difficulties on industrial expansion, however, than of a long-term trend wherein the South's two least industrialized states consistently showed the greatest percentage improvement.

When absolute totals of the number of new jobs created in each state were considered, Arkansas and Mississippi did not appear to be growing so rapidly, the former falling significantly in rank after 1960 (and the late 1950s Little Rock affair) and the latter remaining near the bottom throughout the period. Alabama's industrial growth rate appears to have been unaffected by the Birmingham crisis and the antics of Governor Wallace. A look at states with reputations for slightly more moderation finds Georgia making significant gains after 1960 (and the Atlanta and University of Georgia integration decisions in 1961). Texas, North Carolina, and Tennessee remained near the top in absolute growth in manufacturing employment throughout the period. The moderate states appeared to have grown faster after 1960, but except for Georgia, these states were growing faster than the states resistant to integration before civil rights agitation began.

If the negative impact of racial conflicts on industrial promotion efforts was so difficult to document statistically, why were reporters and liberal crusaders able to produce so many testimonials from executives who

Table 7   Rankings and Growth in Manufacturing Employment in the South

| | 1954–1960 | | 1960–1967 | |
	Absolute	Percentage	Absolute	Percentage
Virginia	5	9	6	12
North Carolina	3	5	2	8
South Carolina	9	10	7	10
Georgia	10	11	4	6
Florida	1	1	5	1
Kentucky	8	5	9	7
Tennessee	4	5	3	4
Alabama	6	8	8	10
Mississippi	11	4	10	2
Arkansas	7	2	11	3
Louisiana	13	13	12	13
Oklahoma	12	12	13	9
Texas	2	3	1	5

NOTE: Rankings were computed from figures in U.S. Bureau of the Census, *Statistical Abstract of the United States, 1958* (p. 782), *1964* (p. 770), *1972* (p. 714) (Washington, D.C.: U.S. Government Printing Office, 1958, 1964, 1972).

swore to shun troubled areas? The answer probably lay in the fact that many industrialists believed that protecting their corporation's progressive image demanded that they appear to reject communities that were not cooperating in desegregation efforts. Many companies declined to risk the kinds of criticism, boycotts, or demonstrations directed against Hammermill because of its willingness to locate in an area where racial prejudice was so blatant.

Hammermill was not the only large company embarrassed by an investment in southern communities where protests focused national attention on institutionalized discrimination. Crown-Zellerbach Corporation, which operated a massive paper plant in Bogalusa, Louisiana, received a flood of unfavorable publicity when its board chairman declined to support desegregation protests in that city. After spokesmen for the Congress of Racial Equality castigated Crown for its "completely irresponsible" behavior, however, there was some evidence that the company did play a low-key role in securing repeal of Bogalusa's segregation ordinance. United States Steel came under heavy fire for its failure to exert positive influence in the Birmingham crisis. The Congress of Racial Equality and the National Association for the Advancement of Colored People pressured companies to stay out of Mississippi and boycott goods produced there.[52]

Despite extensive media coverage of the civil rights struggle, among location theorists and experts questions related to race were raised so seldom that they rarely appeared in questionnaires about how plant site decisions were made. In a 1963 survey, sixty-four of three hundred corporation presidents planning plant moves in the next five years expressed a preference for a Deep South location. The Mid- and Deep South regions ranked second and third, respectively to the East, North, and Central areas, as prime locations. When asked to rank the factors involved in their decisions about where to place new plants, the corporate heads gave heaviest weight to community attitudes toward industry and employer-employee relations (a euphemism for low levels of unionization). The industrial leaders assigned a much lower rank to political calm and stability, though they placed it well ahead of factors like local and state tax concessions.[53]

Whether such surveys reflected concern about racial turmoil is difficult to determine because of the vague wording of the questionnaires. A poll of manufacturers who had located in Tennessee in the 1960s was one of the few to make any direct reference to the question of race. In this study, only 4 of 308 corporate executives claimed to have given any consideration to the community's progress in making racial adjustments as they made their location decisions. Had the survey contained the item "record of racial turmoil," the results might have been more enlightening still, for there was little evidence to contradict Winthrop Rockefeller's assertion that "the industrial prospect doesn't give a hoot whether your schools are segregated or not, but he wants no part of disorder and violence."[54]

52. Gelber, *Black Men and Businessman*, 77–79; *Wall Street Journal*, February 2, 1965, p. 1.

53. Atlanta *Constitution*, October 11, 1963, p. 52.

54. Ronald E. Carrier and William R. Schriver, *Plant Location Analysis: An Investigation of Plant Locations in Tennessee*, Bureau of Business and Economic Research, Memphis State University (Memphis: Memphis State University Press, 1969), 39; "Business Citizenship," 62.

In the apparent belief that incoming industrialists preferred stability and the appearance of harmony to the confrontations that could lead to meaningful progress for blacks, many industrial promoters lent their support to early desegregation efforts only because they wished to avoid embarrassing protests. There was some suspicion that industry-minded moderates used tokenism not only to keep the peace but to keep segregation as well. The peaceful desegregation of which Atlanta's Mayor Hartsfield was so proud and of which others made so much involved just nine black students. Segregation flourished in the moderate climate forged by Luther Hodges, and it was the 1964–1965 school year before 1 percent of North Carolina's blacks attended integrated schools. Despite the snail's pace of integration in the Tarheel State, in 1962 advisers encouraged North Carolina Governor Terry Sanford to stress the state's progressive record in race relations when he visited Lancaster, Pennsylvania, in pursuit of a proposed branch plant of an RCA facility. The aides urged Sanford to assure RCA executives "that North Carolina leads the South, has had and will have no strife."[55]

In the absence of continuing pressure from protesters or the courts, many promotional leaders who had urged peaceful desegregation made no further effort to accelerate integration or promote interracial understanding. Liberal journalist Hodding Carter complained in 1964 that the Mississippi businessmen who had issued a statement after Oxford had done nothing since. White leaders in Augusta refused to go beyond their initial call for peaceful tokenism and actively resisted the election of black officials, a development they would later cite as a sign of progress. Influential whites made little effort to assist Augusta blacks economically, and rather than admit the continued existence of racial problems, development officials directed attention to efforts to beautify the city's parks and showplaces. This superficial concern with the image of Augusta prevailed throughout the 1960s, partially because black leaders failed to generate any significant protest effort after 1962. By 1970, however, the illusion of a progressive, harmonious Augusta went up in the flames of a destructive and bloody riot that left six blacks dead and many others of

55. For a skeptical assessment of the "moderate" leadership provided by southern business and professional leaders, see Calvin Trillin, "Reflections: Remembrances of Moderates Past," *New Yorker*, LIII (March 21, 1977), 85–97; "Summary of Prospect, Radio Corporation of America, August 8, 1962," in Sanford Correspondence.

both races injured. Unwilling to admit that such a terrible thing could happen in a community with such a history of "good race relations," Mayor Millard Beckum surveyed a still smoky city teetering on the brink of more violence and insisted, "Everything is calm and we are desperately trying to make them more calm."[56]

Beckum's obsession with maintaining an image of order and stability, even as events about him starkly refuted his claims, provided further evidence that some development leaders had become advocates of racial moderation only because they feared the bad publicity that was certain to accompany large scale protests and violent interracial confrontations. Harry S. Ashmore provided this explanation for the moderate influence exerted by promoters:

> It is not that the bustling gentlemen at the local Chambers of Commerce or the state Industrial Development Commissions are particularly concerned with race as a moral problem; on the contrary, they, like most of their fellow southerners, wish the matter of integration would quietly go away, and many of them privately share the views of the [citizens] councilmen and the Klux. But they also recognize that sustained racial disorder would be fatal to their effort to lure new industries and new capital from the non-South, and that the existing level of tension isn't doing their handsomely mounted promotional campaigns any good.[57]

An important study of the attitudes toward desegregation of eighty industry-minded businessmen in five southern cities showed almost all respondents to favor segregation, although they opposed extreme measures to retain it. They presumably rejected physical violence and even closing the schools, but the survey produced no evidence that enthusiasm about new industry made southern businessmen willing to take a position more moderate than simple opposition to extremism. Many development leaders seemed less concerned about the suffering that racial violence would cause than the impression it would make on northern investors. With tongue in cheek, Ashmore quoted one such booster: "One lynching and we've wasted two hundred thousand dollars in magazine advertising." A Birmingham leader seemed angrier at "outside agitators" than at the perpetrators of the violence of 1963: "We're going to be all right if we can

56. Muse, "Confidential Memo," February 6, 1964; Cobb, "Politics in a New South City," 112–22, 141–43, 191–94; "A Senseless Waste," Newsweek, May 25, 1970, p. 41.
57. Harry S. Ashmore, An Epitaph for Dixie (New York: W. W. Norton and Company, 1958), 118.

just get Martin Luther King, Governor Wallace and President Kennedy out of here and keep them out."[58]

Boosters who feared damaging publicity often tried to preserve the peace by pressuring blacks to remain silent. The Lake Charles *American Press* worried that civil rights protests were threatening Louisiana's future at a time when the state stood "on the threshold of great progress" and placed responsibility for ending demonstrations on the shoulders of black leadership. L. O. Crosby, Jr., of Picayune, Mississippi, declared, "Our Negro people should be told what they are doing against themselves in allowing the national leaders as well as their state leaders to portray Mississippi in the present light." Crosby urged blacks to help themselves by getting more training and to restrain their protest activities in the interest of the state's industrial growth.[59]

If industrial leaders were not particularly concerned with progress toward racial equality and if local industrial promoters counseled moderation largely out of a desire to stave off embarrassing protests and confrontations, how important was the desire for new industry in bringing about racial progress in the South? Although it seldom accomplished more than a peaceful transition to purely token desegregation, concern about a location's image in the eyes of new industrial investors did encourage economic leaders to help their communities and states take their all-important first steps. As self-serving and hollow as the moderation of boosters and civic officials in Atlanta or Augusta may have been, it was surely preferable to the tragic silence of the economic elite in Birmingham or New Orleans. Few industrial promoters appeared to experience a genuine change of heart on matters of race as a result of their concerns about growth, but widespread support for development efforts provided an important escape hatch for southern economic and political leaders who were searching for a face-saving rationale for the painful but inevitable sacrifice of rigid and total segregation.

The South's past and its commitment to white supremacy could not

58. M. Richard Cramer, "School Desegregation and New Industry: The Southern Community Leaders' Viewpoint," *Social Forces*, XL (May, 1963), 384–89; Ashmore, *An Epitaph*, 119; "The Economic Fallout over Alabama," Louisville *Courier Journal*, September 22, 1963 (SERS clippings).

59. "Louisiana's Racial Problems," Lake Charles *American Press*, July 25, 1965, in Louisiana State University Library Clipping File, Baton Rouge; "Crosby Points to Miss. Needs," New Orleans *Times-Picayune*, January 28, 1965 (SERS clippings).

be discarded casually, but the postwar years had produced encouraging signs of progress toward the nation's economic mainstream. Many southern leaders reasoned that if segregation could not be saved, a futile defense of a moribund institution should not be allowed to prevent the South from grasping the prosperity that finally seemed within reach.

Chapter 6

BETTER TOWNS, BETTER WORKERS, BETTER INDUSTRY

The Civil Rights movement helped to remove or, at least, partially obscure what had been the major blemish on the South's image. Still, there were other significant problems that seemed to impede industrial progress. Many southern communities gave the physical appearance of backwardness and indifference, and the region's public facilities and institutions were generally inadequate. Undemocratic political structures insulated rural lawmakers and state officials from urban pressures to abandon their demagogic shenanigans and modernize their governmental practices. Educational programs lagged far behind the nation as a whole, a regrettable condition in a region whose human capital was sorely underdeveloped.[1] Nineteenth-century urban and community leaders had often supported their calls for local improvements with assertions that such changes would accelerate economic growth. In response to suggestions that hopes for more rapid and economically beneficial growth might hinge on the elimination of physical and institutional deficiencies, post–World War II development spokesmen advocated reforms designed to enhance the South's appearance, moderate its political irresponsibility, and improve the quality of its industrial expansion.

As they worked to attract new industry, promoters often found it difficult to dispel the notion that most southern towns were socially backward and physically shabby. In order to convince investors that not every com-

1. These themes are stressed in Nicholls, *Southern Tradition.*

munity in the South resembled that of Erskine Caldwell's *Tobacco Road*, local boosters enthusiastically accentuated the positive and urged others to do the same. Plant executives and location experts agreed that community pride could be a key factor in the plant location decision. By themselves, however, pride and self-assurance were not sufficient, especially if there was glaring evidence to the contrary. A community's self-esteem and spirit must be reflected in its appearance and in the quality of its services and facilities. An Alabama mayor made just this point: "Peculiarly, we spend thousands of dollars in an effort to attract industries to our cities. But when representatives of those industries arrive, they too frequently find a city shoddy in appearance, with streets full of chuck holes and bumps."[2]

Not only did such conditions make a bad impression psychologically but to employers they meant a potential problem with worker productivity and satisfaction. A General Electric community-relations expert put it this way:

> How much chance does a foreman have of getting a good day's work out of Jim Adams if he has come in a half hour late after bouncing to work over rutted and littered streets and threading his way through the daily traffic jam that stretches for block after block to the plant? Or how courteous will your secretary or receptionist be if she has stood first freezing for 20 minutes on a street corner, then packed in an old bus for three-fourths of an hour and started her day off with ten screaming corns? . . . Where do you think the thoughts of your copywriter will be if his youngster is one of forty-five in an overcrowded classroom presided over by some crank of a teacher who should have been retired a long time ago?[3]

Location experts were fond of citing the case of Union City, Tennessee, which was "jilted" by a company whose executives decided to locate a $17 million plant elsewhere. When questioned about this decision, company spokesmen told a local leader, "There is nothing wrong with your city that a good city government couldn't cure." One Georgia expert warned small-town leaders in his state that a reputation as a speed trap was no asset in attracting industry. A state development staffer was horrified when a local official in a South Carolina town admitted to a prospective investor that much of his city's revenue came from fines levied on

2. Earl Sneed, "The Education of a Mayor," *Alabama Municipal Journal* (February, 1965), 5.
3. "What Industry Needs in the City Plan," *Tennessee Planner*, IX (April, 1949), 128–29.

misbehaving Negroes. Hoping to encourage local leaders to make their communities more attractive locations for industry, state agencies encouraged cooperation:

> Real towns are not made by men afraid
> Lest someone else gets ahead;
> When everyone works and nobody shirks,
> You can raise a town from the dead![4]

More than one expert suggested that local chambers of commerce should exert pressure for reform if there were problems with city or county governments. The Georgia Certified City Program was an excellent example of a promotionally oriented group's efforts to link economic and industrial growth to civic improvement. Sponsored jointly by the Georgia Power Company, the Georgia Municipal Association, and the Georgia Institute of Technology's Engineering Experiment Station, the plan offered a locality the opportunity "to win recognition as a superior location for industry and business." The Certified City Program helped leaders identify those civic improvements necessary to enhance their town's attractiveness to industry and business. In order to receive certification a community needed to measure up to a number of criteria on a checklist that included general appearance, fire protection, education, planning, and recreational facilities.[5]

In Mississippi the code word for progress was M-E-R-I-T, a program that called on local leaders to "Measure Needs-Establish Priorities-Recruit Manpower-Initiate Action-To Build Tomorrow's Community." The ninety-two communities participating in 1965 measured themselves against standards of "Beautification, Education, Fire Protection, Health and Sanitation, Housing and Construction, Long Range Planning, Municipal Finance, Police and Traffic, Recreation and Streets." Between 1960 and 1964, thirty-one Mississippi towns improved their libraries, thirty-five set up beautification projects, and seventy-three improved their sewage treatment facilities. Across the South, state development agencies

4. "This Town Was Jilted," *Changing Times*, IV (October, 1950), 20; Kenneth C. Wagner, "What Has *Your* City Done to Secure More Industrial Payrolls?" *Georgia Municipal Journal*, XIII (April, 1963), 16; Dan T. Henderson to Governor Timmerman, memorandum, February 17, 1955, in Timmerman Correspondence; Tennessee State Planning Commission, *Partners: Industry and the Tennessee Community—a Guide to Community Industrial Development* (Nashville: n.p., October, 1947), iv.

5. Winfred G. Dodson and Robert B. Cassell, "Civic Progress Standards of Georgia Certified City Program," Georgia Institute of Technology, Engineering Experiment Station, Industrial Development Division, 1974, in Library of Congress, Washington, D.C., iv.

and the industrial development divisions of banks, railroads, and power companies sponsored similar programs designed to make southern cities and towns excellent places to live as well as work.[6]

Although most organized industrial recruitment efforts seemed to arise in cities or towns, by the mid-1960s there were approximately seven thousand organized rural development groups in the United States. In addition, many metropolitan booster organizations had programs designed to spruce up their hinterlands. The Albany, Georgia, Chamber of Commerce had an agricultural development committee that conducted a contest among rural units in the vicinity to determine which farm community had made the most significant improvements. Elsewhere, rural development groups organized volunteer fire departments, sponsored roadside cleanup campaigns, and constructed picnic areas.[7]

Leaders of southern communities proved willing to support almost any physical or institutional improvement that seemed likely to make their towns more attractive to investors. After Union City lost its prospective industry, the manager of the local chamber of commerce went to the company for some straight answers about why the firm took its new plant elsewhere. The company responded with several reasons. Officials claimed that they had actually been concerned that the city's taxes were too low to support an acceptable level of public services. It was small wonder that Union City could offer only "a picture show and pool rooms" for recreation and had no swimming pool, no parks, or municipal golf course. The executives had also been upset by the downtown slum, clearly visible from their hotel window, as well as the evidence that the community seemed to have the worst schools of the eight potential locations being considered. In addition to their concern about local government, the executives had also worried about visiting the new plant because Union City had no regular air service.[8]

In response to the comments made by the industry spokesmen, the chamber of commerce formed the Aims and Object Committee to oversee a community improvement crusade that led among other things to construction of a new high school, a swimming pool, and a hospital. The city

6. *Mississippi* (Jackson: Goodwin Advertising, n.d.), 91; C. E. Wright, "Area Development by Utilities," 768–70.
7. H. McKinley Conway, *Area Development Organizations* (Atlanta: Conway Research, 1966), 77–79.
8. "This Town Was Jilted," 20.

also opened five playgrounds, began a downtown cleanup, and asked the Civil Aeronautics Board to authorize airline service to Union City.[9]

Lawrenceburg was another Tennessee city whose leaders learned the importance that industries sometimes attached to a prospective location's amenities. In response to suggestions from industrialists and businessmen, Lawrenceburg leaders supported construction of a new hospital, a hotel, and an auditorium. Local promoters finally attracted the attention of an electronics company interested in a site for a plant that would employ fifteen hundred people. Company scouts had been pleased by the improvements Lawrenceburg had made, but they saw no golf course. Promoters sensed that a Georgia town that sported a course might get the plant and made a last-minute effort to remedy their town's deficiency. In two weeks they collected over $60,000 to finance a golf course, called in local farmers to do the planning, and within two months Lawrenceburg had a nine hole layout. The electronics firm took its plant to Georgia anyway, but boosters at least had some new "bait" for industry. In a subsequent promotional brochure readers learned that Lawrenceburg offered "a new hospital, a bountiful supply of soft water, a large surplus of labor, and one of the best golf course layouts in the mid-South."[10]

In addition to physical improvements and upgraded facilities, the desirability of attracting new industry often stimulated political reform at both the state and local levels. In 1946 Augusta, Georgia, experienced a political revolt led by the Independent party, a group dominated by veterans, many of whom were middle-class businessmen and professionals. The Independents succeeded in ousting the Cracker party, an entrenched machine that had controlled city government for several decades. Whereas the Crackers practiced benevolent but often wasteful and occasionally corrupt despotism, the Independents assured voters that they would give Augusta a more efficient and modernized government and would work to attract the industry that had shunned the city during the Cracker years. Successful in their challenge, the Independents instituted city-manager government only to have it voided by virtue of a legal technicality. Nonetheless, they delivered on their pledges of dignified,

9. *Ibid.*

10. "You Gotta Have a Golf Course," *Business Week*, June 25, 1955, pp. 86–87. For a general discussion of the increased importance of amenities as a factor in industrial location, see Edward L. Ullman, "Amenities as a Factor in Regional Growth," *Geographical Review*, XLIV (January, 1954), 119–132.

businesslike conduct of public affairs, and they supported a number of improvements and extended services that promised to make Augusta a more appealing location for industry.[11]

The initial breakthrough in promoting economic progress came in 1951 with the construction of a huge nuclear plant near Augusta at Barnwell, South Carolina. When plant construction was completed, however, the local economy lagged, and Augustans turned for mayoral leadership to Millard Beckum, who led in the formation of the Committee of 100, which was instrumental in bringing a Continental Can plant to the Augusta area. Under Beckum's leadership the Independents pushed for further improvements designed to enhance Augusta's attractiveness to industry. Although they failed to gain approval for the use of convict labor to prepare industrial sites, boosters did succeed in getting the local airport enlarged so that it could accommodate jet traffic. The local papers joined the crusade for new industry, warning that the city's illegal garbage dumps were enough to make Erskine Caldwell say, "I told you so!" The papers also pushed the sale of liquor by the drink as a progressive measure certain to impress industrialists and conventioneers and argued that one more way to please sophisticated executives was to construct a cultural center.[12]

Augusta's post–World War II "GI Revolt" was not unique. In Hot Springs, Arkansas, Sid McMath led a 1946 political rebellion that launched him on the way to the governor's mansion. As Arkansas's chief executive between 1949 and 1953, McMath combined a program of improvements and image building with a vigorous industrial development crusade. McMath's highway improvement plan was so successful that automobile companies had to stop bragging that their products were sturdy enough to pass "the Arkansas mud test." DeLesseps S. Morrison enjoyed strong support from veterans in a successful 1946 campaign for mayor of New Orleans, but a number of his backers were concerned primarily with the commercial and industrial development of the Crescent City. Many citizens seemed convinced that former mayor Robert Maestri's corrupt and inefficient administration had been responsible for the city's economic stagnation.[13]

11. James C. Cobb, "Colonel Effingham Crushes the Crackers: Political Reform in Postwar Augusta," *South Atlantic Quarterly*, LXXIX (Autumn, 1979), 507–519.
12. Cobb, "Politics in a New South City," 82–89.
13. Lester, *A Man for Arkansas*, 137; Haas, *DeLesseps S. Morrison*, 27.

Louisiana provided the best example of a state whose poor image apparently retarded its industrial growth. A reputation for high taxes, free spending, and a shady and ineffective government that was openly hostile to business had dogged the state since the tumultuous era of governor and then senator Huey P. Long. Officials made an effort to refurbish Louisiana's image in 1940 with the establishment of a Department of Commerce and Industry charged with bringing in new plants. The new agency's executive director promised that industry would now find state government "cooperative rather than antagonistic" and that "punitive laws and political and legislative interference would be discarded in favor of the extended hand of welcome and aid." Such promises notwithstanding, the Pelican State made little progress in improving its reputation. As its regional neighbors registered impressive gains, Louisiana languished, ranking last among the southern states in absolute growth in manufacturing employment during the period 1954–1960. Louisiana gained only nineteen thousand manufacturing employees during this period, whereas Oklahoma, the next slowest growing state, gained twenty-five thousand.[14]

An example of the costliness of Louisiana's undesirable image was the 1964 decision of Schlitz Breweries to locate a $15 million plant in Longview, Texas, instead of Shreveport. Shreveport's boosters lamented the loss of the investment, as well as the three hundred jobs it would have created, but when they questioned Schlitz officials as to what their city lacked, they were told the fault lay with their entire state rather than just their city. Schlitz refused to "buy" Shreveport for the same reasons it shunned other Louisiana cities—instability in state government, unfavorable corporate income and property taxes, and an inefficient public school system. Actually, the tax considerations may have been primary. Schlitz calculated that the Texas location would save the company $500,000 a year in taxes. Company officials made it a point, however, to stress their concerns about state government and the public schools.[15]

In the late 1940s prominent citizens, frustrated at the political and governmental chaos that plagued their state, expressed interest in a

14. Ernest Lee Jahncke, *Smokestacks and Payrolls: An Address Before the Members of the Southeastern Regional Clearing House Association, Baton Rouge, October 25, 1940* (Baton Rouge: n.p., 1940), 5; U.S. Bureau of the Census, *Statistical Abstract of the United States, 1958* (p. 782), *1972* (p. 714) (Washington, D.C.: U.S. Government Printing Office, 1958, 1972).

15. "Many Lessons Can Be Learned from the Schlitz Case," Shreveport *Times*, May 3, 1964, in Louisiana State University Library Clipping File, Baton Rouge.

statewide fact-finding organization. In March, 1950, the presidents of the state's four largest colleges invited 120 leaders from law, business, education, and government to a meeting that led to the organization of the Public Affairs Research Council, a private association supported solely by member donations. Although it concerned itself with good government generally, PAR was most intent on identifying and advocating the reforms needed to make the state more attractive to industry.[16]

PAR researchers began to crank out a number of studies, surveys, and reports designed to alert citizens about what was wrong in Louisiana. One of the more widely read of these issues was the organization's attempt to pinpoint the crucial factors that affected industrial development in the state. The PAR report stressed not the basic economic considerations that influenced plant location decisions, but the areas where public policy makers could take steps to make Louisiana more attractive. The group's survey uncovered dissatisfaction with the state's poor business climate and record of governmental waste and instability. PAR experts also suggested that the fact that only one-third of Louisianians over twenty-five years old had high school diplomas made many industrialists feel that the state's labor supply, though abundant, might be unproductive or difficult to train. The council's experts marshaled impressive evidence that Louisiana would never realize its industrial potential until it could boast of responsible, honest government, equitable taxation, and improved schools.[17]

PAR fought an uphill battle to improve Louisiana's image. Its experts challenged Governors Earl Long and Jimmy Davis on their revenue estimation policies and took credit for the state's belated adoption of "one of the most sophisticated approaches to revenue estimation in the nation." In a similar vein, in 1970 PAR's investigation of organized crime in Louisiana revealed that there had been no prosecutions for income tax evasion in the last twenty-five years. PAR also substantiated charges that even some members of the state's revenue department were paying no income taxes and that certain governors had "forgiven" the taxes of some of their campaign contributors. These revelations led finally to an improved collection system and dramatic reform within the state's revenue

16. Public Affairs Research Council of Louisiana, *Everything You Always Wanted to Know About PAR—But Didn't Know Who to Ask* (Baton Rouge: n.p., n.d.).

17. Public Affairs Research Council of Louisiana, *Factors Affecting Louisiana's Industrial Development* (Baton Rouge: n.p., 1962), 51, 59.

department. PAR researchers also took credit for reforms in highway construction procedure, expansion of vocational-technical education, and even improved decorum in the state legislature.[18]

In Georgia the concerns of growth-oriented urban leaders helped to launch a court fight to free that state from the political demagoguery encouraged by rural overrepresentation in the legislature and in the state's primary elections. This imbalance of power resulted from the county unit system, which allotted each county two unit votes for each of its legislative representatives. Candidates were elected not on popular, but on unit votes with the winner of a county's popular vote receiving its unit votes. Because the Constitution of 1877 gave no county more than three representatives or less than one, candidates who could secure the support of a large number of rural counties could outdistance an opponent who relied largely on urban support. The result was that many political figures, like Eugene Talmadge, who bragged that he never campaigned in a county with a streetcar in it, not only snubbed urban areas but often flayed them publicly to the delight of rural voters.[19]

Liberals argued that the county unit system retarded social progress in Georgia by insulating state political leaders from the moderating influence of urban voters. As Atlanta took on increased economic importance in the state, region and nation, its leaders began to worry that the Georgia capital's prospects for future growth were being undercut by the county unit system's tendency to encourage rustic, reactionary politics. Demands for reapportionment mounted throughout the 1950s. Georgia had lost the lead among southeastern states in manufacturing growth in the mid-fifties and in 1961 Georgia-born General Lucius Clay, president of Continental Can Corporation, warned business and development leaders that the county unit system was an impediment to promotional efforts. Clay conceded that the archaic plan had helped to maintain conservative politics, but he told his audience, "Atlanta is regarded as a modern, progressive business center. Thus, outside industry cannot understand why it has such a relatively weak voice in the political life of the state." Clay warned that this concern created "a feeling of uncertainty as to the future

18. Public Affairs Research Council of Louisiana, 25 *Years of Political Reform* (Baton Rouge: n.p., 1975).

19. For a brief analysis of the county unit system's impact on Georgia politics, see Numan V. Bartley and Hugh D. Graham, *Southern Politics and the Second Reconstruction* (Baltimore: Johns Hopkins University Press, 1975), 47–49.

political atmosphere in the state and industry is always apprehensive of political uncertainties." Urban promoters had long considered the county unit plan a thorn in their sides and they enthusiastically supported the court suit that toppled the unit system in 1962.[20]

The reforms supported by development leaders helped to make politics and government more modern and sophisticated but not necessarily more responsive to all the needs of southern society. Promoters opposed demagoguery and corruption but preached fiscal conservatism and "efficiency." They favored extension of services and other improvements that would appeal to investors and middle-class residents but shunned expensive social welfare programs aimed at blacks or low-income whites. Business leaders were all for urban renewal but usually did their best to see that slums were transformed into attractive commercial and industrial property rather than low-cost housing for the poor. The demise of the county unit system and other antiurban subterfuges enhanced the political influence not only of low-income city dwellers but of more affluent, conservative whites who had fled to the suburbs. In most cases developers supported efforts to make southern politics more respectable, if not more relevant, without undermining the stability that they felt was vital to their promotional efforts.

As southern industrial promoters surveyed the social and institutional deficiencies that seemed to stand in the way of more rapid and desirable economic development, their gaze quickly came to rest on the public schools. The region's reputation for antiintellectualism dated back to the antebellum period and had received occasional nurture from critics like H. L. Mencken, as well as from the demagogic antics of various southern political leaders. If the South was not hostile to education, it often appeared indifferent. With the nation's highest dropout rate and lowest per-pupil expenditures for public schools, the region's almost un-American disregard for the importance of educational progress seemed at odds with its professed desire for industrial expansion.

Industrial promoters were well aware of the South's undesirable reputation in the realm of education, but in the years before the federal government played a major role in supporting the public schools, boosters had few means of upgrading the image of southern education. The low taxes that kept political perennials in office and, presumably, helped to

20. Atlanta *Journal*, May 28, 1961, p. 11.

attract new industry also helped to deny southern public school systems the revenue needed to even approach, let alone enter, the national mainstream. Promotional advertisements could only stress increased school enrollment as evidence of the region's progress, as if to say, "more and more of us are going to school now," before progressing to the more pleasant subjects of cheap labor and low taxes.

Although proponents of regional progress had long called for overhauling and upgrading southern school systems, the need had not seemed so great as long as southern promoters set their sights largely on low-wage, labor-oriented industries that evaluated employees primarily on the basis of loyalty and stamina. As the focus shifted in the late 1950s and early 1960s to more sophisticated, better-paying industries, it appeared that the quality of local schools might be a critical determinant of a community's overall attractiveness to new industry. Citing the importance of good schools, one corporate spokesman remarked: "There are all sorts of places that look like good sites in the boondocks of such states as Louisiana. They have water, sulphur, gas—everything we need. But you can't get anyone to go there to work."[21]

By the late 1950s and early 1960s, competition for grades and college admissions heightened the concerns of upper-middle-class parents about settling in areas with deficient schools. General Motors and Minnesota Mining and Manufacturing let it be known that they scanned a community's schools before choosing it for a plant location. The Celanese Corporation even examined average college board scores among a school system's pupils as it looked at competing localities. Most firms claimed to give special consideration to areas served by universities or junior colleges. The Southern Association of Colleges and Schools pointed to the potentially negative impact on a community's image as a location for new industry if its schools were on the verge of losing their accreditation.[22]

When industrialists were questioned about the importance they placed on a prospective site's educational facilities, they almost invariably claimed that schools were an important consideration. When asked to rank schools against more basic criteria such as labor and taxes, however, executives admitted that schools were essentially an intangible, secondary location factor. For some of the major industries that had been at-

21. *Wall Street Journal*, September 23, 1965, p. 12.
22. *Ibid.*

tracted to the South, schools carried no weight whatsoever in the location decision. In a survey of 105 corporate board chairmen, representatives from labor-intensive industries like apparel and textiles conceded that they did not examine local schools when they selected a site for a new plant. Others, like shoe manufacturers, gave education only minimal weight in their decisions. Predictably, the firms that considered education most seriously when picking a site were the technically oriented ones in fields like aerospace and electronics. Executives also gave primary attention to the local educational system when they decided to build or expand research facilities. When locational decision-makers looked at educational factors, they examined existing facilities and their potential for keeping pace with the area's growth. They also looked at a community's proximity to colleges and universities as well as vocational-technical schools.[23]

Few openly opposed development leaders when they affirmed their belief that improvements in the quality of southern schools would pay off in new and more desirable industrial development in the region. Yet even by the late 1960s the South had a long way to go if it was to bring its schools in line with national standards. Table 8 shows that in 1940 per-pupil expenditures in southern systems were only 50 percent of the national average. This figure had climbed to 70 percent in 1950 but rose only 1 percent in the next decade. By 1968 average per-pupil expenditures in the South stood at 78 percent of the national mean. These gains were impressive in terms of the relative progress since 1940, but the intensity of the South's commitment to educational improvement was still called into question by figures that showed that only five states in the region exceeded 80 percent of the national average for per-pupil expenditures in 1968.

Development spokesmen advocated reforms and improvements in the public schools, but the tradition of low taxation remained a key element in the southern promotional package, and most who crusaded for industrial development warned that tax rates must be held down. Thus, although industrial promoters recognized the need for improvements in public education, their active support for these improvements was restricted by their commitment to kep taxes low enough to please incom-

23. Paul A. Montello, "The Importance of Educational Factors in Industrial and Business Site Selection," in Dick Howard (ed.), *Guide to Industrial Development* (Englewood Cliffs, N.J.: Prentice-Hall, 1972), 355–56.

Table 8   Per-Pupil Expenditures in the South

State	1940	1950	1960	1968
Virginia	$43.80	$145.56	$274	$554
North Carolina	39.56	140.82	237	461
South Carolina	34.08	122.39	220	427
Georgia	34.12	123.37	253	508
Florida	58.12	181.27	318	554
Kentucky	39.93	120.82	233	475
Tennessee	37.77	132.17	238	461
Alabama	30.55	117.09	241	403
Mississippi	24.89	79.69	206	346
Arkansas	27.43	111.71	225	441
Louisiana	51.06	214.08	372	618
Oklahoma	53.85	207.05	311	547
Texas	59.50	208.88	332	493
Southern average	41.13	146.53	266.15	483.69
National average	81.50	208.83	375	623
Southern average as a percentage of national average	50%	70%	71%	78%

SOURCE: U.S. Bureau of the Census, *Statistical Abstract of the United States, 1942* (p. 137), *1953* (p. 122), *1963* (p. 115), *1968* (p. 120) (Washington, D.C.: U.S. Government Printing Office, 1942, 1953, 1963, 1968).

ing industries. Nonetheless, development leaders helped to win a general acknowledgment of the need for better schools in the South, and in so doing, made it easier for incoming executives to accept assurances that the region would soon bring its educational facilities up to national standards.

The desire for new industry had its most significant and direct impact on education in the area of vocational training. As successful as the appeal to low-wage industries seemed to have been in creating new jobs, critics doubted that the proliferation of such plants would ever trigger the rapid industrial agglomeration the region really needed. Without higher-wage firms, southern income levels would continue to lag, and the absence of effective demand would continue to retard economic growth. In order to attract more better-paying industries the southern states would first have to be able to supply adequate numbers of well-trained workers.

Such a goal entailed expanding vocational-technical education programs and extending their curricula beyond a traditional agricultural orientation. This idea gained increasing acceptance throughout the postwar period, but in the absence of widespread demand for more skilled workers, supporters found it difficult to sell thrifty legislators on the notion that a more attractive supply of labor meant more and better industries in their states.[24]

One important stimulus for expanded support for vocational education in the South was the experience of Florida, which had always focused its promotional pitches on the attractive climate and life-style it offered. By the mid-1950s Florida had proven itself the southern state most appealing to industries desiring skilled, intensively trained workers. The Sunshine State had managed to land several aircraft plants, as well as a number of related electronic industries. As the space age dawned and a host of supply firms moved down to be near the Cape Canaveral space flight operations, industrial promoters began to realize that Florida, especially its southern half, was attracting more better-paying, highly technical industry than the South at large. Although Florida had begun to emphasize research and development and vocational education, its primary attractions remained physical. Many well-trained, highly paid personnel proved willing to relocate in Florida although they would move to no other southern state. Some skilled workers even came to the state hoping to find suitable jobs after their arrival, the result being that, more than any of its neighbors, Florida offered an adequate supply of experienced, skilled workers, an asset reflected in its industrial growth.[25]

Envious boosters in other southern states recognized the importance of high-quality labor in the Florida success story. In 1960 Lieutenant Governor Garland T. Byrd concluded that an absence of trained personnel

24. For a survey of these criticisms, see Clarence Danhof, "Four Decades of Thought on the South's Economic Problems," in Melvin L. Greenhut and W. Tate Whitman (eds.), *Essays in Southern Economic Development* (Chapel Hill: University of North Carolina Press, 1964), 61–68; John P. Walsh, "Surveying Vocational and Training Facilities," *Industrial Development*, IV (July, 1957), 5–8; "Industrial Education Centers Planned to Meet Growing Demands of Industry," Raleigh *News and Observer*, March 2, 1958, in University of North Carolina Library Clipping File, Chapel Hill.

25. Florida Development Commission, "Case Histories: Florida's Attraction for Engineers, Scientists, and Other Skilled Personnel" (undated mimeo in Library of Congress, Washington, D.C.); James R. Tarr, "Occupational Migration Flows into and from Florida, 1965–1970" (Ph.D. dissertation, Florida State University, 1977), 161–62; Richard M. Alt, "Factors Affecting Industrial Development," *Industrial Development*, III (May–June, 1956), 34.

may have cost Georgia a share of the space-related industry that wound up in the state to the south.[26] Obviously, none of its regional neighbors could make themselves as climatically and physically attractive as the Sunshine State, but if a way could be found to supply better-trained workers, then perhaps more complex industries could be induced to stop short of moving all the way to Florida. Specialized, state-supported vocational training seemed to be the answer.

In accepting responsibility for training programs geared specifically to the particular needs of new industries, the southern states were merely moving, as they had in the area of subsidization, to institutionalize a practice that had long been in existence. Cities and communities that had supported subsidies by public revenue, private subscription, or payroll deductions had often also provided free training, occasionally with the kinds of abuses that occurred in Ellisville or Brookhaven, Mississippi.

Just as the institutionalization of subsidy programs brought the promise of order and stability to the crusade for new industry, the development of state-administered training programs for new industries aimed at providing high quality workers who would be rewarded rather than exploited. More importantly, perhaps, such training efforts would eliminate the costs of on-the-job instruction for new workers, costs that would otherwise be borne by the relocating plant. The ultimate goal of expanded vocational training programs was to make it as painless and inexpensive for a higher-wage industry to move south as it already was for a lower-paying, labor-intensive one. In the early postwar period, southern states began to expand their vocational offerings beyond the traditional farm shop courses to offerings that included welding, metalworking, draftsmanship, and other more factory-oriented pursuits. In addition, promoters supported industrial arts activities and other efforts to propagate the gospel of industrialism among southern youth.[27]

Although more stress on vocational training at the secondary level was important, there was need for greater emphasis on more specialized postsecondary preparation that could be offered only by an expanded system of technical schools and junior colleges. All of the southern states had such institutions, but in 1960 none had enough of them to provide the needed support if the state pursued a comprehensive program de-

26. Atlanta *Journal*, March 18, 1960, untitled clipping in University of Georgia Library Clipping File.
27. Associated Industries of Georgia, *Annual Report, 1957* (n.p: n.p., n.d.).

signed to attract skill-related manufacturing plants to all parts of the state. Thus during the 1960s southern legislators cooperatively approved expenditures designed to place regional vocational-technical education centers within a reasonable driving distance of every citizen. By the end of the decade, most states were nearing this goal. Tennessee, for example, had twenty-nine training facilities spread across the state from Memphis to Bristol in major metropolitan regions and less well known locations such as Hohenwald, Dickson, and Oneida. As did its neighbors, the state also made use, whenever possible, of its community colleges and even its four-year colleges and universities in its training programs.[28]

Southern vocational-technical schools tried to provide offerings keyed to the future needs of the areas they served. Administrators hoped that careful planning would result in a supply of workers well trained for the opportunities they would encounter. Such a situation would please prospective employers and allow the region's youth to remain near home instead of having to search elsewhere for promising occupations. It was not possible, however, to predict with complete accuracy the types of industry that would come into any state or the area in which the new facility might locate. What was needed was a flexible program designed to respond rapidly to the labor needs of any new industry anywhere in the state. In other words, to be really competitive for more desirable kinds of plants a state should be able to guarantee a conveniently located, personalized training program that minimized delays in initiating production as well as early losses due to labor inefficiency.

One of the pioneering responses to the need for a flexible but effective industrial training program came from South Carolina. In 1960 Governor Ernest F. Hollings urged the legislature to take steps to insure that the state had a supply of labor sufficiently skilled to attract the kind of new plants that would free South Carolina's economy from its dependence on the low wages paid by the textile industry. A joint legislative study committee, which included future governors Robert McNair and John West, took a step in Hollings' direction. Their report concluded that the state's 50 percent dropout rate and its low percentage of college graduates (fewer than 5 percent of first-graders would finish college) meant that a large segment of the population failed to receive optimum benefits from educational programs. By greatly expanding technical-vocational train-

28. Tennessee Division for Industrial Development, *Education in Tennessee* (Nashville: n.p., n.d.), n.p.

ing South Carolina might give its workers more marketable skills that would appeal to the kinds of industries anxious to purchase those skills.[29]

At the committee's recommendation, in 1961 the legislature authorized a new program overseen by the Advisory Committee for Technical Training and Instruction. What emerged was a quick-response training program designed to respond to the needs of incoming industry through a system of special schools. A staff of experts took responsibility for supplying these training centers with equipment and materials from a central depot as well as setting up classrooms, hiring instructors, recruiting local personnel, and overseeing their training. Such a program meant that a new plant might open with an already trained work force eager to demonstrate its new talents in profitable production. The plan operated solely at state expense, and early beneficiaries like Firestone Steel, Smith-Corona Marchant, and Lockheed were quickly singing its praises. Promoters were soon telling industrialists, "You can start up in the black in South Carolina," and similar programs began to appear in other southern states.[30]

Although there were some variations, most start-up programs followed a similar pattern. After the site was selected, state officials would meet with the company's designated training coordinator to work out details concerning equipment and manpower needs. If possible, instruction would utilize actual production equipment transported at state expense. State officials also preferred to use foremen and supervisors as instructors, reimbursing the company for their time. Start-up executives would recruit potential workers by coordinating the efforts of the company's personnel department and the state's employment agency. The state would accept responsibility for determining whether applicants possessed the mental and physical skills and psychological qualities required for the available jobs. Trainees received no salary while attending the classes and had no guarantee of a job when the program ended. Final personnel decisions rested solely with the company, and state officials knowingly recruited more people than were needed to fill the anticipated number of jobs. Still, either because they had no job or because they hoped for a better one, the trainees were willing to invest two to three hours on as

29. Lynda Chastain. "A Dream Whose Time Had Come," *Impact: Technical Education in South Carolina*, XI (April-May, 1978), 2–3.

30. *Ibid.*, 3–11; South Carolina State Board for Technical and Comprehensive Education, *Start Up in the Black in South Carolina* (n.p.: n.p., n.d.).

many as three nights a week learning to perform a job that they might not get.[31]

The states met their responsibilities under the program by providing competent instructors, the necessary equipment, and even individualized training manuals that would serve the special needs of the new plant's labor force. Preparation of the instructional literature often involved the cooperation of the state's department of education. In Mississippi, for example, the State Division of Vocational and Technical Education and the Jackson Branch of Hinds Junior College prepared a training program for a new Milwaukee Electric Tool Corporation plant. In order to prepare workers to manufacture parts for the "sawzall," a hand-held electric saw, the training manual began with a very basic approach: "You probably have seen electric power tools before. But, did you know that there are more than 70 people who will be involved in manufacturing, assembling, packing and shipping these saws?" Using precise and simple language and employing photos and diagrams, the manual carried the student through the various stages of the construction process in which he would be involved as an employee.[32]

It is difficult to determine the average savings each new plant enjoyed as a result of a start-up program, but the Arkansas Industrial Development Commission provided some reasonable hypothetical figures. Costs of training 100 new employees for 100 hours at a training wage of $3.00 per hour added up to $30,000. Five supervisor-instructors at $200 a week for six weeks added another $6,000. Rent, utilities and overhead would run near $50,000. Training manuals would cost $2,000, and production material for trainees, another $3,000. Thus, the total savings to the hypothetical firm as a result of Arkansas's training program would be $91,000, a sizable sum for a medium-sized plant.[33]

The savings afforded by state-financed worker training programs help to explain why so many industrialists praised start-up training programs and cited them as important location factors. South Carolina's model pro-

31. Tennessee Division of Vocational-Technical Education, *Tennessee Industrial Training Service* (Nashville: n.p., n.d.); Kentucky Bureau of Vocational Education, Division of Interagency Relations, *The Kentucky Industrial Training Program Is Off and Running!* (n.p.: n.p., n.d.).

32. Kent Brooks, *D-Handle Portable Electric Power Tools*, Research and Curriculum Unit, Mississippi State University (Mississippi State: Mississippi State University Press, 1973).

33. Arkansas Industrial Development Commission, *Arkansas Invests in Your Profitability Through the Arkansas Industry Training Program* (Little Rock: n.p., n.d.), 10.

gram, for example, served 485 companies between September, 1961, and June, 1977. More than 59,000 workers received training for new jobs, and as planners had hoped, more than 50 percent of these people went to work in non-textile-related plants. A flexible, effective training program was certain to enhance worker productivity in any new plant and, it was hoped, dispel the notion that the preference of southern workers for agrarian pursuits made them unsuited for any but the most basic industrial tasks. Manufacturers who had opened plants in South Carolina between 1967 and 1971 ranked the state's training program as the fifth most important factor influencing their location decisions.[34]

On the surface the attempt to upgrade labor skills seemed a significant departure from the traditional emphasis on cheap labor. Yet even with a higher skill level, southern workers remained a bargain. Incoming industries were all too happy to cooperate by keeping their salaries in line with prevailing wages in established plants. The South's new class of better-trained laborers drew higher wages than those who had toiled for years in textile and apparel plants, but even these more skilled workers took home less money than their counterparts elsewhere. Advertisements continued to stress the docility and loyalty of southern labor and promoters still gave private assurances that large-scale unionization was not in their state or area's foreseeable future. Start-up programs always recruited and trained more personnel than could be immediately employed and the policy of tailoring vocational-technical curricula to local industry's labor needs only increased the likelihood of a surplus of trained workers. A recent study of worker training in North Carolina found administrators and instructors concerned primarily with satisfying the "expressed and anticipated" desires of industry. Thus, there was little attention to the trainee's needs or his reaction to the program.[35]

Just as start-up training represented no drastic departure from the past emphasis on cheap labor, the program continued the South's reliance on subsidies as location incentives. State-financed training enhanced the prospect of profits for any company. The establishment of ongoing courses in pertinent skills at area vocational-technical schools also amounted to an indirect subsidy by lessening the likelihood of expen-

34. Chastain, "A Dream," 6; Joan Hoffman, *Racial Discrimination and Economic Development* (Lexington, Mass.: Lexington Books, 1975), 30.

35. Anne Rogers Moore, "Industrial Training in North Carolina: Case Studies in New and Expanding Industries, 1975–1977" (Ed.D. dissertation, North Carolina State, 1977), 85–87.

sive on-the-job training for future employees. Clearly, the major beneficiaries of state-supported labor-improvement programs were the incoming
industries, which found capable employees who could be paid less than
the national average for the tasks they performed. At the same time,
these new firms also received all of the advantages the South had to offer
in the way of taxes, nonunionism, and generally lower costs of construction and operation.

In its first years, South Carolina's industrial development program did
not affect blacks and whites equally. None of the earliest centers were
built in the low-country counties where most blacks lived, a fact reflected
in responses to a 1971 survey wherein 18 percent of the blacks interviewed were not convinced of the importance of the training program to
the state's economic development. Only 11 percent of whites participating in the survey gave this response. A study of economic development
and discrimination in South Carolina credited the training program with
qualifying blacks for more lucrative, nonfarm employment but also noted
that blacks were still far less likely to move into higher-paying jobs than
whites.[36]

All but the most conservative southern development leaders viewed
start-up training and improved vocational-technical education as steps in
the right direction, but many thought further steps were necessary. At
the end of the 1950s the realities of the jet age and the possibilities of the
space age pointed to a proliferation of more sophisticated manufacturing
operations. While the South's garment, textile, and lumber plants depended on gradual improvements in labor techniques to improve production, more complex operations generally experienced rapid technological
change because of the energies and resources they devoted to research.
The emergent, fast-growing industries of the sixties and seventies would
require more than well-trained work forces. They would need research
facilities and could benefit from the assistance of scientists and engineers
at southern universities. The long-term challenge of achieving economic
parity with the nation at large led developers to urge that the South's educational and research facilities and personnel be upgraded and pressed
into service in the crusade for new and better industry.[37]

36. Hoffman, *Racial Discrimination*, 33, 54–55; Louis Harris and Associates, "Priorities for Progress in South Carolina," Study No. 2130, October, 1971 (mimeo in South
Carolina State Library, Columbia), 14, 17.
37. Cameron Fincher, "Research in the South: An Appraisal of Current Efforts,"

The South of the future was a more attractive daydream as a land of research and engineering facilities than as a festering mass of sweatshops. Unfortunately, however, the region could not upgrade its industrial mix by simple wishful thinking, and there were major impediments to making this dream a reality. The South's allocation of its research resources reflected its agrarian past and perspective. Southern universities were much more likely to provide agricultural experiment facilities than those keyed to the needs of industry. As for private research centers, most southern industries seemed to place little emphasis on research or at least relied on centers located elsewhere. In the nation at large in 1948 there were fifty-two industrial researchers for every ten thousand wage earners, but in the South there were only ten. Thus, it was not surprising that southerners received patents at a rate less than one-third of that for the nation at large. To many concerned proponents of growth, the proper course of future action for the South seemed clear. The region would have to transcend its traditional hostility to "the use of intellectual processes as a means to technological and social innovation and advancement." If the South was to accelerate its move toward the nation's economic mainstream, it must do so by providing a "suitable climate for invention, discovery and innovation."[38]

The desire to attract higher quality, more sophisticated industries to the South bore its most impressive fruit in North Carolina. The Raleigh–Durham–Chapel Hill area was particularly blessed with research facilities because it was home to three major universities, Duke University, the University of North Carolina, and North Carolina State College, all situated within fifteen miles of each other. In the mid-1950s former successful businessman Luther Hodges committed his gubernatorial administration to industrial advancement of the Tarheel State and marshaled every resource at his disposal to achieve his goal. Hodges assured industrialists that North Carolina was more advanced socially and culturally than other southern states, and he received the cooperation of university officials in dealing with individual prospects.[39]

The governor clearly viewed his state's three major universities as an

Georgia State College, School of Arts and Sciences, Research Paper No. 5, October, 1964 (mimeo in possession of the author), 1–4.

38. Fincher, "Research in the South," 8–11, 22; Nicholls, *Southern Tradition*, 162.

39. Luther H. Hodges, *Businessman in the Statehouse* (Chapel Hill: University of North Carolina Press, 1962), 203.

important selling point for new industry, particularly the type of prestigious facilities he most hoped to attract. Thus, Hodges responded favorably to a suggestion by famed University of North Carolina sociologist Howard Odum that his school and North Carolina State College jointly support a research institute for the development of southern resources. Somewhat later Romeo Guest, a Greensboro contractor, actually sketched out a triangular plat with a university at each corner. His company then printed a brochure emphasizing the area's research potential. Guest began to spread his idea around, highlighting the industrial development possibilities it offered. These dreams of a research center might never have come true, however, without the efforts of Governor Hodges, to whom admirers referred as the actual "daddy" of the project. Only a few months after he learned of Guest's ideas, Hodges set up the Governor's Research Triangle Committee, "a nonstock, nonprofit, benevolent, charitable and educational corporation."[40] The Triangle Committee was charged with facilitating cooperation between the three universities and industrial research operations in order "to bring to the attention of industry throughout the country the unique and undeveloped advantages" of North Carolina and especially the Raleigh–Durham–Chapel Hill area.[41]

Hodges' search for funds to buy the land for the research center ended with Karl Robbins, a retired North Carolina textile magnate living in New York. In 1957 the Research Triangle Committee announced happily that Robbins had acquired four thousand acres to be developed into a research park at an initial expense of more than $1 million. The park would be located three miles from the Raleigh-Durham Airport with convenient railroad and major highway access as well.[42]

By 1958 development of the Triangle had begun and Hodges directed his efforts toward the establishment of the Research Triangle Institute, which was to be the heart of the park. This nonprofit research facility was to be located at the center of the park and financed by privately donated funds raised by the concerted efforts of Hodges and the Research Triangle Institute Committee. In the same year, the Institute Committee chairman, banker Archie Davis of Winston-Salem, proposed that the park be purchased from Robbins and his co-investors and turned into a non-

40. *Ibid.*, 204–205; "Certificate of Incorporation of Research Triangle Committee, Inc.," in Hodges Correspondence.
41. "Certificate of Incorporation."
42. "Press Release, the Governor's Office, State Capital, Raleigh, North Carolina, for release: AMs of Wednesday, September 11, 1957," in Hodges Correspondence.

profit, nontaxpaying corporation. Funds for the purchase and for building the institute came from private sources like the Richardson Foundation, from which Hodges solicited a contribution of $50,000 in the hope that such large donations would trigger others. The Triangle Committee explained to the foundation that the new park represented "the most inspiring proposal for undergirding the economic well-being of the state and the Southeast that has been devised." Although the wealthy Hodges did not hesitate to solicit large donations, during the first year of fund raising many of the gifts came from individuals or corporations in much smaller amounts. When the project's funds reached $2 million, the newly chartered Research Triangle Foundation borrowed $1.3 million more and used the money to buy the land from the owners at the original price and to begin construction of the Research Triangle Institute.[43]

Although Hodges and other influential supporters of the Research Triangle project quickly proved themselves skillful fund-raisers, the park, obviously, had to be sold to industrial prospects, or it would become merely another "ahead of its time" idea that failed. Along with Hodges and the members of the various Triangle committees, the administration and faculty of the three schools involved played an active role in approaching potential occupants of the new park. By mid-1958, the "sales crew" had made approximately 150 contacts with business executives, explaining the Research Triangle concept and attempting to gauge the responses they received.[44]

Dr. George L. Simpson, the Research Triangle Committee's director, was on loan from the University of North Carolina, but he quickly adapted to the business of courting new industry for the park. When Simpson visited the research offices of Kimberly-Clark in Racine, Wisconsin, he took along Dr. James Bethel, a professor of wood technology at North Carolina State. The company's initial response was courteous but noncommittal. After Bethel suggested a possible solution to one of the company's problems with bark removal, however, the executives expressed more interest, and they raised the possibility of visiting the Triangle. The sales team also utilized the expertise of faculty members journeying about the country in other capacities. A. C. Menius, Jr., who travelled extensively for the Atomic Energy Commission in 1958, put in a

43. Susan Lewis, "Triangle Dream Being Fulfilled," Raleigh *News and Observer*, December 19, 1965, in University of North Carolina Library Clipping File, Chapel Hill; Capus A. Waynick to H. Smith Richardson, April 25, 1958, in Hodges Correspondence.

44. Hodges to Joseph D. Page, May 5, 1958, in Hodges Correspondence.

good word for the Research Triangle with the various nuclear firms he contacted. Dean K. E. Penrod of Duke visited pharmaceutical houses in the summer of 1958, mentioning the Triangle as he went. Professors Bill Little of UNC and Bill Stevenson of NC State College also did a limited amount of travelling on behalf of the project.[45]

Simpson and other Triangle representatives also made presentations to firms as diverse as General Electric, Union Carbide, and Atlantic Refining. The hard work began to pay off in the late fifties and early sixties as Chemstrand opened a research center and was quickly joined in the park by the American Association of Textile Chemists and Colorists and a United States Forest Service Research Center. In 1960, Dr. George Herbert, formerly associate executive director of the prestigious Stanford Research Institute, became head of the Research Triangle Institute. Although the future looked rosy for the Triangle, Hodges and his cohorts had no patent on the research park concept. By the end of 1960 twenty-three such areas had been developed and plans for sixteen more were announced in 1961. By May, 1963, industrial researchers viewed the Research Triangle as merely one of the "newly emerging centers" competing for the government research dollars and for expanding research firms.[46]

The park's fortunes took a turn for the better in 1963 when former governor Hodges resigned his post as secretary of commerce and accepted appointment as the "dollar a year" chairman of the Research Triangle Foundation. When Hodges took over, the foundation's assets consisted largely of land, which was not being sold. Sensing the need for speedy action, Hodges used his business ties and his prestige as a former cabinet member to gain a hearing from International Business Machines, which opened a facility in the Triangle in 1965. Technitrol, which supplied circuit boards to IBM, came shortly thereafter. Hodges' expertise in dealing with the Washington bureaucracy no doubt aided considerably in the attraction of several governmental facilities, including the National Environmental Research Center.[47]

With Hodges at the helm of the promotional campaign, the park's di-

45. Pearson Stewart to R. M. Hanes, May 6, 1958, June 10, 1958, both in Hodges Correspondence.

46. "New York—September 10, 1958," in Hodges Correspondence; Sidney Stapleton, "Research Park: Getting a Jump on Tomorrow," Durham *Morning Herald*, December 12, 1971, in University of North Carolina Library Clipping File, Chapel Hill.

47. Stapleton, "Research Park."

rectors found that they were soon able to turn away industries that were more manufacturing than research oriented. The Triangle contributed significantly to the 28 percent population increase and the thousand-dollar jump in per capita income in the local area between 1961 and 1971, and Research Triangle boosters noted also that several plants that seemed too "process-oriented" for the park had been induced to locate elsewhere in the Tarheel State. By the early seventies the Research Triangle Park was the site of some of the most impressive research being conducted in the entire nation. Monsanto developed its brand of artificial turf in the park, and researchers of other firms made progress on projects like an artificial membrane used to aid heart transplant patients and a self-sterilizing paper container that could be activated by as little heat as that supplied by ordinary sunlight.[48]

By 1977 there were twenty-two research facilities in the park, and six more were on the way. IBM, which had come in the leaner years of the mid-sixties, was the most manufacturing-oriented occupant and employed 3,300 people. On the other hand, Airco employed only seven researchers to analyze industrial gases. The park had also become a mecca for federal research offices, including the Environmental Protection Agency's main research center and the National Center for Health Statistics. The Triangle's promoters obviously expected that these government facilities would attract other grant-seeking research firms, and with the park's sites still less than one-third occupied, Triangle officials could afford to view future prospects selectively.[49]

The park's success significantly altered the Raleigh–Durham–Chapel Hill area's demographic makeup by attracting highly educated, well-paid professionals. Many younger research personnel welcomed the opportunity to complete further graduate study at one of the three universities. By the mid-1970s the local population included more Ph.D.s per 100,000 people than any metropolitan area in the country. To complement the advantages offered by the park itself, promoters emphasized the area's social and cultural atmosphere and supported local efforts to strengthen the latter even further. Governor Hodges stressed the importance of amenities to research scientists. Triangle Committee Director Simpson wrote a pamphlet highlighting not only the scientific but cultural resources of the Triangle as well. Another promotional item, "A Full Life in the Re-

48. *Ibid.*
49. "A Park That Reversed a Brain Drain," *Fortune*, XCV (June, 1977), 148–53.

search Triangle of North Carolina," emphasized the area's cultural and educational advantages in a sales pitch aimed at the scientist's wife. Readers who feared that they might find life in North Carolina a bit "rustic" for their tastes were informed that "national touring artists, companies and lecturers are frequent visitors and many national companies of New York plays come to the area."[50]

Triangle officials realized that the opportunity to work and associate with highly trained intelligent people was one of the area's greatest attractions. They assured incoming researchers that they were joining an intellectually vibrant community and convinced the American Academy of Arts and Sciences that the Triangle Park was the best location for its proposed National Humanities Center. The academy eventually agreed, choosing the Raleigh–Durham–Chapel Hill area over Washington, Boston, and Philadelphia. The center itself was intended as an institute for advanced study and research in the humanities. Described as "a think tank with an arrow," the $1.5 million center accepted its first group of scholars and associates in September, 1978.[51]

The Research Triangle concept was not unique. Research and development expenditures reached $80 billion in the 1950s, and centers sprouted up all over the country to compete for the research dollars of private industry and the United States government. The desire to attract government funds led to the construction of the Virginia Science Center, a publicly owned research park, and the Virginia Association Research Center, sponsored jointly as a facility for graduate study by the University of Virginia, the College of William and Mary, and Virginia Polytechnic Institute. Both the Science Center and the VARC hoped to enjoy the spin-off benefits of the National Aeronautics and Space Adminstration's Langley Research Center, where the Mercury manned space flight project had been masterminded. Other research centers aimed at private industry's research dollar. In 1967 a Georgia development official hailed the University of Georgia's research park as the kind of facility that would appeal to sophisticated industries as well as laboratories and research institutions of larger corporations.[52]

50. *Ibid.*; George L. Simpson, "Scientific and Cultural Resources of the Research Triangle of North Carolina," in Hodges Correspondence; *A Dynamic Concept for Research: The Research Triangle Park of North Carolina,* supplied by the North Carolina Department of Commerce and Industry, Raleigh, North Carolina.

51. Susan Larson, "Humanities Center to Become Haven for Intellectuals," Durham *Sun,* January 6, 1977, in University of North Carolina Library Clipping File, Chapel Hill.

52. Donald I. Rogers, "The Research Center Business," New York *Herald Tribune,* June

By the end of the 1960s, much of the South's educational system was involved in direct or indirect support of the more sophisticated industries in the region. Cooperation between educators and development leaders was yet another example of the extent to which the southern states committed their public resources and relevant institutions to the crusade for industrial progress. The Florida State Chamber of Commerce went so far as to enlist the aid of the state's librarians, who were expected to help meet "the information needs of business and industry."[53]

The desire for industrial growth contributed to some significant innovations in the South after World War II. Communities were beautified, educational programs were upgraded and extended, and government became more modernized and sophisticated. These improvements suggested a realization that, in order to alter its traditional pattern of slow growth, the South was going to have to improve its facilities and institutions and its human resources as well. Yet, the spirit of reform that accompanied the accelerated crusade for new industry in the South bore a certain resemblance to the business progressivism of the 1920s. Talk as they might about making the South a better place in which to live, southern public officials and promotional leaders were reluctant to risk the region's reputation for stability and conservatism on improvements and other projects that did not seem directly related to the industrial recruitment effort. Government's role as an agent of industrial prosperity had expanded dramatically in the postwar period, but despite the ostensible emphasis on progress the poor and disadvantaged of both races continued to receive little attention from political leaders who practiced laissez-faire in the social arena while they moved their state and local governments into even closer partnerships with business and industry.

Although limited in nature, the changes supported by development leaders nonetheless contributed to a significant improvement of the South's image in the eyes of potential investors and the nation at large. Refurbished towns, as well as improved schools and other public facilities, combined with a moderating racial climate to make the southern

5, 1963, clipping supplied by Peninsula Industrial Committee (Virginia); Robert G. Worden to Allen Stephenson, August 11, 1967, in Georgia Department of Industry and Trade Correspondence.

53. "Proceedings, First Florida Conference on Information Resources, Sponsored Jointly by the Council of 100 and the Florida State Chamber of Commerce with the Cooperation of the Florida Library Association, Tampa International Inn, Tampa, Florida, January 31, 1965" (mimeo in Library of Congress, Washington, D.C.).

states more attractive places to live. Meanwhile, subsidized worker training and research and development assistance encouraged more sophisticated, skill-intensive industries to capitalize on the labor, tax, and general cost advantages that a Dixie location still offered. As the 1970s began, a broadened state role in facilitating industrial development, coupled with important social and political innovations, seemed to place the South at the threshold of an era of unparalleled growth and prosperity.

Chapter 7

THE EMERGENCE OF
THE SUNBELT SOUTH

Prior to World War II the South's courtship of competitive, low-wage, labor-intensive industries had not produced the accumulation of investment capital, consumer buying power and skilled labor necessary for the region's economy to reach the "take-off" point of rapid, self-sustaining growth. On the other hand, the region's long-term commitment to conservative government, low taxes, and promanagement labor policies had nonetheless made it ripe for such growth. All that was lacking was the sharp external stimulus usually necessary for takeoff. In the case of the South the triggering impulse may have been the large military allocations and technological innovations accompanying World War II. In the postwar decades more and more investors turned southward in response to lower operating costs, burgeoning markets nurtured by increased federal expenditures, and a favorable business climate sustained by continued popular and governmental support for industrial development.[1]

By the 1970s the South's sales pitch to new industry was a curious blend of the old and the new. The familiar assurances of cheap, nonunion labor, low taxes, and unfettered operation persisted alongside an appeal to more sophisticated industries based on promises of tailor-made work forces and research assistance, both provided at state expense. As the re-

---

1. Bernard L. Weinstein and Robert E. Firestine, *Regional Growth and Decline in the United States: The Rise of the Sunbelt and the Decline of the Northeast* (New York: Praeger, 1978), 44–65. See also E. Blaine Liner and Lawrence K. Lynch (eds.), *The Economics of Southern Growth* (Durham, N.C.: Seeman Printing, 1977).

gion began to shed its benighted reputation, it also held out the prospect of relaxed life-styles and lower living costs to an increasing number of Americans willing to forgive the Sunbelt South for its past transgressions and overlook its enduring deficiencies.

The cornerstone of the Sunbelt South was Florida, which since the 1920s had based its appeal to industry on its ability to provide an attractive, comfortable life-style for both employers and workers. Glossy development advertisements assured industrialists that they would have little trouble persuading key personnel to pull up stakes and move to Florida. Smugly asserting that "people of the highest caliber like the idea of working in Florida," developers presented impressive evidence to support their claims. For example, when Pratt and Whitney began searching for a site for a new jet aircraft engine plant, it circulated notices soliciting applications from qualified engineers in New England, the Midwest, California, and Florida. The response from the Sunshine State exceeded most of the others by twenty-five to one, and because Pratt and Whitney needed two thousand engineers, their decision to locate a $42 million plant near Palm Beach was not a difficult one.[2]

As the space industry boomed in the early 1960s, Florida's population increased by nearly three thousand people per week, many coming in search of new jobs and more pleasant living conditions. In addition to a large pool of skilled labor and managerial talent, the rapid growth of Florida's population and its tourist influx provided a growing consumer market that industries could not ignore. By the early 1970s, Florida had replaced Virginia as the southern state with the highest per capita income. Industrial prosperity bred more of the same as the state continued to attract a healthy mix of new plants and a host of new citizens to run them. The in-migrants raised both educational and income levels in the Sunshine State, and its industrial structure featured considerably more capital-intensive operations than did the South as a whole. Although cheap, nonunion labor continued to be an important consideration to incoming industries, in a 1962 survey of four hundred executives 65 percent cited markets and anticipated growth of markets as the most influential factor in their decisions to locate in Florida.[3]

2. Florida Development Commission, *Florida: Profile for Profit* (Tallahassee: n.p., n.d.), 1–13; Florida Development Commission, "Case Histories."
3. Florida Development Commission, *Florida*, 7, 12; Richard E. Herrington, "Florida Regional Industrial Growth, 1960–1968" (M.S. thesis, Florida State University, 1970),

Revenue from "tourist taxes" on gasoline, alcohol, and general sales lightened the tax burden on citizens and corporations, and like the other southern states, Florida pledged the cooperation of politicians all the way from the county courthouse to the statehouse. Stable government, a growth-minded legislature, state-supported worker training and research assistance, and a right-to-work law made the business climate in Florida "as good or better than the weather."[4]

Florida's development efforts also benefitted from the state's image in comparison to the rest of the South. Unlike its regional neighbors, particularly Georgia, which was known for speed traps and service station "clip joints," the Sunshine State maintained an air of sophistication, and the influx of migrants and retirees seemed to dilute both accents and regional peculiarities. In the late 1950s Governor Leroy Collins had set a tone of moderation that endured despite the extensive publicity given Martin Luther King's arrest for leading demonstrations in St. Augustine in 1964. As one observer noted, "Florida's Democrats rarely engaged in the demagogic race-baiting typical of many Deep South states. But in the postwar era many of their candidates found ways to tap the strain of ultra-conservatism evident in Florida life—a kind of fiscal conservatism, anti-governmentalism, opposition to any kind of welfare, nationalistic patriotism, and mild racism."[5]

Respectable conservatism was a vital part of the state's business climate, and its reputation for racial moderation meant that a Florida location was unlikely to subject an industry to criticism or boycott from civil rights organizations. Thus, Florida's developmental arsenal included all or most of the weapons wielded by its regional competitors plus a more favorable physical setting and a more sophisticated but nonetheless conservative political and governmental climate. By the end of the 1960s its recent rapid gains and its excellent prospects for the future made it the state that came closest to being the industrial paradise that all the southern states claimed they were.

If the rest of the South was going to follow in Florida's footsteps, it would have to muster the concentrated buying power needed to trigger

---

48–49; Tarr, "Occupational Migration Flows," 161–62; Melvin L. Greenhut and Marshall R. Colberg, *Factors in the Location of Florida Industries*, Florida State University Studies, XXXVI (Tallahassee: Florida State University Press, 1962), 66.

4. Florida Development Commission, *Florida*, 36–37.

5. Tebeau, *A History*, 441–45; Peirce, *The Deep South States*, 446.

an agglomeration of consumer-oriented industries. Although they suffered by comparison with the Sunshine State, neighbors to the north did their best to share in some of the spin-offs from Florida's growth. An increasing number of industries found that many southern locations could provide access to Florida's burgeoning population without sacrificing connections to mid-Atlantic, northeastern, or mideastern markets in the bargain. Most of the remainder of the South could never match Florida's natural advantages, but the advent of air conditioning made humid summers more bearable and the winters in any southern state were certain to be milder than those in the Northeast or Midwest.

Recognition of the South's climatic and geographic advantages was a positive sign, but as late as the early sixties an uncertain racial future seemed to undermine promoters' efforts to sell their states as "good places to work and live." The ugly scenes of Little Rock, New Orleans, Birmingham, and Selma, to name but a few, hardly projected an image of harmonious race relations. Yet after massive resistance had yielded to the skillful tokenism endorsed by growth-minded southern political and economic leaders and diehards like Bull Connor and Ross Barnett had died hard, the South emerged in the early 1970s as a region that had been resurrected, albeit against its will.

Through protests and court suits southerners had resisted forced busing to achieve racial balance, and in many communities white children had deserted the public schools for segregation academies. Still, viewed against a backdrop of more than two centuries of dogged adherence to white supremacy, the South's post-1960 progress in racial integration was nonetheless significant. The tendency to focus on what the region had done, rather than what it still needed to do, was reinforced by the Nixon administration's "southern strategy," which was designed to attract the "white backlash" support that had propelled George Wallace into the national political spotlight and had accelerated the growth of republicanism in the South. As the White House applied the brakes to the integration bandwagon and dismantled the social programs that had been vital elements of the Great Society's efforts to help blacks throw off the burden of their disadvantaged past, it became clear that the Nixon administration's policy of benign neglect entailed no further assaults on southern racial sensibilities. C. Vann Woodward observed that "self-righteousness withered along the Massachusetts-Michigan axis" after Boston and a number of northern cities experienced bitter conflicts over issues like busing and open housing. Feeling frustrated and threatened by black assaults on segregation and discrimination outside the South, nonsouthern whites found it easier to appreciate the progress that had been made in southern race relations.[6]

The inclination to forgive, forget, and even applaud the South was reinforced by the disillusioning experiences of Vietnam and Watergate. The Vietnam War destroyed the myth of American omnipotence and left the nation's sense of nobility and self-sacrifice in a shambles. There ensued an agonizing self-inventory that failed to produce comforting explanations for the failure in Indo-China. Public opinion polls had indicated that the South had been the region most supportive of the Vietnam involvement. Once the conflict had been terminated, however, southern spokesmen generally refused to share in the morbid self-scrutiny that became almost a national pastime. A nation that had prided itself on a victorious past now knew the humiliation of defeat, a burden with which the South had been familiar for over a hundred years. Not surprisingly, it was the southern states that emerged from the Vietnam trauma with the fewest apparent scars.[7]

The South's reaction to Watergate and the other Nixonian excesses was similar to its response to the Vietnam debacle. Although friendly to the president, Senators Howard Baker of Tennessee and Herman Talmadge of Georgia distinguished themselves by public displays of objectivity while they served on the Senate's Watergate Committee. Committee Chairman Sam J. Ervin's record of resistance to civil rights measures was forgotten as he presided over the hearings, quoting the Bible and craftily discrediting much of the city slicker double-talk dispensed by uncomfortable Watergate witnesses.[8] Despite the performances of Ervin, Baker, and Talmadge, most southern representatives generally refused to apologize for their defense of Nixon just as they declined to join other prominent spokesmen in an orgy of disillusionment and self-flagellation like the one that followed the Vietnam War.

For many southerners, it seems, support for the Vietnam War and an

6. For a discussion of the rise of southern republicanism, see Bartley and Graham, *Southern Politics*, 136–38; C. Vann Woodward, "The South Tomorrow," *Time*, September 27, 1976, p. 98.

7. Woodward, "The South Tomorrow," 98.

8. For a brief discussion of Ervin as a folk hero, see Jack Temple Kirby, *Media-Made Dixie: The South in the American Imagination* (Baton Rouge: Louisiana State University Press, 1978), 137–38.

embattled president, especially a sympathetic one, had been simple acts of patriotism and therefore no cause for remorse. For Americans at large, however, Watergate helped to shatter much of what self-assurance Vietnam had left them. National pride and idealism had taken another direct hit, and again, even for those who spent a great deal of time searching, no easy explanation presented itself.

The uncertainties that seemed to paralyze American society at large in the post-Watergate era were in sharp contrast to the confident purposefulness displayed by southern spokesmen. Politically, the region had moved away from the confrontation politics of George Wallace and Lester Maddox to the moderate progressivism of Reubin Askew and Jimmy Carter. The latter, whose presidential bid elicited first mirth and then grudging admiration, represented an individual embodiment of the oft-revived notion that the South might be able to exert a redemptive influence on the nation at large. A survivor who had weathered the civil rights showdown by avoiding identification with either the revolutionaries or the reactionaries, Carter exuded both quiet confidence and almost ostentatious humility. The former Georgia governor seemed to epitomize the best southern traits—an abiding religious faith and a sincere concern for his fellow human beings, both black and white. These laudable qualities were supplemented by Carter's energy and commitment to efficiency, which led one writer to dub him the "Yankee from Georgia," an appropriate symbol of a reunified nation.[9]

Carter's successful quest for the nomination and his subsequent victory were accompanied by a flood of favorable media analyses of the resurrected, triumphant South. "We Ain't Trash No More," one writer exulted, and a larger-and-more-attractive-than-life South appeared in the formerly neoabolitionist pages of *Time* magazine and *Saturday Review*, which proclaimed, "The South as New America." Even the traditionally critical New York *Times* gushingly welcomed the South back into the mainstream of American life, cooing over the fact that every southern city had "some transplanted Yankees who have adopted open collars, drawling speech and bourbon mixed with Coca-Cola," while native southerners had "taken up Scotch whiskey" and were "experimenting with skis." The theme of sectional reunion that novelists and the popular press had

9. William Lee Miller, *Yankee from Georgia: The Emergence of Jimmy Carter* (New York: Times Books, 1978).

stressed in the late nineteenth century had resurfaced in tandem with the ascendance of a new "New South."[10]

As regional peculiarities became intriguing and amusing rather than burdensome, a new southern mystique emerged. Enduring racial problems, maldistribution of earning power, and the ugly effects of rampant growth were usually mentioned in these reconsiderations of the South, but the primary emphasis was upbeat. A favorite topic was the fact that after 1970 a century-old pattern had reversed itself, as the number of blacks returning to the South exceeded the number moving out. Sympathetic writers suggested that a significant number of blacks were returning to the South not only because of increased economic opportunity but also because they had found the region more hospitable than the urban North. Continuing racial difficulties took a backseat to testimonials by blacks who had moved south to escape the rat race of northern urban life. *Time* magazine devoted its September 27, 1976, issue to "The South Today" and presented a largely positive appraisal of life in the region. For example, in an article entitled "The Good Life" a writer noted that, despite its industrial progress, the South remained "a largely rural land of spectacular beauty and prolific resources for recreation and sentient delight" where "life seems to move more slowly . . . because southerners take more time to enjoy it."[11]

The increased popularity of country music and the media's brief love affair with Billy Carter indicated that yesterday's repulsive redneck had suddenly developed rustic charms. Popular performances by Burt Reynolds in a variety of "good ole boy" roles suggested that, though unpolished, most working-class white southerners were at heart harmless, fun-loving, and well intentioned. *Time*'s tribute to the southern redneck portrayed him as a latter-day version of Jefferson's salt-of-the-earth agrarian hero: "Behind his devil-may-care light-heartedness . . . runs a strain of innate wisdom, an instinct about people and an unwavering loyalty that makes him the one friend you would turn to." On television, *The Waltons* reminded troubled Americans that strong family ties had always

10. New York *Times*, February 11, 1976, p. 1; Larry L. King, "We Ain't Trash No More," *Esquire*, CXXVI (November, 1976), 89–90, 152–56; Reg Murphy, "The South as the New America," *Saturday Review*, September 4, 1976, pp. 8–11. See also Gene Burd, "The Selling of the Sunbelt: Civic Boosterism in the Media," in David C. Perry and Alfred J. Watkins (eds.), *Urban Affairs Annual Review*, XIV (1977) (Beverly Hills, Calif.: Sage, 1977), 129–49.

11. "Reverse Migration," "The Good Life," *Time*, September 27, 1976, pp. 50, 32.

been important in the South. The various movie versions of *Walking Tall*, the story of an impulsive but courageous southern sheriff, were especially appealing in a decade when law and order had received much emphasis.[12]

The discovery of the admirable, adorable South paralleled the maturation of a growing tendency to view the United States from a regional rather than a national perspective. The Northeast, Mid-Atlantic, and Industrial Midwest were now lumped together as the "Old Manufacturing Belt" where the bulk of American heavy industry had grown to maturity. By the end of the 1960s, the southern tier of states from Florida and the Carolinas all the way to southern California were being discussed in terms of their excellent prospects for future industrial and economic growth, growth that promised, or threatened, to eclipse the accomplishments of a now-stagnant or decaying Industrial North. Most future investment appeared headed not to the colder, more densely populated states that had been the nation's industrial cornerstone for well over a century, but to the warmer, less-developed states of "the Sunbelt."

In 1969 Kevin Phillips described the Sunbelt as the states of Arizona, California, Florida, and Texas, although he referred occasionally to individual cities or areas in Georgia, New Mexico, and even Tennessee as a part of this new quasi region. Phillips summed up his analysis of the political and economic ascendance of the Sunbelt: "Long ago in the hot valleys of the Tigris-Euphrates and other Near East cradles of civilization, human culture began in the warm womb of a land where people could live without technology, but during the millennium far greater civilization evolved in temperate zones where climate, like necessity, mothered progress and invention. Today, however, a reverse trend is afloat. Spurred by high pensions, early retirement, increased leisure time and technological innovation, the affluent American middle class is returning to the comforts of the endless summer, which they can escape at will in swimming pools and total refrigeration."[13] Phillips demonstrated that the Sunbelt's promising future as a major force in national politics was related to its rapid population growth, and he boldly drew a group portrait of those

12. "Those Good Ole Boys," *Time*, September 27, 1976, p. 47; Kirby, *Media-Made Dixie*, 142–46, 151–53.
13. Kevin P. Phillips, *The Emerging Republican Majority* (New Rochelle, N.Y.: Arlington House, 1969), 437. See also Carl Abbott, "The American Sunbelt: Idea and Region," *Journal of the West*, XVIII (July, 1979), 5–18.

who moved to the region: "The persons most drawn to the new sun culture are the pleasure seekers, the bored, the ambitious, the space-age technicians and the retired—a super slice of the rootless, socially mobile group known as the American middle class."[14]

Although he called it the "Southern rim," in 1975 Kirkpatrick Sale presented a climatic, geographic, economic, and social picture of the Sunbelt. Sale described an area south of a line running from the top of North Carolina on to San Francisco, north of which winter high temperatures normally fell below 60 degrees. This lower third of the nation contained all of the nation's tropical and semitropical regions, its average annual temperatures exceeded 60 degrees, and its residents usually enjoyed from 250 to 350 days of sunshine per year. Sale's imaginary line roughly approximated the 37th parallel, and it marked the northern border of a section that included thirteen states—all of the former members of the Confederacy, except Virginia, plus, according to Sale, "the two territories with the greatest Confederate sympathy," Oklahoma and New Mexico. The Sunbelt line continued on to the coast to take in Arizona, southern Nevada, and California as well. Sale disparagingly contrasted the "bumptious, Baptist cowboy" culture of the southern rim with the patrician restraint of its regional antithesis—the Northeast.[15]

As delineated by both Sale and Phillips, *the Sunbelt* included a number of southwestern and western states, but in the 1970s the term became increasingly interchangeable with *the South*. For nearly a century southern boosters had been attempting to create a bandwagon effect by claiming that the region's industrial base was experiencing rapid growth, the message to potential investors being, "Get on before it's too late!" Although periodic reports of southern industrial progress appeared in the national media throughout the fifties and sixties, widespread acknowledgment of the South's rise came only in the mid-1970s. Actually, surveys indicated that the entire post–World War II period had witnessed a rate of relative economic expansion in the South well ahead of the national pace. The region's real surge in industrial growth came, however, in the mid-sixties as enough industries moved south to serve the relatively affluent and rapidly expanding Florida consumer market. This influx ap-

14. Phillips, *The Emerging Republican Majority*, 437.
15. Kirkpatrick Sale, *Power Shift: The Rise of the Southern Rim and Its Challenge to the Eastern Establishment* (New York: Random House, 1975), 9–14.

parently gave the South the long-sought "critical mass" necessary to accelerate its growth.[16]

The key to Florida's rapid industrial development had been a population explosion fueled by in-migration. For other southern states to even approach Florida's achievements, many of those who left the region seeking greater opportunity elsewhere would have to be retained while new residents were being drawn southward. The South's postwar industrial progress slowed population losses by the mid-1950s, and a significant increase in in-migration beginning around 1970 gave the region a net gain from migration of 2.9 million people between 1970 and 1976. Between 1950 and 1975, the average rate of economic expansion in the South was 4.4 percent annually, as compared to a 3.4 percent rate nationally over the same period. The healthiest sign for southern optimists was the remarkable diversity of the region's broadening industrial base. Betweeen 1970 and 1975 every industry but mining grew faster in the South than in the nation as a whole.[17]

The results of this balanced growth showed up in statistical measures of general prosperity in the South. Per capita incomes increased by 500 percent between 1955 and 1975, as opposed to only a 300 percent rise nationwide. Median family incomes rose by 50 percent between 1965 and 1975, while the national increase was only 33 percent. With bank assets soaring, the South's traditional lack of sufficient capital promised soon to be a problem of the past. By the mid-seventies financial experts predicted that between 1975 and 1986 half again as many jobs would be created in the South as in the North or West.[18]

Indicative of the maturity of the southern economy and the increased sophistication of promotional techniques was the fact that by the early 1970s the South was claiming half the annual foreign industrial investment expended in the United States. At the end of 1972, foreign firms had invested more than $5 billion in the South and within two years this figure had risen to nearly $8 billion. By 1978 many states were attracting as much as $1 billion annually, with South Carolina, North Carolina, and Virginia leading the way in numbers of plants and petroleum-rich Louisi-

16. Gurney Breckenfield, "Business Loves the Sunbelt (and Vice Versa)," *Fortune*, XCV (June, 1977), 133.
17. Weinstein and Firestine, *Regional Growth*, 5; Breckenfield, "Business Loves," 133; "Reverse Migration," 50; "Surging to Prosperity," *Time*, September 27, 1976, pp. 72–73.
18. New York *Times*, January 9, 1977, p. 42.

ana ahead in terms of aggregate value of foreign investments. Southern states soon found it worth their while to establish foreign-based development offices. Georgia quickly opened such outposts in Brussels, Tokyo, São Paulo, and Toronto. Because of its central location, Brussels was a popular site for these offices as the fierce competition for new plants spread across Europe.[19]

By the mid-seventies English industries had built fifty-seven plants in the South. The English investments, valued at $1.25 billion, were largely confined to textiles and tobacco, and nearly half were in the two Carolinas where West German companies were also heavy investors. No southern state proved more successful at attracting foreign plants than South Carolina, which by the end of the 1970s was drawing nearly 40 percent of its total annual industrial investments from outside the United States. Palmetto State promoters had attracted plants from Japan, Italy, the Netherlands, Austria, Belgium, and France and were proud of the fact that there was more West German industrial capital in their state than anywhere else in the world except West Germany.[20]

A number of factors encouraged increased European industrial investments in the United States. As the German mark and the Swiss franc increased in dollar value, American construction costs became cheaper. At the same time political instability and the prospect of growing socialist influence pushed nervous industrialists toward the United States. A Japanese spokesman explained that years of fighting import quotas and tariffs had convinced textile interests in his country that they should commence operations in the United States "using southern labor, southern materials, and Japanese machines."[21]

After European companies decided to build a new plant in the United States, why did they choose a site in the South? Developers pointed to factors like cooperative, business-minded state and local governments. A South Carolina source told of some foreign executives who inquired about tax rates and suddenly found themselves in the office of the state tax commissioner sipping Coke and getting answers. Cooperative customs

19. George Adcock, "Is International Status Taking the South by Surprise?" *South*, II (July/August, 1975), 34, 36; "Recruiting Industry Abroad," *South*, V (April 1, 1978), 31; *Georgia Department of Community Development* (n.p.: n.p., n.d.).

20. Adcock, "International Status," 36, 41; "Recruiting Industry Abroad," 32; "S.C. Industry Now Multilingual," Columbia (South Carolina) *Record*, August 23, 1977, University of South Carolina Library "South Caroliniana" Clipping File, Columbia.

21. "S.C. Industry Now Multilingual"; Adcock, "International Status," 35.

officials in Charleston also helped South Carolina's Michelin Tire Corporation to get equipment unloaded and inspected within forty-eight hours after a freighter docked. In France it often took two, maybe even three, weeks to accomplish the same thing.[22]

South Carolina achieved its success in wooing new industry by providing the same red-carpet, kid-glove treatment afforded all industrial prospects by the southern states. Governor John C. West provided a state plane for an English executive's visit to Charleston and then presented him with a pair of souvenir cufflinks. West promised a Swiss industrialist that "all state agencies will support your interests on a continuing basis in all respects." When a French investor was jailed by the Jamestown police for speeding and reckless driving, an aide suggested that Governor West might call him in France "just to express regrets" about the "unfortunate incident." Other governors were just as involved in foreign recruitment as West, and most took European junkets trying to sell their states. State legislatures were as cooperative with foreign prospects as domestic ones. South Carolina lawmakers, for example, pleased their state's transplanted European executives by lifting the limit on tax-free liquor imports, thereby allowing the industrialists to keep a good supply of their favorite wines without having to pay extra taxes on them.[23]

In addition to government cooperation, southern developers could also offer both immediate and long-term savings in expenditures. North Carolina's Department of Conservation and Development put together a pamphlet entitled *Douze raisons pourquoi les sociétés étrangères ont établi des opérations industrielles profitables en Carolina du Nord, U.S.A.* Although the language was different, French readers learned (just as any American plant executive would have) that the twelve reasons why foreign operations had been profitably established in North Carolina included low construction costs, industrial training programs, and an ample supply of labor. Lower taxes also helped, as did property tax waivers and exemptions. The region's milder climate and attendant energy savings were also a plus. The Canadian trade consul in Atlanta explained that his country's investors were just beginning to learn "how delightfully warm it is down here." He also explained the South's growing market at-

22. "S.C. Industry Now Multilingual."
23. Peter Windham to John C. West, September 4, 1971, "BB" to "MJT," memorandum, September 29, 1971, both in John C. West Correspondence, South Carolina State Archives, Columbia; New York *Times*, August 1, 1976, p. 2F; "Recruiting Industry Abroad," 31–32; "S.C. Industry Now Multilingual."

traction: "Canadians have always built plants in the U.S. when the market got big enough; so we're just following our markets into the South with our plants."[24]

Markets were no doubt important, but the major selling point of any southern state remained its labor supply. Noting the irony in the fact that a Japanese-owned firm in Macon, Georgia, would soon be manufacturing "Maus-Maus [sic] to be sold in Honolulu to Japanese tourists," a Japanese consul explained why his country's investors were interested in opening new plants in the southern states: "The South has the only reserve of good labor left in the U.S. Southern labor is in fact cheaper to us than Japanese labor." With their capabilities enhanced by state-supported training programs, southern workers formed an eager and productive manpower pool. A number of foreign investors appreciated the fact that southern labor showed little inclination to organize. In dealing with non-American companies southern promoters could hardly afford to emphasize low union membership by speaking of native-born labor, but they found suitable euphemistic substitutes. One official explained that foreign employers found "the southern work attitude is more like their own way of doing business." Another felt that these new employers liked South Carolina's "first generation, off-the-land workers" whose attitudes seemed to say, "I'm doing a job. I believe in God."[25]

Michelin Tire Corporation chose Greenville, South Carolina, as the site for its first American plant because, with only 2 percent of its work force organized, the South Carolina Piedmont seemed the safest possible refuge from the United Rubber Workers. A Michelin vice-president denied that his company had settled in the South to exploit cheap labor, and the tire corporation did prove to be one of the more generous employers in the vicinity, both in terms of salaries and fringe benefits. Still, Michelin paid its employees less than its American competitors paid workers in their northern plants. Long noted for its secretiveness and eccentricity, Michelin found South Carolina officials most understanding when they were refused admittance to plants or when reports circulated that man-

24. Adcock, "International Status," 36; International Section of the North Carolina Division of Commerce and Industry, *Douze raisons pourquoi les sociétés étrangères ont établi des opérations industrielles profitables en Carolina du Nord, U.S.A.* (n.p.: n.p., n.d.). See also Arkansas Industrial Development Commission, *Arkansas Europe: Arkansas Industrial Development Commission, Progress Report, July, 1975–June, 1976* (Little Rock: n.p., 1976).
25. Adcock, "International Status," 35; New York *Times*, January 29, 1978, Sec. 3, p. 1.

agement had declined to call the fire department after what appeared to be a dangerous fire at its Greenville facility. Michelin's management liked the Carolina Piedmont and its loyal workers so well that it also placed a research center there. By the end of 1978, Michelin employed about 5,500 workers in its South Carolina operations, most of them locally recruited in an area known for decades as the domain of low-wage textile firms like J. P. Stevens.[26]

South Carolina's courtship of foreign industry bore its most impressive fruit in the former textile mill town of Spartanburg, a city of about fifty thousand. Before local developer Richard E. Tukey, a transplanted New Yorker, began his crusade to bring in foreign companies that built textile machinery for local plants, area workers seemed condemned to labor in dreary, unhealthy mills that shut down frequently and sometimes never reopened. In the early sixties Swiss and German machinery producers came in, but the major development was the arrival from Germany in 1965 of Hoechst Fibers, which built a $200 million plant and promptly became the nation's fourth largest producer of polyester. By the mid-1970s Spartanburg had attracted twenty-four foreign companies that employed four thousand local workers. Average income doubled between 1965 and 1975, and unemployment almost disappeared. Spartanburg County's population increased by 22 percent between 1960 and 1976, and in the same period the value of taxable industrial property increased by 322 percent, with the gigantic Hoechst Company alone contributing a sum in excess of that paid by thirty of South Carolina's forty-six counties.[27]

The influx of foreign firms also brought cultural diversity to the Spartanburg area as the plant executives became involved in community service, politics, and social life. A once-provincial mill town now sported exotic shops and delicatessens reminiscent of a New York or Chicago. Instead of eggs, grits, country ham, and red-eye gravy, a Sunday breakfast in Spartanburg might now include English tea, Vienna rolls, and Swiss jam.[28] Not all communities were as fortunate as Spartanburg in their dealings with non-American industries, and the courtship of European and Japanese firms undercut efforts to make the South less dependent on

26. New York *Times*, January 29, 1978, Sec. 3, pp. 1–7.
27. *Ibid*., August 1, 1976, p. 2F; Roul Tunley, "In Spartanburg the Accent Is on Business," *Reader's Digest*, CIV (January, 1974), 165–68.
28. Tunley, "In Spartanburg,"166.

absentee investors, but by the end of the 1970s foreign investments had helped to rejuvenate local economies throughout the region.

Instead of receiving praise for the belated success of their efforts, by the mid-seventies southern development leaders began to encounter mounting jealousy and resentment, eventually manifested in attempts to destroy or counteract some of the factors favoring Dixie's growth. The ascendance of the Sunbelt paralleled the decline of the old Manufacturing Belt (the tier of industrial states from Connecticut to Wisconsin), whose political and economic leaders found it difficult to appreciate the southern success story while their own constituents complained of population losses, unemployment, and urban blight.

In the mid-1970s several well-publicized analyses of the South's good fortune linked it to the demise of the Industrial North. Early in 1976 shortly after updated census statistics showed a population shift in favor of the South and West, the New York *Times* began a series of six articles replete with glowing descriptions of the South's newfound economic prowess. In uncritical fashion the *Times* adopted the language of the chamber of commerce to stress life-style advantages and to give particular emphasis to the solid base of the South's boom, making it clear that Dixie was now the place to be and to invest. One of the articles looked at the region's rapid population growth, pointing out that, during the previous ten years, more than eight million people had moved into the Southeast, far outnumbering out-migrants who, by and large, were poorer and less educated than the newcomers who replaced them.[29]

The *Times* related the South's population growth to federal spending and rattled off the sources of the southern bonanza. For example, the Tennessee Valley Authority had harnessed the Tennessee River, providing both jobs and low-cost electric power. Since World War II, the South had been a major beneficiary of military spending. In Georgia, Louisiana, Mississippi, and Tennessee, the defense industry was the largest single employer. Huntsville, Alabama, had been a cotton textile town of but 16,000 in 1950, but the coming of the Marshall Space Flight Center helped to bring in Chrysler, International Business Machines, and Rockwell International, to name but a few of the firms that had energized the area's economy and expanded its population to more than 140,000. At

29. New York *Times*, February 8, 1976, p. 42. See also New York *Times*, February 9–13, p. 1.

various times, the writer noted, the space and defense industries had accounted for 70 percent of Huntsville's total employment.[30]

After World War II, many southern congressmen followed the lead of Mendel Rivers, who managed to get twelve military installations located in his South Carolina district. The *Times* opined that the successful courtship of the military was likely to continue because of the region's abundant open land and unabashed affection for the armed services. Available evidence indicated that the Sunbelt had spent the last three decades "first in line at the pork barrel," and although observers had warned of rising northern opposition to southern "milking" of the federal treasury, they speculated that the southern states would "continue to thrive on an uneven exchange with Washington." The flow of federal money into the South went hand in hand with Census Bureau predictions of a pronounced "shift of income from North to South" as expansion and diversification of southern industry proceeded at a rate well ahead of the national average.[31]

While the projected growth rates and the acknowledged momentum of the South's economy pointed to a bright future for Dixie, exactly the reverse was true for the Northeast and North Central states. By the middle of the 1970s this area was still home to 70 percent of the nation's five hundred largest corporations, but the region was nonetheless showing signs of economic decay. The New York metropolitan area was losing people at the rate of two thousand per week. Other large cities like Chicago, Cleveland, Pittsburgh, and Detroit also were suffering heavy losses, as were smaller ones like Bangor, Akron, Allentown, Grand Rapids, and Evansville. Out-migration seemed to drain these cities of talent and human resources in a time of proliferating urban fiscal crises, leaving a shrunken tax base and a largely untrained, disadvantaged central city population for whom there were few economic opportunities. As more than one observer noted, the Northeast and Midwest had absorbed most of the impoverished southern out-migrants only to have the tax base necessary to accommodate this influx shift steadily toward the South.[32]

In mid-1976 two well-publicized magazine articles fanned the flames of interregional antagonism even more. *Business Week* warned of "The Second War Between the States," noting that, while a gradual migration

30. *Ibid.*, February 9, 1976, p. 24.
31. *Ibid.*
32. *Ibid.*, February 13, 1976, p. 14.

of industry and population from the relatively affluent Northeast to the deprived South and West had helped to unify the country, the accelerating redistribution of people and plants had "burst beyond the bounds that can be accommodated by existing political institutions." Conflict loomed at a time when the nation appeared more culturally and ideologically unified than ever before, but even though it would be a largely political contest with income and jobs at stake, the new struggle for economic supremacy, or even parity, promised to be both bitter and divisive. Clearly resentful, a northeastern economist charged, "The Northeast is not getting federal assistance and in the Southeast and Southwest where they have no fiscal problem at all, it's flowing right in.' *Business Week*'s charts appeared to affirm this pronouncement.[33]

The observation that the Northeast and Midwest were losing factories to the South and West did nothing to salve raw northern feelings. The writer observed that in the past two decades, Akron-based rubber companies had moved plants closer to southern markets, in the process reducing the Akron area's rubber-worker force by about 50 percent. Heavy stress on the South's nonunion climate highlighted another seemingly unfair advantage of the "right-to-work region." The loss of plants and a brain as well as tax drain led a midwestern social problems expert to moan, "The industrial Midwest is simply bleeding to death."[34]

Business Week's prediction of renewed sectional conflict over new industry received significant notice, but ironically, it was the *National Journal*, a Washington weekly with a circulation of just over three thousand, that created the biggest stir with its June 26, 1976, article, "Federal Spending: The North's Loss Is the Sunbelt's Gain." The *Journal*'s writers chronicled a dramatic shift of people and jobs toward the South and West. Although they admitted "other economic factors are equally if not more important," they focused primarily on the role of federal spending in this phenomenon. Looking at defense contracts and salaries, federal expenditures for highways and sewers, and welfare and retirement payments, the authors calculated that the Northeast (Maine, New Hampshire, Vermont, Massachusetts, Rhode Island, Connecticut, New York, New Jersey, and Pennsylvania) had received $863 in federal disbursements per resident in fiscal 1975, the Midwest (Ohio, Indiana, Illinois, Michigan, Wisconsin, Minnesota, Iowa, Missouri, Kansas, Nebraska, South Dakota,

33. "The Second War Between the States," *Business Week*, May 17, 1976, pp. 92, 96.
34. *Ibid.*, 98.

and North Dakota) had received $706, the South (Delaware, Maryland, Virginia, West Virginia, North Carolina, South Carolina, Georgia, Florida, Kentucky, Tennessee, Alabama, Mississippi, Louisiana, Arkansas, Oklahoma, and Texas) had received $918, and the West (Montana, Idaho, Wyoming, Colorado, Utah, Nevada, Arizona, New Mexico, California, Oregon, Washington, Alaska, and Hawaii) had received $1,119.[35]

The *National Journal* article also pointed out that the southern states took in $11.5 billion more in federal funds than they paid out in taxes, while the net gain for the Pacific and Mountain states was $10.6 billion. In comparison ten Midwestern and Mid-Atlantic states suffered an aggregate deficit of $30.8 billion. Put another way, in the Northeast where per capita federal tax burdens were 12 percent above the national average in 1975, per capita federal disbursements were 4 percent below. In the Midwest, taxes were only 5 percent above the mean, but government spending was 20 percent less. In the South, federal spending was 2 percent below the national norm, but the tax load was 14 percent lighter. In the West the tax burden was 1 percent greater than in the nation as a whole, but federal spending was approximately 21 percent greater. Although federal tax collections might seem to be positively correlated with income, the *Journal's* writers argued that cost-of-living differentials made the South's income disadvantage "largely illusory."[36]

In constructing their case for a pattern of discriminatory federal spending, the authors of the *National Journal* article alluded only briefly to basic economic factors that might be responsible for the Sunbelt's ascendancy. The southern states benefitted from population growth that had expanded the demand for goods, an ample supply of cheap labor, the greater availability of energy, and the growing obsolescence of older manufacturing facilities in the North.

It was not until the early 1970s that a concerted effort began to eliminate alleged interregional inequities in spending. In 1973 the formation of the New England Congressional Caucus marked the opening salvo in a battle by Manufacturing Belt states to regain their influence on spending policies that might affect their region. Still, despite the clear implications that they were receiving less than their fair share of the federal pie, midwestern and northeastern political leaders were slow to act. For ex-

35. "Federal Spending: The North's Loss Is the Sunbelt's Gain," *National Journal*, VIII (June 26, 1976), 879, 884.
36. *Ibid.*, 881, 883.

ample, Senator Richard Stone of Florida introduced a bill in December, 1975, calling for annual updating of population statistics for state and local government units as a means of more accurately allocating federal grants. Stone's measure passed the Senate by voice vote with the support of many northeastern members who were unaware that the new policy would shift large amounts of federal money away from their region toward the faster-growing South.[37]

The New York *Times* series on the Sunbelt and the *Business Week* and *National Journal* articles did a great deal to help those trying to persuade northeastern and midwestern political leaders to spring to the defense of declining constituent economies. One regional leader commented, "It's a strange phenomenon. . . . We started talking about this issue 3½ years ago. But it was not until the New York *Times* ran its sunbelt series and *Business Week* came out with its special report that people began to see it as a problem." Still, efforts to utilize regional cooperation to combat alleged discriminatory federal spending practices produced no immediate victories. Despite the assertions of economic experts that the region was bleeding to death, the Industrial Midwest showed the least inclination to organize. With fifty-seven large metropolitan areas, it was often hard for the advocates of cooperation to create a sense of state, much less regional, interests. Six midwestern governors issued a joint statement citing the urgent need for concerted action to reverse their region's decline, but very little subsequent action was taken.[38]

In the Middle Atlantic states, efforts to band together for the common economic good proved more successful. In June, 1976, the governors of New York, New Jersey, Pennsylvania, Connecticut, Rhode Island, Massachusetts, and Vermont met to establish the Coalition of Northeastern Governors. The governors called attention to their concerns with a statement that reminded federal officials of the problems that their region faced: "As the nation in the past recognized the development needs of the Western frontiers and the rural South, so now the nation must acknowledge a similar commitment to the older yet still vibrant Northeast." Governor Milton Shapp of Pennsylvania expressed some of the sectional resentment that had spurred the formation of the coalition when he com-

37. John L. Moore, "Washington Pressures/Business Forms Economic Study Unit to Support Bipartisan New England Caucus," *National Journal*, V (February 17, 1973), 226; "Keeping Pace with the Population," *National Journal*, VII (December 27, 1975), 1765.
38. "Federal Spending," 891, 889.

plained, "It was largely tax dollars from our urban states that built the Tennessee Valley Authority. Now we find the lower cost of T.V.A. power used against us to attract our industry."[39]

In order to correct the imbalance in federal spending, the north-eastern governors pledged to educate congressional representatives about the need to protect regional economic interests. They also called for the establishment of a Northeast Economic Development Corporation. Governor Hugh Carey of New York, the prime mover in the governors' organization, had tried to form such a group throughout his fourteen years in Congress because he feared that failure to respond to the needs of his region left only one alternative—the Northeast would be preserved as "a great national museum" where tourists might see "industrial plants as artifacts." They might also visit "the great railroad stations where the trains used to run." "This can't be allowed to happen," concluded Carey; "we must be compensated." The New England Congressional Caucus also worked to protect Manufacturing Belt interests. The dominant figure in the caucus was Representative Michael Harrington of Massachusetts, who actually hoped to form a single coalition that included the states stretching from Wisconsin to New England and the Mid-Atlantic region.[40]

At the end of the 1970s northeastern and midwestern political leaders were making up for lost time in their efforts to equalize the regional distri-bution of federal funds. By February, 1979, twelve coalitions had launched efforts to redirect federal monies to the Northeast and Midwest. All of these organizations engaged in considerable lobbying in behalf of their particular region or subregion, but they also relied heavily on changes in the formulas for allocating federal grant funds. Their efforts in this area had first borne fruit in 1977 when Congress amended the Community Development Block Program to direct more money into northern cities and created the Urban Development Action Grant Program to aid the na-tion's most severely distressed urban areas.[41]

When the Block Program came into being in 1974 the allocation formula for grants to individual cities was weighted 50 percent by the number of persons with poverty income, 25 percent by the amount of

39. *Ibid.*, 889; New York *Times*, January 9, 1977, p. 41.
40. New York *Times*, January 9, 1977, p. 41; "Federal Spending," 889.
41. Patricia J. Dusenbury, "Regional Targeting," Southern Growth Policies Board, Febru-ary, 1979 (mimeo in possession of Southern Growth Policies Board, Research Triangle Park, N.C.).

Table 9   Percentage of Cities Above the Mean for Economic Distress
Indicators, by Region

Distress Indicator	Northeast	North Central	South	West	Total
Percent poor	21.8%	9.5%	70.1%	15.7%	31.3%
Pre-1940 housing	79.0%	58.4%	13.0%	9.6%	39.4%
Per capita income change (1969–1974) lag	62.9%	32.1%	5.2%	33.9%	31.8%
1970–1975 population change lag	69.4%	46.7%	24.7%	17.4%	39.2%
Unemployment	68.5%	32.8%	35.1%	55.7%	46.7%

SOURCE: Harold Bunce, "UDAG Variables and Central City Hardship," Department of Housing and
Urban Development, June, 1977, as quoted in Dusenbury, "Regional Targeting," 4.

overcrowded housing, and 25 percent by total population. The 1977
amendment added an alternative formula and allowed officials to choose
the one that would provide the largest amount of aid for their city. The
new method of computing the extent of an urban area's eligibility for assistance gave 50 percent weight to the percentage of its housing built before 1940, 30 percent to the percentage of the population below the poverty line, and 20 percent to below-average population growth. Instead of
relying primarily on poverty, the new Urban Development Action Grant
Program utilized criteria that emphasized slow population growth, per
capita income, manufacturing employment, unemployment, and pre-
1940 housing. As Table 9 shows, under the new formula the lagging
growth rates of the Northeast and North Central regions made them
prime candidates for increased federal aid.[42]

In addition to attempting to influence federal spending policies in a
direction that would stimulate growth outside the South, nonsouthern
states also accelerated their own promotional efforts. Table 10 presents
some of the results of a recent comparative analysis of state expenditures
for industrial development, which showed that, if the southern states had
once provided more financial support for such programs than did states
elsewhere, their competitors had all but caught up by the early 1970s. In
fact, Pennsylvania's per capita investment in development was more than
6.5 times the southern and national average. The southern states re-

42. *Ibid.*, 6, 10.

Table 10   Southern States' Expenditures for Industrial Development,
1967–1974

State	Per Capita Expenditures	Percent of State Budget
Kentucky	.62	.36
South Carolina	.56	.33
Georgia	.41	.31
Mississippi	.38	.21
Arkansas	.34	.25
North Carolina	.13	.22
Alabama	.29	.16
Louisiana	.22	.12
Virginia	.21	.11
Florida	.20	.17
Tennessee	.18	.15
Oklahoma	.35	.17
Texas	.05	.04
Southern average	.30	.20
U.S. average (47 states*)	.34	.17

SOURCE: Digby, "State Government and Economic Development," 91–92.
*The average excludes figures for Alaska, Hawaii, and Pennsylvania because of their extremely high level of industrial expenditures ($2.44, $2.42, and $2.27 per capita respectively).

tained only a slight edge in the percentage of the total state budget devoted to industrial promotion.[43]

The northern counteroffensive seemed to catch the Sunbelt South's representatives off-balance temporarily, but the media prophecy of civil war for industry quickly became a self-fulfilling one. New England representatives had explained their initial efforts to band together by pointing enviously to the cohesiveness of the southern bloc in Congress—"The southerners always band together, why can't we?" Yet it was the proliferation of regional interest coalitions in the North that led southern political and economic leaders to decide it was they who needed to be organized. Representative John Buchanan of Alabama called for the South to

43. Michael Franklin Digby, "State Government and Economic Development: An Analysis and Evaluation of the Virginia Industrial Development Program" (Ph.D. dissertation, University of Virginia, 1976), 91–92.

create "a countervailing force," while Senator Russell Long of Louisiana put it more simply by warning, "If our people don't get along and start working together, then we're going to suffer for it."[44] Interstate cooperation for accelerated but controlled growth had long been a favorite suggestion of southern planners, but competition among the states and concern about sacrificing independence had impeded efforts to create a central organization to coordinate regional growth policies. By the early seventies, however, southern governors were more willing to cooperate in order to benefit from pooled resources and a commitment to orderly, desirable growth. In December, 1971, nine southern governors signed executive orders creating the Southern Growth Policies Board. By 1978 the organization included Alabama, Arkansas, Florida, Georgia, Kentucky, Louisiana, Mississippi, North Carolina, Oklahoma, South Carolina, Tennessee, and Virginia. Governors of member states shared a revolving chairmanship on an annual basis, and in 1973 the board settled into its central office in the cozy confines of Research Triangle Park. A $225,000 challenge grant from the Ford Foundation was more than matched by contributions from member states and private sources in the South.[45]

Each SGPB state had five board members, including the governor, a state senator, a state representative, and two citizens appointed by the governor. The board employed a full-time staff to administer programs and conduct research, and its "Statement of Regional Objectives" urged member states "to accept responsibility at the state level for planning for growth, adopting and implementing public policies to prevent harmful results and to encourage the beneficial aspects of growth." In 1974 a special "Committee on the Future of the South" presented an impressive detailed report outlining objectives not only for economic growth but for institutional and social progress as well.[46]

The Southern Growth Policies Board played a major role in the South's response to the New England–Midwestern counterchallenge. Staff members prepared a number of position papers aimed at rallying influential southerners for the struggle to maintain the pace of the region's growth. Charging in 1978 that "federal policies have already been modified because of misleading data and misinterpretations of good data," E. Blaine

44. John L. Moore, "Washington Pressures," 228; Albuquerque *New Mexican*, March 1, 1979, p.1.

45. Southern Growth Policies Board, *Annual Report, 1977: The South in the Seventies* (Research Triangle Park, N.C.: n.p., 1977), 13.

46. *Ibid.*

Liner, executive director of the board, tried to clear the air with a paper entitled "The Snowbelt and the Seven Myths." Liner systematically attacked northern contentions that the South was receiving a disproportionate share of federal funds or stealing industry from the North. He also challenged assumptions that poverty was no longer a problem in the South and that northern cities were more in need of aid than southern ones. SGPB researchers were soon complaining that the introduction of the pre-1940 housing formula had cost southern cities over $100 million and estimating that other changes in various grant assistance allocation criteria might produce a loss that ran into the billions. They also found that the so-called poverty rate was being computed inaccurately by dividing 1970 poverty population figures by the 1975 total population, thereby camouflaging the extent of deprivation in the fast-growing South.[47]

Early in 1978 at a White House Conference on Balanced National Growth and Economic Development, Georgia Governor George Busbee, then chairman of the SGPB, represented the southern position in a panel debate which also included Senator Daniel P. Moynihan of New York, one of the leading advocates of changes that would make the federal grant allocation process more favorable to the North. In a session entitled "Beyond Sunbelt-Frostbelt: Regional Policy for a Changing Economy," Busbee and Moynihan called for an end to the rhetorical jousting surrounding the interregional rivalry, but each continued to plead his area's case. Busbee argued that the South needed a fair share of federal funds "to avoid the problems of urban decay and social disintegration that have recently plagued the North." The Georgia governor also noted that while his constituents were having difficulty funding public kindergartens, New York City continued to provide its residents with a tuition-free college education even as it faced bankruptcy. Other southern spokesmen forgot the federal revenue that had been sent their way when they asked, "Now that the South and the Southwest are making economic progress, why should Sunbelt taxpayers bail out the Northeast?"[48]

The Sunbelt-Snowbelt clash heated up the already simmering contro-

47. E. Blaine Liner, "The Snowbelt and the Seven Myths," Southern Growth Policies Board, January 24, 1978 (mimeo in possession of Southern Growth Policies Board, Research Triangle Park, N.C.); Dusenbury, "Regional Targeting," 4–12; E. Blaine Liner, "Presentation to the Southern Governors' Association," February 27, 1979 (mimeo in possession of Southern Growth Policies Board, Research Triangle Park, N.C.).

48. "Busbee, Senator Debate," Southern Growth: Problems and Promise, VI (Winter, 1978), 1, 3; New York Times, January 9, 1977, p. 41.

versy over alleged "plant piracy" by southern promoters. Several recent studies have argued that neither the decline of the Manufacturing Belt nor the ascendance of the Sunbelt was directly related to the transfer of established facilities. In fact, only 1.5 percent of northern job losses between 1969 and 1972 resulted from industrial out-migration. The major sources of the decline were firm closings, which cost the North more than half the jobs lost during this period, and the contraction of other operations, which accounted for nearly 45 percent of the losses.[49]

A recent estimate suggested that 8 percent of the jobs in any community disappeared annually because of plant failures or contractions. The major difference between the directions taken by the southern and northern economies resulted from the number of new jobs being created in each region. Between 1969 and 1972 new jobs contributed only 4.6 percent to employment in the North as compared to 7.6 percent in the South. Meanwhile plant expansions produced 14.1 percent of the new jobs in the South and only 11.2 percent in the North. Thus, researchers argued, it was not established facilities lured away from the Manufacturing Belt, but investments in new and expanded plants that were creating most of the Sunbelt South's new employment opportunities.[50] This attempt to repudiate charges of industrial piracy was somewhat misleading. Industrialists perceived the South as a highly favorable environment for new business and industrial ventures, and they were obviously tempted to liquidate obsolete or marginally profitable facilities in the North and reinvest in new projects in an area whose now-vibrant economy was experiencing a self-reinforcing boom. Thus, the South may not have been robbing the Manufacturing Belt of established plants, but its appeal to investors almost certainly led to some plant closings and the transfer of jobs to the southern states.

The South's 1.6 percent growth in manufacturing employment between 1970 and 1975 contributed less to the Sunbelt boom than did population growth, which spurred the rapid expansion of the service and

49. Breckenfield, "Business Loves," 142; Carol L. Jusenius and Larry C. Ledeber, *A Myth in the Making: The Southern Economic Challenge and Northern Economic Decline* (Washington, D.C.: United States Department of Commerce, Economic Development Administration, November, 1976), 24, 27.

50. Breckenfield, "Business Loves," 142; Peter M. Allaman and David L. Birch, "Components of Employment Change for States by Industry Group, 1970–1972," Working Paper #5, Inter-Area Migration Project, September, 1975, Joint Center for Urban Studies of MIT and Harvard University (mimeo in Massachusetts Institute of Technology Library, Cambridge), 11–18.

wholesale and retail trade industries. The South's wholesale and retail employment gains were more than three times higher than the North's during the first half of the 1970s, and new jobs appeared in service industries at more than twice the northern rate. Public employment also figured heavily in the South's advances in the 1970s. Federal civilian jobs increased in the region by 5.4 percent between 1970 and 1975, while the North suffered a 3 percent loss during the same period. Still, despite claims that an expanded federal payroll was responsible for the South's economic surge in the 1970s, per capita federal employment in the region remained constant and approximately equal to the national average between 1970 and 1975. During the same period, state and local government employment expanded more than twice as fast in the South as in the northern tier of states from Connecticut to Wisconsin.[51]

The impact of interregional plant migration may have been exaggerated, but the Sunbelt South was definitely luring workers and consumers away from the Manufacturing Belt. During 1973 and 1974, 90,800 more workers covered by Social Security moved from eleven northern states to the Sunbelt South than in the opposite direction. By far the biggest loser was New York, whose net out-migration of 27,500 workers to the South even included a few residents lost in the exchange of migrants with Mississippi. New York, New Jersey, and Pennsylvania were the northern states hardest hit by out-migration. Florida was the chief beneficiary of all this movement, receiving 57,300 more workers than it lost during 1973 and 1974. In fact, more than 62 percent of the South's net gains came in Florida where in-migration accounted for 90 percent of population growth between 1970 and 1975.[52]

The migration patterns of the 1970s favored the South, but the numerical importance of this influx of new citizens was exaggerated. Without fast-growing Florida, 65.5 percent of the Sunbelt South's population growth in the first half of the 1970s would have been the result of natural increase. Interregional mortality rates differed little, but the birth rate was 1.5 percent higher in the South than in the North, suggesting that even if no migration had occurred in either direction between 1970 and 1975, the southern population would still have grown more rapidly.[53]

51. Jusenius and Ledeber, A Myth, 23–25.
52. Ibid., 34, 38–39; Breckenfield, "Business Loves," 135.
53. Jusenius and Ledeber, A Myth, 4.

Table 11   Net Migration, South in Relation to North, 1973–1974 (× 100)

	CT	MA	RI	NY	NJ	PA	OH	IN	IL	WI	MI	Southern States' Net Total
FL	+12	+32	+1	+229	+79	+99	+20	+24	+20	+6	+51	+573
GA	+9	+20	−4	+31	+21	−3	+8	+16	+6	0	+13	+117
NC	+2	+29	−1	+61	+25	−13	−2	+7	+1	+1	+5	+115
SC	+5	−10	−4	+2	0	−12	0	0	+1	+1	+3	−14
VA	−2	+6	−9	+13	+1	+18	+9	+2	+7	0	+2	+47
AL	+5	+1	−4	−7	−3	−1	+8	+6	+8	+4	+4	+21
KY	−3	−5	+1	−5	+1	+7	−8	+19	+6	−5	+1	+9
MS	−1	+1	−4	+1	−3	−12	+11	+9	−8	−2	−11	−19
TN	+2	+3	−2	+56	−15	+5	+11	+1	+19	+1	+3	+84
LA	−3	+2	−1	−9	+1	0	+4	−3	−4	−1	−1	−15
AR	+1	−12	+1	+7	−4	+1	+6	+3	−9	+2	−3	−7
OK	+4	−12	0	−2	−1	−1	−5	+7	−5	+4	−1	−12
TX	+5	+1	−7	+5	+11	−33	−14	+35	+13	+2	−9	+9

SOURCE: Jusenius and Ledeber, *A Myth*, 38–39.

Although regional differences in birth rates contributed to the quantity of the South's population growth, migration was nonetheless a key factor in explaining the improved "quality" of that growth. Those who moved southward tended to be above average in income and educational levels, while those continuing to go north were more likely to be below average in these areas. The southward migration of managers and professionals pointed to an expected relationship between population shifts and increasing investment in new business and industrial ventures. The same association was suggested by a .666 Spearman rank-order correlation between a state's net migration (1970–1976) and its percentage of growth in nonagricultural employment (1970–1977). The *National Journal* painted a sinister portrait of a sly South exchanging unproductive, potentially impoverished residents for more affluent, contributive ones: "The Northeast and Midwest gain dependent, low-taxpaying populations and lose significant numbers of middle class taxpayers, the South and West gain taxpaying residents. Taxes, as a result, go up in the Northeast and the Midwest, but can be held more stable because of the broadening tax base in the growing regions."[54]

Those who opposed efforts to eliminate the disparities in federal spending among the regions pointed to the fact that for all the hoopla about prosperity, the Sunbelt South states were still the nation's poorest. Despite recent gains, average per capita income in every state remained below the national average in 1975. On the other hand, only two states (Wisconsin and Indiana) in the northern tier were below the national mean and then only by four percentage points. In contrast, eleven southern states were actually more than ten points below the national figure. In response to the assertion that lower living costs offset lower incomes in the South, experts noted that even after cost-of-living adjustments only Texas, Florida, and Virginia had per capita incomes above the national average while four southern states showed figures that were still 10 percent below the norm. Those figures suggested why, as late as 1970, 43.7 percent of the poor people in the United States lived in the Sunbelt South as opposed to 31.1 percent in the North. Rather than overtaking the North, the South was still struggling to catch up. Policies designed to direct beneficial federal spending away from the region threatened to preserve the remaining income disparities.[55]

Money from Washington had clearly contributed to southern economic progress in the period after World War II. Military expenditures during the war and the proliferation of military installations in the decades that followed provided a significant infusion of needed capital. The large number of military bases in the region also resulted in significant in-migration. Many military personnel had no choice but to come to the South, but when discharged many also chose to stay, perhaps to remain near an armed forces installation in order to take advantage of post hospitals and exchanges. Other federal expenditures played a significant part in southern economic progress. The Tennessee Valley Authority was a boon to the industrial growth of a large part of Tennessee and Alabama. Loans from the Area Redevelopment Administration and the Small Business Administration helped to subsidize many new manufacturing operations in the South.

Although federal spending had complemented Dixie development ef-

54. This correlation was computed from figures given in Weinstein and Firestine, *Regional Growth*, 8–9, 12–13; "Federal Spending," 888.
55. Jusenius and Ledeber, *A Myth*, 6, 11.

forts, northern critics exaggerated Washington's role in the economic drama of the seventies. Representatives of the Industrial North naturally associated the South's post-1960 progress with their own region's decline, but the demise of the Manufacturing Belt was the result of developments and phenomena far broader and more significant than industrial piracy and federal favoritism. The once-vibrant North had fallen prey to all the ills associated with highly developed industrial capitalism. Because the northern states seemed to offer so many more opportunities, they continued to attract underproductive residents even as investment possibilities diminished and living conditions deteriorated because of increased costs, congestion, and pollution.

As more affluent residents began to escape urban-industrial centers, a costly commitment to social welfare programs pushed taxes higher for those who remained. A high degree of worker organization and escalating living expenses kept labor costs high. Naturally, as their northern facilities became obsolete, an increasing number of companies chose to forego modernization of the old plant in favor of constructing a new facility in the South where labor and living were less expensive and the consumer and industrial markets were growing more rapidly. The energy crisis accentuated the South's climatic advantages, while the 1974–1975 recession did its greatest damage in heavy-manufacturing-dominated areas of the North.

As ominous as the future seemed for the northern states, a 1978 study argued that the various sections of the country were merely headed toward economic convergence. The Sunbelt South and the Manufacturing Belt were moving toward a more equal sharing of the wealth, and as the regions approached parity, the growth of the formerly underdeveloped South and West had actually begun to slow, as had the decline of the northern industrial tier. New England's share of personal incomes had dropped by 23 percent between 1930 and 1950 but fell by only 4.5 percent in the twenty years that followed. Moreover, disparities in federal spending were actually becoming less acute. In 1952 the southeastern states received 50 percent more in federal funds than they had paid out, a margin that shrank to 11 percent in the 1974–1976 period.[56] However accurate these findings may have been, representatives from northern

56. *Wall Street Journal*, October 6, 1978, p. 22. See also Max Moise Schreiber, "The Development of the Southern United States: A Test for Regional Convergence and Homogeneity" (Ph.D. dissertation, University of South Carolina, 1978), 147–53.

states found little comfort in them as they faced continued pressure to restore the economic vitality of the areas they represented.

The Sunbelt boom resulted from the interaction of seemingly contradictory influences. On the one hand, an influx of relatively affluent consumers combined with the cumulative impact of a high birth rate and increased federal spending to supply the momentum that neo–New South promotional strategies had failed to muster. On the other, the traditional development policies that had once confirmed a pattern of slow growth had also preserved the cost advantages and favorable business climate that made Dixie even more appealing to market-conscious industrialists. The Sunbelt ballyhoo of the late 1970s suggested that the realization of Henry Grady's dreams might at last be close at hand. Like Grady's New South, however, the Sunbelt South retained its ties to a past characterized not only by bright hopes but by recurrent disappointments. Thus, it remained to be seen whether the region could actually reach the nation's economic mainstream in the 1980s and, in so doing, make prosperity a permanent feature of a new "southern way of life."

Chapter 8

WHY INDUSTRY CAME SOUTH

If so much of the South's growth in the late 1960s and the 1970s could be traced to attractions such as population expansion, surplus labor, low taxes, and climatic advantages, how significant were industrial development efforts in promoting the emergence of the Sunbelt South? Did subsidies, sales pitches, and kid-glove treatment make any difference, or would the South have been "bought" even if there had been no efforts to "sell" it?

Although there has been considerable disagreement as to which factors have been the major determinants of industrial location, researchers and theorists have based their thoughts on a common assumption—that decisions about where new plants would be built were made only after a rational consideration of the costs and benefits involved. Thus, most attempts to explain plant location decisions focused primarily on economic factors. The major disagreement concerning these decisions has centered on which economic consideration was given priority. From the beginning, theorists have cited a number of potential influences on the migratory habits of American industry, the major ones being the availability of markets for the goods to be produced, a suitable labor supply, and the necessary raw materials. Other miscellaneous factors normally mentioned that related to the cost or convenience of construction were tax rates, transportation, fuel supply, waste disposal, and climate.[1]

Some of the strongest evidence that the South's expanding markets

1. For a survey of the literature of industrial location research, see Leonard F. Wheat, *Regional Growth and Industrial Location* (Lexington, Mass.: Lexington Books, 1973), 6–20.

were its primary attractions for industry came from a study published in 1949 by the National Planning Association. This survey included data gleaned from interviews with officials of more than fifty major firms that had built plants in the South since World War II. Responses indicated that approximately 45 percent of the plant locations discussed had been chosen because of the attraction of the South's growing markets. On the basis of their interviews, the authors concluded, "The major force attracting plants to the South in recent years had been the growing volume of expenditures of both final consumers and industry." Although the region had suffered historically from insufficient consumer demand, income payments rose by 187 percent from 1940 to 1947, an increase nearly 40 percent higher than the national average. Per capita income remained well below the national mean, but rapid population growth nonetheless fed an expanding consumer market.[2]

After World War II both Ford and General Motors realized that an Atlanta area location would place their new automobile assembly plants near a significant pool of buyers. The Ready Foods Corporation found it cheaper to open a dog food plant in Charleston than to try to supply the Southeast out of its Chicago facility. The market research department of the Armstrong Cork Company estimated that the center of an expanding southern market for asphalt tile was within a few miles of Jackson, Mississippi, where the company built a $700,000 plant in the late forties.[3]

Textile supply production facilities like the Celanese plant at Rock Hill, South Carolina, responded to the growth of that industry in the strip of states from Virginia down through Georgia. Mechanization of southern agriculture not only contributed to a regional labor surplus but also attracted the attention of firms like International Harvester, which built a new tractor plant in Louisville in 1947. Because market-oriented industries clustered in areas experiencing significant industrial and population growth, cities like Atlanta were likely to keep growing once their booms began.[4]

The National Planning Association study indicated that raw materials and natural resources had lured 30 percent of the surveyed plants to the South. Paper firms attracted by plentiful supplies of pulpwood fell into

2. McLaughlin and Robock, *Why Industry Moves South*, 26–32. For another study emphasizing markets, see Harvey S. Perloff *et al.*, *Regions, Resources, and Economic Growth* (Baltimore: Johns Hopkins University Press, 1960).

3. McLaughlin and Robock, *Why Industry Moves South*, 35–36, 39–40, 42.

4. *Ibid.*, 40, 45.

this category. Sulphur and phosphorous deposits proved important to incoming chemical operations, and other plants with significant energy demands had been swayed by more than adequate reserves of petroleum, natural gas, and hydroelectric power. Twenty-five percent of the new plants studied had been little concerned with markets or raw materials but had sought locations where labor costs were low. Firms manufacturing textiles, apparel, and shoes, for example, needed low-wage workers because of intense competition within their respective industries.[5]

A major analysis that appeared a few years later rejected the NPA survey's assertion that expanding markets had become the primary cause of industrial growth. Instead, economist Victor Fuchs claimed that between 1929 and 1954 the three major locational determinants had been climate, labor, and raw materials. Fuchs credited one-third of the interregional shifts of industry in this period to resources (among which he included climate) and raw materials. He attributed another one-third of northeastern losses and southern gains to low wages and weak unions, which were important to certain industries. For example, Fuchs demonstrated that the South Atlantic states gained 116,021 jobs in the cotton, pulp and paper, and woolen industries between 1929 and 1954, while New England lost 114,754 jobs in these same industries. Fuchs's claims received support from a survey of industrial migration to the South that categorized firms as market- or non-market-oriented according to the distances from their plants to the markets they served. This study concluded that market-sensitive plants were only beginning to have a significant impact on southern development in the early 1960s.[6]

The most recent comprehensive analysis of industrial location in the United States was Leonard F. Wheat's *Regional Growth and Industrial Location*, which appeared in 1973. Using data drawn primarily from the census and the *Statistical Abstract of the United States*, Wheat revived the notion that markets were the key to southern industrial expansion by analyzing influences on regional growth patterns. He found that markets accounted for 55 to 75 percent of the growth registered between 1947 and 1963 and affirmed earlier indications that climate had become an im-

5. *Ibid.*, 53–66, 75–76, 79–83.
6. Victor R. Fuchs, *Changes in the Location of Manufacturing in the United States Since 1929* (New Haven: Yale University Press, 1962), 259, 204; Francisco DeAraujo Santos, "Factors Affecting the Shift of Manufacturing Industries to the Southern Region of the United States from 1954 to 1963" (Ph.D. dissertation, Columbia University, 1971), 50, 68, 103.

portant locational consideration, attributing 14 to 28 percent of regional growth (most of it in the South and West, naturally) to favorable mean temperatures in January.[7]

Labor, which Fuchs had found so important, ranked only a distant third in Wheat's survey, accounting for but 3 to 9 percent of regional growth. Wheat made it a point to inform readers that as far as industrial migration to the South was concerned, cheap labor may have had a negligible net effect if its negative impact on per capita income were considered. He reasoned that although low-wage southern labor had appealed to textile and apparel firms, better-paying, consumer market–oriented industries were more interested in areas where workers had larger paychecks to spend. Thus, in the long run, depressed southern wage levels may have been as much a burden as a blessing to industrial recruitment efforts. Wheat argued that wage differentials probably had little to do with overall southern growth: "If wage levels in the South were to climb suddenly to the national average, I doubt that manufacturing growth in the South would suffer at all (although the composition would change)." Given the obvious disagreement concerning the causes of southern industrial growth, it was not surprising that a synthesis of nine post–World War II plant location surveys yielded no conclusive distinctions between the respective importance of markets, labor, or raw materials as locational considerations.[8]

As this summary indicates, plant location studies were abundant, but they produced nothing approaching a consensus as to why industries chose southern locations. Broad analyses of industrial migration also tended to obscure the significant site requirement variations among plants as well as the fact that these requirements often changed over a period of time. Ample labor supplies and expanding demand brought some industries southward while changes in production technology and the resulting obsolescence of older plants figured prominently in other decisions to migrate. A 1966 study found, for example, that in addition to low wages, changes in manufacturing techniques had also drawn both the hosiery and knit goods industries to the South.[9]

Resource-oriented manufacturers naturally cited the existence of the

7. Wheat, *Regional Growth*, 183–89.
8. *Ibid.*, 192–97; Morgan, "The Effects of State and Local Tax and Financial Inducements," 50.
9. Bobby Ross Eddleman, "The Rate of Relocation as a Determinant of Southern Area Industrial Growth" (Ph.D. dissertation, North Carolina State University, 1966), 88.

Table 12   Relative Importance of Certain Factors to Firms Locating in Tennessee

Rank	Factor	Percentage Citing as Important
1	Low Cost and Availability of Labor	65.6
2	Low Cost of Electric Power	36.0
3	Favorable Labor-Management Relations	35.7
4	Community Leaders Cooperation	32.2
5	Low Cost of Bulding and Land	19.8
6	Low Freight Cost, Finished Product	17.9
7	Available Existing Plant	17.5
8	Favorable Community and State Tax Structure	17.2
9	Low Cost of Financing Plant Through Revenue or General Obligation Bonds	16.9
10	Available Existing Building	16.6
11	Community Concessions	14.0
11	Greater Demand in Area	14.0
11	Greater Demand Potential in Area	14.0
14	Low Cost of Raw Materials or Components	13.3
15	Size of City	10.1
16	Availability of Low Cost Raw Materials	9.1
17	Community Facilities	8.5

Source: Carrier and Schriver, Plant Location Analysis, 39.

desired raw materials in the areas they chose. When quizzed, petrochemical companies identified raw materials as the factor that most influenced their decisions to move into Louisiana. In explaining why Continental Petroleum put a refinery in Lake Charles, executives stressed both the availability of oil and the area's accessibility to cheap barge transportation and foreign markets.[10]

Table 12 is based on a 1969 study of plant location decisions in Tennessee in which nearly 66 percent of the 308 responding firms cited labor costs and availability as crucial considerations in their recent decisions to locate in Tennessee. Predictably, this item seemed most crucial to execu-

10. James W. Bateman, "Why Continental Chose Lake Charles as Optimum Site for Higher Alcohol Plant," Petroleum Refiner, XL (April, 1961), 147–49.

tives in apparel and other labor-intensive industries. The survey also indicated that Tennessee's nonunion climate continued to be an enticement to firms whose labor costs were a significant part of their production expenses. Cost factors other than labor also appeared to be of some importance. The availability of inexpensive electric power (supplied by TVA) was an important factor, as were land, buildings, freight, and raw materials expenditures. Demand ranked lower than the major cost-oriented factors, suggesting that, while it was a significant consideration, it was not the major attraction to new industries considering a Tennessee location. The survey also indicated that local facilities, cultural atmosphere, and quality of life were secondary factors that came into play only after more basic requirements had been met.

Of all the industries that became concentrated in the South none showed a more consistent labor-cost orientation than textiles. A poll of firms that located in South Carolina between 1965 and 1974 showed construction and labor costs, room for expansion, labor productivity, and highway facilities as the state's major attractions for industry. The 240 industrialists who responded to the survey provided little basis for the persistent assertions of theorists that the growing regional market was responsible for the South's industrial growth. In fact, the survey reinforced the continuing reputation of textile-laden South Carolina as a haven for industries seeking low-wage, nonunion labor. Nearly 95 percent of those polled considered labor costs a significant influence on their decisons and nearly 85 percent paid attention to the extent of unionization in the state.[11]

The most recent study of location factors within the textile industry indicated that labor considerations remained the primary factor in plant location decisions. A weighted ranking of the opinions of eighty-five textile executives showed labor relations, availability of semiskilled and unskilled labor, and state labor laws among the top five site selection priorities. Proximity to customers, a market consideration, and accessibility of raw materials ranked twenty-sixth and twenty-seventh in a list of thirty factors. Approximately 80 percent of the executives polled expressed a continuing preference for a southern location.[12]

11. Charles Thomas Ziehr, "The Importance of Incentives on the Location of Manufacturing in South Carolina" (M.S. thesis, University of South Carolina, 1975), 50.
12. Elbert Lee Menees, "The Location of the American Textile Industry" (Ph.D. dissertation, University of South Carolina, 1976), 399–400.

Differences in demographic, climatic, and economic conditions often resulted in considerable variation in locational factors within individual states. Demand-oriented firms that hoped to continue to supply a national market moved into North Florida, while those interested in serving a more localized market located in South Florida where growth was most rapid. Fabricated metals and other industries catering to the construction industry also tended to cluster in the faster-growing southern part of the state. Lumber mills and wood products plants sprang up near supplies of timber regardless of location.[13]

Northeast Georgia was an area that could serve the needs of both labor- and market-oriented plants. Residents showed no reluctance to leave farming for industrial work. Between 1940 and 1950 the percentage of the labor force employed in agriculture declined by seventeen points while the percentage working in manufacturing increased by twelve. Most of the growth in manufacturing employment came in labor-intensive industries, with apparel, livestock feed, metal products, and textile plants accounting for 89 percent of new employment in the 1950s. Apparel plants had moved into small towns, hiring women (80 to 90 percent of apparel workers were white females) who either were unemployed or wanted to stop commuting to jobs in larger towns nearby.[14]

The nonunion climate of northeast Georgia helped a great deal in the attraction of new plants. Flanked on the east by South Carolina's ardently antiunion textile belt, the area was a safe distance from the union-attracting presence of Atlanta to the west. One owner argued that, for every ten miles a new plant's executives put between their operation and Atlanta, they could expect an additional two years of freedom from union activity. On the other hand, highway connections to Atlanta were excellent. This was an important consideration to the Monroe Auto Equipment Corporation, which built a large plant in the nonunion town of Hartwell near the South Carolina border. The Hartwell location temporarily kept the company out of reach of Atlanta-based unions while the community's highway accessibility put the shock-absorber plant within an easy hundred-mile drive of one of its major customers, the Ford Motor Company plant at Hapeville near Atlanta.[15]

Although most plant location surveys sought the opinion of econo-

13. Greenhut and Colberg, *Factors in the Location*, 58.
14. Northam, "An Analysis of Recent Industrialization," 115, 221, 224.
15. *Ibid.*, 115, 132–33.

Table 13   Factors South Carolinians Believe Important to Their State's Development

Factor	Rank	Percentage Citing as Very Important
Good natural resources	1	76
Availability of land	2	70
Labor force willing to be trained for skilled jobs	3	68
Good highways and other transportation facilities	3	68
South Carolina's technical training program	3	68
Good year-round climate	6	59
Good race relations	6	59
Efforts of state development board	7	57
Favorable tax rates for industry	8	54
Low wage rates	9	50
High costs and bad working conditions "up North"	10	47
Ability of South Carolina's politicians to get government contracts	10	47
Lack of labor unions	11	43

SOURCE: Harris and Associates, "Priorities for Progress," 17–19.

mists or the executives who made site-selection decisions, a study conducted in August, 1971, presented the opinions of 855 South Carolinians randomly polled on questions related to their state's economic progress. As Table 13 shows, those interviewed felt the Palmetto State had a great deal to offer new industry. Natural resources, available land, a willing work force, good highways, and state-sponsored technical training were cited as the most important advantages the state offered. "Good race relations" ranked higher than did the efforts of the State Development Board, low taxes, low wages, or the absence of unions.

The fact that South Carolinians felt that low-wage, nonunion conditions were less important than a number of other factors contradicted not only the results of several surveys of the state's industrialists but some of the other responses given in the 1971 poll. For example, 82 percent of the respondents agreed that southerners received less pay for the same work than their counterparts in other areas of the country. In addition, 66 percent felt that manufacturers were receiving "breaks" at the expense of employees and that the state government should insist on higher salaries. South Carolinians were proud of the many natural and man-made advantages their state had to offer new industry, but although they were less willing to admit it, they also realized that a number of companies were still coming to the state expecting to take advantage of its cheap, docile labor.[16]

The emphasis that plant location polls gave to basic economic factors raised questions about the importance of state and local promotional organizations in stimulating industrial growth. Even developers often disagreed as to the relative effectiveness of state and local agencies. For example, the Mississippi Agricultural and Industrial Board felt it was responsible for much of the state's growth, but many local boosters claimed to have secured new plants without much or any help from the board. The director of the North Mississippi Industrial Development Association claimed that only ten of his forty-four contacts with prospects between October, 1965, and July, 1966, had come as a result of board efforts. A survey of fifty mayors and sixty-nine chamber of commerce heads in Georgia showed they felt the Georgia Power Company and the state's Department of Industry and Trade were by far the most important state-level development organizations, although the State Chamber of Commerce, the Georgia Institute of Technology's Engineering Experiment Station, and the Citizens and Southern Bank were also listed as relatively effective in their promotional activities. When these same leaders rated types of local development groups, chambers of commerce, development authorities, utilities, and banks headed the list.[17]

A 1972 survey of seventy companies concerning seventy-one plant location decisions showed that executives considered some (but not all) of the services and information provided by state, local, and private development organizations to be of little value. Approximately 81 percent of the responding executives acknowledged some sort of contact with a chamber of commerce or other local group while 59 percent had been in touch with the state development office. Local organizations had been more involved in the 48 midwestern plant location decisions, but state, utility, and railroad promoters had been more active in the South. According to more than half of the respondents, unsolicited visits and telephone calls

16. Harris and Associates, "Priorities for Progress," 57, 59.
17. Joyner and Thames, "Mississippi's Efforts," 442; Ellis, "A Survey of Georgia Industrial Developers," 78.

had been of little value in locational decision-making. On the other hand, nearly half admitted unsolicited market reports were useful, and a large number found assistance such as visit itineraries and site and community data to be of significant value.[18]

When the responses to the survey were broken down according to the size of the relocating plant, some important distinctions emerged. Heads of smaller firms considered unrequested information far more valuable than did representatives of larger companies. Similarly, half of the executives of smaller operations had made use of information about available buildings, while only a few from larger firms had found such information to be of value.[19]

The survey seemed to indicate that development organization services had been best utilized by the smaller companies that had little experience in choosing a relocation site. Larger, older corporations were less dependent on developers for assistance. Thus, the author found it ironic "that industrial developers could have the most influence on location projects of small companies and small companies most need their help, but most industrial developers spend the greatest amount of their time trying to assist large companies where their influence . . . is quite minimal."[20] This conclusion should have been particularly important to southern promotional officials who often seemed obsessed with enhancing their reputations by landing large plants of major manufacturers.

An obsession with larger firms was one of the criticisms raised in another survey of the reactions of industrialists to the activities of state development agencies in the Southeast. Still, 71 percent of the 493 respondents agreed that if potential locations in more than one state proved equally attractive, the role of the state development agency could be crucial. The executives found the assistance provided by state and local agencies to be of roughly the same value.[21]

A study of fifty-six manufacturers locating in Mississippi between 1960 and 1970 showed that promotional policies and incentives were more important to some firms than others. For example, although 53 percent of those polled claimed they definitely or probably would have come

18. Dick Howard, "Manufacturers' Attitudes Toward Industrial Development Information," in Dick Howard (ed.), *Guide to Industrial Development* (Englewood Cliffs, N.J.: Prentice-Hall, 1972), 203, 212–13, 215.

19. *Ibid.*, 215.

20. *Ibid.*, 221.

21. Thomas, "State Industrial Development Organizations," 379–82.

to Mississippi had its industrial development program not existed, 36 percent said just the opposite. Moreover, executives of four of the seven plants in the sample employing five hundred or more people admitted that Mississippi's bonding and tax subsidy programs had brought them to the Magnolia State. Although 88 percent of the industrialists mentioned labor supply as a major consideration in making the move to Mississippi, 37 percent also cited the state's industrial development policies. When the plants were divided according to wage scales, it was clear that development incentives had been more attractive to firms paying an average wage of no more than a hundred dollars per week. Forty-two percent of these companies would not have come to Mississippi without the state's promotional package, as compared to the 33 percent of the remainder of the sample that would have gone elsewhere under the same circumstances.[22]

The Mississippi survey's suggestion that it was low-wage industries that found subsidies most attractive reinforced the findings of a South Carolina poll cited earlier. This study showed that new industries in the textile-dominated Palmetto State gave more weight to incentives and concessions than earlier general analyses of industrial location had indicated. More than two-thirds of the respondents conceded that tax exemptions were important and nearly as many revealed that the state's start-up training program had been a significant factor in their decisions. Over half had paid attention to the fact that the state planning board offered several forms of assistance to new plants and more than a third had been pleased with South Carolina's revenue bond financing program.[23]

The responses of Mississippi and South Carolina industrialists seemed to support the old maxim that "good industries don't need or accept handouts." Yet, a 1969 analysis of the potential impact of subsidies demonstrated that revenue bonds could offset dramatically the labor expenses of any plant where equipment and materials, rather than labor, accounted for most of the operating costs. On the other hand, for labor-oriented industries revenue bond benefits would not cancel out the effects of wide differences in wages between alternative locations. Thus, for manufacturers of apparel, leather goods, and textiles, bond financing would com-

22. Clyde Thomas White, "An Economic Study of the Industrial Development Policies of the State Government of Mississippi, 1960–1970" (D.B.A. dissertation, Mississippi State University, 1973), 95–96, 99.
23. Ziehr, "The Importance of Incentives," 50.

pensate for differences in labor costs only in the range of 3 to 5 percent while capital-intensive industries like plastics or clay (which hired fewer workers but paid them better) might expect a labor expense offset of 30 to 56 percent.[24]

Assuming a "purely economic" decision about a new plant site, revenue bond financing would not cause an industrialist to choose a location where labor, tax, or other costs were significantly higher than in an alternative one. If the choice was to be made between areas of nearly equal operating expenses, however, the revenue bonds might be of some influence. It is important to remember that the southern states where bond use was most common, were also the states where labor and tax costs were lowest. Thus, revenue bonds may have supplemented the South's other advantages and helped to compensate for minor deficiencies in the quality of labor or strength of markets.

Evidence that well-known, capital-intensive firms had begun to respond to industrial bond subsidies by the early 1960s appeared in a study of development bond financing in Alabama. Out of the 212 firms participating, 46 (21.7 percent) were major national corporations whose stocks were listed on either the New York or American Stock Exchange. After 1960 the size of capital investments made by bond-subsidized operations in Alabama rose sharply. Between 1952 and 1960 the average investment per job created was $2,448, but in the period 1961–1968 this figure rose to $20,473, an increase of 740 percent.[25] These firms might have chosen an Alabama site had bond financing not been available, but their acceptance of the subsidy probably indicated that they considered it significant.

The attractiveness of subsidies was not necessarily so dependent on the type of operation as the type of expenses it involved and the relative importance of these expenses in terms of overall costs and profits. Competitive industries, wherein companies were sensitive to practically all cost variations, were thus more likely to respond to subsidies than industries that could pass a location's cost disadvantages on to consumers. Researchers often seemed to forget that even capital-intensive operations had labor and tax costs. If such industries became competitive enough all

24. William J. Stober and Laurence H. Falk, "The Effect of Financial Inducements on the Location of Firms," *Southern Economic Journal*, XXXVI (July, 1969), 34.

25. Alabama Business Research Council, *Industrial Development Bond Financing*, 33, 36.

such expenses could influence profits and, therefore, plant location decisions. For example, as the American automobile and electronics industries faced increasing foreign competition, a southern location that offered low-interest financing, cheaper labor, and lower taxes became more
attractive because of the savings it offered in not one, but all of these
areas.

Because the states continued to offer incentives and companies continued to accept them, it seemed reasonable to assume that certain concessions and assistance did help to influence the location decision. There
was, however, considerable disagreement as to which inducements were
most effective. One recent study measured state involvement in promotion statistically and then compared the extent of a state's commitment to
its actual rate of industrial growth. The author theorized that the intensity of a state's support for economic development could explain as much
as 25 percent of its growth, but only nineteen of twenty-nine development advantages and incentives appeared to contribute to industrial expansion. Except for the availability of speculative buildings and free land,
financial subsidies seemed little related to growth, and only a few of the
various kinds of tax exemptions seemed effective.[26]

At the end of the 1960s the Arkansas Industrial Development Commission asked state development officials and leading industrialists for a
ranking of the ten most effective incentive-assistance programs drawn
from a list of sixty then in effect in various states. Table 14 indicates that
state developers felt revenue bond financing was by far the most effective
location inducement, followed at a distance by publicly financed training
programs, state-sponsored industrial development authorities, privately
supported industrial development credit corporations, and freeport exemptions on goods in transit. Industrialists placed more emphasis on tax
exemption and moratorium plans. A comparison of rankings based on the
number of times an inducement was ranked by both developers and executives yielded a relatively weak positive correlation (.173). This suggested that those who attempted to attract industry and those who determined which locations had the most to offer were not in close agreement
about the most effective incentives and inducements.[27]

26. Digby, "State Government and Economic Development," 246–49.
27. Richard A. Duvall, "Industry, States Rate Incentive, Assistance Programs," *Industrial Development*, CXXXVII (November/December, 1968), 26–30. This Kendall rank-order
coefficient (sig. .046) was computed from the ratings presented in this article.

Table 14   Top Ten Incentives for Industrial Location

State Developers' Rank		Industrialists' Rank
1	City or county revenue bond financing	28
2	State-supported training of industrial employees	13
3	State-sponsored industrial development authority	20
4	Privately sponsored development credit corporation	40
5	Inventory tax exemption on goods in transit (freeport)	7
6	Tax exemption on manufacturer's inventories	2
7	State right-to-work law	8
8	Tax exemption on raw materials used in manufacturing	4
8	University R & D facilities available to industry	18
9	City and/or county-owned industrial park sites	41
10	State recruiting, screening of industrial employees	21

Industrialists' Rank		State Developers' Rank
1	Tax exemption or moratorium on land and capital improvements	16
2	Tax exemption on manufacturers' inventories	6
3	Tax exemption or moratorium on equipment and machinery	3
4	Tax exemption on raw materials used in manufacturing	8
5	Corporate income tax exemption	7
6	Sales/use tax exemption on new equipment	18
7	Inventory tax exemption on goods in transit (freeport)	5
8	State right-to-work law	7
9	Accelerated depreciation on industrial equipment	38
10	Incentive for compliance with pollution-control laws	19

SOURCE: Duvall, "Industry, States Rate Incentive, Assistance Programs," 26–27.

NOTE: The rankings are weighted and the table is based on the number of times an incentive was rated from one to ten.

Lack of agreement concerning the importance of industrial develop-ment incentives raised the question of what actions, if any, communities might take to improve their chances of attracting new industry. Here again, there was disagreement. A study of 296 manufacturing plants that located in rural Tennessee between 1964 and 1973 utilized a regression analysis that compared a community's characteristics with its employ-ment patterns. Noting that more than one half of the net increase in jobs came in the apparel and manufacturing industries, the author showed that areas with higher quality public services and facilities were not nec-essarily those that were most successful in attracting new plants and concluded "community leaders can influence the employment expansion of plants very little by manipulating community variables."[28]

Ironically, a similar analysis of industrial growth in nonmetropolitan counties of both Tennessee and Kentucky concluded that a community had "the potential to improve its chances of attracting industry if it is will-ing and has the necessary financial and leadership resources to do so." By employing a linear probability function, the author calculated that local financing and the existence of a designated plant site controlled by an industrial development group could enhance a community's chances of attracting a new industry by as much as 55 percent. In many cases, espe-cially those involving large plants, improvements in education and fire protection seemed capable of offsetting nonmodifiable variables like the lack of access to interstate highways or metropolitan areas. Sites and fi-nancing seemed more important to labor-oriented industries than did the absence of a college or lack of access to an interstate. There was also con-siderable geographic variation in regard to the effectiveness of modifiable characteristics in attracting industry. In the eastern regions of both Ten-nessee and Kentucky an abundance of labor had outweighed any com-bination of community-created factors. On the other hand, in the western counties of both states the availability of financing and suitable sites had been of considerable importance in bringing in new industry.[29]

Regardless of their actual effectiveness as plant location induce-ments, subsidies and other forms of assistance reflected a state or com-

28. Danny Lloyd Gunter, "Factors Affecting Employment Patterns in Manufacturing Plants in Rural Tennessee, 1964–1973" (Ph.D. dissertation, University of Tennessee, 1975), 98.
29. David R. Kelch, "Industrial Location in the Nonmetropolitan Communities of Ken-tucky and Tennessee, 1970–1973" (Ph.D. dissertation, University of Kentucky, 1978), 115, 148, 151–54.

munity's earnest desire for new industry. Since the Grady era, southern industrial promoters had stressed the importance of an attractive business climate. In 1975 Fantus, the plant-location consulting firm, developed a list of criteria by which the state business climates could be ranked. Fantus used corporate, property, income and unemployment tax rates, as well as workmen's compensation payments, welfare expenditures, labor relations histories, and the extent of promanagement labor laws in defining a good business climate. As Table 15 shows, the study placed eight of the southern states among the top twelve, or excellent, business climates, and all but Louisiana fell into the top twenty-four, which included both excellent and good business climates.

When a state's business climate ranking was compared to its ranking in terms of its percentage growth in manufacturing employment between 1970 and 1977, the resulting rank order correlation (.568) suggested a noteworthy positive association. On the other hand, there was little apparent relationship between a state's ranking in per capita expenditures for promotion and its standing in the Fantus poll or its recent growth in manufacturing employment.[30]

An Industrial Development Research Council survey confirmed the Fantus analysis. Corporate executives involved in site selection placed the states into three categories—"Cooperative," "Indifferent," and "Antigrowth." Seven of the top-rated states in the Fantus listing were described as cooperative in the IDRC survey, and all of the twelve lowest-ranking Fantus states were labeled antigrowth.[31]

More than three decades of polling, calculating, and theorizing have produced mounds of industrial location research, but the conclusions to be drawn from these data are anything but clear. Many of the problems with the surveys are related to the vagueness of questions, responses, and estimates of the importance of various location factors. For example, in most studies it was difficult to determine whether an item's importance should be assessed on the basis of the number of times it was chosen as a primary, first-choice consideration, or the total number of times it was

30. This Spearman rank-order correlation (sig. .000) was computed utilizing a copy of the Fantus Rankings supplied by the Alabama Development Board and manufacturing employment figures given in Weinstein and Firestine, *Regional Growth and Decline*, 16–18. Per capita promotion expenditures taken from Digby, "State Government," 91–92, correlated with the Fantus ranking at −.064 (sig. .333) and with 1970–1977 increases in manufacturing employment at −.388 (sig. .003).

31. Weinstein and Firestine, *Regional Growth*, 136–39.

Table 15   Fantus Business Climate Rankings, 1975

1	Texas
2	Alabama
3	Virginia
4	South Dakota
5	South Carolina
6	North Carolina
7	Florida
8	Arkansas
9	Indiana
10	Utah
11	North Dakota
12	Mississippi
13	Georgia
14	Iowa
15	Tennessee
16	Arizona
17	Nebraska
18	Colorado
19	Missouri
20	Kansas
21	Oklahoma
22	Kentucky
23.5	New Mexico
23.5	Wyoming
25	Idaho
26	Louisiana
26.5	Ohio

SOURCE: Alabama Chamber of Commerce, *Alabama Ranked Second Nationally for Good Business Climate* (n.p.: n.p., April, 1976).

placed in one of the categories identifying it as a significant influence. Industrial location surveys also failed to provide any evidence to support the validity of their findings and, therefore, offered no explanation why some of the firms that had cited markets or raw materials as primary locational factors had built their plants in areas that by no means provided the best possible access to consumers or production resources. Very few such studies made any effort to distinguish between factors that made an entire region attractive and those that led an industry to choose a particular site within that region.[32]

Attempts to assess the importance of low-wage labor in bringing new industry to the South were characterized by a considerable amount of superficiality and naïveté. For example, in 1949 the authors of the NPA study concluded that labor had been less important than raw materials and markets in attracting new industry to the South. Moreover, even the labor-oriented plants had placed more emphasis "on availability and on labor attitudes than on wage rates."[33]

While it was true that the post–World War II boom made the South's labor surplus more inviting, the NPA researchers and countless others who followed in their footsteps showed limited perception in interpreting the responses they received concerning southern labor. Researchers presented their findings on plant location without a clear understanding of the euphemistic language of industrial promotion, a language frequently employed in their own survey questionnaires. In the minds of industrial executives phraseology like "labor climate," "availability," "productivity" (output compared to wage rate), "attitudes," or even "favorable political climate" and "community attitude toward industry" could be translated into "low-wage, nonunion labor." Researchers also consistently failed to acknowledge the likelihood that any industrialist would be reluctant to concede that his company had moved to the South primarily to take advantage of cheap labor or tax exemptions. When surveys posed such embarrassing questions flatly, the euphemisms often outranked the "bottom line" response. In a 1964 study of favorable location factors in the South Carolina Piedmont, for example, "low wages" ranked behind "amicable labor relations" and "availability of labor" and was given the same weight as "South Carolina labor laws."[34]

Plant location studies were also potentially misleading because they presumed that a firm's primary requirements as listed by an executive in response to a questionnaire were the requirements that had encouraged

32. T. E. McMillan, Jr., "Why Manufacturers Choose Plant Locations vs. Determinants of Plant Locations," *Land Economics*, XLI (August, 1965), 239–46; Ronald E. Carrier and William Schriver, "Plant Location Studies: An Appraisal," *Southwestern Social Science Quarterly*, XLVII (September, 1966), 136–40.

33. McLaughlin and Robock, *Why Industry Moves South*, 67.

34. Clinton H. Whitehurst, Jr., "Industrialization in South Carolina's Rural Piedmont Counties: The Plant Location Decision," *Business and Economic Review*, Bureau of Business and Economic Research, University of South Carolina, X (January, 1964), 5.

this executive to place his plant in its current location. In fact, many companies doubtless found several potential locations that offered the necessary access to markets or raw materials. At that point decision-makers may have begun to assess the relative merits of each site in terms of labor costs, tax rates, subsidies, or quality of community services. Thus, when more than one site could fulfill a firm's major needs, considerations that might otherwise be secondary could become crucial. Finally, only a few surveys recognized the possibility that personal factors might influence an executive, especially of a small firm, to choose one location over another. Decisions about where to build a new plant occasionally hinged on an industrialist's personal likes and dislikes relating to a community's recreational facilities or even to restaurants. Such intangible, noneconomic influences on plant location might not be acknowledged, but they existed, especially in cases where competing sites were approximately equal in terms of the economic benefits they offered.

With the weaknesses of plant location surveys in mind, it is nonetheless possible to reach some tentative conclusions about the reasons for southern industrial growth after World War II. First, as the preceding chapter indicated, population growth and the resultant expansion of consumer markets made the major contribution to the emergence of the Sunbelt South. Second, although it appeared to become less important as population and buying power increased in the region, abundant, low-wage, nonunion labor was a persistent factor. My 1978 interviews with nine state development officials in the South produced almost unanimous off-the-record admissions that cheap labor was still one of their state's major attractions to new industry. Raw materials accounted for pockets of industrial growth in areas where these resources were plentiful. Man-made factors like subsidies and tax concessions were probably more significant than surveys suggested and could be crucial after basic economic requirements had been met. Finally, no single factor like markets, labor, or concessions could be identified as the single most important. As the Fantus ranking suggested, the South's growth was closely related to its ability to provide a highly desirable combination of markets, cheap labor, low taxes, and cooperative state and local governments.

Promotional efforts informed potential investors of the basic economic advantages of a southern location while subsidies and other forms of assistance combined with the solicitous and hospitable attitudes of development leaders to underscore the region's earnest desire for new industry.

In the midst of heated competition for industry a state or community that did not engage in extensive promotional activity was likely to be labeled as indifferent or antigrowth. Such a reputation, no matter how undeserved, was extremely difficult to disprove. At the end of the 1970s while the rest of the South was enjoying rapid industrial expansion, development leaders in Louisiana were still struggling to overcome their state's anticorporate image.[35] Once publicly supported efforts to seduce, subsidize, and otherwise accommodate new industry became the norm, leaders of industry-hungry states and communities had little choice but to participate. In a sense the promotional effort became an important advertisement for the all-important business climate. As such, it was clearly related to the dramatic emergence of the Sunbelt South.

35. *Wall Street Journal*, June 9, 1978, p. 1.

Chapter 9

THE PRICE OF PROGRESS

The emergence of the Sunbelt South gladdened the hearts of southern development leaders, but it also heightened the concerns of those charged with maintaining the unspoiled natural environment that had helped to make the region an attractive alternative to the Manufacturing Belt. When Henry Grady and other development advocates formulated the guidelines for bringing industry to the late-nineteenth-century South, they promised investors not only a plentiful supply of cheap labor but an abundance of natural resources and raw materials that could be utilized practically without constraint. Freedom to exploit the region's resources and contaminate its air and water became an important element of the South's favorable business climate wherein, free from regulations, industry could be its own boss. Preserving such a permissive atmosphere proved more difficult, however, when environmental problems emerged as a major public concern because, in addition to encouraging and facilitating industrial development, state government was given the responsibility of preventing incoming plants from releasing pollutants into the air and water.

For the most part, prior to the late 1960s southern developers made it a point to ask few questions about a new industry's environmental impact even if the anticipated facility would obviously cause pollution. Some communities did more than just ignore environmental considerations. Local promoters not only provided nominal rents and protection from competition when Union Camp came to Savannah in 1935 but also agreed "to secure the necessary action and if possible legislation on the part of the governmental bodies concerned, to protect and save you

[Union Bag] harmless from any claims, demands or suits for the pollution of air or water caused by the operation of the plant. . . . It is agreed that in case litigation arises or suits are brought against you on account of odors and/or flowage from the proposed plant that the Industrial Committee of Savannah will pay all expenses of defending such suits up to a total amount of $5,000."[1]

When the South Carolina legislature went into special session in 1956 to pave the way for Bowater Paper's new plant at Rock Hill, there was little chance that the state's newly strengthened pollution laws would be allowed to get in the way. The state's Pollution Control Authority cooperated in rolling out the red carpet for Bowater by exempting the company from the provisions of the law it would have found most burdensome. Governor George Bell Timmerman, Jr., and state development officials apparently paid little heed to critics who charged them with selling the state's birthright for "a mess of pottage."[2]

Efforts to enact air pollution control laws in North Carolina and Georgia in 1967 illustrated the difficulties involved in providing statutory protection for the environment in states that were hungry for new industry. In both states, the bills legislators began with stated emphatically that protecting the environment was a major contribution to the public health and general welfare of the citizenry. Both promised significant improvements in the regulation and curtailment of air pollution, until they were modified by the lawmakers after considerable input from industry.

The North Carolina measure was not introduced until copies had been circulated among affected industries and Department of Conservation and Development officials. The result was a speedily revised bill in which "maintenance of a proper environment in which people may live and work" had given way to providing the "maximum employment and full industrial development of the state." Another change promised prevention of injury to plant and animal life "to the greatest degree practicable." Finally, air pollution abatement would not be mandatory if a hearing demonstrated the impossibility or unfeasibility of eliminating the activities causing or contributing to the pollution. This provision exempted industries in cases where the cost of reducing contamination seemed "unduly burdensome in comparison with the pollution abate-

1. Fallows, *The Water Lords*, 159.
2. J. Roy Pennell to Timmerman, May 26, 1956, A. G. Kennedy to Timmerman, May 29, 1956, both in Timmerman Correspondence.

ment results which can be achieved." Such qualifications on enforcement confronted the state courts with some stiff challenges to their interpretive skills, challenges that seemed likely to provide protection for an accused industry. The revised statute also altered the administrative policy board that would oversee enforcement. Gone was one of the conservationists stipulated for the eleven-member board along with one from a thirteen-person advisory group. A representative of county government replaced the former; the latter's place went to a spokesman for industry, which already had five seats on the advisory council.[3]

The story of Georgia's 1967 effort to regulate pollution was strikingly similar. A relatively strong bill died in committee, but Glenn Kimble, a representative of the Union Camp Paper Corporation proposed a replacement measure. Explaining that he presented this substitute "in behalf of all Georgia industry," Kimble explained that his proposal would "prevent the crippling of segments of our economy by trying to reach Utopia too fast," and with only a few changes, Kimble's suggestion became law. This new law authorized pollution control "consistent with providing for maximum employment and the full industrial development of the State" and prevented the Georgia Air Quality Branch from forbidding the burning of forest land, a step that might greatly inconvenience paper companies like Union Camp. Like its North Carolina counterpart, the Georgia bill made both the need for continued industrial development and the feasibility of abatement important enforcement considerations. The modification of both of these state pollution laws reflected a dual concern for the interests of existing industries and the impact of pollution regulation on future industrial growth.[4] A North Carolina editor explained that supporters of meaningful pollution statutes were up against "too many chambers of commerce who want—occasionally they desperately need—the economic stimulus of factories and processors. Moreover, industrial development has become a competitive interstate game played for political as well as economic stakes. And even governors are subject to the common denominator rule which holds that what is allowed elsewhere may be tolerated among their own constituents."[5]

The industry-hungry southern states seemed least likely to make

3. Tom Inman, "Air Polluters Win First Round," Raleigh *News and Observer*, March 30, 1967, in University of North Carolina Library Clipping File, Chapel Hill.
4. Fallows, *The Water Lords*, 146–48.
5. Inman, "Air Polluters."

stringent demands on incoming plants, but by the end of the 1960s environmental protection had become a significant concern in Dixie as in the rest of the nation, especially as media attention focused on the worst examples of industrial pollution in the region. A Ralph Nader study demonstrated that Savannah's guarantees to Union Camp had produced ugly and foul-smelling results, especially in the Savannah River, which ran through the city. By 1969 Union Camp accounted for 80 percent of the industry-related contamination in Savannah and 70 percent of the waste discharges most deadly to marine life. These effluents, consisting of wood sugars, cellulose, and natural wood adhesives, were so dangerous to fish because they dissipated the oxygen in the water as they decomposed. The Savannah also received all of the city's raw sewage, the discharges from a Continental Can plant, and 690,000 pounds of sulfuric acid daily from an American Cyanamid facility. American Cyanamid's pollution potential became even more apparent in March, 1972, when two members of a Corps of Engineers dredging crew were overcome by a thick cloud of sulfur dioxide that engulfed the river. It was small wonder that the Savannah gave off a heavy, offensive stench and that the fish that survived could not be eaten because of their oily taste. At points the water's acid content was high enough to sear human skin, and one cautious canoeist left the stream in Savannah because of his concern about the water's effect on his rubberized Kayak.[6]

Savannah's industries were not the only polluters of the river. Upstream 160 miles, at industry-hungry Augusta, the Olin Corporation had leaked mercury wastes into the Savannah. Concentrations became so heavy that fish downstream as far as Savannah had absorbed dangerous levels of the poisonous chemical. As a result, late in the summer of 1970, fishing was prohibited in the entire stretch of water between the two cities.[7]

In tiny St. Mary's on the Georgia coast, the Gilman Paper Company, which had migrated from Vermont in the early forties, poisoned both the air and the water. St. Mary's was almost totally dependent on Gilman and therefore townspeople tolerated not only the smell but the thick, acrid smoke that killed Spanish moss, ruined the chrome on automobiles, and even flecked the paint on their houses. Gilman did its greatest damage to animal life in the North River, once an unspoiled tidal stream but now

6. Fallows, *The Water Lords*, 7–10; Atlanta *Constitution*, March 15, 1972, p. 2A.
7. Fallows, *The Water Lords*, 8.

such a hostile environment for aquatic life that some claimed that a crab thrown in the water would immediately crawl out and die.[8]

As of late 1970, Gilman was making no apparent effort to clean up its wastes on the North River. In 1967 the plant manager had spoken out against the regulations imposed by the Georgia Water Quality Control Board. He began in much the same fashion as an employer requesting protection from unions by citing his firm's economic importance to the area: "It can be safely stated that not less than 75 percent of the economy of Camden County is directly dependent on Gilman Paper Company." He asked why the plant, which employed 1,625 workers, should make a "very major expenditure" to clean up the river since the cleanup would "contribute virtually nothing to any segment of the population?" Finally, he argued that it would be foolish to shift the river from its valuable role as receptacle of waste and concluded, "The current and potential value of North River lies solely in waste treatment and limited navigational use."[9]

Under pressure to bring in new plants and payrolls, development officials were often too ready to accept a company's assurances that its operations would produce no pollution. When he made the announcement in 1967 that the Farmers Chemical Association was locating a fertilizer plant at Tunis, North Carolina, Governor Dan K. Moore gave assurances that the facility would be engineered for maintenance of a clean environment and that no pollution would result. East Carolina University President Leo Jenkins also hailed the plant as a desirable new industry, and when the company promised that no waste by-products would result from their operations, no public official disputed this claim. Problems arose quickly, however, when green slime began choking the nearby Chowan River. In July, 1971, the North Carolina Board of Water and Air Resources claimed that the Farmers Chemical plant was discharging inadequately treated waste into the Chowan. As the controversy erupted, a Chowan area newspaper, the Ahoskie *Herald*, claimed that it had been misled: "The reason the plant was located on the river was to use the Chowan for barging in phosphates, we were told." Actually, Farmers Chemical seemed to be flushing about one-half ton of nitrogen a day into the river.[10]

In the initial stages of the controversy, local plant officials insisted that

8. *Ibid.*, 102–104.
9. *Ibid.*, 105–106.
10. Raleigh *News and Observer*, August 27, 1972, Sec. IV, pp. 3–4.

their main priority was continued operation. Two of them called together local businessmen, reminded them of the plant's contribution to the area's economy, and warned that punitive action by state water quality officials could jeopardize the construction of a multimillion-dollar natural gas facility that had once been slated to locate near Farmers Chemical. Only when the controversy reached corporate headquarters did company executives pledge their full cooperation in alleviating the pollution problem.[11]

The Raleigh *News and Observer* noted the irony of the enthusiasm with which the plant had been lured to North Carolina, recalling the successful efforts of boosters to secure from the legislature a tax exemption for the $6 million worth of natural gas the company used annually. The *Observer* conceded that the plant had "made its unwholesome presence an economic asset to the area" by employing 350 people (three-fourths of whom received less than the state's low average wage), but nonetheless charged Farmers Chemical with "sorry corporate citizenship." Much of the responsibility for the despoliation of the Chowan also belonged to "state and local officials and industry boosters," who "worked mightily and to the accompaniment of much public applause" to lure a polluting industry to North Carolina.[12]

At Selma, Alabama, the Hammermill Paper Company, which George C. Wallace had courted so ardently, proved to be a mixed blessing. Although it did bring new payrolls and pay new taxes, it also created serious pollution problems. Its smoky, acidic emissions often kept the air so cloudy that an instructor at nearby Craig Air Force Base complained, "The smog so often prevents my student pilots from flying that it is difficult to complete the training course in the established amount of time."[13]

Louisiana also had its share of industrial pollution problems. A 1971 survey concluded: "Industrial development has resulted in the discharge of virtually every conceivable type of manufacturing waste into the state's streams in alarming amounts." Researchers estimated that 65 percent of industrial discharges received less than adequate treatment and cited such results as "off flavors" in lower Mississippi River drinking water supplies and inedible, oily-tasting fish taken from the same waters. Sci-

11. *Ibid.*, October 22, 1972, Sec. IV, p. 3.
12. *Ibid.*, August 27, 1972, Sec. IV, p. 4.
13. Leslie Allan, Eileen Kohl Kaufman, and Joanna Underwood, *Paper Profits: Pollution in the Pulp and Paper Industry* (Cambridge, Mass.: MIT Press, 1972), 210.

entists eventually found sixty-six chemicals in a section of the river used by New Orleans for its water supply. Some of these seemed linked to what one expert described as the "hellaciously high" cancer rates in Louisiana. The brown pelican had disappeared from the Louisiana, Mississippi, and Texas Gulf Coasts, apparently because of a toxic substance that had entered its food chain. Numerous rivers, lakes, and bayous had been spoiled by mercury and by oxygen-consuming wastes from paper mills and food-processing plants. Perhaps the greatest danger came from frequent oil spills and leaks, not to speak of the occasional fires. Even the drilling mud used by petroleum companies posed a problem to coastal oyster beds.[14]

The 1960s had been a decade of torrid interstate competition for industry. Industrial bonds, tax concessions, and other incentives had spread out of the South to every part of the nation. Governors and political leaders at all levels listed industrial promotion as one of their top priorities. By the end of the decade, however, zeal for more smokestacks had been tempered by mounting concern for the environmental impact of continued industrial "progress." As the leading development journal observed in 1970, "Glad-handed, back patted, applauded and lauded in years past, industry has all at once become America's bad boy." The writer concluded that this change of heart was apparently the work of environmentalists who had succeeded in making American industry "a whipping boy." This emergent concern about pollution had manifested itself in 1970 in the form of restrictions that many developers saw as threats to industrial expansion throughout the nation.[15]

Stricter regulations resulted in part from a desire to protect relatively unspoiled areas of the South and also from a concern among states'-rights-conscious legislators that failure to enact effective antipollution measures might lead to federal intervention. For example, certain amendments to the Clean Air Act of 1970 empowered the Environmental Protection Agency to step in where state pollution control programs were not doing the job. The EPA actually took such action in November, 1971, when the particulate level in Birmingham's air climbed near the federal

14. Vernon L. Strickland to William T. Hackett, Jr., memorandum, March 17, 1971, in Louisiana Department of Commerce and Industry Uncatalogued Correspondence, Louisiana State Archives, Baton Rouge; New Orleans *Times-Picayune*, June 19, 1977, p. 1.
15. Linda L. Liston, "Fifty Legislative Climates Turn Stormy as States Fire Up Pollution Control Programs," *Industrial Development*, CXXXIX (November/December, 1970), 1.

maximum. The state's tough new air pollution statute had not yet been implemented and a federal judge responded to the crisis with an injunction that prevented twenty-three local plants from discharging any material into the air.[16]

Passed in 1971, Alabama's new environmental laws indicated a toughened stance against pollution. The new water quality law provided for daily fines up to $10,000, the highest in the Southeast. The law also permitted civil action to recover damages resulting from the loss of fish and wildlife and allowed the state to demand restitution for the costs of cleanup operations. Finally, the act reorganized Alabama's water quality board, which had been dominated by employees of firms with waste discharge permits or state officials with obvious proindustry biases.[17]

Florida was the first of the southeastern states to enact a provision that permitted citizens to file suit against governmental agencies to require them to enforce pollution laws. Under the state's environmental protection act of 1971, individuals could also bring charges against polluting industries. Apparently motivated in part by environmental concerns, Florida legislators also slashed state expenditures for industrial promotion in 1971. All the southeastern states also moved toward a system of industrial zoning in the early 1970s by requiring that sources of contaminants could be operated only after an official permit had been issued. Issuance of a permit required detailed information from the company concerning the types of emissions produced by the new facility as well as the steps that would be taken to control them.[18]

Conflicts over pollution often consisted of agency warnings followed by company pleas for more time to meet deadlines, which in turn elicited more warnings. Occasionally, however, industrialists chose to shut down their plants rather than attempt to comply with state guidelines. This was the case at Saltville, Virginia, in 1970 when the Olin Corporation elected to close its soda ash production facility. The company's explanation was that there was "no technological or economical or otherwise practical" means of complying with Virginia's new water quality regulations. State officials were obviously disappointed with Olin's decision because it threatened to slice in half the company's $8 million annual payroll and its yearly

16. Linda L. Liston, "The Southeast: Economic Imperatives Bow to Environmental Integrity," *Industrial Development*, CXL (September/October, 1971), 6–7.
17. *Ibid.*
18. *Ibid.*

expenditures of $14 million for materials, services and supplies in the Saltville area.[19]

In order to avoid economic shocks like the one that occurred at Saltville, a number of southern states utilized close cooperation between development and pollution control agencies to screen out environmental undesirables. North Carolina's Division of Economic Development automatically referred potential polluters to the state's water and air pollution control officials who outlined the protective measures necessary before the company could open a plant in the Tarheel State. In Georgia a spokesman for the Air Quality Control Branch claimed that state developers would not recruit an industry that seemed uncooperative toward pollution control officials. Georgia Governor Jimmy Carter informed his constituents that he had told a group of New York industrialists, "We don't want any industry or factory in Georgia . . . that is not prepared to cooperate fully with us in complying with Georgia's air and water pollution laws." In environmentally conscious Florida, developers made it clear that it was their policy to recruit new plants selectively and that while they made no official effort to discourage certain industries, they provided no help in the establishment of plants likely to contribute to pollution problems. Promoters claimed this approach got the message across so effectively that few unacceptable industries even made inquiries in Florida.[20]

The new and important interrelationships between pollution control and industrial development became apparent when the director of Tennessee's Division of Air Pollution Control reproached his counterpart at the Division for Industrial Development:

> It has been my understanding that the Division of Air Pollution Control would be advised when members of your staff had knowledge of a new industry locating in Tennessee. Since no such notification has been received in quite some time, I wonder if this procedure has been abandoned or if such reflects a lack of new industrial development. It would be most desirable that new industries be aware of requirements for air pollution control so they may make orderly plans for compliance with regulations, rather than having to make hasty makeshift plans at the last minute, or even worse, beginning construction or operation in violation of regulations and hence being subject to possible legal action.[21]

19. Richmond *Times Dispatch*, July 8, 1970, p. 1.
20. Atlanta *Constitution*, November 25, 1971, p. 2A; Atlanta *Journal*, August 4, 1974, p. 1E.
21. D. P. Roberts to James H. Alexander, November 6, 1970, in Tennessee Division for Industrial Development Correspondence.

The steps taken by the southern states in the early seventies to provide statutory safeguards against industrial pollution were a significant departure from the old hands-off attitude about industry's impact on natural resources and the environment. Still, heightened concern over pollution did not mean that state and local political and economic leaders were ready to give environmental purity precedence over industrial growth. Southern promotional advertisements still made it clear that new industries would find state governments sympathetic to their problems in pollution control. In an article prepared for the *American Banker*, Tennessee Governor Winfield Dunn criticized "unreasonable fanatic groups crying for the impossible to be done overnight" and placing "the entire responsibility for meeting their idealistic demands upon industry." Dunn assured industrialists that such fanaticism was uncommon in his state, where citizens and public officials managed to protect the environment without becoming "unreasonable about it."[22]

Despite the official rhetoric about selectivity and the need for environmental purity, a 1972 survey showed South Carolina, which ranked tenth nationally, to be the southern state with the most adequate pollution control program. Except for Texas (fourteenth), Kentucky (sixteenth), and Florida (seventeenth), no other state in the South was in the top twenty, and Oklahoma, Alabama, Arkansas, Louisiana, and Mississippi ranked forty-second, forty-fourth, forty-fifth, forty-sixth, and fiftieth respectively. The strong commitment to any and all types of industrial development had been tempered somewhat by environmental concerns, but it was still correct in 1972 to conclude that "most southern states are interested in recruiting industry instead of scaring them with strict pollution control regulations."[23]

Although they faced pressure to be more selective about the types of plants they recruited, many state developers still felt they could not afford to be choosy. For example, as of 1974, promoters in Louisiana promised to help any industry interested in their state. Louisiana had a number of pollution problems, but its relatively high unemployment rate encouraged developers to cooperate with almost any potential investors. Many northeastern coastal states rejected proposals for offshore oil terminals

22. "An Article for the American Banker by Winfield Dunn, Governor, State of Tennessee, 1969" (typescript in Tennessee Division for Industrial Development Correspondence).
23. S. R. Jarrett, "How the States Stack Up in Pollution Control," *Industrial Development*, CXLI (September/October, 1972), 4–5.

and refineries, but Louisiana, Alabama, Mississippi, Georgia, and South Carolina all made an effort to secure such a port in the early seventies.[24]

The zeal for environmental purity that emerged in the early 1970s may have been weakened by the recession of 1974–1975, which temporarily slowed the Sunbelt South's boom. At any rate, there were numerous examples in the latter half of the seventies to suggest that state agencies had not always been successful in detecting and curtailing industrial pollution. Virginia Fibre Corporation's paper mill at Riverville in Amherst County gave off such a stench that it affected a four-county area. The Virginia Air Pollution Control Division received more than two hundred complaints about the smell, and when it held a public hearing on the matter late in 1976, more than five hundred people attended. Out of the hearing came a consent order that required the company to follow state guidelines in correcting the problem. Although it seemed similar to the cases of dozens of other paper mills throughout the South, Virginia Fibre's was significant because the plant had opened in 1975, long after enforcement and technology were supposed to have solved such problems. In July, 1976, a scientific report charged that emissions from Union County, Arkansas, bromine plants were killing the needles on loblolly pines and doubling the maturation period of the trees. In 1977 Allied Chemical Company pled guilty to over nine hundred violations of federal water pollution laws after investigators found harmful levels of kepone, an inert poison, in the water around Hopewell, Virginia.[25]

Environmental protection had also become a problem as the southern states wooed foreign industries. In 1969 Georgetown, South Carolina, a seaside town of thirteen thousand, became the beneficiary of South Carolina's then-fledgling program to attract international investment when German-owned Georgetown Steel began operations. The fact that the mill had been built in the downtown area upset a number of local residents, 3,500 of whom signed a petition requesting an investigation of the company. There was a heavy dust covering homes and buildings, and the South Carolina Pollution Control Authority quickly found the facility in violation of state air quality standards.[26]

The Georgetown area had a large underemployed black population,

24. Atlanta *Journal*, August 4, 1974, p. 1-E.

25. Ben Critzer, "Paper Mill Odor Affects 4 Counties," Charlottesville *Daily Progress*, February 15, 1976, in University of Virginia Library Clipping File, Charlottesville; Arkansas *Gazette*, July 22, 1976, p. 5A; New York *Times*, February 5, 1977, p. 8.

26. New York *Times*, July 2, 1972, Sec. III, pp. 1–2.

and by no means all local residents objected to the mill. Some reminded critics that local residents had been glad enough to get the plant in 1969. Layoffs at the International Paper Company plant, another pollution law violator, had caused unemployment to rise dramatically. Anxious to relieve the local economic distress, the state had arranged for the construction of docking and materials-handling facilities at a cost of $1.5 million. Development officials had also persuaded the Corps of Engineers to dredge a half-mile waterway in order to connect the new plant to the Georgetown harbor. Local businessmen were pleased with the $10 million annual payroll, and local government had benefitted from a $400,000 yearly tax contribution. Workers who remembered the days of unemployment or underemployment agreed that "without the mill people would have nothing to do but cut wood."[27]

South Carolina's courtship of foreign industry produced another environmental controversy that provided a classic example of the often complex interactions between a new industry, an economically deprived population, and an established employer with a vested interest in maintaining the status quo. In 1969 the Badische Analin and Soda Fabrik Company (BASF), which already had operations in New Jersey and Michigan, announced its intention to locate a $100 million petrochemical plant in Beaufort County, South Carolina. The company had chosen the site because it offered eighteen hundred acres of land (much of it state-owned), as well as the five million gallons of fresh water the plant would use each day. The area also offered railroad and coastal access, a free trade zone, and a large supply of labor.[28]

State developers were delighted by the BASF announcement for several reasons. First, the impoverished coastal area had been widely publicized in recent United States Senate hearings on poverty and hunger. Second, the state owned land in the area, which it had been anxious to sell to an incoming industry for some time. Finally, the BASF plant would help the State Development Board keep alive its record of bringing over $500 million worth of industry into the state each year. Anxious to please BASF executives, state development officials promised to construct both a thirteen-mile railroad spur and a strip of four-lane highway to the plant

27. *Ibid.*

28. Oliver G. Wood, Jr., *et al.*, *The BASF Controversy: Employment vs. Environment*, Bureau of Business and Economic Research, University of South Carolina, Essays in Economics Series, No. 25 (Columbia: University of South Carolina Press, 1971), 1–2.

site. Dredging of the Colleton River and construction of a new docking facility were part of the package, as was a five-year exemption from state corporate income taxes. The company later promised to build a second plant in the area, provided it could be given a free trade exemption allowing it to import forty thousand barrels of naphtha a day.[29]

The first objection to the proposed facility came from the developers of the nearby Hilton Head Island resort who charged that the plant would pollute the environment and devastate the local fishing and recreation industries. The resort's backers discussed the possibility of using the proposed site as a recreational facility and promised to help recruit lighter industry for the area if BASF plans were not carried out. Hilton Head developers and residents also charged that the plant was being allowed too large an exemption from state and local taxes and that the company's proposed pollution control budget was inadequate.[30]

Supporters of the project countered with evidence of its potential benefits, including a United States Chamber of Commerce forecast that "the influx of 1,000 employees in Beaufort will result in a population increase of 3,590; more than $4,000 more in personal [per capita] income; 30 more retail establishments; 1,000 more households; 970 more passenger car registrations; $3,310,000 more retail sales per year; 910 more school children; $2,290,000 more in bank deposits; and 650 more jobs over and above what the plant will employ."[31]

A study that showed neighboring North Carolina's chemical workers earning $146 per week as compared to $72 per week for textile employees came into play, for the BASF facility would provide better-paying jobs in a state where 50 percent of all manufacturing employment was in textiles. The State Development Board commissioned an economic study that showed the Beaufort area with fifty-eight thousand jobs in 1980 if the plant were constructed and only thirty-six thousand if it were not. Local residents presented a "welcome" petition containing nearly seventy-five hundred signatures to BASF, leading a local pharmacist to observe, "I would say 80 percent of the people in Beaufort County are in favor of BASF—Those who aren't rich." NAACP spokesmen supported the construction of the plant because the area's underemployed black population was especially impoverished. Black leaders pointed out that the con-

29. *Ibid.*, 2, 8–9.
30. *Ibid.*, 9–11.
31. *Ibid.*, 8–9.

tinued domination of the local economy by the resort industry would only condemn blacks to "jobs as maids, janitors and servants for the wealthy with no hope of upgrading themselves in the future." Meanwhile, the editor of a Columbia newspaper felt certain that "the image of South Carolina in industrial circles was not enhanced" by the controversy.[32]

Despite strong support from state officials and the local populace, in January, 1971, BASF finally announced it would not locate in the Beaufort area. The Hilton Head developers had succeeded in protecting their interests, and shortly thereafter they concluded that the recreational facility they had considered building on the site might prove noisy and otherwise annoying to resort residents and guests. Having thus preserved the "natural beauty" of the coastal region, the resort promoters had also helped to maintain a surplus of cheap labor to serve as maids, janitors, and greenskeepers. In a purely material sense, the underemployed labor force of the Beaufort area had suffered the greatest loss. The proposed BASF facility's economic impact would have more than compensated for the loss of low-paying jobs in the recreation and fishing industries. On the other hand, no price tag could be attached to what the plant might have done to the environment, although, in fact, surprisingly little was ever known about the facility's actual pollution potential. The State Development Board had pushed the project, the State Pollution Control Authority had provided little guidance, and the opposition had capitalized on prevailing sensitivity to environmental issues by prophesying ecological disaster.[33]

The cases of Georgetown Steel and BASF suggested one of the less-publicized reasons for the South's success in attracting foreign industry. Highly developed nations like West Germany and Japan were beginning to export their heavy, polluting industries. As the Japanese consul general in Atlanta candidly noted, "Older industries, like textiles are being phased out in Japan and exported to other countries. . . . We will put these high-pollution industries where there is space and water enough to handle them . . . like here in the South."[34] Thus, foreign investors appreciated not only the South's cheap labor and low taxes but also its apparent ability to absorb industries that produced large amounts of wastes and contaminants.

32. *Ibid.*, 15, 17, 19–20.
33. *Ibid.*, 21, 62–69.
34. Adcock, "International Status," 36.

As they tried to balance economic needs against their obligations to state pollution control statutes, southern development leaders found their tasks complicated by the expanded federal role in environmental protection. In spite of the South's impressive gains during the postwar period, there remained in the 1970s sparsely populated rural areas where industrial activity was at a minimum. Pollution hardly seemed a problem in such locales where citizens were considerably more interested in jobs and a better standard of living than in the pristine quality of air and water, which they took for granted. Developers from unpolluted areas probably felt that stiffened national pollution regulations would have little effect on their efforts until 1972 when the Supreme Court handed down its decision in the case of *Sierra Club* v. *Ruckelshaus*. This opinion simply left standing a ruling of the Circuit Court of Appeals of the District of Columbia that the intent of the Clean Air Act of 1970 was to prevent significant deterioration in the quality of clean air even in locations where pollution levels were far below federal maximums.[35] Development leaders from less-industrialized areas had hoped that their states and communities would be able to bring in new industry until pollution levels approached national limits, but the *Sierra Club* decision seemed to shackle them with a no-growth policy.

In 1976 the debate over enforcement of federal pollution laws took on more sectional overtones when the Environmental Protection Agency announced its "swap-off" provision which allowed areas not yet in compliance with the Clean Air Act of 1970 to bring in new industry so long as existing air quality did not deteriorate as a result. In effect, this policy allowed new pollution if it would be offset by improvements in the existing level of air quality. This might be accomplished by better emissions control in established plants or by the purchase of an outdated facility that could then be shut down, thereby removing a source of pollutants that would soon be replaced by the incoming plant.[36] The swap-off provision held out certain advantages for an already industrialized area. Instead of halting growth in order to prevent air quality deterioration, obsolete plants could be exchanged for new ones. On the other hand, underdeveloped areas were now less likely to receive the overflow benefits from environmental restrictions on growth in the Manufacturing Belt.

Development aspirations of less-industrialized areas faced another challenge in 1976 in the form of proposed amendments to the Clean Air

35. *Congressional Record*, 95th Cong., 1st Sess., Vol. 123, pp. 9,421–422.
36. New York *Times*, November 11, 1976, pp. 1, 24.

Act of 1970 that would have tightened regulations by implementing the *Sierra Club* decision to prevent "significant deterioration" of air quality in localities where the air was cleaner than required by federal law. The amendments also sought to maintain the unspoiled nature of national parks and protected streams by placing strict limits on the levels of new emissions allowed within specified distances of either. Both these provisions, of course, were likely to have the greatest impact in relatively unindustrialized portions of the South and West.[37]

Representatives of the areas whose future development seemed most threatened by the proposed amendments led the opposition in 1976. Joining western senators, a Dixie contingent argued that the new measures would create a federal land-use policy and thereby severely curtail state and local decision-making prerogatives. Senator Jesse Helms of North Carolina charged that if the amendments passed, "federal bureaucrats will be able to exercise control over every locality and region in the country, determining what areas will grow economically and those which will not grow, regardless of the needs of the people who live in the area." Helms quoted a number of southern political and business leaders who opposed the concept of "no significant deterioration." Conservative textile industrialist Roger Milliken made a similar point when he charged that the proposed amendments could "seriously impair the continued orderly development of our less populated areas." Senator James Allen of Alabama claimed that a number of his constituents had urged him to oppose the amendments.[38]

One of the most outspoken critics of the proposed Clean Air Act amendments was Georgia Governor George Busbee, who saw an ulterior motive behind the "no significant deterioration" provisions: "The northern states see what's happening in the South. We're getting our fair share of new industry and new jobs and they're doing everything in their power to set up trade barriers." According to Busbee's scenario, jealous northern representatives were "trying to do their dirty work behind the white knight cloak of environmental protection." In reality, the Georgia governor asserted, the controversy over the amendments was "nothing but a replay of the old discriminatory freight rate battle in a new format."[39]

37. *Ibid.*, August 5, 1977, p. 9; *Congressional Record*, 95th Cong., 1st Sess., Vol. 123, p. 1.654.

38. *Congressional Record*, 94th Cong., 2nd Sess., Vol. 122, pp. 13,148–150, 13,157–160.

39. Atlanta *Constitution*, November 20, 1975, p. 7C.

Other growth-conscious southern leaders echoed Busbee's criticisms, though with less emphasis on conspiracy. Governor Cliff Finch of Mississippi charged that the amendments would "virtually halt economic development in our state." Arkansas's Governor David Pryor, the Arkansas Industrial Development Commission, and even the state's leading pollution control official went on record as opposed to the amendments. Development leaders in North Carolina also protested the amendments on the grounds that they would complicate efforts to industrialize economically depressed rural areas while encouraging further industrialization in areas where there was already a pollution problem.[40]

Senator William L. Scott of Virginia, who proposed to delete the "no significant deterioration" provisions from the amendments, produced a stack of editorials from his state's newspapers, all of them supporting Scott's position. Scott's proposal was defeated, but it received the votes of seventeen senators, all of them from states south of the Mason-Dixon Line or west of the Mississippi River. The 1976 attempt to attach the "no significant deterioration" stipulation to the Clean Air Act failed in the Senate because of a filibuster not, ironically, by southern representatives, but by Senators Jake Garn and Orrin Hatch of Utah, who saw the amendments as a threat to the economic development of a state that had plenty of clean air and national park acreage but also needed jobs.[41]

The amendments finally passed in 1977 after Garn and Hatch agreed not to filibuster, but only after Scott had again offered an unsuccessful substitute amendment that reflected the fears of some southern and western spokesmen that certain underdeveloped rural areas in their states would be penalized by the new, stricter air quality requirements. Along with his colleagues, including James Eastland of Mississippi, Jesse Helms of North Carolina, and Strom Thurmond of South Carolina, Scott proposed to allow state and local governments to set pollution standards in areas where air was cleaner than federal law required. Returning to a familiar theme among southern politicians, Scott stressed states' rights, arguing that residents of a locality should have the option to accept or reject new industry "rather than have the decision made for them by an unelected federal official in Washington." Although Scott claimed to be

40. *Congressional Record*, 94th Cong., 2nd Sess., Vol. 122, p. 13,159; Arkansas *Gazette*, January 4, 1976, p. 3E, April 29, 1976, p. 9A; Raleigh *News and Observer*, September 23, 1976, Sec. I, p. 5.

41. *Congressional Record*, 94th Cong., 2nd Sess., Vol. 122, pp. 13,163–168, 13,185; New York *Times*, October 2, 1976, p. 7.

defending a political principle, when pressed, he referred to the economic considerations behind his suggestion: "I am thinking about an area such as we have in King and Queen County, Virginia, an area where the principal industry, I believe, is tree farming. I suppose there must be thousands of counties throughout our country where they have no major industry. Suppose the people of these areas would want to construct a factory which would have a degree of pollution. Yet the factory if established, would not interfere with maintaining federal standards. Should not the people of the locality be permitted to determine whether or not they want a factory?" Scott's amendment again received only seventeen votes, all from representatives of southern or western states.[42]

As passed, the Clean Air Act Amendments of 1977 incorporated provisions to prevent significant deterioration even in areas where air quality was acceptable. The revised act also included the swap-off alternative although the necessity of meeting federal standards by the end of 1982 seemed to indicate that new industries could be introduced only after trade-offs that eliminated more old pollution than was being introduced by the new facility. Thus, after obsolete or unprofitable operations had been bought out or reduced in scale, heavily industrialized areas also seemed to face a future without growth. On the other hand, the prohibition of significant deterioration might also discourage companies from opening new plants if continued operation of their older facilities were at all feasible. Such a development would obviously be a blow to hopes for continued industrial growth in the South.[43]

Southern charges that the new environmental restrictions were part of a conspiracy against their promotion efforts were largely exaggerations. The significance of these new provisions was not lost, however, on northern observers who were concerned that the South was industrializing at their region's expense. A New York *Times* editorial noted that the revised Clean Air Act "would have a major impact on the rural South; much of the region's industrial growth has been going on miles from the nearest towns to take advantage of relatively cheap land and labor." Praising the new law for serving the national interest, the writer added, "And

42. *Congressional Record*, 95th Cong., 1st Sess., Vol. 123, pp. 9,421–428 (quotation from 9,423).
43. New York *Times*, August 5, 1977, p. 9; Carlton B. Scott, "Clean Air Act Amendments Loom as Threat to Industrial Expansion," *Industrial Development*, CXLVII (July/August, 1978), 9–12; "Clean Air Act Amendments of 1977," typescript in possession of Southern Growth Policies Board, Research Triangle Park, North Carolina.

we can't complain if what's good for the nation is also good for the North." [44]

It appeared to many that the costs of compliance with federal pollution control statutes might also slow the pace of southern industrial development. Escalating emissions restrictions put the price tag for industrial pollution control in 1974 alone at $6.5 billion. Southern promoters had been successful in attracting new facilities to their states, but would industries continue to expand so rapidly with the pollution control costs so high and threatening to go higher? In the long run, the southern states dealt with industrial pollution control expenses in much the same way that they had responded to the problem of enticing new industries in the years before protecting the environment was a prominent concern. They began a series of subsidies and incentives designed to offset the costs and inconvenience of emission control. By 1971 Alabama, Georgia, Florida, North Carolina, and Tennessee offered state *ad valorem* tax exemptions on all pollution abatement facilities. In addition to *ad valorem* exemptions, Georgia and North Carolina permitted "fast write-offs" by allowing corporations to deduct from their taxable incomes a significant portion of the cost of new pollution control equipment. Industries requesting such concessions were required to secure permits from state air and water quality boards. [45]

As a supplement to the tax breaks on pollution control equipment the southern states turned to an old friend, the industrial revenue bond. The use of such bonds for construction of large plants had been curtailed significantly in 1968, but Congress had specifically excluded air and water pollution control facilities when it confined tax-exempt status to industrial issues of $1 million or less. As a result, bonds to finance pollution control equipment fit nicely into plans to make protecting the environment as painless as possible for new industries. By 1971 Florida and Georgia had already authorized the use of revenue bonds to support pollution abatement projects, and the practice spread rapidly across the South and the nation as a whole. By 1978 only Washington lacked a provision for pollution control funding through the use of industrial revenue issues. [46]

44. New York *Times*, August 20, 1977, p. 20.
45. John E. Petersen, *The Tax-Exempt Pollution Control Bond* (Chicago: Municipal Finance Officers Association, 1975), 3.
46. Liston, "The Southeast," 11; "The Fifty Legislative Climates," *Industrial Development*, CXLVII (January/February, 1978), 7.

The exclusion clause in the 1968 congressional amendment limiting the general use of such bonds provided a major loophole through which by 1975 the states were squeezing about $2 billion in pollution control issues annually. Savannah floated $32.5 million worth of bonds to help American Cyanamid and Union Camp clean up their emissions. Other well-known firms like Amoco, Monsanto, DuPont, and United States Steel also accepted subsidies to help them keep down the costs of pollution control. In 1974 Exxon, the largest domestic oil company, sold $100 million worth of bonds to finance pollution abatement improvements at its Baton Rouge, Louisiana, refinery. Because the 5.9 percent interest paid by these bonds was 2 percent below the prevailing rate on nonexempt securities the company expected to enjoy a $50 million saving over the twenty-two-year life of the securities.[47]

Cumulative sales of industrial revenue bonds had totalled only $1.6 billion when congressional restrictions were imposed in 1968, but analysts warned that yearly expenditures for emission control equipment could climb as high as $15 billion by the end of the 1970s. Thus, pollution control bonds posed the same problem that escalating industrial development issues had raised: they drove up interest rates on other tax-free securities and hence increased the cost of other municipally financed projects. Moreover, tax losses due to revenue bond issues in 1973 totalled approximately $66 million. Experts warned of a "bond explosion" that could push these losses as high as $1.5 billion by 1980.[48]

Skyrocketing expenditures for emission control suggested that environmental pollution was one of the most serious concerns of the 1970s, but it was difficult to determine how deeply most southerners felt about the issue, especially if clean air and water could be preserved only at the expense of new payrolls. A 1971 survey of South Carolinians' opinions concerning environmental protection and industrial development yielded confusing results. Approximately 28 percent of the respondents admitted that they considered air pollution a "very serious" problem within the state, and 31 percent conceded that it was at least a "somewhat serious" concern. Yet, only 11 percent thought dirty air a crucial problem for their own communities. Anxiety about water pollution followed a similar pat-

47. Petersen, *The Tax-Exempt Pollution Control Bond*, 1; *Wall Street Journal*, July 8, 1974, p. 24, February 27, 1975, p. 20, April 23, 1976, p. 22.
48. Petersen, *The Tax-Exempt Pollution Control Bond*, 1–2.

tern although 66 percent of those polled felt water quality was more of a concern than it had been ten years before.[49]

Only 8 percent of the sample felt that the state was doing an excellent job in controlling pollution, whereas 36 percent charged that the state was enjoying poor or only fair results in its efforts. Blacks were less concerned about the environment than the need for more jobs, but overall, nearly three-fourths of the South Carolinians questioned agreed that state government should exert tighter controls over the type of industry it recruited and the sites where this industry would be located.[50]

Such responses provided a strong suggestion that, even in a relatively less developed state like South Carolina, citizens saw the need to protect their environment from industrial contamination. It was at this point that the results of the survey became particularly confusing, however, because those who participated also overwhelmingly supported continued recruitment of all sorts of industries. Sixty-six percent urged further efforts to attract heavy manufacturing plants, including chemical operations whose heavy use of water made them potential polluters. A surprisingly large number also favored bringing in more nuclear and petroleum-related industries. Despite the fact that nearly three-fourths of the respondents called for tighter control of industrial location, nearly 60 percent could think of no areas from which industry should be banned. An overwhelming 89 percent of those polled urged that industrial recruitment continue, and despite the significant doubts about contemporary pollution control efforts, nearly three-fourths insisted it was possible to have the population and the economy expand at their present rates without sacrificing pleasant living conditions within the state.[51]

J. Bonner Manly, the director of the State Development Board, explained the survey results with the observation that South Carolinians "are not concerned about the preservation of the environment of the state at the exclusion of industrial development because, for the most part, past growth has not entailed the horrors of big city life."[52] Manly's simple explanation notwithstanding, to the extent they seemed to be calling for more environmental safeguards at the same time as they were demand-

49. Louis Harris and Associates, "Priorities for Progress," 132, 136, 139.
50. *Ibid.*, 31, 145, 152.
51. *Ibid.*, 33, 35, 124, 171, 176.
52. "The Fifty Legislative Climates," *Industrial Development*, CXLI (November/December, 1972), 14.

ing continued industrial growth, South Carolinians wanted the best of both worlds. While it is possible that the survey participants were calling for a new and more sophisticated approach to industrial development that would avoid environmental deterioration, it is also possible and altogether probable that a great number of them simply failed to see the potentially conflicting nature of their desire to protect the environment and their even stronger support for continued industrial expansion.

The dangers of a headlong and perhaps shortsighted pursuit of industry came home to many South Carolinians at the end of the 1970s. South Carolina had begun its courtship of nuclear plants by attracting the Du-Pont Corporation's Savannah River atomic weapons facility to Barnwell in 1951. The Savannah River Plant employed eight thousand people by the end of the 1970s and had stimulated dramatic population growth in the surrounding area. The importance of cheap, plentiful electric power in attracting new industries led the state's two major utilities, Duke Power and Carolina Power and Light, to construct nuclear generating plants. By 1979 nearly 50 percent of South Carolina's electric power came from nuclear sources as compared to a 10 percent average nationwide. Meanwhile, Westinghouse had constructed the world's largest uranium fuel fabrication plant in Columbia and Chem-Nuclear Systems had established a facility for low-level radioactive waste storage.[53]

Hoping to build on an already sizable nuclear base, state and local developers had jumped at the chance to land a $70 million Allied General Nuclear Services fuel recovery plant, which was to be located near the DuPont facility at Barnwell. South Carolina lawmakers held joint legislative hearings on the matter in 1971 and 1972, hearings that environmentalists charged were stacked in favor of the company and supporters of the project. A critical observer also pointed out that at the time Allied General was seeking approval to locate at Barnwell, two of the members of the State Development Board were former nuclear industry employees.[54]

As the state legislature's Nuclear Study Committee considered the impact of the proposed facility, Governor John C. West received word that several scientists at state universities had been pressured to withhold their objections to the nuclear operation. An attorney charged that one of

53. Suzanne Rhodes, "Barnwell: Achilles Heel of Nuclear Power," *Southern Exposure*, VII (Winter, 1979), 45–46; New York *Times*, April 1, 1979, p. 30.
54. Rhodes, "Barnwell," 45.

the opponents of the Barnwell facility received a phone call threatening him with the loss of his faculty position at one of the state's colleges. The attorney also provided Governor West with a letter from famed chemist Linus Pauling warning that it would be impossible to make the Barnwell plant "safe for local residents or for other people in the world." [55]

Despite the undercurrent of opposition, South Carolina accepted the reprocessing facility, only to have it fail to be licensed because of President Jimmy Carter's 1977 moratorium on nuclear reprocessing. By 1979 Allied had succeeded in interesting the Department of Energy in the purchase of the plant as a storage facility for spent reactor fuel rods, but new opposition to this plan arose with the revelation that the plant had been constructed over an earthquake-susceptible geologic fault and an underground stream that was part of the area's water supply. [56]

Two valve blowouts occurred at South Carolina's Oconee County nuclear power facility in 1973, and in 1977 a mechanical failure and human error at the same plant led to the dumping of radioactive water from the plant into Lake Hartwell, a huge reservoir with significant shoreline in both Georgia and South Carolina. Accidents such as these increased public consciousness of the dangers of further expansion of the nuclear industry in the state, but the crowning blow came with the potentially disastrous accident in March, 1979, at Three Mile Island near Harrisburg, Pennsylvania. Newly inaugurated Governor Richard Riley responded to the Pennsylvania scare by curtailing waste shipments into his state, and his press secretary lamented former governor James Edwards' attitude about the nuclear industry, which he described as "keep bringing this waste in here, it's gold, let's get all of it we can!" As South Carolinians pondered the events at Three Mile Island, *The China Syndrome*, a film that dramatized the danger of a serious accident at a nuclear plant, clearly caused even more reflection on the willingness of former state officials to accept any and all nuclear operations with few questions asked. [57]

South Carolina was not the only southern state whose residents became concerned about nuclear pollution. A 1976 Environmental Protection Agency study of a low-level waste dump near Morehead, Kentucky,

55. Townshend M. Belser to John C. West, August 12, 1971, Linus Pauling to [?], June 21, 1971, both in West Correspondence.

56. Rhodes, "Barnwell," 47.

57. New York *Times*, April 1, 1979, p. 30.

found that significant amounts of plutonium had escaped in less than 10 years from a facility designed to contain it for 250,000 years. An alarmed state government finally purchased the storage area and closed it at a cost to the taxpayers of $1.25 million.[58]

At the end of the 1960s residents of the Athens, Alabama, area had accepted TVA assurances that the nuclear power plant being built at nearby Brown's Ferry would be safe. Said one resident: "Everybody figured the plant meant more jobs and industry. You were snubbed if you said anything against it." By 1978, however, the facility had been the scene of numerous mishaps, some so bizarre as to be comical had they not also been potentially serious to community health and welfare. Not only were there several problems related to inadequate structural support but in October, 1973, fourteen hundred gallons of radioactive waste spilled into the Tennessee River, and in August, 1975, radioactive cobalt 60 leaked from the plant and became part of a rain cloud that promptly dumped it on Athens, briefly raising radiation levels to greater than five times the normal reading. Earlier in 1975 a fire that took six hours to extinguish had burned through enough control cables to raise the possibility of a loss of coolant, and a "melt-down" that could have spread radioactive materials over a large part of the surrounding area. Finally, in December, 1977, a workman's overshoe fell into the water surrounding a reactor core and threatened to block the flow of coolant around the fuel rods. Enough local residents became concerned about the dangers the plant posed that the local civil defense director formulated an evacuation plan to deal with any serious threat to the public safety.[59]

Although the poor reputation of TVA's Brown's Ferry operation seemed to indicate increased concern about the nuclear industry in the South, residents of Soddy, Tennessee, embraced their local TVA facility with open arms. Despite extensive coverage of the Three Mile Island scare, the plant was constructed without significant protests even from residents of Chattanooga, which was only fourteen miles away. The fact that Soddy built two new public schools within a mile of the plant indicated that a TVA official was correct in describing the area as "nuclear country." An observer remarked, "East Tennesseeans believe nuclear power will be to them what oil is to Houston."[60]

58. William Reynolds, "The South: Global Dumping Ground," *Southern Exposure*, VII (Winter, 1979), 51.

59. *Wall Street Journal*, April 18, 1978, pp. 1, 34.

60. New York *Times*, May 17, 1979, pp. 1, 12.

The controversy surrounding the nuclear industry in the South at the end of the 1970s exemplified the problems faced by southern industrial developers in the age of environmental protection. The old emphasis on untrammeled use of the South's natural resources and raw materials had been expanded to include assurances of low-cost electric power. Influential utility companies had invested heavily in nuclear plants, which they promised would reap a harvest of new and expanded industry. It was also abundantly clear to developers in the 1970s that the South's favorable business climate was a key factor in its recent economic achievements. Thus, too dramatic a response to citizen concerns about nuclear industries threatened to tarnish a proindustry reputation built on cooperation and assistance, rather than regulation. On the other hand, the Sunbelt South's economic backbone was its newfound ability to attract and retain productive workers and consumers, many of whom chose to reside in the South because of the opportunity to live in an area unspoiled by congestion and pollution. The danger of nuclear catastrophe, however remote, was clearly a threat to the image of relaxed, uncomplicated living that had been such a boon to recent development efforts.

The environmental pressures of the late sixties and early seventies confronted southern state governments with the difficult responsibility of regulating industry while preserving their traditional roles as agents of industrial expansion. Stern public pronouncements and stiffened regulations made it clear by the end of the 1970s that polluting industries were not as welcome in the South as they once had been, but southern developers still managed to convey the impression that their state governments continued to place a higher priority on growth than environmental protection. A Georgia advertisement informed European readers in 1979, "Government should strive to improve business conditions, not hinder them. So Georgia has streamlined its operations for greater efficiency. That's why we can preserve our natural resources, yet still be responsive to private enterprise. Our one-stop environmental permitting service issues all required state and federal EPA permits."[61]

---

61. *Economist*, CCLXX (March 17–23, 1979), Survey 3.

Chapter 10

A NEW SOUTH WITH OLD PROBLEMS

The problem of maintaining a reputation for cooperating with industry without sacrificing a relatively uncontaminated natural environment was but one of the dilemmas facing southern developers at the beginning of the 1980s. The growth of the sixties and seventies had been based on population expansion and an attractive business climate nurtured by continued reliance on traditional development policies. Forced to weigh the benefits of these policies against their restrictive tendencies, southern leaders found themselves confronting the question of how cheap labor, low taxes, and minimal constraints on growth could be rationalized in the face of expectations of rapid improvement in the general standard of living, expanded public services, social stability, and all the other factors that influence the quality of life in any region.

The most obvious example of the persistence of the New South development tradition was the emphasis on low-wage, nonunion labor that continued to characterize industry-seeking efforts. As long as southern communities based their appeals to new industries on a surplus of cheap, unorganized workers, chambers of commerce and local development commissions had experienced no difficulty in wooing new plants while shooing away union agents. When the emphasis shifted toward attracting more sophisticated, high-wage operations, however, booster organizations found themselves in a dilemma. Executives of the large, nationally known and better-paying firms that came south to serve a rapidly expanding market sometimes came expecting unionization or at least willing to accept it as the easiest means of avoiding labor trouble in their other plants where work forces were organized. Yet, even in the 1970s the South's economy continued to be dominated by low-wage industries that had relocated with at least a tacit assurance that they would not have to compete for labor with better-paying plants. Thus, many communities maintained a policy of recruiting only nonunion operations. As one observer noted, "The industry hunters want to put high-wage industries in, but their salaries are paid by people who are in low-wage industries and they have to take that into consideration."[1]

Many of North Carolina's local industrial developers were as committed to keeping out unions as to bringing in industry. In 1977 the Person County Economic Development Commission voted to welcome a Brockway Glass Company beer bottle plant to Roxboro only if the work force would not be unionized. Eventually built in Danville, Virginia, the plant would have brought three hundred new jobs, many with a four-dollar-per-hour starting salary, into the Roxboro area. A local banker explained the commission's decision: "A lot of people around here have jobs who wouldn't have them if a strong union came in here and drove those other industries out."[2]

When a Greenville, South Carolina, construction executive learned that the Philip Morris Tobacco Company was preparing to build a local plant that would employ twenty-five hundred well-paid but probably unionized workers, he told one of the city's bankers, "Let's run those bastards off; somebody else will come." A Greenville lawyer agreed: "The industrial climate of South Carolina is based on non-unionization. If Philip Morris were here with unionized workers and families, this would no longer be a non-union community." Perhaps the greatest irony of all lay in the opposition to Philip Morris expressed by the Michelin Tire Corporation, whose appearance on the Piedmont scene in 1974 had caused concern among established employers that the French firm's higher wages, better benefits, and susceptibility to unionization might disrupt the local labor situation.[3]

Communities in the Carolinas had no monopoly on discouraging unionized industries. The Greenville, Mississippi, Industrial Foundation made no attempt to conceal its opposition to unions. The foundation's chairman claimed that he had companies begging to come to his city, but

1. Raleigh *News and Observer*, September 11, 1977, in University of North Carolina Library Clipping File, Chapel Hill.
2. *Wall Street Journal*, February 10, 1978, p. 1.
3. Cliff Sloan and Bob Hall, "It's Good to Be Home in Greenville . . . But It's Better if You Hate Unions," *Southern Exposure*, VII (Spring, 1979), 89.

he suspected that a number of firms never contacted him because they knew that a unionized plant would be unwelcome in Greenville. A Fantus Company executive confirmed that every southern state had a healthy share of Greenvilles: "There are literally scores of companies that have been turned away from southern towns because of their wage rates or their union policies."[4]

There was no clearer evidence of the Sunbelt South's deep-seated antipathy toward organized labor than the successful resistance of the J. P. Stevens Company to the unionization of its employees. The nation's second largest textile producer, by 1976 Stevens employed forty-four thousand workers in eighty-five plants, mostly in the Carolinas. Stevens' salaries were in line with those paid elsewhere in the southern textile industry where wages remained, on the average, about $1.42 per hour below the national norm for manufacturing labor, and the company's retirement benefit payments were considered quite low. One retiring employee of twenty-four years expected a monthly pension of twenty-four dollars, and another remarked: "After 37 years of faithful service, I have a plaque, $1,360 and brown lung."[5]

The Stevens Company had been under steady assault since 1963 by the Textile Workers' Union of America, and when workers at seven Stevens plants at Roanoke Rapids finally voted for TWUA representation in August, 1974, the New York *Times* hailed the union victory as "a major step toward unionization of the largely unorganized and traditionally low-wage textile industry."[6] Not until six years later, however, did the Roanoke Rapids workers actually receive a collective bargaining contract and even then Stevens officials were quick to point out that the agreement provided no benefits not available to employees in the company's nonunion plants.

Stevens resisted unionization by resorting to every type of coercion and harassment within and beyond the law, demonstrating that in the antiunion climate of the South, winning a collective bargaining election was often only the first step for the union. Such a victory elicited an automatic challenge from employers like Stevens. If a representative of the

4. *Wall Street Journal*, February 10, 1978, p. 1.
5. Elton Manzione, "Organizing J. P. Stevens: On-the-Road with the Union," unidentified newspaper clipping in University of North Carolina Library Clipping File, Chapel Hill, p. 5.
6. J. Gary DiNunno, "J. P. Stevens: Anatomy of an Outlaw," AFL-CIO, *American Federationist*, LXXXIII (April, 1976), 1, 4.

National Labor Relations Board upheld the election results, the company asked for a reconsideration, then a hearing before the entire NLRB. Months later, the NLRB would still be considering a motion to hold another election. By stonewalling even after some plants had voted for unionization, the company took the risk that the delay in engaging in collective bargaining would yield a savings in wages, fringe benefits, and expenditures for improved working conditions that would outweigh any fines or penalties that Stevens might be forced to pay. The National Labor Relations Board found J. P. Stevens guilty of fifteen separate labor law violations between 1965 and 1976, forcing the firm to award $1.3 million in damages to workers whose legal rights had been violated. Company officials paid the price without lengthy protest, secure in the knowledge that the penalty payments could be listed as operating expenses for income tax purposes.[7]

The NLRB charged Stevens with terminating prounion employees, as well as harassing them and denying them overtime. The company apparently shut down a Statesboro, Georgia, operation because its work force voted for a union. Stevens officials were found guilty of wiretapping the phones of organizers, and the company faced accusations of firing a fifty-year employee who refused to try to persuade his union activist son to leave town. Stevens also used racial propaganda to thwart unionization. For example, on April 25, 1973, the company sent its Roanoke Rapids employees an antiunion letter containing a message for blacks that was really an attempt to scare white workers: "A special word to our black employees. It has come repeatedly to our attention that it is among you that the union supporters are making their most intensive drive—that you are being insistently told that the union is the wave of the future for you especially—and that by going into the union in mass, you can dominate it and control it in this plant, and in these Roanoke Rapids plants as you may see fit."[8] With white workers in a three-to-one majority, black control of a union was unlikely, but by raising the specter of Negro domination Stevens had resorted to a time-honored means of thwarting change in the South.

As Stevens stood fast against a torrent of unfavorable national publicity, it received the customary local support accorded union-besieged

7. *Ibid.*, 4.
8. Manzione, "Organizing J. P. Stevens," 1, 5; DiNunno, "J. P. Stevens," 3–8; Henry P. Leifermann, "The Unions Are Coming," *New York Times Magazine*, August 5, 1973, p. 25.

employers in the South, especially from newspapers like the Columbia, South Carolina, *State*, which dismissed the campaign to organize Stevens as "a power play, pure and simple, to get an economic stranglehold on Stevens and ultimately on the southern textile industry." The editor expressed confidence that the "level-headed" textile workers of the Carolinas would reject the union and its "promises of labor's heaven on earth." The Greenville *News Piedmont* referred to a nationwide consumer boycott of J. P. Stevens as "evil . . . deplorable . . . tyrannical" and later warned that, if unionization gained a foothold in Greenville, "individual workers' rights would be trampled in a mindless union." The editors urged Stevens employees not to "fall for the false siren song of union rocks and shoals waiting as sharks to snare unwary travelers."[9]

At the end of the 1970s the South Carolina textile belt's aversion to organized labor was still so deeply rooted that tactics such as those utilized by J. P. Stevens were upheld and explained in classes at state-supported Clemson University. Clemson offered a seminar for textile executives entitled "The Organizing Drive and the Union-Free Environment," which a critical writer suggested might be more candidly dubbed "The ABC's of Union-Busting." The seminar, "tailored especially for employers of the 75 percent of the U. S. work force who, while eligible to join unions, have not done so," was best suited for middle management executives "having the responsibility for maintaining a union-free environment in their companies and organizations." Participants learned of delaying, harassing tactics that might be employed without fear of legal reprisal. Under certain circumstances, instructors urged executives to break the law. A speaker inquired, "Wouldn't you willfully violate the law if you could destroy the union in the process? Of course you would." Other tips included how to mislead employees about the freedoms they would lose by joining the union and how to scare them "legally" with a veiled threat of a plant closing.[10]

Clemson's sponsorship of such a seminar was indicative of the extent to which the school's fortunes were intertwined with those of the Piedmont textile community. University President Robert C. Edwards had

9. "Assault on Textiles," Columbia (S.C.) *State*, June 14, 1976, University of South Carolina Library Clipping File, Columbia; Sloan and Hall, "It's Good to Be Home," 91.

10. John Norton, "Clemson's School for Unionbusters," Columbia (S.C.) *State*, University of South Carolina Library Clipping File, Columbia, 7–8. Greenville's Furman University also offered such a seminar. See Sloan and Hall, "It's Good To Be Home," 92.

Table 16   Nonagricultural Workers Belonging to Unions, 1976

State	Percentage of Nonagricultural Workers Unionized
Alabama	19.0
Arkansas	15.5
Florida	13.1
Georgia	14.2
Kentucky	24.7
Louisiana	16.2
Mississippi	12.0
North Carolina	6.8
Oklahoma	13.5
South Carolina	6.6
Tennessee	18.3
Texas	12.0
Virginia	13.6
United States Average	24.8

SOURCE: U.S. Bureau of the Census, *Statistical Abstract of the United States, 1979* (Washington, D.C.: U.S. Government Printing Office, 1979), 427.

once been affiliated with Deering-Milliken and continued to serve as a director of Dan River Mills. Clemson also offered an extensive textile management program and served as a major supplier of junior executives for local plants.[11]

By the end of the 1970s antiunionism had supplanted racism as the South's most respectable prejudice. Senator Strom Thurmond of South Carolina, a former segregationist, found it easier to cope with black voting than with the threat of unionization. Said one labor leader, "He'll accept blacks now, but you still don't see Strom shaking hands with union people."[12] The outcast status of union supporters in the South became clear when membership statistics were examined. As Table 16 shows, near the end of the seventies the two Carolinas were the least unionized states in the South. Except for Kentucky, where much union member-

11. Sloan and Hall, "It's Good To Be Home," 92.
12. Washington *Post*, April 30, 1978, p. 4-B.

ship was attributable to the presence of the United Mine Workers, no state had as much as 20 percent of its nonagricultural work force enrolled in labor organizations.

From a purely pragmatic standpoint, low levels of unionization were clearly beneficial to development efforts. Many companies still came south to escape or temporarily elude unions. Yet, unfair and sometimes illegal resistance to unionization not only gave management an upper hand in dealing with labor but also helped to depress wages. Ironically, by keeping itself a bastion of hostility to unions, the Sunbelt South invited the continuing assaults of organizers who realized, given the southward shift of growth momentum, that the weakness of unions in Dixie was undermining the position of organized labor in other parts of the nation. It was unlikely that labor organizers would conquer the South in the 1980s, but so long as the region presented itself as such a tempting, if formidable, target, its long-term labor future would remain unsettled.

Persistent antiunionism was not the only vestige of the South's economic past that undercut efforts to raise wage levels in southern industry. The slow growth of earlier decades had left some areas with labor surpluses so large that they were not significantly reduced even by the relatively rapid expansion of the 1970s. For a large number of rural southerners industrial employment still meant a drive of fifty miles or more each day. When Anheuser-Busch announced three hundred openings at its new facility at Williamsburg in the early seventies, twelve thousand Virginians submitted their applications.[13] On the one hand, a seemingly limitless pool of willing workers was a clear advantage as developers tried to sell industrialists on a southern location. On the other, this enduring abundance of labor was a natural influence in favor of depressed wages.

So long as large parts of the South maintained a surplus of underemployed, unskilled labor, promises to recruit "bigger 'n' better" industries were unrealistic and, in many cases, inappropriate. Chronic high unemployment areas were most in need of plants that would create large numbers of jobs. Higher-paying, research-oriented facilities like those located in North Carolina's Research Triangle were likely to import many of their employees and hire relatively few local workers. The Triangle's

13. "The New Rich South: Frontier for Growth," *Business Week*, September 2, 1972, pp. 35–36; John C. Brooks, "Remarks to James Sprunt Institute Forum on the Rural South in Transition," Kenansville, N.C., October 25, 1979 (typescript in possession of the author), 6.

growth encouraged a few firms to move in manufacturing plants to be near their research facilities and fostered spin-off expansion in service industries in the Raleigh area, but its impact was not sufficient to lift the state from its bottom-rung position in manufacturing wages per employee.[14]

Large national firms accounted for nearly 84 percent of the total capital investment by bond-subsidized industries in Alabama between 1952 and 1968, but created only 44 percent of the jobs. On the other hand, the state and locally based companies that contributed less than 8 percent of the capital spending accounted for nearly 43 percent of the employment. These percentages confirmed some surprising facts that were just beginning to be publicized at the end of the 1970s. For example, few developers seemed aware that only approximately 6 percent of the nation's firms employed more than fifty persons and that most new jobs were created by companies employing fewer than twenty. As for "big name" industries, the top one thousand companies on the *Fortune* magazine listing averaged an increase of only seventy-five jobs each between 1970 and 1976. These statistics underscored the difficulty of boosting wage levels in the South by recruiting plants of larger, better-paying firms. Such operations rarely created enough jobs for indigenous workers to have much impact on local pay scales, particularly in high labor-surplus areas with an entrenched cheap-labor tradition. A 1979 report illustrated the overall "drag" effect of a low-wage economy by showing that average wages in North Carolina's better-paying industries actually declined slightly from $256 to $253 between 1962 and 1976.[15]

Though less victimized by conscious discrimination after the Civil Rights Movement, the Sunbelt South's blacks still found it difficult to share in the region's growth. Developers seemed unable to steer industries into impoverished rural areas with high concentrations of blacks, whom employers spurned as poorly trained and union prone. Many blacks left these enduring pockets of poverty for southern cities where opportunities for unskilled workers often failed to meet expectations and where overcrowding and dramatic contrasts in standards of living con-

14. Emil Malizia, "The Earnings of North Carolina Workers," *University of North Carolina Newsletter*, LX (December, 1975), 1–4; Barbara Koeppel, "Something Could Be Finer Than to Be in Carolina," *Progressive*, XL (June, 1976), 20–23.

15. Alabama Business Research Council, *Industrial Development Bond Financing*, 43; *Washington Post*, May 29, 1979, p. 17A; Breckenfield, "Business Loves," 142–43.

tributed to tensions that manifested themselves in rising crime rates, expanding ghettoes, and a white exodus to the suburbs.[16]

Urban development leaders often failed to recognize such problems and occasionally followed policies that exacerbated them. Beaming local boosters credited the Research Triangle for the fact that 60 percent of the workers in Raleigh and Wake County, North Carolina, held white-collar jobs in 1975. Promoters were less pleased, however, with reports appearing in 1974 and 1975 that showed Raleigh with one of the nation's highest interracial income differentials for cities its size. Local blacks objected to the Raleigh Chamber of Commerce's written policy of opposition to unions, ostensibly formulated to protect the area's image of affluence and sophistication from an influx of blue-collar industries. Feelings ran especially high after revelations that local developers had turned a cold shoulder to both Xerox and Miller Brewing Company, possibly sacrificing two thousand well-paying jobs in the process.[17]

Like the cheap labor element of the southern sales pitch, the commitment to low taxes and government frugality seemed to play a significant role in the industrial growth of the post–World War II South. Yet, critics persisted in asking how underfinanced governments could provide the expanded services and facilities needed to accommodate new growth or meet the needs of those who did not share in the region's newfound prosperity. Table 17 summarizes a 1977 Southern Regional Education Board study that demonstrated that the fast-growing Sunbelt South was utilizing only about 79 percent of its taxing potential at the state and local level, a figure only 82.6 percent of the national average. When the South's tax effort was broken down according to type of tax, it was clear that neither property nor individual and corporate income levies were generating enough revenue. On the other hand, despite its high poverty rate, the Sunbelt South overworked the sales tax, which hit the poor especially hard. The SREB statistics revealed that Mississippi, the poorest state in Dixie, was utilizing nearly 165 percent of its sales tax capacity.[18]

16. Breckenfield, "Business Loves," 144; New York *Times*, February 6, 1977, p. 22. Ironically, as whites moved into better-paying jobs, blacks found opportunities in the textile industry. Reese Cleghorn, "The Mill: A Giant Step for the Southern Negro," *New York Times Magazine*, November 9, 1969, p. 34.

17. Steve Berg, "Written Policy Against Unions Unique Here," Raleigh *News and Observer*, November 17, 1975, in University of North Carolina Library Clipping File, Chapel Hill.

18. Kenneth E. Quindry and Niles Schoening, *State and Local Tax Ability and Effort, 1977* (Atlanta: Southern Regional Education Board, 1979), 87.

Table 17 Percentage of Taxing Ability Utilized

Tax	South	Nation	Mid-Atlantic
General Sales	107.60	98.00	90.80
Property	57.52	100.00	117.80
Income—Individual	52.41	82.50	130.00
Income—Corporate	70.33	92.00	122.60
Tax Effort as Percentage of Ability Per $1,000 Personal Income	78.82	95.37	112.64

SOURCE: Quindry and Schoening, *State and Local Tax Ability and Effort*, 86–87, 90–91.

Interregional comparisons clearly demonstrated Dixie's tax advantages, but the correspondingly low level of services posed a problem as the South's economy expanded. New industries required new streets, more water and sewage treatment capability, and better fire protection. A fast-growing population needed all these, plus improved schools, hospitals, and transportation systems.

In spite of a poorer-than-average population, on a per capita basis the Sunbelt South actually received slightly less federal welfare support than the northern states. Lower federal welfare expenditures in the South may have been due to the reluctance of conservative state and local governments to participate in programs that required a financial contribution on their part. Critics pointed out that the South led the North nearly two to one in receipt of federal funds that required no state matching expenditures. Without federal assistance impoverished southerners would have suffered even more because in 1977 southern state and local governments spent only $100.31 per capita (63 percent of the national average) on social welfare, as compared to a northern figure of $186.09 (116 percent of the national average).[19] Many boosters who flashed "I told you so!" grins at the news that black out-migration had been reversed probably failed to grasp the full significance of this phenomenon. Not only was the South now exporting fewer of its undertrained, less-affluent residents but many former southerners who fell into this category were returning.

19. Jusenius and Ledeber, *A Myth*, 34; "Federal Spending," 881–82; Bureau of the Census, *Statistical Abstract of the United States, 1979*, p. 296.

Table 18 Quality of Life Rankings for the Southern States

State	1931	1972	Change in Ranking 1936–1972
Alabama	47	47	0
Arkansas	44	48	−4
Florida	36	34	+2
Georgia	45	44	+1
Kentucky	40	45	−5
Louisiana	41	43	−2
Mississippi	48	50	−2
North Carolina	42	46	−4
Oklahoma	35	39	−4
South Carolina	46	49	−3
Tennessee	43	38	+5
Texas	38	41	−3
Virginia	37	35	−9
Average	41.4	43.5	—

SOURCE: Ben Chieh-Liu, *The Quality of Life in the United States, 1970: Index, Rating, and Statistics* (Kansas City: Midwest Research Institute, 1975), 23.

As spiritually pleasing as black reverse migration was, it was also an added burden on the region's already inadequate social welfare programs, especially those in urban areas that were absorbing a large part of the black influx.

As promoters emphasized cheap labor and low taxes, they neglected to explain that maintaining these advantages for industry helped to perpetuate less than advantageous living conditions for southerners at large. Indicators based on registers of individual well-being, equality, living environment, economic vitality, education, public welfare, and quality of government still showed the South far behind the rest of the nation. A 1972 *Lifestyle Magazine* survey placed Florida, the highest ranking southern state, thirty-fourth in overall quality of life, followed closely by Virginia (thirty-fifth). As Table 18 shows, the remaining southern states dominated the bottom one-third of the listing. Even more telling were the reconstructed rankings from 1931, which, instead of progress, showed an overall deterioration of relative positions among the states of the Sunbelt

South. Similar surveys ranked most southern cities well below those of comparable size in other parts of the nation.[20]

Such statistical comparisons notwithstanding, the South's rapid population growth indicated that, in an era of lowered expectations, many Americans apparently felt that Dixie's pluses outnumbered its minuses. The question for the 1980s and beyond, however, remained that of how long severely strained public services and institutions, as well as significant economic, social, and political inequities, could be squared with the resurrected image of the South as a land of pleasant living.

Even when viewed against the backdrop of a regional experience checkered with contradictions and inconsistencies, the Sunbelt South remained a paradox. Its recent gains and excellent prospects for future growth, as well as many of its most serious deficiencies, were closely related to the policies that had shaped its economic development. Until Paul Gaston noted the status quo orientation of the "New South Creed," the possibility that the pursuit of industrial expansion could have a conservative as well as liberalizing effect was seldom considered by observers who blamed rural, agrarian influences for the South's shortcomings and theorized that only urbanization and industrialization could save the region from itself.[21]

Attempts to determine the relative importance of change and continuity in the South's post-Reconstruction experience have defined continuity largely in terms of the survival of planter influence. Looking in 1941 at late-nineteenth-century efforts to promote industrialization, Wilbur J. Cash argued that "far from representing a deliberate break with the past, the turn to Progress clearly flowed straight out of that past." Convinced that the twentieth-century South had yet to escape the shadow of the plantation, Cash asserted that behind the noise of skyscraper construction in towns like Charlotte and Spartanburg, he could hear "the gallop of Jeb Stuart's Cavalrymen." Ten years later C. Vann Woodward rejected Cash's portrait of a South bent on achieving industrial modernization under the social and political dominance of conservative planters.

20. Ben Chieh-Liu, *Quality of Life Indicators in the U.S. Metropolitan Areas, 1970* (Summary) (Kansas City: Midwest Research Institute, 1975), 10–11, 24–25, 38–39.

21. Paul M. Gaston, *The New South Creed: A Study In Southern Mythmaking* (New York: Alfred A. Knopf, 1970). For arguments stressing the positive impact of urbanization and industrialization, see Yinger and Simpson, "Can Segregation Survive?" and Nicholls, *Southern Tradition*. For a discussion of the tendency to expect too much from urbanization and industrialization, see James C. Cobb, "Urbanization and the Changing South: A Review of Literature," *South Atlantic Urban Studies*, I (1977), 253–66.

Woodward described a post-Reconstruction shift of power away from a weakened planter class to a new group of middle-class industrialists "with little but a nominal connection with the old planter regime." In 1970 Paul Gaston explained that the New South movement's leaders paid homage to a mythical antebellum heritage largely as a means of affirming their regional loyalties and encouraging sectional reconciliation while they worked to transform the South into a society where "whirring cotton mills and crimson blast furnaces were preferred to magnolias and moonlight."[22]

Some recent studies have challenged Woodward and Gaston's interpretations and reaffirmed Cash's by arguing that the South's late-nineteenth-century crusade for industrial growth was heavily influenced by a still-viable planter class. In an examination of Alabama between 1860 and 1885, Jonathan M. Wiener described a coalition of planter and industrial interests that led Alabama down the "Prussian Road," a politically and socially repressive, economically self-restrictive path in industrial development. In his study of late-nineteenth-century North Carolina, Dwight B. Billings, Jr., argued that affluent landholders had demanded that the state's economy conform to a pattern of "conservative modernization" comparable to that which occurred in Germany and Japan. Billings extended his analysis into the twentieth century and noted the success of Tarheel promoters in grafting the textile industry onto the state's "agrarian social structure." Pointing to contemporary North Carolina's high industrialization and low wages and union membership, Billings argued that the old development tradition had yet to be shattered.[23]

If the problems that plagued the Sunbelt South at the end of the 1970s seemed to reinforce the arguments of Billings and Wiener by suggesting considerable continuity between the Old South and the New, the events of the 1980s indicated, paradoxically enough, that the persistent influences of the region's agrarian past were receiving considerable reinforcement from contemporary trends in the world and national

22. Cash, *The Mind of the South*, 183, 225; C. Vann Woodward, *Origins of the New South, 1877–1913* (Baton Rouge: Louisiana State University Press, 1951), 20. See also C. Vann Woodward, *American Counterpoint: Slavery and Racism in the North-South Dialogue* (Boston: Little, Brown, 1971), 261–83; Gaston, *The New South Creed*, 173.

23. Jonathan M. Wiener, *Social Origins of the New South: Alabama, 1860–1885* (Baton Rouge: Louisiana State University Press, 1978), 71–73, 222–27; Dwight B. Billings, Jr., *Planters and the Making of a New South: Class, Politics, and Development in North Carolina, 1865–1900* (Chapel Hill: University of North Carolina Press, 1979), 96–107, 215–32.

economy. The shadows that hung over the Sunbelt at the end of the 1970s and lengthened during the course of the 1980s were those not only of the plantation but of a national economy reeling from the effects of global competition for industrial jobs and new industrial investment.

The relationship between the South's economic problems and the ones besetting the nation at large was nowhere better illustrated than in the manufacturing sector. By the 1980s, forty-eight of the fifty counties with the highest percentage of the work force employed in manufacturing nationwide were located in the South. In an era of industrial contraction and outmigration, however, the distinction of becoming the nation's new manufacturing belt was a dubious one indeed. For example, the South's saturation with textile and apparel industries proved especially disadvantageous as the 1970s drew to a close amid reports of plant closings and heavy job losses in these industries. The Jonathan Logan operation at Spartanburg, South Carolina, had boasted 2,500 employees in 1978, but the company had shut down these facilities entirely by 1985. Between 1979 and 1985, 300,000 textile jobs vanished in the Piedmont textile belt alone.[24]

The downside of the South's overall dependence on traditional manufacturing industries became all too apparent during the 1980s. Although Florida registered a 24 percent increase in manufacturing production workers between 1977 and 1989, job losses in other states held net regional growth in this category to only 1.3 percent. Because more than three-fourths of the jobs created in the South during the 1980s were in services and in wholesale and retail trade, young southerners were much less likely to find a high-wage job in a mill than a low-wage one in a mall.[25]

In order to keep these regional figures in perspective, it is important to note that the employment of production workers in manufacturing fell by approximately 10 percent nationwide between 1977 and 1989. Much of this loss could be traced to international competition, which manifested itself in the importation of cheaper foreign goods as well as the exportation of jobs to cheaper overseas labor markets. An Alabama

24. U.S. Bureau of the Census, *County and City Data Book* (Washington, D.C.: U.S. Government Printing Office, 1983), p. lvii; "Textile Industry Faces Struggle for Survival," *Southern Exposure*, XIII (February, 1985), 4; *USA Today,* September 9, 1985.

25. U.S. Bureau of the Census, *Annual Survey of Manufacturers, 1989* (Washington, D.C.: U.S. Government Printing Office, 1991), 3-4–3-9; Knoxville *News-Sentinel*, October 28, 1990.

spokesman complained in 1982 that "industrial jobs are going out the back door faster than we can get them in the front door." After scoffing for years at complaints by New England representatives that their workers were being squeezed by industrial migration to the low-wage, non-union South, southern political leaders showed no hesitation in condemning competition with cheaper labor in foreign countries as "an abuse of the free enterprise system."[26]

Forced to compete with so-called Third-World nations where industrial workers often earned considerably less than a dollar an hour, the South had become, by comparison at least, a high-wage region. By the 1980s, however, the southern states vied for new industrial investment not only with less developed regions but with more economically mature ones as well. A survey of the various industrial development incentives offered by each of the states in 1990 indicates that, while the South's reputation for hospitality to industry is still well deserved, the business climate has also grown much warmer elsewhere in the nation. Reeling from large-scale job losses and industrial outmigration, the northern states turned readily to many of the enticements and giveaways their political representatives had once deplored when they saw them only in the industrial recruitment arsenals of southern states. Illinois, for example, embraced accelerated depreciation write-offs for new industries, and the city of Indianapolis offered nearly $300 million in subsidies to a United Airlines maintenance facility while McDonnell Douglas sought massive financial aid and other forms of assistance from the nine cities locked in a bidding war for its aircraft construction plant. When General Motors announced a week before Christmas 1991 that it would close as many as twenty-one plants nationwide in the next few years but refused to reveal which plants would be shut down, the company's actions recalled countless examples of footloose plant managers trying to squeeze more tax and wage concessions from desperate southern communities by playing them off against each other.[27]

With interregional competition for industry becoming so heated, big-

26. *Annual Survey of Manufacturers*, 1989, pp. 3–4, 3–9; "When the Bubble Burst in Alabama," *U.S. News and World Report*, April 19, 1982, 104; "Textile Industry Faces Struggle," 4.

27. See "Chart 1: Financial Assistance for Industry," "Chart 2: Tax Incentives for Industry," "Chart 3: Special Services for Industrial Development," "Chart 4: State Incentives for Pollution Control, Other Laws," *Site Selection*, XXXV (October, 1990), 1087, 1092, 1097; New York *Times*, December 18, 19, 1991.

ticket subsidies remained the order of the day throughout the South, especially when large, modern, highly sought-after plants were involved. Toyota's 1985 decision to open an assembly plant in Georgetown, Kentucky, was tied to an incentive package including site, site preparation, highway construction, worker training, and tax concessions estimated in the $350-to-400 million range. Tennessee governor Lamar Alexander was exultant when General Motors announced its decision to locate its state-of-the-art Saturn assembly plant at Spring Hill, near Nashville. Alexander credited General Motors's decision to his state's favorable business climate and bragged that, while New York had wooed the company with a $1.2-billion incentive package, Tennessee "didn't offer a penny." In reality, however, the inducements dangled before General Motors ran into hundreds of millions of dollars. As a result of these concessions, tax losses to Maury County, where the plant was constructed, were put at $57 million for the first decade alone. Other incentives included an estimated $50 million in road construction and $20 million more in worker training. State and local officials predicted a huge payoff in new jobs, but Saturn officials announced that, through a special agreement with the United Auto Workers, the majority of the jobs initially slated for the plant would be offered to UAW members who had been laid off at other General Motors plants around the nation. Boosters insisted that, no matter who filled them, the 6,000 jobs created by Saturn would provide enormous economic benefits. Those who had worked to bring the plant to Tennessee argued that the investment in attracting Saturn would surely pay off over the long haul. Some Spring Hill–area residents, beset by rising taxes and disturbed by a dramatic change in the local lifestyle, were not so sure. Other, more detached observers also pointed out that General Motors's decision to build the plant in Tennessee probably had less to do with the state's generous incentives than with the fact that the location put the plant within approximately 500 miles of 75 percent of the domestic auto market.[28]

The subsidies offered by the southern states merely reflected the enthusiasm—or, in some cases, desperation—with which state and local political and economic leaders continued to pursue new industrial operations. When Alabama governor Guy Hunt announced that American Lei-

28. Atlanta *Journal and Constitution,* October 5, 1986; Carter Garber et al., "Greasing GM's Wheels," *Southern Exposure,* XIV (September/October and November/December, 1986), 45–47.

sure Designs would open a factory in Greenville, he linked the announcement to the spirit of the Declaration of Independence: "America was
founded more than 200 years ago on the principles of freedom and the
right of individuals to pursue personal success. . . . It is fitting, therefore,
that today . . . we gather here in Alabama to announce the birth of a new
business which will give economic freedom to more of our people." Con-
ceding that, despite the fanfare, the plant would employ only eight
people, Hunt responded that "eight jobs may not sound very important,
but it could mean the world to those eight people who are going to start
earning paychecks and providing for their families." Hunt's exuberance
affirmed Earl and Merle Black's observation that "the southern business
creed which has reminded more than one observer of a new 'McKinley
era' exerts a compelling popular appeal extending far beyond its direct
and most obvious beneficiaries."[29]

Liberal social scientists had long looked to the day when the South
would at last boast a bonafide white-collar middle class of sufficient size
and influence to provide responsible progressive political leadership. A
majority of southern workers held white-collar jobs by 1980, but instead
of being committed social reformers, this new bourgeoisie more closely
resembled what Earl and Merle Black called "entrepreneurial individualists." As the Blacks wrote:

> The reigning political philosophy of the new southern middle class is the
> entrepreneurial version of the individualistic political culture, a blend of con-
> servative and progressive themes. In its emphasis on low rates of taxation,
> minimal regulation of business, and resolute opposition to unions and redis-
> tributive welfare programs for have-nots and have-littles, the current political
> ideology retains important continuities with the traditionalistic political cul-
> ture. Its progressive element consists in its willingness to use governmental
> resources to construct the public infrastructure—highways, airports, har-
> bors, colleges and universities, research parks and health complexes—that in
> turn stimulates and makes possible additional economic growth.[30]

This narrow, growth-oriented progressive inclination had definite limits, however. Many development advocates had long maintained that the
South's hopes for long-term economic expansion were dependent on significant improvement in the quality of its educational system. Yet no

29. Tuscaloosa *News,* June 8, 1988; Earl and Merle Black, *Politics and Society in the
South* (Cambridge, Mass.: Harvard University Press, 1987), 297.
30. Earl and Merle Black, *Politics and Society,* 296–97.

matter how vocal their advocacy of education reform, they often re-mained equally adamant in their insistence on maintaining the low levels of taxation that were deemed essential to maintaining a good business climate. When Mississippi governor William Winter introduced an edu-cational reform package in 1981, he grounded his appeal for the program in the widespread belief that Mississippi's only hope for economic im-provement lay in making dramatic progress in education. Citing this per-ception, Winter sought to fund his program through increased severance taxes on petroleum and natural gas. Opponents of this tax turned the tables on Winter, however, contending that higher taxes would stifle Mis-sissippi's efforts to recruit new industry. When the legislature finally en-acted a watered-down version of Winter's plan, it turned to the state's already overworked and notoriously unpredictable sales tax as the source of revenue. Although the entrepreneurial individualists of the South's new middle class continued to stress educational improvements as a key to economic progress, because an investment in education offered only a potential long-term payoff rather than a guaranteed, immediate one, ad-vocates of education reform operated at a decided disadvantage. A 1991 poll in economically and educationally troubled Louisiana showed, for example, that 42 percent of the respondents felt the current economic situation in the state was a serious problem, while only 13 percent saw education in the same terms.[31]

Although developers promised more and better jobs by-and-by, in the short run their overriding emphasis on the business climate was any-thing but a plus for southern workers. Twelve of the thirteen southern states maintained their right-to-work status as the 1980s drew to a close. In addition, these states consistently ranked lowest in disability, work-men's and unemployment compensation, and other programs potentially beneficial to labor. Indeed, a southern state's favorable business-climate ranking usually translated into a less-than-hospitable environment for in-dustrial workers (see Table 19).[32]

One of the keys to the contrasts between the climate for business and the climate for workers was the persistently rabid antiunionism of the

31. James C. Cobb, *Industrialization and Southern Society, 1877–1984* (Lexington: University of Kentucky Press, 1984), 140–41; "New Priorities Seen as Southern Voters Defeat Two Pro-Education Governors," *Chronicle of Higher Education,* XXXVIII (Novem-ber 20, 1991), A28. See also Atlanta *Journal and Constitution,* March 12, 1989.

32. Kenneth Johnson and Marilyn Scurlock, "The Climate for Workers," *Southern Ex-posure,* XIV (September/October and November/December, 1986), 28–31.

Table 19　Business Climate v. Worker Climate in the South

State	Business Climate Ranking	Worker Climate Ranking
Alabama	29	50
Arkansas	15	48
Florida	6	41
Georgia	8	44
Kentucky	30	47
Louisiana	39	45
Mississippi	10	51
North Carolina	7	43
Oklahoma	25	39
South Carolina	11	49
Tennessee	13	47
Texas	18	34
Virginia	12	29

SOURCE: Kenneth Johnson and Marilyn Scurlock, "The Climate for Workers," *Southern Exposure*, XIV #5–6 (September/October and November/December, 1986), 29.

South's political and economic leadership and the apparent reluctance of southern workers to join unions even when given the opportunity. The percentage of the southern labor force belonging to unions fell from a thirteen-state average of 13.9 in 1984 to 12.6 in 1988. In the latter year, union membership in both the Carolinas stood well below 5 percent of the work force. This continuing union weakness was more than a regional phenomenon, however; between 1984 and 1988 the percentage of union membership among manufacturing workers nationwide fell from 27.3 to 24.9.[33]

In addition to suggesting that a southern location might offer a safer haven from union organizing onslaughts, the ardent pro-business stance of southern political leaders was easily interpreted as evidence of a lenient attitude toward a variety of corporate abuses. Motorists encountering signs proclaiming "Kentucky Is Open for Business" were likely to sense that the word "wide" should precede "open" in that message. The some-

33. U.S. Bureau of the Census, *Statistical Abstract of the United States* (Washington, D.C.: U.S. Government Printing Office, 1990), p. 418.

times bitter fruits of such an attitude were apparent enough in the fire that flashed through the Imperial Food Products, Inc., plant in Hamlet, North Carolina, on September 3, 1991, killing twenty-five workers whose escape routes were blocked by an illegally locked door. State worker-safety officials subsequently admitted they had not inspected the plant a single time during its eleven years of operation. The nonreciprocal nature of North Carolina's relationship with Imperial Foods was underscored by the fact that the company, which closed after the fire, had never contributed to the local United Way and owed the economically devastated town more than $21,000 in back taxes, water and sewer charges, and police protection fees at the time it closed.[34]

The South's ongoing commitment to a favorable business climate also helped sustain the perception of a permissive attitude toward polluting industries. In 1989 the governing board of the Georgia Department of Natural Resources responded to pressure from the Environmental Protection Agency by instituting more stringent restrictions on the release of dioxin into the state's waterways. Lawyers for several of Georgia's paper mills protested that their clients would have to spend $100 million in order to comply with the new regulations. At that point, the commissioner of the Department of Natural Resources reportedly asked officials at the paper mills to suggest a dioxin release level they could meet without spending great sums of money. Five months later, the DNR board replaced the tougher requirement with one 554 times weaker than the one recommended by EPA. Only when EPA announced that Georgia's standard was unacceptable and threatened to impose its own regulations did the Georgia board adopt a somewhat stronger stance. Georgia officials reportedly took this action, however, after they had ascertained that the paper mills could "live with the new standard," which remained one of the weakest in the nation. Such a "write-your-own-regulations" approach suggested why a 1991 survey of 256 environmental indicators put the southern states solidly at the bottom of a fifty-state ranking. Alabama, Louisiana, Mississippi, Texas, and Tennessee occupied the bottom six ranks in the survey, and only Florida at eighteenth and North Carolina at twenty-third were in the top half of the poll. The authors concluded that "of all the regions, only the South maintains a backward resistance to positive policies in the face of extraordinary levels of poisons."[35]

34. New York *Times*, November 25, 1991.
35. Atlanta *Journal and Constitution*, October 30, 1990; Atlanta *Constitution*, August 12, 1991.

The persistence of this lenient, look-the-other-way attitude toward corporate misbehavior reflected the extent to which intense national and global competition for new industries made it difficult to place more demands on employers coming into the South. Nowhere was this reality more obvious than in the region's continued reputation as a haven for low-wage employers. Whereas the earnings of white-collar workers in southern metropolitan areas had largely converged with those of their counterparts elsewhere in the nation by the end of the 1980s, for blue-collar workers in nonmetropolitan locations, major discrepancies remained. The absolute gap between the hourly wages of southern and nonsouthern production workers in manufacturing firms stood at $1.32 in July 1981, and ten years later the figure was almost exactly the same.[36]

In remote rural areas with large, unskilled black populations, job seekers often found it difficult to find steady work at any wage. Developers continued to face difficulties in recruiting industries for such communities throughout the 1980s. Between 1977 and 1982, employment grew twice as fast in counties where less than 25 percent of the population was black than in those where more than 50 percent was black. One such area was the Mississippi Delta, where the mechanization of agriculture had left an economic void that relocating industries showed little inclination to fill. Boeing Aircraft promised to create 600 jobs when it accepted an $18-million subsidy to open an aircraft repair facility at Greenville in 1985. Most of the jobs failed to materialize, however, and Boeing left the area in 1989. Greenville lost another major employer in 1991, when officials at the Schwinn Corporation, long seen as one of the Delta's most progressive and stable employers, announced that it was closing its Greenville facility and expanding its operation in Taiwan.[37]

At one point, the Delta had shown signs of developing its own home-grown industry as catfish growing and processing expanded rapidly

36. Charles Hirschman and Kim Blankenship, "The North-South Earnings Gap: Changes during the 1960s and 1970s," *American Journal of Sociology*, LXXXVII (September, 1981), 388–403; Robert S. Goldfarb, Anthony M. J. Yezer, and Sebastian Crewe, "Some New Evidence: Have Regional Wage Differentials Really Disappeared?" *Growth and Change*, XIV (January, 1983), 48–51; U.S. Department of Labor, Bureau of Labor Statistics, *Employment and Earnings*, XXVIII (September, 1981), p. 96; *Ibid.*, XXXVIII (September, 1991), pp. 108–12.

37. Stuart A. Rosenfeld and Edward M. Bergman, *After the Factories: Changing Employment Patterns in the Rural South* (Research Triangle Park, N.C.: Southern Growth Policies Board, 1985), 27; Jackson *Clarion-Ledger*, August 25, 1985, November 30, 1988, August 11, 1991.

during the 1980s. By the end of the decade, however, the industry was facing rebellion from a unionized, predominantly black work force whose leaders complained of low wages, harassment, and unsanitary working conditions. Workers at the Delta Pride catfish plant in Indianola claimed victory after winning small wage concessions in a bitter strike in 1990, but gloomy predictions of a saturated market and slumping producer prices suggested that in the future such gains would be hard won indeed. The Personnel Department at Delta Pride (where the average annual wage was more than $4,400 below the minimum poverty-level income for a single parent with three children) actively encouraged employees to apply for welfare assistance, thereby suggesting how distressingly commonplace the paradox of the working poor had become in the low-wage South. Here again, however, conditions in the South merely reflected trends that were national in scope. Across the nation the percentage of workers earning less than the Census Bureau's designated poverty level for a family of four rose from 12.1 percent in 1979 to 18 percent in 1990.[38]

During the 1980s, progress toward significant reduction of poverty in the South was modest at best (see Table 20). In five states, including Mississippi, which was already the nation's poorest, the poverty rate actually rose during the decade. Overall, the South's percentage of the nation's poor declined only from 39.1 in 1980 to 37.2 in 1990. The total number of southerners living in poverty actually rose by 8.9 percent between 1980 and 1990, but the relationship between regional and national economic trends became clear enough during the 1980s as the number of nonsoutherners with incomes below the poverty level grew by 18.5 percent, a figure more than twice as high as the one for the South.[39]

Although Texas led the nation in the creation of new jobs during the 1990–91 recession, the number of Texans living in poverty increased by nearly 20 percent during the 1980s (see Table 20). Elsewhere, North Carolina's overall employment growth rate of 23 percent between 1983 and 1987 included a 47 percent increase in dynamic Wake County, where Raleigh is located, and a 12 percent decline in Graham County,

38. Michael Alexander, "Fishy Business," *Southern Exposure*, XIV (September/October and November/December, 1986), 32–34; Atlanta *Journal and Constitution*, October 30, 1990; New York *Times*, December 10, 1990; Memphis *Commercial Appeal*, December 16, 1990; *USA Today*, May 12, 1992.

39. U.S. Bureau of the Census, *Poverty in the United States, 1990*, Current Population Reports, Series P-60, No. 175, (Washington, D.C.: U.S. Government Printing Office, 1991), pp. 219–21.

Table 20   Percentage of the South's Population Living in Poverty, 1980 and
1990, and Percentage Change in Number of Persons Living in
Poverty, 1980 and 1990

State	1980	1990	Change
Alabama	21.2	19.2	−5.1
Arkansas	21.5	19.6	−2.5
Florida	16.7	14.4	+12.1
Georgia	13.9	15.8	+3.8
Kentucky	19.3	17.3	+10.4
Louisiana	20.3	23.6	+9.7
Mississippi	24.3	25.7	+15.8
North Carolina	15.0	13.0	−5.5
Oklahoma	11.5	15.6	+18.5
South Carolina	16.8	16.2	+2.6
Tennessee	19.6	16.9	−5.8
Texas	15.7	15.9	+19.5
Virginia	12.4	11.1	+9.0

SOURCE: U.S. Bureau of the Census, *Current Population Reports, Poverty in the United States: 1990* (Washington, D.C.: Government Printing Office, 1991), pp. 219, 221.

whose entrenched poverty was all too characteristic of rural Appalachia. Such statistics underscored the striking unevenness of the South's economic development pattern. Surveying economic conditions in the South, one journalist warned, "It is dangerous to generalize about a region where South Florida, the Mississippi Delta, and the Texas Oil Patch have about as much in common as Moscow, Las Vegas, and Beirut."[40]

With so many of its isolated, impoverished rural areas still hungry for industrial development, and with so much of its existing industry concentrated in low-wage, labor-intensive operations likely to be eyeing new and even cheaper operating locations elsewhere in the world, and, finally, with so much of its recent expansion occurring in service-sector jobs in metropolitan areas, the South moved into the 1990s facing the prospect of major demographic changes. The region's traditional pattern of industrial dispersal left employment in manufacturing more than 30 percent higher in the nonmetropolitan South than in the nation as a whole

40. *Wall Street Journal,* January 15, 1989; New York *Times,* February 28, 1992.

in 1980. This statistic seemed likely to change significantly in the face of plant closings and massive layoffs, the potential result being an influx of job seekers into metropolitan areas whose increasingly service-dependent economies and remarkably lean educational and social welfare budgets (kept so in part by the desire to maintain an attractive business climate) might prove inadequate to meet the demands they were likely to face.[41]

As the decade drew to a close, the specter of economic decline hung over the entire nation, and a number of states, both inside the South and out, joined in the heated pursuit of the superconducting supercollider, "the largest and costliest scientific instrument in the world" and a big-ticket, high-tech project with total costs estimated at $4.4 billion. More than any similar single event in the 1980s, the story of the intensely competitive courtship of the supercollider illustrated both the extent and the limits of the South's progress toward economic independence and self-sustainability after a half century dedicated to the zealous pursuit of industrial development. On the one hand, the decision to locate the supercollider near Waxahatchie, Texas, twenty-five miles south of Dallas, seemed to suggest that pronouncements concerning the end of the Sunbelt boom were premature, especially in light of indications that the site was chosen because the Dallas–Fort Worth area (though suffering through an economic downturn at the time) was one of the nation's top producers of military electronics and telecommunications equipment. In the final analysis, however, it was not the success enjoyed by Texas in wooing the supercollider but the failure of Alabama and Mississippi to land the project that revealed the most about conditions in the majority of southern states at the end of the 1980s.[42]

The joint Mississippi-Alabama proposal called for the superconducting supercollider to be located not far from Columbus in eastern Mississippi near the Alabama line. If the project came to this essentially rural area, the two states pledged themselves to institute an impressive (and expensive) list of improvements. Alabama promised to spend approximately $413 million on improvements to highways, public primary and secondary education (including a school for the "gifted and talented"

41. James C. Cobb, "The Sunbelt South: Industrialization in Regional, National, and International Perspective," in Raymond A. Mohl, ed., *Searching for the Sunbelt: Historical Perspectives on a Region* (Knoxville: University of Tennessee Press, 1990), 38.
42. New York *Times*, November 11, 1988.

youngsters of those scientists and engineers who would move into the area to work on the project) as well as community colleges, worker training, and university-level instruction and research. Mississippi's commitment was even more imposing. The poorest state in the union promised to spend $500 million on short-term improvements to infrastructure and public facilities and pledged itself to overall expenditures in the neighborhood of $2.1 billion. Clearly intended to alleviate concerns about education, transportation, and the overall quality of life in a relatively remote rural area, these proposed improvements were to be enacted only *after* the two states had landed the project. The primary, up-front selling point offered by the area was neither man-made nor man-enhanced. It was instead Selma chalk, an indigenous clay formation known to be soft but stable and therefore nearly ideal for the construction of the fifty-three-mile tunnel that the Supercollider required.[43]

Throughout his career as a proponent of industrial development, Henry Grady illustrated the economic dependence of the nineteenth-century South with the parable of a funeral in Pickens County, Georgia, where everything utilized in the burial, down to the shovel that dug the grave, was imported from the North. Save for the corpse, all Georgia had supplied was the hole in the ground. More than a century after Grady told his story for the last time, while one southern state could offer an attractive concentration of high-tech industries, all Alabama and Mississippi could provide for the supercollider project was a good place to dig a hole in the ground.[44] When Grady was telling his Pickens County funeral tale to such good effect in the 1880s, his story seemed to emphasize the economic problems that resulted from the South's historic dependence on single-crop agriculture and the resultant quasi-colonial relationship with the North. More than a century later, the failure of the Alabama-Mississippi supercollider campaign seemed to send the same message.

By the end of the decade, however, students of southern economic history were less inclined to blame contemporary deficiencies solely on the old agricultural or plantation tradition than on the broader economic context in which the South's economic odyssey had unfolded. Early in 1991 North Carolina development leaders sought to recruit a $500-million United Airlines maintenance hangar for Greensboro. The projected

43. Jackson *Clarion-Ledger*, December 30, 1987.
44. Gaston, *The New South Creed*, 70–71.

facility was to employ 6,000 unionized workers making fifteen dollars or more per hour. It would also pay an estimated $4 million per year in local inventory taxes. Yet a number of business groups in the area expressed opposition to the new hangar on the basis of the threat it posed to the state's reputation as a haven for nonunion industry. Such reports seemed hardly less frequent in the 1980s than they had been in the preceding decades, and a concerned North Carolina editor noted that fifty years earlier W. J. Cash had observed "the universal assumption in the business community and the people in general that the preservation of cheap labor was imperatively necessary to Progress." The Greensboro incident seemed to reaffirm Cash's insistence on the continuity of the plantation mentality in the South, but when contemporary southern economic or political leaders show such diehard resistance to unionization, their actions are related not only to the region's agricultural heritage but to a global and national economy characterized by intense competitiveness and industrial mobility on a grand scale. As Gavin Wright observed, "Whether the South ever becomes highly unionized . . . is an open question. But if it does not, it will be a sign of the late twentieth-century American times, not the persistence of the Old South."[45]

Further suggesting the manner in which conditions in the world economy helped to sustain a conservative, sometimes reactionary attitude among southern employers, Wright agreed with those who cited the South's continuing status as a colony, but he quickly added that "the South is not a colony to any other geographic entity but to placeless global organizations and markets" and noted as well that "what these writers say about the South is true for the country as a whole." In Wright's view, the South and the entire nation as well were only two of numerous economies that were, ironically enough, "coming to resemble the economy of the antebellum South when slave owners were ruthless and footloose because their wealth was portable."[46]

Wright's analogy suggested that the mobility of capital, rather than the persistence of the planter class, linked the economy of the Old South with that of the various "New" Souths that followed. Other scholars have argued that changing conditions in the nation and the world at large may

45. Charlotte *Observer,* February 10, 1991; Gavin Wright, *Old South, New South: Revolutions in the Southern Economy since the Civil War* (New York: Basic Books, 1986), 264.
46. Wright, *Old South, New South,* 273.

have helped to reinforce certain characteristics and circumstances that have otherwise been attributed to the persistence of planter influence in the South. David Carlton noted perceptively that "discussions of the New South in recent years have tended to view its social characteristics, from 'paternalism' to low wages, to worker powerlessness, as internally generated, the creations of a persistent ruling class." In Carlton's view, however, the "revolution from above" that Billings had described in North Carolina was not "sponsored by southern junkers so much as imposed upon them." In a similar vein, James C. Cobb stressed the importance of "an evolving national and international economy that helped to make certain elements of the social and political organization of a fading plantation society not just compatible with but almost integral to the establishment of a new industrial one."[47]

In its formative years, the South's industrial tradition was indeed heavily influenced by both the economic and social legacy of the plantation. At the end of Reconstruction, however, the southern states lacked investment capital, skilled labor, and significant consumer buying power. These deficiencies encouraged recruitment of labor- and resource-exploitative industries, thereby nurturing a self-reinforcing pattern of slow growth wherein the potential for social and political disruption was minimal. Within this context both planters and manufacturers found it mutually advantageous to maintain an abundant, controlled labor supply, eliminate the prospect of a political challenge from below, and perpetuate fiscal policies that kept taxes low and governments small. (Reduced to its essentials, the so-called good business climate of which southern politicians remained so protective in the 1990s still bore a striking resemblance to the planter-industrialist policy rapprochement of the 1880s.)

As agriculture declined steadily in economic importance in the post-Depression years, the region's industrial tradition remained intact because manufacturers continued to insist on policies that would encourage further expansion without destroying the stability and special advantages they cherished. By the 1930s the South's strategies for industrial growth were so thoroughly intertwined with so-called plantation traditions such as white supremacy, minimal government, and regional chauvinism that political and economic leaders resisted threats to one as

47. David L. Carlton, "The Revolution from Above: The National Market and the Beginnings of Industrialization in North Carolina," *Journal of American History*, LXXXVII (September, 1990), 474; James C. Cobb, "Beyond Planters and Industrialists: A New Perspective on the New South," *Journal of Southern History*, LIV (February, 1988), 68.

threats to all. For example, labor unions promised to impede development efforts, subject the region to increased Yankee influence, and undermine white supremacy. Likewise, more spending for public welfare would scare away tax-conscious industrialists and elevate blacks at the expense of whites. In the long run, the commitment to industrial development and the determination to preserve the southern way of life were often complementary rather than contradictory impulses.

The desire for new industry spawned several innovative programs and eventually paved the way for token desegregation in some southern cities, but development leaders seldom moved beyond the steps necessary to quell or forestall civil rights protests. Moreover, the economic conservatism that was so much a part of the growth ethos virtually guaranteed that local business leaders would be slow to embrace programs designed to provide social uplift for the disadvantaged of any race. By the mid-1970s the much-trumpeted Sunbelt success story raised hopes that the South's long-awaited day of deliverance from backwardness and poverty might be at hand. Unfortunately, however, many of the same forces that spurred the apparent nationalization of the South's economy also manifested themselves in the decided southernization of the nation's economy as mounting global competitiveness forced even firms that were once relatively free-spending and socially responsive to adopt a more narrowly self-interested and cost-conscious posture in their dealings with workers and state and community leaders throughout the United States.

Historians who continue to argue about whether W. J. Cash could really hear the gallop of Jeb Stuart's cavalrymen behind the building of skyscrapers in the post–World War I Piedmont might add relevance and depth to their discussions of continuity and change in the New South by examining not only the South's plantation tradition but its industrial tradition and the broader national and international context in which these two became largely indistinguishable from each other. Only by looking outward as well as inward can we begin to understand fully why, long after the plantation's demise, the leaders of the New South persisted in their ill-fated efforts to achieve a developed economy at the expense of a developed society. Such an understanding promises a firmer grasp of the contradictions and contrasts that mark the southern economy in the 1990s and, beyond that, a clearer sense of why in recent years the socioeconomic and political outlines of the nation's future seem so ominously reminiscent of the South's past.

BIBLIOGRAPHY

MANUSCRIPTS

Alabama Planning and Industrial Development Board Correspondence. 1964. Alabama State Archives, Montgomery.

Alabama State Planning Commission Records. Uncatalogued typescripts. Alabama State Archives, Montgomery.

Almond, J. Lindsay, Correspondence. 1959. Virginia State Archives, Richmond.

Collins, Leroy, Correspondence. 1955. Florida State Archives, Tallahassee.

Georgia Department of Industry and Trade Correspondence. 1967. Georgia State Archives, Atlanta.

Governor's Correspondence. 1946. Florida State Archives, Tallahassee.

Hodges, Luther H., Correspondence. 1954–1958. North Carolina State Archives, Raleigh.

Louisiana Department of Commerce and Industry Correspondence. 1971. Louisiana State Archives, Baton Rouge.

Mississippi Board of Development Records. 1941–1942. Mississippi State Archives, Jackson.

Mississippi Industrial Commission Records. 1937–1938. Mississippi State Archives, Jackson.

North Carolina Division of Commerce and Industry Correspondence. 1946–1950. North Carolina State Archives, Raleigh.

Sanford, Terry, Correspondence. 1961. North Carolina State Archives, Raleigh.

South Carolina Development Board Correspondence. South Carolina State Archives, Columbia.

Tennessee Division for Industrial Development Correspondence. 1967–1970. Tennessee State Archives, Nashville.

Timmerman, George Bell, Jr., Correspondence. 1956–1958. South Carolina State Archives, Columbia.

Virginia Department of Conservation and Development Correspondence. 1959. Virginia State Archives, Richmond.

Wallace, George C., Correspondence. 1963–1965. Alabama State Archives, Montgomery.

Warren, Fuller, Correspondence. 1952. Florida State Archives, Tallahassee.

West, John C., Correspondence. 1971. South Carolina State Archives, Columbia.

White, Hugh L., Correspondence. 1952–1965. Mississippi State Archives, Jackson.

Wright, Fielding, Correspondence. 1951. Mississippi State Archives, Jackson.

GOVERNMENT DOCUMENTS AND REPORTS

Allbritton v. *City of Winona*, 180 Mississippi 100, 178 So. 799.

Allbritton v. *City of Winona*, 303 U.S. 627 (1938).

Congressional Record. 82nd Cong., 2nd Sess., Appendix, Vol. 98, Pt. 8.

Congressional Record. 90th Cong., 2nd Sess., Vol. 114, Pt. 6.

Congressional Record. 95th Cong., 1st Sess., Vol. 123.

Congressional Record. 83rd Cong., 1st Sess., May 1–27, 1953, Vol. 99, Pt. 4.

Congressional Record. 89th Cong., 1st Sess., Vol. 111, Pt. 2.

Congressional Record. 94th Cong., 2nd Sess., Vol. 122.

Congressional Record. 95th Cong., 1st Sess., Vol. 123.

Green v. *Frazier*, 233 U.S. 253 (1920).

Jusenius, Carol L., and Larry C. Ledeber. *A Myth in the Making: The Southern Economic Challenge and Northern Economic Decline.* Washington, D.C.: United States Department of Commerce, Economic Development Administration, November, 1976.

Mississippi Agricultural and Industrial Board. *First Biennial Report to the Legislature.* Jackson: n.p., 1945.

————. *Eighth Biennial Report to the Legislature, 1958–1960.* Jackson: n.p., 1960.

Mississippi House Journal. Extraordinary Session, 1936.

Mississippi Senate Journal. Extraordinary Session, 1936.

Roterus, Victor. "Community Industrial Development—a Nationwide Survey," in U.S. Congress, Senate Committee on Banking and Currency. 86th Cong., 1st Sess. *Development Corporations and Authorities.* Washington, D.C.: U.S. Government Printing Office, 1959.

South Carolina House Journal. Extra Session, Beginning Monday, June 4, 1956.

U.S. Bureau of the Census. *Census of Governments, 1967.* Vol. 4, No. 5. *Compendium of Government Finance.* Washington, D.C.: U.S. Government Printing Office, 1969.

————. *Statistical Abstract of the United States.* Washington, D.C.: U.S. Government Printing Office, 1942, 1953, 1958, 1960, 1963, 1964, 1968, 1972, 1979.

U.S. Department of Labor. *Growth of Labor Law in the United States.* Washington, D.C.: U.S. Government Printing Office, 1962.

NEWSPAPERS

Albuquerque *New Mexican*, March 1, 1979.

Arkansas *Gazette*, 1956 and 1976.

Atlanta *Constitution*, 1961–1975.
Atlanta *Journal*, 1960, 1961, and 1974.
Charlottesville *Daily Progress*, February 15, 1976.
Columbia (S.C.) *Record*, August 23, 1977.
Columbia (S.C.) *State*, June 14, 1976.
Des Moines *Register*, February 8, 1981.
Durham *Morning Herald*, December 12, 1971.
Durham *Sun*, January 6, 1977.
Forest Park (Ga.) *Free Press*, September 9, 1961.
Jackson *Daily Clarion-Ledger*, 1944, 1951, and 1963.
Jackson *Daily News*, 1940–1950.
Lake Charles *American Press*, July 25, 1965.
Louisville *Courier Journal*, September 22, 1963.
Macon *Telegraph*, August 6, 1962.
Memphis *Commercial Appeal*, January 4, 1958.
New Orleans *Times-Picayune*, January 28, 1965, and June 19, 1977.
New York *Herald Tribune*, June 5, 1963.
New York *Times*, 1935–1979.
Ocala *Star Banner*, August 21, 1960.
Oklahoma City *Times*, October 6, 1962.
Oxford (Miss.) *Eagle*, November 3, 1955.
Raleigh *News and Observer*, 1956–1977.
Richmond *Times Dispatch*, 1958, 1959, and 1970.
Savannah *Morning News*, October 2, 1947.
Shreveport *Times*, May 3, 1964.
The State (Columbia, S.C.), June 14, 1976.
Wall Street Journal, 1952–1978.
Washington *Post*, July 9, 1961, April 30, 1978, and May 29, 1979.

Clipping Files
Florida State University Library, Tallahassee.
Southern Educational Reporting Service (microfilm), University of Georgia Library, Athens.
University of Mississippi Library, Oxford.
University of North Carolina Library, Chapel Hill.
University of Virginia Library, Charlottesville.

BOOKS

Allan, Leslie, Eileen Kohl Kaufman, and Joanna Underwood. *Paper Profits: Pollution in the Pulp and Paper Industry.* Cambridge, Mass.: MIT Press, 1972.
Ashmore, Harry S. *An Epitaph for Dixie.* New York: W. W. Norton, 1958.
Bartley, Numan V. *The Rise of Massive Resistance.* Baton Rouge: Louisiana State University Press, 1969.
Bartley, Numan V., and Hugh D. Graham. *Southern Politics and the Second Reconstruction.* Baltimore: Johns Hopkins University Press, 1975.

Billings, Dwight B., Jr. *Planters and the Making of a New South: Class, Politics, and Development in North Carolina, 1865–1900.* Chapel Hill: University of North Carolina Press, 1978.

Black, Earl. *Southern Governors and Civil Rights.* Cambridge, Mass.: Harvard University Press, 1976.

Brownell, Blaine A. *The Urban Ethos in the South, 1920–1930.* Baton Rouge: Louisiana State University Press, 1975.

Cash, Wilbur J. *The Mind of the South.* 2nd ed. New York: Vintage Books, 1969.

Coleman, Kenneth, ed. *A History of Georgia.* Athens: University of Georgia Press, 1977.

Conway, H. McKinley. *Area Development Organizations.* Atlanta: Conway Research, 1966.

Crain, Robert L. *The Politics of School Desegregation: Comparative Case Studies of Community Structure and Policy Making.* Chicago: Aldine, 1968.

Dabney, Virginius. *Below the Potomac: A Book About the South.* New York: D. Appleton Century, 1942.

Fallows, James M. *The Water Lords.* New York: Grossman, 1971.

Fuchs, Victor R. *Changes in the Location of Manufacturing in the United States Since 1929.* New Haven: Yale University Press, 1962.

Gaston, Paul M. *The New South Creed: A Study in Southern Mythmaking.* New York: Alfred A. Knopf, 1970.

Gelber, Steven M. *Black Men and Businessman: The Growing Awareness of a Social Responsibility.* Port Washington, N.Y.: Kennikat Press, 1974.

Gilman, Glenn. *Human Relations in the Industrial Southeast: A Study of the Textile Industry.* Chapel Hill: University of North Carolina Press, 1956.

Gottman, Jean. *Virginia at Mid-Century.* New York: Henry Holt, 1955.

Haas, Edward F. *DeLesseps S. Morrison and the Image of Reform: New Orleans Politics, 1946–1961.* Baton Rouge: Louisiana State University Press, 1974.

Heard, Alexander, and Donald S. Strong. *Southern Primaries and Elections, 1920–1949.* Freeport, N.Y.: Books for Libraries Press, 1970.

Hellman, Daryl A., Gregory H. Wassall, and Laurence H. Falk. *State Financial Incentives to Industry.* Lexington, Mass.: Lexington Books, 1976.

Hodges, Luther H. *Businessman in the Statehouse.* Chapel Hill: University of North Carolina Press, 1962.

Hoffman, Joan. *Racial Discrimination and Economic Development.* Lexington, Mass.: Lexington Books, 1975.

Hoover, Calvin B., and B. U. Ratchford. *Economic Resources and Policies of the South.* New York: Macmillan, 1951.

Howard, Dick, ed. *Guide to Industrial Development.* Englewood Cliffs, N.J.: Prentice-Hall, 1972.

Kennedy, Stetson. *Southern Exposure.* Garden City, N.Y.: Doubleday, 1946.

Kirby, Jack Temple. *Media-Made Dixie: The South in the American Imagination.* Baton Rouge: Louisiana State University Press, 1978.

Kousser, J. Morgan. *The Shaping of Southern Politics: Suffrage Restriction and the Establishment of the One-Party South, 1880–1910*. New Haven: Yale University Press, 1974.

Lepawsky, Albert. *State Planning and Economic Development in the South*. Kingsport, Tenn.: Kingsport Press, 1949.

Lester, James E., Jr. *A Man for Arkansas: Sid McMath and the Southern Reform Tradition*. Little Rock: Rose, 1976.

Liner, E. Blaine, and Lawrence K. Lynch, eds. *The Economics of Southern Growth*. Durham, N.C.: Seeman Printing, 1977.

McGill, Ralph. *The South and the Southerner*. Boston: Little, Brown, 1963.

Marshall, F. Ray. *Labor in the South*. Cambridge, Mass.: Harvard University Press, 1967.

Mason, Lucy Randolph. *To Win These Rights: A Personal Story of the CIO in the South*. Westport, Conn.: Greenwood Press, 1970.

Miller, William Lee. *Yankee from Georgia: The Emergence of Jimmy Carter*. New York: Times Books, 1978.

Moes, John E. *Local Subsidies for Industry*. Chapel Hill: University of North Carolina Press, 1962.

Newby, I. A. *The South: A History*. New York: Holt, Rinehart, and Winston, 1978.

Nicholls, William H. *Southern Tradition and Regional Progress*. Chapel Hill: University of North Carolina Press, 1960.

Oates, Mary J. *The Role of the Cotton Textile Industry in the Economic Development of the American Southeast, 1900–1940*. New York: Arno Press, 1975.

Peirce, Neal R. *The Deep South States of America: People, Politics, and Power in the Seven Deep South States*. New York: W. W. Norton, 1974.

Perloff, Harvey S., et al. *Regions, Resources, and Economic Growth*. Baltimore: Johns Hopkins University Press, 1960.

Phillips, Kevin P. *The Emerging Republican Majority*. New Rochelle, N.Y.: Arlington House, 1969.

Quint, Howard H. *Profile in Black and White*. Westport, Conn.: Greenwood Press, 1958.

Sale, Kirkpatrick. *Power Shift: The Rise of the Southern Rim and Its Challenge to the Eastern Establishment*. New York: Random House, 1975.

Silver, James W. *Mississippi: The Closed Society*. New enlarged edition. New York: Harcourt, Brace, and World, 1966.

Swain, Martha H. *Pat Harrison: The New Deal Years*. Jackson: University Press of Mississippi, 1978.

Tebeau, Charlton W. *A History of Florida*. Coral Gables: University of Miami Press, 1971.

Tindall, George B. *The Emergence of the New South, 1913–1945*. Baton Rouge: Louisiana State University Press, 1967.

Twelve Southerners. *I'll Take My Stand: The South and the Agrarian Tradition*. New York: Harper Brothers, 1930.

Weinstein, Bernard L., and Robert E. Firestine. *Regional Growth and Decline in*

the United States: The Rise of the Sunbelt and the Decline of the Northeast.
New York: Praeger, 1978.

Wheat, Leonard F. *Regional Growth and Industrial Location.* Lexington, Mass.: Lexington Books, 1973.

Wiener, Jonathan M. *Social Origins of the New South: Alabama, 1860–1885.* Baton Rouge: Louisiana State University Press, 1978.

Wofford, B. M., and T. A. Kelly. *Mississippi Workers: Where They Come From and How They Perform.* University: University of Alabama Press, 1955.

Woodward, C. Vann. *American Counterpoint: Slavery and Racism in the North-South Dialogue.* Boston: Little, Brown, 1971.

———. *Origins of the New South, 1877–1913.* Baton Rouge: Louisiana State University Press, 1951.

ARTICLES

Abbott, Carl. "The American Sunbelt: Idea and Region." *Journal of the West,* XVIII (July, 1979), 5–18.

Adcock, George. "Is International Status Taking the South by Surprise?" *South,* II (July/August, 1975), 31–41.

Alt, Richard M. "Factors Affecting Industrial Development." *Industrial Development,* III (May-June, 1956), 24–35.

"Area Development Ads: Some Good and Bad Attempts to Blight Our Countryside Further." *Industrial Marketing,* LIII (May, 1968), 67–76.

"Bargains for Industry." *American Society of Planning Officials Newsletter,* XVIII (August, 1952), 1–2.

Bateman, James W. "Why Continental Chose Lake Charles as Optimum Site for Higher Alcohol Plant." *Petroleum Refiner,* XL (April, 1961), 147–49.

"The Battle for New Industry." *Steel* (December 4, 1957), 61–68.

Block, Joseph. "Regional Wage Differentials, 1907–1946." *Monthly Labor Review,* LXVI (April, 1948), 371–77.

Breckenfield, Gurney. "Business Loves the Sunbelt (and Vice Versa)." *Fortune,* XCV (June, 1977), 132–46.

Brown, Joe David. "Birmingham, Alabama: A City in Fear." *Saturday Evening Post,* CCXXXVI (March 2, 1963), 12–18.

Burd, Gene. "The Selling of the Sunbelt: Civic Boosterism in the Media." In David C. Perry and Alfred J. Watkins, eds., *Urban Affairs Annual Review,* XIV (1977) Beverly Hills: Sage, 1977.

"Busbee, Senator Debate." *Southern Growth: Problems and Promise,* VI (Winter, 1978), 1, 3.

"Business Citizenship in the Deep South." *Business Horizons,* V (Spring, 1962), 61–66.

"'Buy Industry' or 'You May Not Get It,' Says Lafayette Mayor Who Learned the Hard Way." *Tennessee Town and City,* VIII (July, 1957), 6, 46.

Carrier, Ronald E., and William Schriver. "Plant Location Studies: An Appraisal." *Southwestern Social Science Quarterly,* XLVII (September, 1966), 136–40.

Chastain, Lynda. "A Dream Whose Time Had Come." *Impact: Technical Education in South Carolina*, XI (April-May, 1978), 1–20.

Cleghorn, Reese. "The Mill: A Giant Step for the Southern Negro." *New York Times Magazine*, November 9, 1969, pp. 34–35, 142, 145, 147, 156.

Cobb, James C. "Colonel Effingham Crushes the Crackers: Political Reform in Postwar Augusta." *South Atlantic Quarterly*, LXXIX (Autumn, 1979), 507–519.

———. "Urbanization and the Changing South: A Review of Literature." *South Atlantic Urban Studies*, I (1977), 253–66.

"Committee of 100 Has Accomplished Much in Augusta Area." *Georgia Magazine*, II (April-May, 1959), 30–31.

"Companies Rush for Cheaper Money." *Business Week*, June 11, 1966, pp. 114–21.

"Corporate Advertising Picture of the 50 States' Development Programs." *Public Relations Journal*, XX (October, 1964), 28.

Couch, Robert F. "The Ingalls Story in Mississippi, 1938–1958." *Journal of Mississippi History*, XXVI (August, 1964), 192–206.

Cramer, M. Richard. "School Desegregation and New Industry: The Southern Community Leaders' Viewpoint." *Social Forces*, XL (May, 1963), 384–89.

Crepas, Kenneth J., and Richard A. Stevenson. "Are Industrial Aid Bonds Fulfilling Their Intended Purpose?" *Financial Analysts Journal*, XXIV (November-December, 1968), 105–109.

Danhof, Clarence. "Four Decades of Thought on the South's Economic Problems." In Melvin L. Greenhut and W. Tate Whitman, eds. *Essays in Southern Economic Development*. Chapel Hill: University of North Carolina Press, 1964, pp. 7–68.

Davenport, Walter. "All Work and No Pay." *Colliers*, C (November 13, 1937), 9–10, 70–75.

———. "With Labor Thrown In." *Colliers*, C (November 27, 1937), 16–17, 79–80.

DeVyer, Frank T. "Labor Factors in the Industrial Development of the South." *Southern Economic Journal*, XVIII (1951), 189–205.

DiNunno, J. Gary. "J. P. Stevens: Anatomy of an Outlaw." AFL-CIO. *American Federationist*, LXXXIII (April, 1976), 1–8.

Duvall, Richard A. "Industry, States Rate Incentive, Assistance Programs." *Industrial Development*, CXXXVII (November/December, 1968), 26–30.

"The Economic Consequences of BAWI." *Business Week*, April 26, 1952, p. 180.

Emmerich, Oliver J. "Balancing Agriculture with Industry." *Nation's Business*, XXV (February, 1937), 23–24, 92–93.

———. "Collapse and Recovery." In Richard Aubrey McClemore, ed. *A History of Mississippi*. Vol. II. Hattiesburg, Miss.: University and College Press of Mississippi, 1973, pp. 97–119.

"Federal Spending: The North's Loss Is the Sunbelt's Gain." *National Journal*, VIII (June 26, 1976), 878–91.

"The Fifty Legislative Climates." *Industrial Development*, CXLI (November/December, 1972), 10–15.

"The Fifty Legislative Climates." *Industrial Development*, CXLVII (January/February, 1978), 2–14.

Fuchs, Victor R., and Richard Perlman. "Recent Trends in Southern Wage Differentials." *Review of Economics and Statistics*, XLII (August, 1960), 292–300.

Fuller, Helen. "Atlanta Is Different." *New Republic*, CXL (February 2, 1959), 8–11.

———. "New Orleans Knows Better." *New Republic*, CXL (February 16, 1959), 14–17.

Gaillard, Frye. "I'll Be Dead . . . Before They Pay." *Progressive*, XL (June, 1976), 22.

Garwood, John D. "Are Municipal Subsidies for Industrial Location Sound?" *American City*, LXVIII (May, 1953), 110–11.

"The Go-Getters of Fort Smith, Arkansas." *Fortune*, LXIX (April, 1964), 120–21.

"The Good Life." *Time*, September 27, 1976, pp. 32–39.

"Hammermill and Race-Troubled Selma Point Up Negro's Basic Problem." *Pulp and Paper* (March 1, 1965), 52.

Harding, Vincent. "A Beginning in Birmingham." *Reporter*, XXVIII (June 6, 1963), 13–19.

Harris, Louis C. "Don't Overlook the Newspaper's Role." *Industrial Development*, CXXXVI (March-April, 1967), 21–23.

Hibbs, Ben. "Progress Goes Marching Through Georgia." *Saturday Evening Post*, CCXXXVI (February 16, 1963), 69–73.

Holmquist, Richard C. "Gimmies and Gimmicks: A Penetrating Analysis of the Right-and-Wrong-Ways to Attract New Industries." *Commonwealth.* XXIX (May, 1962), 17–19.

"Hotter Bidding for New Plants." *Business Week*, December 16, 1961, pp. 126–31.

"How Ads Relocate U.S. Industry." *Printer's Ink*, CCLXXVIII (March 9, 1962), 23–28.

Howard, Dick. "Manufacturers' Attitudes Toward Industrial Development Information." In Dick Howard, ed. *Guide to Industrial Development*. Englewood Cliffs, N.J.: Prentice-Hall, 1972, pp. 199–221.

"How New Plants Help." *Nation's Business*, L (December, 1962), 88–89.

"Industrial Growth: But Not the Most Profitable Kind." *Business Week*, November 28, 1959, pp. 130–33.

Jarrett, S. R. "How the States Stack Up in Pollution Control." *Industrial Development*, CXLI (September/October, 1972), 2–6.

Joyner, Bill P., and Jon P. Thames. "Mississippi's Efforts at Industrialization: A Critical Analysis." *Mississippi Law Journal*, XXXVIII (1967), 433–87.

"Keeping Pace with the Population." *National Journal*, VII (December 27, 1975), 1765.

Kennedy, John F. "New England and the South: The Struggle for Industry." *Atlantic Monthly*, CXCIII (January, 1954), 32–36.

King, Larry L. "We Ain't Trash No More." *Esquire*, CXXVI (November, 1976), 89–90, 152–56.

Koeppel, Barbara. "Something Could Be Finer Than to Be in Carolina." *Progressive*, XL (June, 1976), 20–23.

Leifermann, Henry P. "The Unions Are Coming," *New York Times Magazine*, August 5, 1973, pp. 10–11, 25–26.

Lichtenstein, Eugene. "Higher and Higher Go the Bids for Industry." *Fortune*, LXIX (April, 1964), 118–21, 160–64.

Liston, Linda. "Fifty Legislative Climates Turn Stormy as States Fire Up Pollution Control Programs." *Industrial Development*, CXXXIX (November/December, 1970), 1–15.

———. "Proliferating Industrial Parks Spark Plant Location Revolution." *Industrial Development*, CXXXIX (March-April, 1970), 7–11.

———. "The Fifty Legislative Climates Come Under Fire. *Industrial Development*, CXXXVIII (November/December, 1968), 15–22.

———. "The Southeast: Economic Imperatives Bow to Environmental Integrity." *Industrial Development*, CXL (September/October, 1971), 6–21.

Long, W. H. "40,000,000 Being Spent to Lure More Industry and Tourists." *Public Relations*, XXII (August, 1966), 29–33.

———. "Why States Are Budgeting Too Little." *Public Relations Journal*, XX (October, 1964), 25–32.

Lowry, Robert E. "Municipal Subsidies to Industries in Tennessee." *Southern Economic Journal*, VII (January, 1941), 317–29.

McMillan, George. "Integration with Dignity: The Inside Story of How South Carolina Kept the Peace." *Saturday Evening Post*, CCXXXVI (March 16, 1963), 16–21.

McMillan, T. E., Jr. "Why Manufacturers Choose Plant Locations vs. Determinants of Plant Locations." *Land Economics*, XLI (August, 1965), 239–46.

Maitland, Sheridan, and James Cowhig. "Research on the Effects of Industrialization in Rural Areas." *Monthly Labor Review*, LXXXI (October, 1958), 1,121–124.

Malizia, Emil. "The Earnings of North Carolina Workers." *University of North Carolina Newsletter*, LX (December, 1975), 1–4.

Marshall, F. Ray. "Impediments to Labor Union Organization in the South." *South Atlantic Quarterly*, LXVII (Autumn, 1958), 409–418.

Massie, Robert. "What Next in Mississippi?" *Saturday Evening Post*, CCXXXV (November 10, 1962), 18–23.

Miller, Helen Hill. "Private Business and Public Education in the South." *Harvard Business Review*, XXXVIII (July-August, 1960), 75–88.

Montello, Paul A. "The Importance of Educational Factors in Industrial and Business Site Selection." In Dick Howard, ed. *Guide to Industrial Development*. Englewood Cliffs, N.J.: Prentice Hall, 1972, pp. 349–382.

Moore, John L. "Washington Pressures/Business Forms Economic Unit to Support Bipartisan New England Caucus." *National Journal*, V (February 17, 1973), 226–33.

Morgan, William E., and Merlin M. Hackbart. "An Analysis of State and Local Industrial Tax Exemption Programs." *Southern Economic Journal*, XLI (October, 1974), 200–205.

Murphy, Reg. "The South as the New America." *Saturday Review*, September 4, 1976, pp. 8–15.

Murphy, Richard T., Jr., and William Lee Baldwin. "Business Moves to the Industrial Park." *Harvard Business Review*, XXXVII (May-June, 1959), 79–88.

"Needed: Investment Capital." *Tennessee Town and City*, VIII (December, 1957), 12.

Nelson, Robin C. "Ads and 007's Lure Industry." *Printer's Ink*, CCXCIV (February 24, 1967), 35–41.

"The New Rich South: Frontier for Growth." *Business Week*, September 2, 1972, pp. 32–37.

Osthagen, Clarence H. "Sunny and Warm—Boykins, Virginia." In Virginia Division of Industrial Development and Planning, "Community Development Seminar, November 14–16, 1962," pp. 63–65.

"A Park That Reversed a Brain Drain." *Fortune*, XCV (June, 1977), 148–53.

Persky, Joe. "The South: A Colony at Home." *Southern Exposure*, I (Summer/Fall, 1973), 14–22.

Powledge, Fred. "Black Man, Go South—Specifically, as Far as Atlanta, for Old Times There Are Now Forgotten." *Esquire*, LX (August, 1965), 72–74, 120–21.

"The Price of Defiance." *Business Week*, October 6, 1962, pp. 31–32.

"Recruiting Industry Abroad." *South*, V (April 1, 1978), 31–32.

"Reverse Migration." *Time*, September 27, 1976, p. 50.

Reynolds, William. "The South: Global Dumping Ground." *Southern Exposure*, VII (Winter, 1979), 49–56.

Rhodes, Suzanne. "Barnwell: Achilles Heel of Nuclear Power." *Southern Exposure*, VII (Winter, 1979), 42–48.

Rogers, Ralph J. "The Effort to Industrialize." In Richard Aubrey McClemore, ed. *A History of Mississippi*. Vol II. Hattiesburg, Miss.: University and College Press of Mississippi, 1973.

Scott, Carlton B. "Clean Air Act Amendments Loom as Threat to Industrial Expansion." *Industrial Development*, CXLVII (July/August, 1978), 9–12.

"The Second War Between the States." *Business Week*, May 17, 1976, pp. 92–111.

"A Senseless Waste," *Newsweek*, May 25, 1970, pp. 36, 41.

Sloan, Cliff, and Bob Hall. "It's Good to Be Home in Greenville . . . But It's Better if You Hate Unions." *Southern Exposure*, VII (Spring, 1979), 83–93.

Sneed, Earl. "The Education of a Mayor." *Alabama Municipal Journal* (February, 1965), 5.

Soffer, Benson, and Michael Korenich. "'Right to Work' Laws as a Location Factor: The Industrialization Experience of Agricultural States." *Journal of Regional Science*, III (1961), 41–56.

"Southern Exposure." *I.U.D. Digest*, VII (Spring, 1962), 104–113.

Stillman, Don. "Runaways—a Call to Action." *Southern Exposure*, IV (Spring, 1976), 50–59.

Stober, William J., and Laurence H. Falk. "The Effect of Financial Inducements on the Location of Firms." *Southern Economic Journal*, XXXVI (July, 1969), 25–35.

"Surging to Prosperity." *Time*, September 27, 1976, pp. 72–73.

Tanzer, Lester. "Dixie Dilemma: Bond Buyers Frown on Public Money Lure for Southern Plants." *Barron's*, August 18, 1952, pp. 15–16.

"This Town Was Jilted." *Changing Times*, IV (October, 1950), 20.

"Those Good Ole Boys." *Time*, September 27, 1976, p. 47.

Tindall, George B. "Business Progressivism: Southern Politics in the Twenties." *South Atlantic Quarterly*, LXII (Winter, 1963), 92–106.

Trillin, Calvin. "Reflections: Remembrances of Moderates Past." *New Yorker*, LIII (March 21, 1977), 85–97.

Tunley, Roul. "In Spartanburg the Accent Is on Business." *Reader's Digest*, CIV (January, 1974), 165–68.

Ullman, Edward L. "Amenities as a Factor in Regional Growth." *Geographical Review*, XLIV (January, 1954), 119–32.

Wagner, Kenneth C. "What Has *Your* City Done to Secure New Industrial Payrolls?" *Georgia Municipal Journal*, XIII (April, 1963), 16–17, 20.

Walsh, John P. "Surveying Vocational and Training Facilities." *Industrial Development*, IV (July, 1957), 5–8.

"What Industry Needs in the City Plan." *Tennessee Planner*, IX (April, 1949), 126–30.

"When Low Taxes Repelled an Industry." *American City*, LXV (August, 1950), 5.

Whitehurst, Clinton H., Jr. "Industrialization in South Carolina's Rural Piedmont Counties: The Plant Location Decision." *Business and Economic Review* (Bureau of Business and Economic Research, University of South Carolina), X (January, 1964), 4–26.

Woodward, C. Vann. "New South Fraud Is Papered by Old South Myth." Washington *Post*, July 9, 1961, p. 3E.

———. "The South Tomorrow." *Time*, September 27, 1976, pp. 98–99.

Wright, C. E. "Area Development by Utilities." *Public Utilities Fortnightly*, LXIV (November 5, 1959), 766–73.

Yinger, J. Milton, and George E. Simpson, "Can Segregation Survive in an Industrial Society?" *Antioch Review*, XVIII (Spring, 1958), 15–24.

"You Gotta Have a Golf Course." *Business Week*, June 25, 1955, pp. 86–87.

OTHER PUBLISHED MATERIAL

Alabama Business Research Council. *Industrial Development Bond Financing: Business and Community Experiences and Opinions*. Center for Business and Economic Research. University: University of Alabama Press, 1970.

Alabama Chamber of Commerce. *Alabama Ranked Second Nationally for Good Business Climate.* N.p.: n.p., 1976.

American Federation of Labor. *Subsidized Industrial Migration: The Luring of Plants to New Locations.* Washington, D.C.: n.p., 1955.

Arkansas Industrial Development Commission. *Arkansas Europe: Arkansas Industrial Development Commission, Progress Report, July, 1975–June, 1976.* Little Rock: n.p., 1976.

————. *Arkansas Invests in Your Profitability Through the Arkansas Industry Training Program.* Little Rock: n.p., n.d.

Associated Industries of Georgia. *Annual Report, 1957.* N.p.: n.p., n.d.

Barnett, Paul. *An Analysis of State Industrial Development Programs in the Thirteen Southern States.* Bureau of Research, School of Business Administration, Division of University Extension, University of Tennessee, XIII. Knoxville: University of Tennessee Press, 1944.

Brooks, Kent. *D-Handle Portable Electric Power Tools.* Research and Curriculum Unit, Mississippi State University. Mississippi State: Mississippi State University Press, 1973.

Carrier, Ronald E., and William R. Schriver. *Plant Location Analysis: An Investigation of Plant Locations in Tennessee.* Bureau of Business and Economic Research, Memphis State University. Memphis: Memphis State University Press, 1969.

Chieh-Liu, Ben. *Quality of Life Indicators in the U.S. Metropolitan Areas, 1970* (Summary). Kansas City: Midwest Research Institute, 1975.

————. *The Quality of Life in the United States, 1970: Index, Rating, and Statistics.* Kansas City: Midwest Research Institute, 1975.

Dunn, Edgar S. *Recent Southern Economic Development: As Revealed by the Changing Structure of Employment.* University of Florida Monographs in the Social Sciences, XIV. Gainesville: University of Florida Press, 1962.

A Dynamic Concept for Research: The Research Triangle Park of North Carolina. Supplied by the North Carolina Department of Commerce and Industry, Raleigh, North Carolina.

Florida Development Commission. *Florida: Profile for Profit.* Tallahassee: n.p., n.d.

Georgia Department of Community Development. N.p.: n.p., n.d.

Georgia State Chamber of Commerce. *Industrial Survey of Georgia, 1970.* Atlanta: n.p., 1970.

Gilmore, Donald R. *Developing the "Little Economies."* Committee for Economic Development, Supplementary Paper, X. New York: n.p., April, 1960.

Greenhut, Melvin L., and Marshall R. Colberg. *Factors in the Location of Florida Industries.* Florida State University Studies, No. XXXVI. Tallahassee: Florida State University Press, 1962.

Hopkins, Ernest J. *Mississippi's BAWI Plan: An Experiment in Industrial Subsidization.* Atlanta: Federal Reserve Bank of Atlanta, 1944.

————. *The Louisville Industrial Foundation: A Study in Community Capitalization of Local Industries.* Atlanta: Federal Reserve Bank of Atlanta, 1945.

International Section of the North Carolina Division of Commerce and Industry. *Douze raisons pourquoi les sociétés étrangères ont établi des opérations industrielles profitables en Carolina du Nord, U.S.A.* N.p.: n.p., n.d.

Jahncke, Ernest Lee. *Smokestacks and Payrolls: An Address Before the Members of the Southeastern Regional Clearing House Association, Baton Rouge, October 25, 1940.* Baton Rouge: n.p., 1940.

Jones, Ethel B. *Effect of High-Wage Unionized Industries on Neighboring Industries.* College of Business Administration, Industrial Research and Extension Center, University of Arkansas. Little Rock: University of Arkansas Press, June, 1962.

Kentucky Bureau of Vocational Education, Division of Interagency Relations. *The Kentucky Industrial Training Program Is Off and Running!* N.p.: n.p., n.d.

Louisville Industrial Foundation. *Forty-third Annual Report.* Louisville: n.p., January 15, 1959.

McLaughlin, Glenn E., and Stefan Robock. *Why Industry Moves South: A Study of Factors Influencing the Recent Location of Manufacturing Plants in the South.* NPA Committee of the South Report, III. Kingsport, Tenn.: Kingsport Press, 1949.

Mississippi. Jackson: Goodwin Advertising, n.d.

National Industrial Conference Board. *The Economic Almanac, 1962.* New York: Newsweek, 1962.

Northrup, Herbert R., and Richard L. Rowan. *Negro Employment in Southern Industry.* Industrial Research Unit, Wharton School of Finance and Commerce, University of Pennsylvania. Philadelphia: University of Pennsylvania Press, 1970.

Patterson, D. Jeanne. *The Local Industrial Development Corporation.* Indiana University Bureau of Business Research, Graduate School of Business. Bloomington: Indiana University Press, 1967.

Petersen, John E. *The Tax-Exempt Pollution Control Bond.* Chicago: Municipal Finance Officers Association, 1975.

Public Affairs Research Council of Louisiana, *Everything You Always Wanted to Know About PAR—But Didn't Know Who to Ask.* Baton Rouge: n.p., n.d.

————. *Factors Affecting Louisiana's Industrial Development.* Baton Rouge: n.p., 1962.

————. *25 Years of Political Reform.* Baton Rouge: n.p., 1975.

Quindry, Kenneth E., and Niles Schoening. *State and Local Tax Ability and Effort, 1977.* Atlanta: Southern Regional Education Board, 1979.

Ross, William D. *Louisiana's Industrial Tax Exemption Program.* Division of Research, College of Commerce, Louisiana State University, *Louisiana Business Bulletin*, XV. Baton Rouge: Louisiana State University Press, December, 1955.

South Carolina State Board for Technical and Comprehensive Education. *Start Up in the Black in South Carolina.* N.p.: n.p., n.d.

Southern Growth Policies Board. *Annual Report, 1977: The South in the Seventies.* Research Triangle Park, N.C.: n.p., 1977.

Stokes, Thomas L. *Carpetbaggers of Industry.* N.p.: Amalgamated Clothing Workers of America, 1937.

Tennessee Division for Industrial Development. *Education in Tennessee.* Nashville: n.p., n.d.

Tennessee Division of Vocational-Technical Education. *Tennessee Industrial Training Service.* Nashville: n.p., n.d.

Tennessee State Planning Commission. *Partners: Industry and the Tennessee Community—a Guide to Community Industrial Development.* Nashville: n.p., October, 1947.

Wallace, Raymond F. *An Analysis of the Balance Agriculture with Industry Program.* State Administration Series, Bureau of Public Administration, Vol. IV, University of Mississippi. University: University of Mississippi Press. 1952.

White, Hugh L. *Address of Governor Hugh L. White Before the Annual Convention of the Mississippi Press Association at Gulfport, Mississippi, June 12, 1936.* N.p.: n.p., n.d.

Wood, Oliver G., Jr., et al. *The BASF Controversy: Employment vs. Environment.* Bureau of Business and Economic Research, University of South Carolina, Essays in Economics Series, No. 25. Columbia: University of South Carolina Press, 1971.

ADVERTISEMENTS

Business Week, July 17, 1937, p. 52; October 16, 1937, p. 28; January 20, 1949, p. 70; March 6, 1954, p. 48; March 8, 1958, p. 124; March 3, 1962, p. 66; March 5, 1962, p. 146; March 5, 1966, p. 126.

Economist, CCLXX (March 17–23, 1979), Survey 3.

Fortune, LV (March, 1957), 236.

THESES AND DISSERTATIONS

Agthe, Donald E. "The Economics of North Florida Industrial Parks." Ph.D. dissertation, Florida State University, 1970.

Cobb, James C. "Politics in a New South City: Augusta, Georgia, 1946–1971." Ph.D. dissertation, University of Georgia, 1975.

Crooke, Jonas Boyd. "The Labor Characteristics of Low-Wage Manufacturing Industries in East Tennessee: The Berkline Corporation." M.S. thesis, University of Tennessee, 1967.

Digby, Michael Franklin. "State Government and Economic Development: An Analysis and Evaluation of the Virginia Industrial Development Program." Ph.D. dissertation, University of Virginia, 1976.

Eddleman, Bobby Ross. "The Rate of Relocation as a Determinant of Southern Area Industrial Growth." Ph.D. dissertation, North Carolina State University, 1966.

Ellis, William Lee. "A Survey of Georgia Industrial Developers Operating at the Local Level in 1969." M.A. thesis, University of Georgia, 1972.

Gunter, Danny Lloyd. "Factors Affecting Employment Patterns in Manufacturing

Plants in Rural Tennessee, 1964–1973." Ph.D. dissertation, University of Tennessee, 1975.

Herrington, Richard E. "Florida Regional Industrial Growth, 1960–1968." M.S. thesis, Florida State University, 1970.

Holley, John Fred. "Elizabethton, Tennessee: A Case Study of Southern Industrialization." Ph.D. dissertation, Clark University, 1949.

Jones, R. G. "Political and Economic Transition in Mississippi: A Preliminary Survey." M. A. thesis, Louisiana State University, 1938.

Kelch, David R. "Industrial Location in the Nonmetropolitan Communities of Kentucky and Tennessee, 1970–1973." Ph.D. dissertation, University of Kentucky, 1978.

Leach, Damonia Etta Brown. "Progress Under Pressure: Changes in Charlotte Race Relations, 1955–1965." M.A. thesis, University of North Carolina, 1976.

Menees, Elbert Lee. "The Location of the American Textile Industry." Ph.D. dissertation, University of South Carolina, 1976.

Moore, Anne Rogers. "Industrial Training in North Carolina: Case Studies in New and Expanding Industries, 1975–1977." Ed.D. dissertation, North Carolina State, 1977.

Morgan, William Edward. "The Effects of State and Local Tax and Financial Inducements on Industrial Location." Ph.D. dissertation, University of Colorado, 1964.

Morrison, Alexander H. "The Impact of Industry on a Rural Area: A Case Study of Development in Warren and Surrounding Counties, 1930–1954." Ph.D. dissertation, University of Virginia, 1958.

Northam, Raymond Mervyn. "An Analysis of Recent Industrialization in Northeastern Georgia." Ph.D. dissertation, Northwestern University, 1960.

Plowman, Edwin Lee. "An Analysis of Selected Strategies Used by the Southern Regional Council in Effecting Social Change in the South." Ph.D. dissertation, Boston University, 1976.

Prince, Jack Edward. "History and Development of the Mississippi Balance Agriculture with Industry Program, 1936–1958." Ph.D. dissertation, Ohio State University, 1961.

Rainey, Ronald Isaac. "A Description and Analysis of the Primary Features of Louisiana's Industry Inducement Program." M.A. thesis, Louisiana State University, 1967.

Ross, William D. "Industrial Promotion by Southern States." Ph.D. dissertation, Duke University, 1951.

Santos, Francisco DeAraujo. "Factors Affecting the Shift of Manufacturing Industries to the Southern Region of the United States from 1954 to 1963." Ph.D. dissertation, Columbia University, 1971.

Schreiber, Max Moise. "The Development of the Southern United States: A Test for Regional Convergence and Homogeneity." Ph.D. dissertation, University of South Carolina, 1978.

Scott, William Irvin. "Why Manufacturers Have Located in Mississippi." M.B.A. thesis, University of Mississippi, 1951.

Shiffler, Larry Wayne. "Negro Participation in Manufacturing: A Geographical Appraisal of North Carolina." M.A. thesis, University of North Carolina, 1965.

Tarr, James. "Occupational Migration Flows into and from Florida, 1965–1970." Ph.D. dissertation, Florida State University, 1977.

Thomas, William Ronald. "State Industrial Development Organizations in the Southeast: An Evaluation of Performance by Industrial Executives." Ph.D. dissertation, Georgia State University, 1971.

Triplette, Ralph R., Jr. "One Industry Towns: Their Location, Development, and Economic Character." Ph.D. dissertation, University of North Carolina, 1974.

White, Clyde Thomas. "An Economic Study of the Industrial Development Policies of the State Government of Mississippi, 1960–1970." D.B.A. dissertation, Mississippi State University, 1973.

Williams, Ned. "Financing Industry in the South: Mississippi's Second BAWI Program." Ph.D. dissertation, Columbia University, 1965.

Wisman, Paul Pence. "The Nature of the Labor Force of a Rural Industry in Virginia: A Case Study of the Stonewall Plant of Merck and Company, Inc." M.S. thesis, University of Virginia, 1950.

Ziehr, Charles Thomas. "The Importance of Incentives on the Location of Manufacturing in South Carolina." M.S. thesis, University of South Carolina, 1975.

UNPUBLISHED REPORTS

Allaman, Peter M., and David L. Birch. "Components of Employment Change for States by Industry Group, 1970–1972." Working Paper #5, Inter-Area Migration Project, September, 1975, Joint Center for Urban Studies of MIT and Harvard University. Mimeo in Massachusetts Institute of Technology Library, Cambridge.

Augusta Chamber of Commerce. "Augusta Industrial Program." Undated typescript in possession of Augusta, Georgia, Chamber of Commerce, Augusta.

Barksdale, William E. "The Saga of A Shoestring Operation." In American Industrial Development Council, "Practitioner's Notes." March, 1973, mimeo in possession of the author.

Brooks, John C. "Remarks to James Sprunt Institute Forum on the Rural South in Transition." Kenansville, N.C. October 25, 1979, typescript in possession of the author.

Cassell, Robert B. "An Industrial Appraisal of Sandersville and Tennille, Georgia." Sandersville-Washington County Chamber of Commerce. June, 1962, typescript in University of Georgia Library, Athens.

"Clean Air Act Amendments of 1977." Typescript in possession of Southern Growth Policies Board, Research Triangle Park, N.C.

Collins, Amy. "Industrial Development in Georgia, 1958–1965." Industrial Development Division, Engineering Experiment Station, Georgia Institute of Technology, 1967, mimeo in Library of Congress, Washington, D.C.

Davis, D. P. "Entertaining the Prospect." In Virginia Division of Industrial Development and Planning, "Community Development Seminar, November 14–16, 1962." Mimeo in Library of Congress, Washington, D.C., 81–82.

Dodson, Winfred G., and Robert B. Cassell. "Civic Progress Standards of Georgia Certified City Program." Georgia Institute of Technology, Engineering Experiment Station, Industrial Development Division, 1974. In Library of Congress, Washington, D.C.

Dusenbury, Patricia J. "Regional Targeting." Southern Growth Policies Board. February, 1979, mimeo in possession of Southern Growth Policies Board, Research Triangle Park, N.C.

Fincher, Cameron. "Research in the South: An Appraisal of Current Efforts." Georgia State College, School of Arts and Sciences, Research Paper No. 5. October, 1964, mimeo in possession of the author.

Florida Development Commission. "Case Histories: Florida's Attraction for Engineers, Scientists, and Other Skilled Personnel." Undated mimeo in Library of Congress, Washington, D.C.

Fort Smith Chamber of Commerce. "Site #9, Fort Smith Chamber of Commerce, Fort Smith, Arkansas." Undated mimeo in possession of Fort Smith, Arkansas, Chamber of Commerce, Fort Smith.

General Assembly Committee on Schools. "Majority and Minority Reports." Atlanta, April 28, 1960, mimeo in University of Georgia Library, Athens.

Georgia Power Company and the Georgia Institute of Technology, Atlanta, comps. "A Comparative Cost Analysis: Cost of Operating a Lighting Fixture Plant in Wheeling, West Virginia, v. Athens, Georgia." Athens, Georgia, Area Chamber of Commerce, September 19, 1962.

Georgia State Chamber of Commerce. "Summary of Industrial Advantages of Edison, Georgia." 1953, typescript in University of Georgia Library, Athens.

———. "Take A Tip from the Beaver, Mr. Businessman." Atlanta, 1965. In University of Georgia Library, Athens.

Harris, Louis, and Associates. "Priorities for Progress in South Carolina." Study No. 2130. October, 1971, mimeo in South Carolina State Library, Columbia.

Jacoway, Elizabeth. "Little Rock Businessmen and Desegregation: Some Preliminary Findings." Unpublished paper delivered at the April, 1978, meeting of the Organization of American Historians.

Liner, E. Blaine. "Presentation to the Southern Governors' Association." February 27, 1979, mimeo in possession of Southern Growth Policies Board, Research Triangle Park, N.C.

———. "The Snowbelt and the Seven Myths." Southern Growth Policies Board. January 24, 1978, mimeo in possession of Southern Growth Policies Board, Research Triangle Park, N.C.

"Proceedings, First Florida Conference on Information Resources, Sponsored Jointly by the Council of 100 and the Florida State Chamber of Commerce with the Cooperation of the Florida Library Association, Tampa International Inn, Tampa, Florida, January 31, 1965." Mimeo in Library of Congress, Washington, D.C.

Soule, Don M. "Comparative Total Tax Loads of Selected Manufacturing Corporations with Alternative Tax Loads Computed for a Hypothetical Manufacturing Corporation and Sixteen Variations Thereof." Bureau of Business Research, University of Kentucky, Lexington. 1960, mimeo in Library of Congress, Washington, D.C.

South Carolina State Planning Board. "An Opportunity for the Woolen and Worsted Industry in South Carolina." Bulletin No. 10, n.d. In South Carolina State Archives, Columbia.

Southern Regional Council. "Leadership Reports," #3, May 11, 1959, #24, February 16, 1961, #42, June 6, 1963. In "Leadership Project" Files, Southern Regional Council, Atlanta.

Tennessee State Planning Commission. "Subsidies for Industries in Tennessee." 1947, mimeo in University of Tennessee Library, Knoxville.

U.S. Advisory Commission on Intergovernmental Relations. "Industrial Development Bond Financing." June, 1963, mimeo in Library of Congress, Washington, D.C.

Williamsburg County Legislative Delegation, County Commission, Industrial Commission, Superintendent of Schools. "Williamsburg County—Industrial Data—1957." Mimeo in South Carolina State Archives, Columbia.

MISCELLANEOUS CORRESPONDENCE

Lyford, W. T., to Robert A. Derose, December 21, 1959. Letter in possession of Marianna, Florida, Chamber of Commerce.

Page, Drewery I., executive vice-president, Owensboro Chamber of Commerce, to the author, April 8, 1977.

Sims, J. M., Jr., to Robert A. Derose, January 15, 1960. Letter in possession of Marianna, Florida, Chamber of Commerce.

Wells, H. W., executive vice-president, Greater Madisonville Area Chamber of Commerce, to the author, May 24, 1977.

BIBLIOGRAPHIC APPENDIX

GOVERNMENT DOCUMENTS AND REPORTS

U.S. Bureau of the Census. *Annual Survey of Manufacturers, 1989*. Washington, D.C.: U.S. Government Printing Office, 1991.

———. *County and City Data Book*. Washington, D.C.: U.S. Government Printing Office, 1983.

———. *Current Population Reports, Poverty in the United States, 1990*. Series P-60, No. 175. Washington, D.C.: U.S. Government Printing Office, 1991.

———. *Statistical Abstract of the United States*. Washington, D.C.: U.S. Government Printing Office, 1990.

U.S. Department of Labor, Bureau of Labor Statistics. *Employment and Earnings*, XXVIII (September, 1981). Washington, D.C.: U.S. Government Printing Office, 1981.

———. *Employment and Earnings*, XXXVIII (September, 1991). Washington, D.C.: U.S. Government Printing Office, 1991.

NEWSPAPERS

Atlanta *Constitution*, August 12, 1991.

Atlanta *Journal and Constitution*, October 5, 1986, March 12, 1989, October 30, 1990.

Charlotte *Observer*, February 10, 1991.

Jackson *Clarion-Ledger*, December 30, 1987.

Knoxville *News-Sentinel*, October 28, 1990.

Memphis *Commercial-Appeal*, December 16, 1990.

New York *Times*, November 11, 1988, December 10, 1990, November 25, 1991, December 18, 19, 1991.

Tuscaloosa *News*, June 8, 1988.

USA Today, September 9, 1985, May 12, 1992.

BOOKS

Black, Earl, and Merle Black. *Politics and Society in the South*. Cambridge, Mass.: Harvard University Press, 1987.

Cobb, James C. *Industrialization and Southern Society, 1877–1984*. Lexington: University Press of Kentucky, 1984.

Wright, Gavin. *Old South, New South: Revolutions in the Southern Economy since the Civil War*. New York: Basic Books, 1986.

ARTICLES

Alexander, Michael. "Fishy Business." *Southern Exposure*, XIV (September/October and November/December, 1986), 32–34.

"Chart 1: Financial Assistance for Industry," "Chart 2: Tax Incentives for Industry," "Chart 3: Special Services for Industrial Development," "Chart 4: State Incentives for Pollution Control, Other Laws." *Site Selection*, XXXV (October, 1990), 1087–88, 1092, 1097.

Carlton, David L. "The Revolution from Above: The National Market and the Beginnings of Industrialization in North Carolina." *Journal of American History*, LXXXVII (September, 1990), 445–75.

Cobb, James C. "The Sunbelt South: Industrialization in Regional, National, and International Perspective." In Raymond A. Mohl, ed. *Searching for the Sunbelt: Historical Perspectives on a Region*. Knoxville: University of Tennessee Press, 1990, 25–46.

———. "Beyond Planters and Industrialists: A New Perspective on the New South." *Journal of Southern History*, LIV (February, 1988), 45–68.

Garber, Carter, et al. "Greasing GM's Wheels." *Southern Exposure*, XIV (September/October and November/December, 1986), 45–47.

Goldfarb, Robert S., Anthony M. J. Yezer, and Sebastian Crewe. "Some New Evidence: Have Regional Wage Differentials Really Disappeared?" *Growth and Change*, XIV (January, 1983), 48–51.

Hirschman, Charles, and Kim Blankenship. "The North-South Earnings Gap: Changes during the 1960s and 1970s." *American Journal of Sociology*, LXXXVII (September, 1981), 388–403.

Johnson, Kenneth, and Marilyn Scurlock. "The Climate for Workers." *Southern Exposure*, XIV (September/October and November/December, 1986), 28–31.

"New Priorities Seen as Southern Voters Defeat Two Pro-Education Governors." *Chronicle of Higher Education*, XXXVIII (November 20, 1991), A28.

"Textile Industry Faces Struggle for Survival." *Southern Exposure*, XIII (February, 1985), 4.

"When the Bubble Burst in Alabama." *U.S. News and World Report*, April 19, 1982, 104.

OTHER PUBLISHED MATERIAL

Rosenfeld, Stuart A., and Edward M. Bergman. *After the Factories: Changing Employment Patterns in the Rural South*. Research Triangle Park, N.C.: Southern Growth Policies Board, 1985.

INDEX

JAMES C. COBB is Bernadotte Schmitt Professor of History at the University of Tennessee, Knoxville. His publications include *Industrialization and Southern Society* and *The New Deal and the South*.